RACING POST BOOKS
Henry Cecil: Trainer of Genius

'Sir Henry Cecil has been a brilliant trainer of racehorses, a charismatic and complex man. Brough Scott's achievement has been to explain Cecil's genius and charisma without shying away from the more complex issues. The result is a wonderfully rounded portrait of one of the most endearing figures in British sport.'
David Walsh, chief sports correspondent of *The Sunday Times*

'This book is a triumph of its genre, and does full credit to both the writer and his complex but so thoroughly engaging subject. It should be required, and enjoyable reading, for both the casual race watcher and the most ardent student of the sport.'
Channel 4 Racing

'The story of Henry Cecil's life is what the whole world of racing has been waiting for. Brough's book is a masterpiece and does the maestro full justice.'
Ian Balding, Derby-winning trainer

'... a classic book about a classic legend.'
The Independent

'... a gem of a book ... Brough Scott has written a brilliantly sensitive, balanced and authoritative book.'
Robin Oakley, *The Spectator*

'Scott's tour of Cecil's inner self is as fascinating as it is illuminating.'
Charlie Brooks, *The Daily Telegraph*

'Brough Scott, the author, has done an excellent job in capturing this re-markable, but flawed, man.'
Country Life magazine

'This is by far the best book on racing I have ever read. It combines a truly extraordinary story one that no novelist would have dared to submit with brilliant writing by an author who is almost as knowledgeable about horses and the turf as his subject. It is a just tribute to a man who deserves to be admired beyond even his achievements.'
Stoker Devonshire, *The Spectator*

'It's a great story, well told.'
Daily Racing Forum

HENRY CECIL

Trainer of Genius

Brough Scott

RACING POST

For my father Mason Hogarth Scott.
1900–1971.
Whose fascination with racing inspired my own,
whose support let me follow my dream,
whose love will never die.

Paperback edition published in 2014 by Racing Post Books
Raceform House, High Street, Compton, Newbury, Berkshire RG20 6NL

First published in Great Britain in 2012

1 3 5 7 9 10 8 6 4 2

ISBN 978-1-909471-40-5

Cover designed by Jay Vincent
Text designed by Soapbox
www.soapbox.co.uk

Frontispiece: Sir Henry Cecil and Frankel after the Greenham Stakes at Newbury, April 2011.

Printed and bound in the UK by CPI Group (UK) Ltd, Croydon, CR0 4YY

www.racingpost.com/shop

CONTENTS

MAP OF BRITISH FLAT RACECOURSES
AND CECIL-RELATED PLACES

Aberdeen
Crathes Castle

Hamilton
Musselburgh
Ayr

Middleham
(training centre)

Newcastle

Malton
(training centre)

Carlisle
Redcar
Catterick
Thirsk
Burton Agnes Stud

Ripon
York
Hambleton Hill and
Cliff Stud (Noel Murless
training)

Beverley
Pontefract
Doncaster

Haydock
Chester
Southwell
Nottingham

Royal Agricultural
College, Cirencester
Wolverhampton
Leicester
Yarmouth

Warwick
Newmarket

Ffos Las
Chepstow
Windsor

Kempton
Epsom

Beckhampton
(Noel Murless training)
Bath
Newbury
Ascot

Folkestone
Lingfield

Salisbury
Canford School

Sandown

Sunningdale School

Brighton
Goodwood

MAP OF NEWMARKET

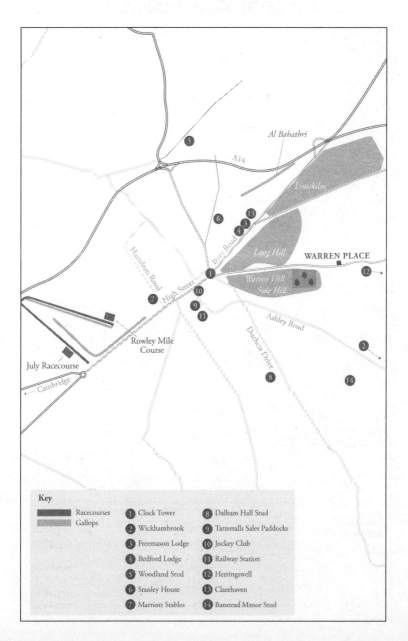

Key

▬ Racecourses			
▬ Gallops			
① Clock Tower		⑧ Dalham Hall Stud
② Wickhambrook		⑨ Tattersalls Sales Paddocks
③ Freemason Lodge		⑩ Jockey Club
④ Bedford Lodge		⑪ Railway Station
⑤ Woodland Stud		⑫ Herringswell
⑥ Stanley House		⑬ Clarehaven
⑦ Marriott Stables		⑭ Banstead Manor Stud

INTRODUCTION

IT WAS a sound they had never heard before. The ovation on that last April afternoon at Newmarket in 2011 was quite exceptional for the horse – but much, much more so for the man. Frankel, the three-year-old colt who had just blitzed his rivals in the 2,000 Guineas, was just six races and eight months into what was to prove an unbeaten career. Henry Cecil seemed to be living his seventh life already, yet this promised to be the very best of them. Nothing beats a resurrection.

It took him a long while to get to the sunlit unsaddling enclosure as everyone had wanted to shake history by the hand. By the time Henry had come down the steps on to the grass of the paddock, Tom Queally had taken the saddle and numbercloth off Frankel's sweat-stained back and the big screen had already replayed proof of an all-the-way victory as awesome as any seen since the 2,000 Guineas began in 1809 with a winner called Wizard. The crowd had been so thunderstruck they had even broken into applause mid-race and cheered horse and jockey on the walk back to the winner's circle. But now they wanted something else. They wanted to greet the extraordinary, captivating, complex, fascinating, flawed, patrician, populist genius that is Henry Cecil.

That moment in the spring of 2011 was a full 36 years after a 32-year-old Henry had legged up Frankie Dettori's father Gianfranco on the Italian-owned Bolkonski to win the 1975 2,000 Guineas and

Frankel and Tom Queally in full flight when winning the 2,000 Guineas in 2011 ...

what was to become the first of a post-1900 record 25 individual British Classic races for H.R.A. Cecil as a trainer. In that time, with its unprecedented heights and its more recent doom-laden lows, the unique mix of aloof, almost autistic concentration and engaging, self-deprecating charm has seared his dandyish figure into the consciousness not just of racing fans but of the wider world. He has blacksmith's hands and an artist's face. He is both a complex and a simple man. He can be dauntingly direct one minute and winningly vulnerable the next. But in the early years of the new century the winning ways seemed to have deserted him as a series of sometimes self-induced blows left him a cancer-ridden ember of his glory days.

In the eighties and nineties he had become the unlikeliest of icons. He was the amazingly posh and unacademic stepson of one royal trainer and the son-in-law of another. He had become a cult interviewee as he coyly diverted the TV plaudits while the big-race

... and in the Newmarket winner's enclosure with Sir Henry Cecil and owner Khalid Abdulla.

winners were led in. But the perfect storm had been brewing awhile. Divorce had been followed by staff defections, owner loss, his twin brother's cancer, drink, depression and a further divorce before, in 2006, cancer hit him too. Henry Cecil's mighty Warren Place stable had sent out 110 winners in 1978, 180 in 1987 and another 100 in 1998. In 2005 he had just 12 successes and the wan, raddled 62-year-old on the hack overseeing just a handful of horses looked a doomed and painful sight. But now he was back. Now he was here.

He wore an elegant navy blue cashmere blazer with narrow charcoal trousers, Gucci shoes and a dark blue shirt with a light speckled tie, above which his rather ravaged face was set severe to hold back the emotions raging beneath the trademark flop of now thinning hair. His tall body was still taut with big-race tension but his head dipped in characteristic mute acknowledgement as he walked very precisely over to shake Tom Queally by the hand – an almost papal welcome to the Classic-winning club. As he did so the swell of approval erupted into a full-scale roar. When it finally subsided a voice called out 'Three cheers for Henry!' and three times the crowd roared its response.

It was a scene unique in the experience of even the most seasoned racegoer, and rightly so. For what Henry Cecil achieved in that moment is not just unprecedented in racing, it is exceptionally rare in life itself. All societies produce a few individuals who through drive and circumstance take themselves to the very top. Of those there is an unhappy but inevitable percentage who then ride the helter-skelter right down to the bottom. Many of those will refocus and enjoy some level of success a second time, but never in racing, and only on very few occasions in the wider world, has anyone climbed back to truly become 'The Man' again. When they do the effect can be almost eerily adulatory. For what has been loved and lost is now found again.

In Henry Cecil's case this was doubly so, for when he first began to emerge from the darkness, the cancer had him so deep in its grip that any success had about it the bitter sweetness of a swansong. Someone had called out 'Three cheers for Henry Cecil!' in June 2007 when Light Shift took the Oaks at Epsom to become his first Classic winner in seven years. But the tearful figure standing on the rostrum had looked so gaunt and stricken that most of us doubted he would make Christmas.

Yet as the numbers and the winners picked up, so too did the man. Despite still needing regular remedial chemotherapy, the prospect of again masterminding as many as 150 thoroughbreds continued to lift him from his bed before dawn. At a time of life when most people at best bask in former glories, he had, with Frankel, moved on to an even higher plane. You could hear a chorus growing around the formerly barely whispered thought that this colt might be the best of all the great ones that had gone before.

For as 2011 progressed the legend only grew. The Queen's Birthday Honours had been published before Royal Ascot and the winner's call was amended to 'Three cheers for Sir Henry!' as Frankel was led back in another triumph, albeit this time a less perfect one. Once again the reporters and TV cameras hung on his every word. Once again readers and viewers delighted in the appealing mix of angst and insouciance with which the old clothes horse talked of the thoroughbreds he so clearly adored. But once again they saw only the outward visible signs of what is a much more complex and contradictory and finally more inspiring story than it may at first appear.

Henry might have a gilded spoon of a background but his early years seemed devoid of promise. Racing might have been a boyhood backdrop but neither it nor horses appeared to be a passion that consumed him. He inherited a famous yard and top-line horses at only 26 but was scuffling around without a stable within a twelvemonth. And while to outsiders he could be the jokey, self-deprecating dandy, in other matters of both a personal and professional kind the single-mindedness that drove him forward could skew his judgement horribly.

For some of us it is hard to give Henry the credit that must undoubtedly be his due. For we are diverted by the early sixties memory of him and his identical twin brother David during their time as occasional attendees of that last gasp of useless sons of gentlefolk, the nine-month 'gin and tonic' estate management course at the Royal Agricultural College at Cirencester. Even loyal contemporaries have no recollection of the twins showing an interest in anything other than wine, women and cigarettes, and precious little in racing. Even when he took over from his royal trainer stepfather Sir Cecil Boyd-Rochfort and saddled Wolver Hollow to win the Eclipse Stakes in his first season, most of us put it down to

The flag flies above Warren Place to mark another Group One winner.

inheritance. And when success continued we tended to ascribe it to the influence of his staunch 'First Mate' of a head lad Paddy Rudkin, and especially to that of Henry's talented and enthusiastic wife Julie, daughter of the other royal trainer Sir Noel Murless.

'No, I never really rated him in those early days at all,' admitted the esteemed Sir Peter O'Sullevan, before continuing with characteristically mellifluous understatement, 'but subsequent events have made me somewhat amend that opinion.' Sir Peter may have been 94 when he gave that verdict but he had not lost either his clarity of thought or his taste for adventure: on the morning of the day when Frankel won glory in the 2011 Sussex Stakes, Peter drove his 'wolf in sheep's clothing' Golf R at over 150mph round Goodwood Motor Racing Circuit.

Mercifully we were travelling at a slightly slower pace at the time of our conversation. The great man's mind quickened as we pondered the key to Cecil's success, for which this book will search. 'It's hard to put a finger on it,' said Peter, that wonderful voice conjuring memories of a half-century of famous races, 'but there is no doubt he has a unique affinity with the thoroughbred, and there must be something very different that has and still drives him. It might not be easy,' he added, as only Peter could, 'but you might have a bit of fun finding out.'

For a year I mixed fortnightly pilgrimages to Warren Place with visits to family, friends, schoolmasters, stable lads, jockeys, punters, race fans and not least master tailor Joseph Ghazal, for whom Henry is a special client, though not necessarily the most famous. As anyone who bothers to trawl through the newspaper cuttings will discover, Henry's life has not been without its dramas on the personal side, but the purpose of this book is not censoriously to rake up old issues but to take a fresh look at what really drives this racing knight.

Just what is it that transformed this apparently ineffectual youth into a hyper-achieving adult? Where, beneath the foppish exterior, lies the dynamo that still drives him as he moves into his eighth decade? How close has he been to the demons that eventually took his twin away? Above all else, what spawned the 'sixth sense' that those who work with him declare is as near as they know to genius?

It would be simpler, if less interesting, if we confined ourselves to the racing discipline. But Henry Cecil is much more than a product of a training apprenticeship. He is the result of one of the most romantic, distinguished, historic and tragically beleaguered of backgrounds, on both sides of his family tree. So even to start to understand the secrets of Sir Henry Richard Amherst Cecil, it is essential to go back to the very beginning.

1

THE EARLY YEARS

THE MIRACLE is that he survived at all.

When 25-year-old Elizabeth Rohays Cecil gave birth in Aberdeen Hospital to Henry and ten minutes later to David on the night of 11 January 1943, it meant she now had four boys under the age of four. What's more, just five days earlier Rohays (as she was always called) had received official confirmation that her 28-year-old husband Henry Kerr Auchmuchty Cecil had been killed in action with the Parachute Regiment in North Africa, some 40 miles west of Tunis.

You might think that stress enough for a young widow whose older brother Sandy Burnett had inexplicably committed suicide at Cambridge University in March 1934 (her adored younger brother Roger was to be killed in Germany in February 1945). You would be wrong. On the night of 21 April, just over three months after the birth of the twins, 30 Dornier 217Es hit Aberdeen – the Luftwaffe's biggest raid on that city of the war. A total of 98 civilians and 27 servicemen were killed and almost 10,000 houses damaged. The casualties would have included another adult and four small boys had a large incendiary bomb that landed right outside Rohays' front door not failed to explode.

Not surprising, then, that despite her parents Major General Sir James and Lady Burnett owning the comparatively safe albeit draughty fortress of Crathes Castle 30 miles to the west, Rohays should decide

Crathes Castle.

to find her boys more amenable lodgings well removed from 'Siren City', a nickname earned by Aberdeen's proximity to the German bomber base at Stavanger in Norway which resulted in 32 raids and 364 air-raid warnings during the war. As it happened, her now late husband's older brother William Cecil, Lord Amherst, had given them the most generous of wedding gifts when they were married at St Margaret's Westminster in December 1938: the strangely moated house and 250 acres of Gesyns Farm at Wickhambrook near the racing capital of Newmarket. The Cecils had been there together in the summer of 1942 while Henry was readying for embarkation to North Africa in November. In the modern argot, the move down south was a 'no brainer', yet without it Rohays would never have met and married her second husband, the Queen's racehorse trainer Sir Cecil Boyd-Rochfort, and the illustrious career of the baby that was to become Sir Henry Cecil would never have begun.

But long before anyone plays the amateur psychologist with any effects these excitements may have had on Rohays and her fledgling family, it is worth taking in how much history was raging around in the gene pool when Henry and his brothers came into the world. Of course racing people sometimes put an inordinate emphasis on breeding. The most famous example of this remains the erudite John Hislop, owner and breeder of the great horse Brigadier Gerard, whose unbeaten six-race exploits in 1971 exceeded even Frankel's triumphs in 2011. John spends the first third of his 350-page tribute explaining how the pairing of his untalented mare La Paiva with the local stallion Queen's Hussar had been a piece of triumphant foresight rather than of simple convenience. If we adopted the same approach with Henry Cecil's parentage, this book would run to several volumes.

The name 'Cecil' is only the start. Before British history lost its compulsory place in the school curriculum every pupil knew of William Cecil, Elizabeth I's secretary of state, and of his son Robert, who did the same job for James I. Of how William's descendants became the marquesses of Exeter and lived at Burghley House and of how Robert's line were the marquesses of Salisbury based at Hatfield, and so the one family became owners of two of the finest stately homes in England.

But if you talked to Henry Cecil, or better still if you sat with his late father's 86-year-old cousin Rear Admiral Sir Nigel 'Os' Cecil in his old rectory on the Isle of Wight, you would discover an awful lot more in their Cecil line than a couple of ancestral piles and a string of eminent politicians. In his coat room the old admiral had a family tree that whisked the Cecils back to William the Conqueror and four centuries further to Rhodri Mawr, King of Wales, whose granddaughter married someone with the unfortunate (to a modern ear) moniker of Sytsylt, which later became Cyssel and then Cecil itself. And once Os got out the sherry the trip would go panoramic: everything from how his uncle (and Henry's great uncle) John Cecil married Cornelia Vanderbilt – and with that came ownership of Biltmore, the largest house in America – to how his grandmother (Henry's great grandmother) Mary Amherst was the oldest of the seven siblings whose existence is immortalised in London's Seven Sisters Road.

Despite being married to Lord William Cecil, the brotherless Mary succeeded her father William, the first Lord Amherst, to become Baroness Amherst of Hackney, and the title of Lord Amherst was then passed to her grandson William whose own son, another William, holds the title to this day.

At this stage all bar ardent genealogists might be tempted to resort to jokes like 'pay attention at the back', but the Cecil/Amherst family tree is worth the attention for two major reasons. Firstly, it reveals the starkness of bereavement. Mary's oldest son and therefore Henry's grandfather, yet another Lord William Cecil, was killed at the Battle of the Aisne in the very first month of the 1914–18 war. This meant that Henry's own father, born in 1914, had, like his son, no memory of the man whose name he carried. Secondly, a chat with the admiral and a look at the picture of the original Lord Amherst lays to rest one of the oldest canards about the twins: that their much darker complexion compared with that of their two older brothers means they are not actually Cecils at all.

It is a story that has been sniggered at for decades in racing circles. Several famous personages have been linked with the idea that the lonely Rohays might have been a bit free with her dazzling charms when Henry Snr was off in uniform. All good fun, but while it is true that the twins have darker skin than their siblings, Os Cecil, who is old enough to have good memories of his cousin, will tell you it is not at all true that they were unlike him in character and it is absolutely untrue that they bear no resemblance to other forebears. Just Google the first Baron Amherst and back at you will stare an image (right) from the 1870s with much of the soulful, slightly pug-faced features of our Henry Cecil. After all, it is his great-great grandfather.

That William Amherst loved to collect things, as Henry does. He was in fact a noted Egyptologist and backed some of the earlier expeditions of Howard Carter, who later discovered the tomb of Tutankhamun under the patronage of Lord Carnarvon. Amherst's bad luck got worse at the end of his life when a dodgy solicitor lost him a fortune and he was only to live six weeks after being forced to sell his treasured collection.

As the war memorial at Medjes-el-bab in Tunisia records, Henry Cecil's father's luck ran out towards the end of 1942, but Os reported he had been pretty unafraid to test it beforehand. 'I remember him being full of fun,' said the old man, showing a picture of his short-trousered self on some 1930s lawn alongside a dashing figure in a white linen suit. 'There were lots of stories about him. One was how at a pompous army reception in Cairo he rather drunkenly prodded at some local potentate's groaning rack of medals, which broke off and cascaded round the floor. But the most celebrated was the night he skidded off a railway bridge in Norfolk and somehow landed safely on the line below after jumping a platform.' Indeed a cutting of the newspaper report hangs on the washroom wall in the house of Henry's oldest brother 'Bow' in Warwickshire.

So Henry's father was a popular daredevil son of privilege not enamoured with hard work. 'It is not at all plain to me,' wrote his tutor at Trinity, Cambridge about the suggestion of a City career, 'that the two years of drudgery in an office to which you refer will not be a great deal better for him than the kind of life which he has led during the last fifteen months.'

Cambridge's closeness to Newmarket meant full exposure to the racing bug and Henry Snr was still only 24 when a filly called Celestial Way, which he shared with the trainer Teddy Lambton, won the important Cheveley Park Stakes.

Maybe things simply happened younger back then because it was a mere two years later, in September 1938, that flirtatious, fancy-free, man-of-the-world Henry Cecil became engaged to the dazzling and vivacious Rohays Burnett whom he had first met at a dance in Aboyne near her home in Scotland when she was just 16. Rohays, talented enough to have considered becoming a ballet dancer when at 'finishing school' in Paris, was quite a catch; not even the most cursory look round Henry Cecil's tartan-draped study can fail to register the importance of this Scottish side of the family. The Cecils may have been major players since Elizabethan times, but the Burnetts go right

back to Robert the Bruce in the early fourteenth century, and to serving David I of Scotland (c.1080–1153) when they first came over from Normandy, probably as 'Bernard'. The Cecils may boast the stately elegance of Hatfield and Burghley, but the Burnetts have been at Crathes since Robert the Bruce gifted them the land in 1323; the mighty castle that glowers down on the River Dee was first completed in 1596. Henry Cecil's father may have lots of peers in his pedigree, but Rohays Burnett's father Sir James (left) was the 13th Baronet of Leys and the 24th Laird of Crathes.

It was to Crathes that the two older siblings, Bow and Jamie, repaired for both Easter and summer holidays; Henry and David and their two-years-younger half-brother Arthur Boyd-Rochfort would usually only come in the summer.

Crathes was not just a castle. In its grounds, Sir James and his wife Sybil had created one of Scotland's greatest gardens, and what with gillies to take the boys fishing on the Dee and gamekeepers to take them grouse shooting on the moors, it was as near to old-fashioned privileged paradise as it is possible to imagine. Especially for four young boys spending their home lives subject to the well-intentioned but restrictive discipline of an elderly stepfather and the rigid routine of Freemason Lodge, one of the country's most famous racing stables.

A passage in the ghosted autobiography Henry brought out in 1983 gives a vivid feel of the impression Crathes made:

How we loved those holidays up there. We would take the night train from King's Cross, leaving London about eight o'clock. For most of the night we lay awake, as the train made its way through the different counties and the increasingly broad accents of the porters and passengers on the platforms told us that we were drawing closer to Scotland. Having thrown our sixpences over the Forth Bridge en route we eventually arrived at Aberdeen about seven o'clock in the morning.

The factor [estate manager] Mr Birnie and the chauffeur Sim were always there to meet us and the first thing we did was to sit down to a fantastic Aberdeen kipper at a nearby hotel. After that we set out on the fourteen-mile journey along the Deeside road to Crathes.

There was always plenty to do at Crathes. The keepers used to take us walking up grouse most mornings and pigeon shooting in the evenings. Then there was a good deal of shooting on the lake and along the burns, and on occasion we would make the higher ground and shoot blackcock and capercaillie. We even had roe deer drives although I never much liked shooting such beautiful creatures.

By all accounts his grandparents had developed some fairly distinctive eccentricities. Sir James, always likely to speak his mind, spoke so fast that he was called 'Maxim' after the quick-firing Maxim gun of the 1880s. For her part Lady Sybil was so magnificently stingy that when she invited the boys to have a Coca-Cola she poured it out in sherry glasses. But their grandparents were children of another time. Sir James had fought with distinction in both South Africa and France, and his wife had accompanied him to China when to protect British interests in the area he had become Brigadier 14th Infantry Brigade, Shanghai Defence Force. From that stay they brought home several exotic additions to what has become one of the world's most beautiful shrub gardens. That and the grounds of Crathes became something of an obsession, but they loved having their grandsons around, and with such a plethora of servants tales of those holidays now ring like days from not one century ago but two.

'It was amazing looking back,' says Henry's older brother Jamie, who at the age of 25 changed his name to Burnett of Leys at his grandfather's request and came up to Deeside to assume the laird's responsibilities. 'It was totally old-fashioned. There was Sandy Sim the chauffeur and before him Christie, who was always drunk, but my grandmother said she would rather be driven by Christie drunk than my grandfather sober. There was a cook, and Scott the butler with a black coat and pinstripe trousers. He would not just stand at table but would come up in the morning and pull the curtains, fold up your clothes and help you on with your coat when you went out. We boys would just have the run of the place. It was wonderful. I remember riding back on the gamekeeper's bike after he had taken us ferreting in the morning and sitting on the handlebars with rabbits slung underneath.'

Idyllic impressions for young boys no doubt, and in their grandfather and his forebears there was also inspiration. Jamie has now triumphantly revived the Burnett history globally on the web, a site he drives under the fine title of 'Representer of the House and Chief of the Name of Burnett Leys'. He has also modernised the estate with property, a sports hall, a business centre, a sawmill and a theatre. The National Trust was given Crathes in 1952 but James remains its most spirited guide, bringing you such luminaries as James Burnett, the younger brother of the 1st Baronet whose work (rather like the Egyptology of William Amherst) preceded that of Darwin. But for missed opportunities no one could match Sir Robert Burnett of Leys, the 11th Baronet, who went to California in 1860 and when he returned to Scotland 15 years later thought he had done well to get $140,000 for the land he had originally bought for just $3,000. Mind you, it's worth a bit more now. It is a large part of Los Angeles.

Yes, in Henry's ancestry, to use the racing terminology, the dam's side is every bit as important as the sire's.

For the most important meeting of his life, Henry was not even there. Mind you, he wouldn't have remembered much about it. You don't when you are only 14 months old.

Henry and David would have been crawling round the Gesyns Farm nursery with their brothers when their widowed mother stepped off the London train at Newmarket that April afternoon in 1944. Rohays was 27, slim, stylish and self-confident, with gorgeous chestnut-red hair. Also alighting was the already renowned figure (twice champion trainer) of Captain Cecil Boyd-Rochfort. He was 57, tall, fit, handsome, immaculate and still maintaining the military bearing that had won him the Croix de Guerre in 1915 – the same year his older brother Arthur won a VC for saving the lives of his platoon by picking up a bomb and throwing it out of the trench before it exploded. Cecil was also the most long-standing of eligible bachelors in this racing heartland where his Freemason Lodge stables housed horses of the King and of American millionaires. On seeing the lady he raised his grey Edward VII-style homburg. The return smile was not one he would ever forget.

He saw it again a week later when the Newmarket racing season had its annual 'rite of spring' Craven meeting at which so many Classic hopefuls start their journey towards fame or oblivion. He made enquiries, he arranged to be introduced. He suddenly felt the freedom of the bachelor was not something that should be maintained. So every Sunday he travelled the eight and a half miles of dipping Suffolk countryside from Newmarket to Wickhambrook to pay court. Not much of a journey you might think, but then you wouldn't be doing it on an upright bicycle that looked as if it must have been around in Edward VII's time.

No concessions to any early-day 'Lycra' cycling kit, either: this was tweed cap, plus fours, shooting jacket, collar and tie. Cecil Boyd-Rochfort had never seen the need to pilot a car, and now there was no petrol and no one to drive him. But Cupid had hit its unlikely target, and how tongues must have wagged as this distinctive figure pedalled steadily up the Ashley Road, off past Cheveley and Kirtling before finally turning left just before Wickhambrook. It would have been a full hour by the time he crossed the bridge over the farmhouse moat to lunch with his new intended.

He was no slowcoach when it came to courting.

By the end of May Rohays had twice been over to stay at Freemason Lodge. In the middle of June, CBR put a bet of £10 at 25-1 on his filly Hycilla in the Oaks, which like all wartime Classics was run at Newmarket's July Course as the Rowley Mile track was an airbase and Epsom was an army camp. Rohays was not the only one smiling as the filly came winging home. She and Cecil were engaged four days later and on Monday, 24 July they were married at St Agnes' Church, Newmarket, with Sir Humphrey de Trafford as best man and Rohays given away by her father Sir James Burnett in full general's uniform. There may have been other and younger suitors, but none had matched the sheer panache with which the old Captain had pressed his suit.

Cover girl: Rohays Boyd-Rochfort in *The Sketch*, July 1947.

Rohays would become a trainer's wife, Henry and his brothers would be stepsons. The first sounds they would remember of a morning would be the clacking of racehorse shoes in the yard beneath their second-floor bedroom. Their first understanding of life would be the rigid and relentlessly evocative routine of a string of thoroughbreds going out on to the wide open spaces of Newmarket Heath, the serious-faced debriefs afterwards, the flurry of expectation when an important owner came to look round, the press build-up to big races, and the laughs and tears when the big days arrived.

The man whom the boys came to call 'Uncle Cecil', and by whom Rohays would have Arthur in July 1945, was much more than a mere racehorse trainer. Indeed he was a man of such distinctive background that unlike most of his peers he in many ways seemed grander than any of his millionaire owners, except perhaps the King and Queen. He was brought up in the magnificent rooms and galleries and sweeping acres of Middleton Park House in County Westmeath, Ireland, which his father George had completed in 1850 with not only architectural delights but such unheard of luxuries as under-floor heating.

His family was at the apex of Eton-educated, horse-mad Anglo-Irish society, with a dash of off-beat heroism never far away, as witnessed by the exploits of the illegitimate son of his Westmeath neighbour and uncle by marriage Sir Thomas Chapman. That boy grew up to be Lawrence of Arabia. Cecil Boyd-Rochfort may have been rather more correct and less historic than that but early events showed he cannot have lacked either drive or charm in what he did. For after going to work at the Chattis Hill stables of his fellow Irishman Atty Persse in Hampshire at 19, at 21 he became assistant trainer to the redoubtable Captain Dewhurst at Newmarket's Bedford Lodge. Then in 1912, at the ripe old age of 25, he was appointed racing manager to Edward VII's millionaire financier friend Sir Ernest Cassel, who was to leave the none too shoddy sum of £7.5 million when he died in 1921 and whose granddaughter Edwina was to become the wife of Lord Mountbatten of Burma.

In 1923 Boyd-Rochfort borrowed £6,000 from his mother and the American millionaire Marshall Field (and paid it off with betting winnings within four years) to buy the Freemason Lodge training stables in Newmarket's Bury Road, which is now the base of multiple champion Sir Michael Stoute, for so long Henry's arch rival in the town. The young tyro duly got his career under way with a double at Pontefract, a track whose Yorkshire friendliness used to be tempered by an unhappy tendency to subsidence because of the coal shafts sunk way beneath. Freemason Lodge itself was a large, rather dour two-storied house built in 1900, but equipped well enough for the bachelor whose first Classic successes came with Brown Betty's 1,000 Guineas in 1933 and Boswell's 1936 St Leger (both horses were owned by another American millionaire, William Woodward), followed by his first two training championships, in 1937 and 1938. But what the house, and indeed the man, was not set up for was the impact of four boys of five and under; and then, when Arthur arrived in 1945, five boys under six.

Looking back, it is amazing that things went as well as they did. Rohays' method of coping with the demands of being a trainer's wife 30 years younger than her husband was to install the boys on the second floor with her old nanny from Scotland and operate on the strictly Edwardian principle that children could have the run of the place during playtime but meals and bedtime were strictly under Nanny's, not parents', rules. 'It was just the way it was,' says Bow Cecil, the oldest brother, before turning to a happiness-filled photo of Rohays and her boys running hand in hand by the stables. 'Our mother was wonderful, terrific fun, and we all adored her, but it was Nanny who brought us up really while Mummy entertained and helped Uncle Cecil. With five of us we always had something to do. We used to go everywhere on our bikes, down to the cinemas for Saturday morning matinee, and thinking back now it is amazing what Uncle Cecil put up with. He was more like a grandfather of course and quite formal, but when you think of it he gave us a huge amount of support.'

That's very much how Henry remembers it. 'We never had anyone to read us a bedtime story or anything like that' is the most wistful comment he will make now, before adding, 'We had a very good upbringing. We entertained ourselves, playing cricket and football and roaring round the house on scooters driving everyone mad. Uncle Cecil was very fair. He was 57 when he married our mother and now I appreciate what he took on. He gave us a marvellous education and he gave me a chance in life.'

It is an important perspective to grasp as we try to imagine the world of Newmarket in the 1940s and 1950s. Picture the hugely tall, famously aloof, utterly Edwardian figure of Cecil Boyd-Rochfort, long lampooned as the grandest man in town, now encumbered not just by an impossibly glamorous young wife but by all the hassle of a pack of tumbling boys.

People had long had fun at the Captain's expense – provided they were out of earshot. He had rigid standards in the stable and outside it and would positively encourage the impression that he was not prepared to suffer fools gladly or converse with people unless he felt like it. He would have been just about the only trainer the public recognised. For it was he, immaculately suited, gold watch chain across the double-breasted waistcoat, gleaming starched collar beneath the firmly tilted chin, who would be photographed alongside the Queen when Epsom and Ascot were featured on the newsreels, which were our biggest source of information in those times. In the Coronation year of 1953 when Henry and David were just ten, it was CBR towering over the young Queen as she watched her horse Aureole circle the paddock before the Derby. It was CBR beside her as the nation willed the colt on to second place behind the Sir Gordon Richards-ridden Pinza just four days after the Coronation itself.

Cecil Boyd-Rochfort might have looked aloof, more royal than the royals, but there was a professional logic to his attitude that only added further distance between him and his detractors. Because, for all the prestige of his owners and the almost teetotal rectitude of his behaviour, he had built an enviable reputation for successfully backing his winners and could feel that sharing this information with others, let alone members of the press, would be entirely counterproductive. So were spawned countless tales of his discomfiture with others, and particularly with anything 'new-fangled', notably his difficulty with the telephone down which he used to bellow as if raising his voice would help it carry down the lines. One evening his barked greeting into the mouthpiece was answered by an American voice (in fact the once dual Derby-winning jockey Tommy Weston) saying, 'Testing transatlantic lines, testing transatlantic lines, repeat after me: "I cannot eat."'

'I cannot eat,' boomed the Captain.

'Testing transatlantic lines,' continued the voice. 'Repeat after me: "I cannot eat my currant bun."'

'I cannot eat my currant bun,' roared Her Majesty's trainer.

'Then you know what you can do with it, Captain,' giggled Weston in triumph.

Such anecdotes are ever the penalty for those who self-consciously carry an aura about them. I still vividly remember my first glimpse of CBR at Newmarket one Sunday afternoon in what must have been 1961. He would have been well into his seventies then but still cut a magnificently uncompromising figure as he sailed down the Bury Road with homburg, overcoat and cane for all the world as if he were a stately yacht beating back to harbour.

'As I grew up I grew ever more in awe of him,' wrote Henry just before his own 40th birthday. 'Although unfailingly courteous to his friends and to his owners, he could be formidable when small boys had exhausted the patience with which he was not liberally endowed. "Be quiet, you will frighten the horses" was a frequent admonition. A stricter man could not be imagined, and my brothers and I were always relieved when it was time for a meal as he took great pleasure in his food and was always calmer and more mellow at the table.'

What is interesting in this and the other brothers' recollections is that while there was awe aplenty there was little actual fear, except for the one well-merited occasion when Henry bought some white mice which duly escaped and within weeks the mighty royal stable was crawling with the creatures. This the pictures do not contradict:

while there is often a slightly posed formality about the photographs, enhanced by the fifties clothing, there is a sort of baffled benevolence about the old man looming high above the pack of little boys. They could be dressed in jodhpurs, shorts or, in one splendid image, cowboy outfits brought back from one of the Boyd-Rochforts' annual winter visits to their wealthy American owners, which usually started with an Atlantic crossing on the Queen Mary. Most evidential of all, given how Henry later spent every day of his working life, is the natural exposure to the rhythms and seasons and challenges of the racing game: Henry and David proudly sitting on their ponies alongside their famous stepfather and, most evocative of all, the two twins sitting on his knee at the Newmarket yearling sales. Then they must have been barely five years old. Well over 60 years later, in the autumn of 2011, I watched Henry's eyes flitting round that self-same auction. How many hours of practice do they say it takes to make a genius?

In Henry's case it seems the very assumption of the access removed any evidence of the ambition. If you examine the early days of great trainers like Michael Stoute, Aidan O'Brien or even Aidan's legendary 'no relation' namesake Vincent O'Brien, they all had either no (in Stoute's case) or very little racing background. They were boys of energy who found a subject that fascinated them and which they used as a ladder to scale the cliffs of life. Henry Cecil was energetic enough but he just seems to have rocked around with his doppelganger David. Jamie thinks he can remember Henry being a bit more interested in pets and ponies than the rest of them, but only marginally so. Of the five it was Bow who actually followed the racing pages a bit. It is to Rohays' and CBR's (and Nanny's) credit that there are no traces of Henry being an unhappy, tortured child secretly developing a skill set that would later lift him to fame. Probably, if not certainly, without CBR providing a high-flying racing universe for Henry to grow up in, no great training career, perhaps no distinction whatever, would have arrived for the toddler who moved into the top floor of Freemason Lodge in the summer of 1944.

Whether the Captain had any thoughts of actually grooming one of the five boys to succeed him at this stage seems unlikely, but his sense of good order made him plan out some education for the children in his care. Later on it would be the standard boarding school route taken by families of his ilk, but to begin with part of the upstairs was commandeered as a classroom and the luckless Mrs East was hired to try to instil some knowledge into a makeshift group that included Hugo Morris, son of a Newmarket stud owner, Geoffrey and Hugh Van Cutsem and Sue Armstrong, sons and daughter of trainers Bernard Van Cutsem and Sam Armstrong. From all reports, particularly his own, if Henry did not show much ambition in general he showed even less aptitude when it came to schooling.

'We were not a great success,' says Henry, laughing at the memory. 'David and I were late developers and I remember that when Mrs East gave out "merit" awards at the end of one term she had useful things like protractors and rulers for Hugh and Hugo while for David and me she had glove puppets of Muffin the Mule. By the time we went to Sunningdale we were some way behind, and anyway David always froze in exams. He just could not do them.'

Sunningdale, rather than their father's old school at Sandroyd in Wiltshire to which Bow and Jamie had gone, was chosen because Mr Fox the headmaster was a keen racing man and Uncle Cecil felt he and Rohays would be able to drop in after Ascot races. Today Sunningdale, an old Victorian house set in its own rhododendron- and conifer-lined grounds off a quiet suburban road half a mile across the A30 from the great golf course with which it shares a name, remains a classic English prep school. On a visit there in 2011 I found a warm, friendly and clearly creative environment very different from the original description of the pupil who was there with his twin brother between 1950 and 1956. 'If Tom Brown's schooldays were anything like mine,' Henry wrote in 1983, 'I can sympathise with his much publicised misfortunes. I hated the compulsory nude swims as well as the cold baths in the summer, and resented the treatment to which our hair was subjected. Besides having to wash it in an indescribable liquid of very high density which the masters called shampoo, it had to be cut by the school barber, a tonsorial butcher who got through twelve victims in ten minutes using hand clippers.

'David and I were very close throughout the miseries of prep school. If he were in trouble I would feel pain and sorrow for him, and as a child, I cried a lot. At least one of the worst of the ordeals there we shared together, for we were almost unmercifully teased because we had to wear hair grips to keep our pronounced fringes out of our eyes.'

A photograph taken at this time of the two of them staring mournfully out from under the Kirby grips makes one want to scream at the unwitting stupidity of teachers and parents: why not cut their hair shorter and so spare the little boys their easily foreseeable humiliation? But, we remind ourselves once again, we are looking back at another time: when the twins appeared as William and Arthur in a sketch called 'The Inky Boys', a co-character was called 'The Blackamoor'; and on another occasion no one thought it uncomfortable to include the song 'Ten Little Nigger Boys'.

The names of Cecil Major and Cecil Minor are invariably towards the bottom of class lists. In the General Paper from January 1956, 'Cecil ma' is 53rd, 'Cecil mi' 56th, and 'Boyd-Rochfort' (Arthur, then ten years old) 66th of 69; second place went to 'Ogilvy' – the actor Ian Ogilvy, one of Henry's best friends who found TV stardom in the 1970s as Simon Templar in *Return of the Saint*. Indeed in all the scrupulously chronicled school magazine reports during the

Cecil twins' Sunningdale sojourn the only sustained compliment comes in laughably bizarre circumstances.

'Cecil ma's skill as a goalkeeper,' goes the report on the first XI's 1955 football season, 'was acclaimed not only here but on the grounds of the schools he visited. During the last few weeks of the season he went into the forward line while his brother deputised for him in goal with almost equal proficiency.' Unfortunately, that glowing tribute comes in the course of a summary whose first two sentences are classics of their kind:

'Looking back on our records during the last fifty years we have been unable to find any season quite so unsuccessful as the past has been for the first XI and the less said the better. In the opening match here Ludgrove won a crushing victory by 10 goals to 0 and this reverse was followed by severe defeats in the following six matches so that by the beginning of November forty-seven goals had been scored against our seven.'

Henry loves this memory of what ended as a season of 13 straight defeats, usually boosting the Ludgrove catastrophe to 14 goals through his own net. But nowadays he is less censorious of the regime. 'It wasn't really too bad,' he says. 'We used to have two gangs and have fights up in Chapel Wood. I was the leader of our gang and Ogilvy and Sykes [Sir Tatton Sykes, the artistic owner of Sledmere House, that eighteenth-century gem in Yorkshire] were my lieutenants. The only thing I hated was when all the other boys went off home during our first half-term and nobody came to pick us up. So David and myself had to stay at the school, and although the masters were very good with us, you would have thought our mother would have planned for us to go to some old aunt at least.'

However well or otherwise the twins fared as individuals, an aptitude for education was so clearly missing that in the spring of 1956 Rohays was informed that for the first time Sunningdale boys

Sunningdale School football First XI, 1955: Henry Cecil, goalkeeper, is in the middle row.

would fail the not exactly onerous entry test to nearby Eton. Once again Uncle Cecil would have to intervene.

As it happened, help was in the family. CBR's older brother Colonel Harold Boyd-Rochfort was a governor of Canford School next to the River Stour in Dorset. Harold had taken over the running of the Middleton Park Estate on the death of his brother Arthur (the VC hero) in 1940 and had bred the grey colt Airborne, who went on to win the 1946 Derby. But through his cricketing connections he had earlier agreed to play an honorary role at the school which before the war was renowned for its riding prowess, took teams to competitions in Olympia and had a full-scale riding school called the Hippodrome.

Canford's impeccably kept archive records the correspondence as the governor gently squeezes a clearly slightly reluctant headmaster to accept his twin nephews provided they put up some sort of performance in the Common Entrance exams. To pass these they were now despatched to an erratic-sounding crammer in Chichester run by a retired couple always referred to as 'His' and 'Hers'.

The Canford records even include an ingratiating letter from Mr Ratcliffe ('His') to Rohays saying of the Cecil twins, 'Everyone is well aware that we are a week before Common Entrance but it's a pleasure to have them here. They are so full of enthusiasm, the French is much better, history still below standard but both are particularly well mannered and very appreciative.' That is not how Henry recalls it. He says he and the other ten boys spent most of their time doing domestic chores, polishing furniture and working in the garden. However, garden duties came to the rescue when 'His' was called away during the actual exam, leaving Henry and David to confer well enough for both to pass and to prompt this comment in a letter from the Canford headmaster Hardy to his opposite number at Sunningdale: 'There was a very clear similarity in their work – how identical are they?'

The archives at Canford, like the rest of the school, are in an admirable state thanks no doubt to the help of a £7.7 million windfall from the sale of an old stone relief stuck up in the Grubber (the school tuck shop). It was thought to be a mere copy before being accepted as the real thing dating back to a ninth-century BC Assyrian monarch rejoicing in the name of King Ashurnasirpal II. However, the documents reveal little of distinction or even of rebellion or idleness about the Cecil twins. 'They are both pleasant boys,' writes their housemaster after a year. 'Both behave sensibly and reasonably competently but I fail to see in what sphere they will ever make a mark in house or school.'

Such faint praise proved to be only a fraction harsh, and unfortunately for two men who later proved to be so naturally interested in design neither of them got caught in the radar of the inspirational art master

Robin Noscoe, to whom the film-maker Derek Jarman ascribed his own salvation from the muscular rigours of Canford (he attended at the same time as the Cecils). David failed to pull up any noticeable trees but Henry was a prefect in his last term, captained his House rowing four and represented the school in cross country and boxing. He also passed nine O-levels – a fact that made the opening line of the school's private valediction seem a bit harsh. 'No brains,' it reads as they leave in the spring of 1960. 'Both are physically strong and vigorous, both seem to be competent and cooperative, friendly and well-mannered, both have a single interest in horses and both are going to study horse flesh.'

By the ordinary schoolboy standards of the time this was mediocrity itself. But there were straws in the wind that prefaced something of Henry's distinctive later personality. Firstly, despite the military heroes in his background, exposure to the Canford Cadet Force instilled in him an anathema to any idea of service life and thereby cut off one possible career option. Similarly the ritual humiliation of the fagging system gave him a desire to have people work with rather than for him. And finally his own memories of the two sports in which he represented the school chime with the sort of issues he would eventually face as a trainer.

'On the day of the school cross country,' he says, 'I had this terrible flu but was determined to run all the same. When we had come on to the final drag across the playing fields I was second behind the best runner in the school. Then,' he added, almost wincing at the recollection, and making it obvious how much he must feel for a horse suffering a similar affliction, 'everything went completely to jelly and I finished twelfth.'

The other memory has its comic side, but its own lesson nonetheless. Henry Cecil, his current fans may be surprised to know, represented Canford in the heavyweight division of their boxing match against local rivals Poole. After four fights it all came down to this final bout and straight away Cecil was so on top that his opponent could do little more than cover up. Into the second round and there was so much more of the same that Cecil finally rabbit-punched his man to the floor with a mighty blow to the back of the neck. The Poole 'fighter' was counted out but Henry was disqualified and the match was lost. 'He just kept cowering away all the time,' says Henry. 'In the end I lost my temper. I should not have done. It never helps.'

Just straws in the wind perhaps, but in hindsight they prove to be significant ones. So too does Canford's final commendation: 'A boy of considerable courage and determination.' And now he was off 'to study horse flesh'. It was a subject on which Uncle Cecil could set the course himself, and in which the pupil might yet have the prospect of prizes.

The path was not as simple, as easy or as straight as hindsight would suggest. The record shows that just nine years after leaving Canford Henry Cecil was making headlines in his first year as a racehorse trainer. By then he had taken over Freemason Lodge from his stepfather, married Julie (the daughter of the other royal trainer Noel Murless) and was already winning the biggest races in the land. At 26, Henry Cecil was the youngest operator in the country, he was a success, everyone must have seen him coming. Well, it did not seem like that at the time.

For the Canford School comment that the twins were going 'to study horse flesh' was more of an observation than a career definition, and Henry's own memory is that on leaving school neither he nor David had any clear ambition of what they should do in life. They had no money of their own, they did not feel themselves cut out for any sort of business, they hated the prospect of the army, so what else was there bar the racing world with which at least they were familiar? It suits Henry's assumed self-deprecating languor to deny any signs of drive or talent in those early days, and first impressions of those two tall, playful, charming, rather clumsy identical twins did little to contradict this. But by his own account a seed had begun to grow.

'During my later days at Canford, I found myself increasingly curious about what was going on at Freemason Lodge,' Henry wrote in a passage that reveals as much about himself as it does about the Edwardian atmosphere in which he was raised.

Although brought up beside a stable yard, I did not have a natural interest in either racing in particular or horses in general. We had been taught to ride, but were of no particular asset to the local pony club. I never hunted and was to be thirty-eight before I jumped a fence on a horse.

However in our middle teens David and I went racing a lot in our holidays. As our interest developed I began to ride out with Uncle Cecil's string. I enjoyed the racing at home at Newmarket most, particularly the Craven meeting, in April, the first of the year on our local course. The atmosphere at the Craven meeting was always full of anticipation with everybody anxious to see whether the two-year-olds of the previous season had trained on well enough to be able to reveal normal improvement on their early form. At home at Freemason Lodge there was the excitement of the owners coming to stay. I shall never forget the way the aroma of their fine cigars filled the smoking room, or how I adored the scent of the hyacinths placed around the rooms by Tom the gardener.

Those owners would have included the Queen, whose victory with Aureole in the 1954 King George VI and Queen Elizabeth Stakes at

Queen Elizabeth the Queen Mother and Her Majesty the Queen with royal trainer Captain Cecil Boyd-Rochfort, Royal Ascot 1954.

Ascot not only took Cecil Boyd-Rochfort to his first post-war training title but afforded racegoers the rare sight of the Queen running as she raced to greet her horse in the winner's enclosure. That success would certainly have registered with the 11-year-old schoolboy locked away at Sunningdale, and when his stepfather became champion again next year there were even better times with a fillies' Triple Crown for Meld, the best filly if not the best horse he ever trained. What's more, the first leg of the Triple Crown, the 1,000 Guineas, was run at Newmarket in April and therefore Henry, his mother and all four of his brothers were celebrating as stable jockey Harry Carr rode Meld into the unsaddling enclosure. It was a first English Classic winner both for Carr and for the filly's remarkable 62-year-old owner Countess Anastasia Mikhailovna de Torby, otherwise known as Lady Zia Wernher of Luton Hoo, the great granddaughter of Tsar Nicholas I of Russia and the grandmother of a very young Fiona Phillips, who was later to marry Henry's older brother Jamie.

Heady memories for any boy, and they can only have been seared deeper when Henry and David became two high-riding, quite stylishly bent figures in the Boyd-Rochfort string. Imagine the excitement for the 15-year-olds at Newmarket in April 1958 when they cheered on the Queen's Pall Mall to win the 2,000 Guineas, and then the excitement and subsequent fear when Alcide, owned and bred by the Captain's best man Sir Humphrey de Trafford, was hot favourite for the Derby only to have his rib smashed by a 'nobbler' to prevent him from running.

Riding out with a thoroughbred racing string is one of the most addictive, evocative and privileged pleasures in any sport. To do it at a major stable where you see Derby favourites, Ascot winners and blue-blooded hopefuls walking and snorting and jig-jogging beside you at every turn is akin to being on the training pitch at Manchester United, or walking a practice round with a group of golf champions before the Open. For an hour and a half you live in the capsule of that 30-strong bunch of horses and riders, hearing their woes, sharing their challenges, relishing their and your dreams of what might be possible with the athletes moving so sweetly between their and your knees.

There is no evidence, bar an entrancing piece of home cine film, that Henry did it particularly well; in any case, he and David soon grew too big and heavy to go down the race-riding path, the default early diversion of the enthusiastic trainer's son. But it is significant that he did it at all. Plenty of subsequent evidence has shown that while not academic he is a highly sensitive, quite sensuous man. To have that riding-out experience across the historic glories of Newmarket Heath where the whole horseracing story began in Charles II's time and whose Warren Hill has fired artists such as Wootton, Seymour and Munnings for three full centuries now is something that was to prove intrinsic to Henry's being.

How could it not when so many famous figures beat their way to his stepfather's door, not the least of them Sir Alfred Munnings, who was impressed with Henry's drawing, a talent now being taken to a more serious level by his younger son Jake? How much more excitement does a teenager need than for the horses being ridden beside him to include not just the four-year-old Alcide, whose 1959 victories were to establish him as the best colt Cecil Boyd-Rochfort ever trained, but also Parthia, who that June was to give the now 72-year-old Captain the Epsom Derby which for so long the fates had denied him?

That year was the last great season of Cecil Boyd-Rochfort's career. Its £109,000 in winnings was his highest-ever annual total, even if it did not match the £145,000 of his great rival Noel Murless, who was later to play so large a part in his stepson's story. That year also saw the final flowering of one of the great training teams of the twentieth or any other century: CBR as trainer, Harry Carr as stable jockey and the tall, dashing, one-time Grand National-winning figure of Bruce Hobbs as assistant. In many ways training racehorses is no more and no less than running an academy of equine excellence, and academies can never depend on the principal alone. The perfect mix for a great racehorse trainer is that he provides the strategic wisdom, the assistant or head lad supplies the operational detail, the jockey delivers on the track, and all three work together in total mutual trust. This triple infusion rarely works perfectly or for long, but when it does all things are possible. It certainly happened in Henry Cecil's glory days, and in the Indian summer of his career something similar began to gel.

So why, when the 17-year-old twins emerged from Canford too big to be jockeys, too blockish for business and too unwilling for the army, did CBR not immediately groom one of them to be his successor? Partly because of the agony of letting go. 'What else would I do?' said the great John Dunlop contemplating life in his seventies as he looked towards the sea from his downland gallops at Arundel in Sussex. Indeed Bruce Hobbs' decision to set up as a trainer on his own was taken only when he realised his mentor was not going to retire any day soon. And partly because, by their own admission, the twins were not exactly clamouring for jobs to do; and probably by the very fact that it still seemed impossible to plan for one twin without the other.

But they had at least shown an interest in 'horse flesh', as well as a clearly burgeoning one in wine, women and cigarettes. Old CBR was probably the world's best-connected man in the realms of 'horse flesh' and it's hard to see how he could have bettered the experiences to which he exposed his two stepsons over the next couple of years. He did not invite them to hang around either his own or another trainer's racing stables but first despatched them into stud life. The idea was for them to get some physical experience of the animal at the heart of it all and so equip them with enough knowledge to be of use to someone in that sphere. True they were often, in Henry's words, 'little more than glorified unpaid labourers' much of the time. But in having to muck out and mix in they would gain some invaluable understanding of the painstaking sweat and slower rhythm of this other life.

For two seasons Henry did the basic daily routines at Lord Derby's Woodland Stud within walking (or in his case scooter-crashing) distance of Freemason Lodge, and at foaling time sat up through the night waiting for mares to give birth. It was hard work but, as the saying goes, that never did anyone any harm, and it also introduced him to 'Tote' Cherry-Downes, another 'GUL' (glorified unpaid labourer) who was to become one of Henry's closest and most influential friends.

For two late summers Henry also went up to Burton Agnes Stud in Yorkshire to help with the preparation of their yearlings for the autumn sales, learning the firm but even-tempered patience needed to get a boisterous young thoroughbred to accept the discipline of being led on daily condition-building walks. He got to know and like the ordinary guys he worked with despite the often vast differences in age and background, and relished the inflated glories of their wartime tales. Especially those of the Woodland Stud's Cherry Pryke, who insisted he should have got a VC for the heroism involved in lugging a three-gallon urn of boiling soup along the Great War trenches and getting it bullet-punctured and his backside scalded in the process.

This undergraduate course in equine management was not confined to England. In the autumn of 1961 Henry worked *un stage*, as the French call it, at Madame Jean Couturie's magnificent Le Mesnil stud near Le Mans which that summer had seen its greatest son, Right Royal V, win the King George VI and Queen Elizabeth Stakes at Ascot, and Henry would have shared in the staff's excitements as the colt then tilted at France's European seasonal showdown, the Prix de l'Arc de Triomphe, only to be run out of it by the Italian star Molvedo. By all reports Henry found the splendidly opinionated Madame Couturie inspirational enough, although he did not enjoy getting scratched to bleeding when having to retrieve fallen birds from thorn thickets on partridge shoots, and certainly did not get the chateau reception somehow afforded me when I visited with my friend Jeremy Hindley some eight years later. It remains the only time in my life when I have gone upstairs to find my clothes laid out, the bath run and the toothpaste squeezed out on to the brush.

Henry might not have been getting luxuries or money but his ageing stepfather was certainly providing him with contacts and sound equine experience. From Le Mesnil he did a stint at the Equine Research Station in Newmarket where he claims his main achievement was failing to administer enough anaesthetic to a four-legged patient and giving the surgeon something close to a heart attack when the beast revived mid-operation. Then in the spring of 1962 CBR played his biggest cards: he arranged for the twins to go to two of the most famous studs in America's famous 'Blue Grass' state of Kentucky, David to Claiborne Farm and Henry to Greentree.

Claiborne, owned by the Hancock family, and Greentree, then owned by Jock Whitney, the American ambassador in London and a long-standing patron of CBR's, were both state-of-the-art nurseries and beautiful temples to the famous thoroughbreds they had raised. Once again Henry's work was little more than basic horse handling and shit-shovelling, but at least the privileged 'Limey' showed he was not afraid to get his massive hands dirty. The twins ended the experience by riding the horse box all the way down to Florida with a bunch of yearlings for the bloodstock sales and then buying a $98 Greyhound bus ticket to make America their oyster.

Being CBR's stepsons, this trip featured a particularly large and impressive pearl in the shape of the 825,000 acres of the King Ranch in Brownsville, Texas. The ranch owner Bob Kleberg Jnr was yet another Freemason Lodge patron and he wrote to the Captain saying, 'I note that your sons Henry and David are in Kentucky and if you will let them know they are welcome to the ranch for a short visit at their convenience I will be glad to have them.' King Ranch, the backdrop for the film *Giant* and the James Michener novel *Centennial*, has almost mythical status in America, and no further proof of their stepfather's influence can be needed than to say that Kleberg himself later took the twins out on a cattle round-up, although Henry admitted his attempts to brand a calf were less successful than his pursuit of the local cowhands' daughters.

Yet despite having connections to die for the boys lacked any cash of their own, a situation they planned to rectify by working as lumberjacks for the Manawaukee Logging Company near Montreal. Their financial predicament was aggravated only once, when David fell for a honeytrap lady who neatly removed his wallet while he was sleeping off her ministrations. Quite what the Manawaukee lumberjacks made of this identical pair of willowy young Englishmen is not recorded and was certainly not understood by the twins as French was the only language. The credit the pair deserved for undertaking such arduous work was not matched by the brains of the company, which discovered that planning permission had been refused only after the crew had painstakingly felled and sawn the forest to construct a new camp. Everything built had to be destroyed.

It appears to have been hard and dirty work where the only chance of a wash was, according to Henry, a stagnant lake with large moose in attendance. Fortunately for their fellow passengers in the first-class cabin that Henry, at last flush with funds, had decided to indulge in, the pair had stayed with a cousin in Toronto for a clean-up, though they kept three heavy months of beard to surprise their family when they got back to Crathes. Nearly half a century on it is hard to sift fact from fable, but even if only part of the story is true Jamie and his guests at the castle must have been pretty shocked when the two ex-lumberjacks came loping up from the station for all the world like two shaggy prodigal sons in search of succour and forgiveness.

They may have gained experience in the previous couple of years but they do not seem to have grown any extra ambition when they discovered that the employment register was not exactly awash with vacancies for 20-year-old would-be stud managers. With no other prospects in mind they somehow not only got their sorely pressed stepfather to send them on the notorious one-year estate management course at Cirencester Agricultural College, they also got him to buy them both a car: a Mini for Henry and a Renault Dauphine for David. The Captain had plenty of reasons to regret both decisions. The cars barely lasted a day, Henry smashing his into a wall and David contriving unwittingly to emulate his father's 1936 railway landing by skidding off a bridge and writing off the Renault in a sheep field. That the twins lasted at Cirencester appears not to have been through any merit of their own but because their high-japes, heavy-drinking, chain-smoking, party-going attitude was standard behaviour. On the morning of a royal visit, the daffodils had been painted red, white and blue. On returning from holiday, the principal found an old Morris Eight sitting on his bed. Not for nothing was this sojourn nicknamed the gin and tonic course.

It is from this time that I retain a blurred memory of two engaging but archetypical examples of those apparently useless sons of the gentry with which Cirencester abounded. Of course I was a bit of a priggish swot by comparison, having just finished Oxford University, and was running and wasting away in an attempt to make my way forward as a jockey. If anyone had told me that one of those genial drunken boys was going to become one of the most successful and driven racing men of the century I would have thought they had been on the wacky baccy, which was just starting to do the rounds in those days.

Plenty of others also took the pessimistic view, like Alan Yuill Walker, now a well-regarded author and pedigree expert but then a racing-mad doctor's son from Hampshire whose father had become GP to the trainer Bill Wightman at Upham near Southampton. Most mornings Alan would have an 11.30am cup of coffee with the Cecil twins at a place appropriately called the Mad Hatter. He used to feel very proud to be close to the stepsons of the famous Captain Boyd-Rochfort, 'but I never flattered myself that they were there because of me. They were there because it was where the students from the Secretarial College would take their break and the girls would be all over them. What's happened since is amazing really because back then Henry didn't seem very interested in racing. If people quizzed him about the Boyd-Rochfort horses he would say, "Oh I don't know, ask Alan." It's hard to believe he could ever have had the drive to do what he has. And yet the record is there for all to see.'

When the twins got back to Newmarket the prospects at first seemed little better. 'What are we going to do with Henry?' somebody asked upon leaving a party where much drink had been taken and little sense shown. 'He just seems so hopeless.' The stepfather had one last deck to play. He secured for Henry the promise of a position with leading bloodstock agent Keith Freeman in Norwich, while David could come and join him as assistant. The thought of being under the old man's thumb was too much for David, so the twins agreed to swap roles. The racing world could now begin to judge just how 'hopeless' Henry would prove to be.

2

RACING APPRENTICESHIP

THEY MUST have made an odd couple. Captain Cecil Boyd-Rochfort, Croix de Guerre, in his late seventies but ever the unbending, utterly Edwardian figure who for half a century had cast a distinctive shadow across Newmarket Heath. Henry Cecil, only 21, the tall, flop-haired stepson whose main claim to fame, if any, was being fairly boisterous at parties and very dangerous in cars.

When Henry joined the stable it was certainly true that CBR needed an assistant. For the departure of Bruce Hobbs in 1960 had been followed by Harry Carr's retirement in July 1964, so removing the second vital part of the team that had given Freemason Lodge three trainers' championships and five British Classics in the 1950s. The Captain's mind was sharp but he was a tired and often lame old man and his tolerance level was declining with age. Cooks, butlers and housemaids came and went. And just as he never learned to drive he never came to terms with the telephone, which he continued to berate in such loud and forceful terms that Weatherbys, the racing secretariat, told him they would cease operations if he did not moderate his language.

His personal position was not eased by the erratic charms of his dazzling but sometimes dizzy consort. Besides being 30 years her husband's junior, Rohays was such a glamorous figure that when, in her forties, she appeared in an advertisement for After Eight mints bearing the slogan 'a girl should resist anything but temptation', the headmistress of Roedean wrote in to object. Not surprisingly, perhaps, her weakness for alcohol increased and, although CBR was wonderfully supportive, it cannot have been easy when Rohays was on one of her moderate days wandering round in a nightgown.

What most people felt the Captain needed was somebody out of the Bruce Hobbs mould who could have serious input into the training system and ensure operational efficiency was kept up both in the stable yard and through all the routines of preparing, planning, transporting and competing at the highest level. Instead CBR opted for his entirely untested stepson who for so many years had been part of the sibling gang that biked around the yard and even climbed over the wall when he was entertaining the Queen in the large conservatory, built to try to compensate for the dark Victorian pokiness of most of the rooms within Freemason Lodge.

It was an act of either inspired selection or dangerous family indulgence, and it's not hard to guess what the majority opinion was. 'It was always going to be very difficult,' says a longstanding member of staff. 'The Captain was very set in his ways and when Henry came he was keen enough, but he was like a big labrador puppy with those huge hands and feet. It was all right to begin with but they were going to be two dogs in the same kennel and that doesn't often work.' To this day Henry refuses to disparage his stepfather, but 'you can't have two trainers' is one of the apparently casual epigrams that often still drop from his lips.

Despite such misgivings and the lessening of the winners' total from 24 in 1964 to just 11 a year later, the first season with

Royal victory in the Eclipse Stakes at Sandown Park, 1965: Canisbay (Stan Clayton) beats Roan Rocket (Bill Williamson).

Henry Cecil as assistant had some headline highlights and saw an almost doubling of prize money from £23,000 to £40,000. Chief beneficiary of this was his most famous patron, Her Majesty the Queen. In 1965 the royal colours were carried to glory in the Eclipse Stakes with Canisbay and in the Yorkshire Cup with a gelding called Apprentice, whose subsequent success in the Goodwood Cup had been preceded by another victory for the Queen by Gold Aura in the Goodwood Stakes. Wise though it may be for Her Majesty never to give interviews, it would be truly fascinating to know what she made of the youthful, rather dressy stepson who was now so often at her trainer's side.

With her sense of history she would have appreciated that Canisbay's Eclipse was the first for a reigning monarch since the great race was incorporated (at twice the then prize money of the Derby) at Sandown in 1886. With her horseman's background she would have been even more impressed by the training achievement of getting Apprentice to win the Yorkshire Cup as not just his first-ever success but in his first race for almost two years after breaking down as a three-year-old. It was the seventh time CBR had saddled a Yorkshire Cup winner and was a supreme example of the patience that has him accepted as one of the greatest trainers of stayers in the history of the turf. No coincidence, then, that 'patience' was the first word Henry Cecil used when asked for the keys to his profession by Clare Balding in a BBC interview preceding Royal Ascot in 2011.

Not that the stepson didn't test the old man's patience to the limit when he joined him. It was not just his dress sense or the usual young man's follies: on one drink-fuelled return journey from Cambridge he entirely failed to navigate the roundabout at the top of the July Course and ended with his car so thoroughly wedged between trees that they had to wake up a posse of stable lads to secretly pull it out. The extra concern was something which was dynamite, for in a town where the principals all compete in the same profession and where success and failure is logged in the newspapers every day, swirling jealousies abound. Moreover, Henry Cecil was going out with Julie, daughter of Noel Murless, the tall, quiet figure up at Warren Place who had been champion trainer four times in the previous seven years and was to be again, three more times in the next six. This courtship, even if it had not quite come to that, was most definitely 'sleeping with the enemy'.

Julie had arrived at Newmarket as a ten-year-old in 1952 when her father moved from Beckhampton in Wiltshire, where he had first topped the trainers' table in 1948. Her first memory of Cecil Boyd-Rochfort was of a large figure blocking out the sun and an unexpectedly kindly voice asking where her pony had come from. Used to roaming free in Wiltshire, she initially found Newmarket restrictive but soon thrived as she began to ride some of the top horses in the Murless string. She has a memory of two little boys in cowboy outfits at the pony club, but when she got to know them better the two she actually teamed up with were Arthur and Henry's twin David. Indeed she still thinks the only reason she linked up with Henry is because something had upset her and she went to cry on David's shoulder but mistook Henry for his younger twin and found the shoulder strangely comforting.

Whatever the case, the fact of a liaison between the children of Newmarket's greatest rivals presented the sort of dilemma and opportunity for gossip such as may be seen today were the son of the Manchester United manager to begin 'walking out' with the daughter of his counterpart at Manchester City. To this end Henry hardly helped his cause one evening by bringing Julie home noisily in the small hours and having his attempt at climbing a drainpipe unhappily interrupted by the master of Warren Place opening the front door, just as his great rival's trespassing stepson lost his grip and crashed to the ground in a drunken heap. 'Go home' are the only reportable words from Noel Murless.

Despite all this the relationship continued to develop, and on 19 October 1966 Henry and Julie were married at St Mary's (below). In the wider world it was two days before the tragedy at Aberfan in Wales, where a rain-sodden slag heap slipped and buried 116 schoolchildren. But at Newmarket it was a day for racing royalty, with Lester Piggott's daughter Maureen acting as bridesmaid and 26-times champion jockey Sir Gordon Richards toasting the bride and groom. However unfocused Henry's aim may have been in the past, it would have to be much tighter now. Not just for his personal responsibility for the daughter of one great trainer, but for the mounting pressure he would feel in his dealings with the other.

For the Captain was not getting any younger, nor any more robust. On his 80th birthday on 16 April 1967 he would receive an engraved

silver cigarette box from the Queen; but the year before that had given Henry two of the harshest possible examples of the disasters that always lurk even in the brightest of training's clear blue skies.

His stepfather had not been well over the winter of 1965/66 and the normal Boyd-Rochfort cruise to Florida was delayed and then substituted by three weeks in the Sicily sun. But CBR's health was buoyed by the well-being of a handsome bay three-year-old called Smooth Sailing, who promised to at last lay to rest the hoodoo over the horses he trained for Harry Guggenheim. This Yale- and Cambridge-educated businessman, ambassador and philanthropist, whose family name has been immortalised by the museums in New York and Bilbao, remained the one American billionaire in the Boyd-Rochfort collection for which the luck would not turn.

Twice in the last decade, with colts named Bald Eagle and Iron Peg, the Captain had trained horses of such promise that they had been favourites for the Classics before they had even run. Twice hope had proved a fickle companion, and now came the third time. When CBR came back from Sicily he was thrilled with the way Smooth Sailing had flourished under his stepson's care and, in one of the thousands of dutiful letters that were his trademark, he was able to tell his almost equally aged patron that his colt was 'a fine horse with beautiful action and certainly gives me the impression that he will be a racehorse. He looks to me far superior to anything I have got here.' On 19 March CBR and his stepson went out to watch Smooth Sailing work. That afternoon, his owner was penned another letter:

This morning, Smooth Sailing was doing a nice exercise gallop, seven furlongs across the Flat, and [stable jockey Stan] Clayton was riding him. He passed us going magnificently on the bit and Clayton said he had never felt him going better. Just after he passed us he crumpled up and his whole hind part seemed to give way and down he went. I felt sure he had broken a bone and Clayton told me he heard it distinctly and two of my boys who were with me also heard it, just like a shot out of a gun. Of course the poor horse lay there and we kept his head down so that he could not get up and telephoned for the vet immediately. He said he had fractured his tibia where it goes into the stifle and the bone was just through the skin. The vet said there was nothing to do but to destroy him.

Such deaths are always shattering. One moment there is half a ton of rippling athlete powering across the turf as 300 years of genetic planning have programmed it to do. The next, a limb has gone and down it crashes, soon to be not just a tyre-punctured vehicle but a great lump of steaming meat. The thoroughbred is such a symbol of hope and vitality that when it is so instantly extinguished there is a choking shock, even in the recollection. Although rare, it has always happened and always will. It is a full 40 years back to the half a dozen or so occasions it happened to me as a jockey, but the image of a broken-necked chestnut called Red Stag lying on the Newbury turf as the field of novice hurdlers thundered away into the distance haunts me still, as does the noise made by the cracking hind leg of a novice chaser called Mine Alone as his weight snapped his limb beneath him as he struggled to get up after we had turned over in the lead at the now defunct racetrack at Wye.

Smooth Sailing haunts Henry Cecil all the way back to March 1966, and five months later the unwanted lightning struck again, this time with different but every bit as unhappy implications for his stepfather and one of his elderly patrons. For while Lady Zia Wernher, the owner of the Triple Crown superstar Meld, could not like Harry Guggenheim be called an unlucky Boyd-Rochfort owner, she had been unfortunate with the products of Meld's half-sister Sonsa, two of whom had suffered fractures at Newmarket. And although such memories may have given the Tsar's great granddaughter pardonable reasons to send Meld's son Charlottown to trainer Towser Gosden on the supposedly more fracture-free Sussex Downs at Lewes, the man who had masterminded Meld to glory cannot have liked it. CBR would therefore have been especially pleased when Meld's two-year-old son Donated was enrolled at Freemason Lodge, not Lewes, thrilled when he began to show promise, and mortified when the Smooth Sailing saga went into an encore. Donated, too, snapped a leg and had to be euthanised on the Newmarket gallops.

'I felt heartbroken,' wrote Henry, 'and I am quite sure that for all his outward composure, the Captain did too. But he consoled me by putting his arm round my shoulders and saying quite simply, "These things happen. That's racing."'

Age and outlook might have given stepfather and stepson their differences, but here was recognition that both their lives depended on the daily dynamic of racehorse care. There were only seven winners that season. They were united in grief.

At a mere 74, Lady Zia was two years younger than the unlucky Harry Guggenheim, but she was a full 24 years younger than Mrs Charles Oliver Iselin. Henry Cecil must have realised that, while his stepfather's age might give him an opportunity (not publicly confirmed until June 1968), it was also likely to remove his principal patrons pretty soon. Indeed in the 1968 season, Mrs Iselin was, with eight horses in training, numerically their largest owner, and she had been 100 years old on 7 January. Among the Iselin entry was a tall dark bay called Wolver Hollow whom CBR had always rated, had probably campaigned too highly, but who at the turn of 1968 was struggling with grass sickness. Every week Henry would make the sad drive with his stepfather to see the horse, who at one stage was little more than skin and bone.

Hope Iselin was quite a player herself. The daughter of one fortune and married to another, a pioneer woman golfer and the first woman to sail in a winning America's Cup yacht, she was appalled when she heard that the district where their magnificent Long Island home stood (after which Wolver Hollow was named) was to be called 'Lower Brookville'. 'I refuse,' she said with magnificent hauteur, 'to live in "Lower" anything. If you must call it something you must call it Upper Brookville.'

In the summer of 1968 Mrs Iselin made one last visit to see her horses at Newmarket. She had winners at Ripon, Yarmouth and Beverley, and then in August Henry took a recovered Wolver Hollow across the Channel and watched the veteran Australian jockey 'Scobie' Breasley coax the Iselin colours home in the coveted Prix Ridgway at Deauville. Afterwards the Captain sent a letter with the good news to his owner, adding, 'There is one thing I have done with which I am sure you will agree, and that is to give my stepson Henry fifty pounds. He has worked so hard and taken such care over all the horses that I think he deserves it.'

The money will have been well received, and so too was one unique statistic about this final big-race success for CBR as a trainer: Scobie Breasley was a 54-year-old grandfather, Boyd-Rochfort was 81 and the horse's American owner had reached her century. The combined ages of Wolver Hollow's connections made a surely unsurpassed total of 235. Henry would need some younger allies to take him forward.

One of them was at Freemason Lodge already. George Winsor had come from Cornwall as a 16-year-old apprentice and had the enviable duty of looking after Wolver Hollow. His long career in racing ended with a horrible fall in the summer of 2010 when a horse broke a leg and fell heavily with him on Newmarket's 'Al Bahathri' all-weather gallop. Cancer meant George died much mourned a year later, but not before his contribution had been publicly recognised at the Godolphin Stable Staff Awards in February 2011.

'Henry was assistant and I was just a stable lad,' George recalled when we talked after the ceremony, 'yet he was always easy to speak to, no airs and graces, although he was more into his clothes and what he was wearing. He could get on with people and it was obvious he would be more relaxed around the place. The Captain was real old school and every evening you had to have your horse standing just right and the box prepared perfectly with a thin layer of straw in the corner with a sprinkling of sand and a twist of straw across the doorway.

'Ninety-five per cent of lads wouldn't know what you were talking about nowadays, but that is the way it was and I enjoyed the owners coming round, especially the Queen. She would always talk to you and I remember doing a little horse of hers called Autograph who won at Folkestone which in those days before the M25 [that motorway didn't open until 1986] meant you had to go through London and the Blackwall Tunnel and it would be a three-day trip: one to go, one to race, and one to return.'

George Winsor went on to be an integral part of the Cecil team; in the glory years he was the neat figure in the blazer with the paddock sheet on his arm in his role as travelling head lad. His portrait of the young Henry rings true even in its reservations. 'He liked a drink and he was a lunatic driver. There was no Newmarket bypass in those days and at weekends the traffic on the A14 would be so chocker that you could walk from Freemason Lodge up to the clock tower at the top of the High Street quicker than a car would travel. Henry had a white Daimler Dart and one day he gave me a lift and went straight down the middle between all the traffic. I thought I would never get over it.'

If George Winsor was the sort of guy a new trainer would want to keep in the yard, Paddy Rudkin was the type you needed to import. At the time Henry came up to him on the Heath and asked him to join him as his future head lad, Paddy was a 28-year-old local farrier's son who had started in racing as an already nine-stone apprentice 14 years earlier. His career had one interruption, or more exactly amputation, when he got the sack for refusing to continue working after 1pm when soaked through on Boxing Day; he then lost a finger when, blacklisted by the racing yards, he got a job in a sawmill.

But what was left of Rudkin was good, stern stuff. He finally got another 'jack-of-all-trades' racing job with ex-jockey-turned-trainer Scotty Pringle where no horse was thought too difficult or any rogue too cute. From there, at the ripe old age of 23, he answered an advert for head lad placed by the stylish Teddy Lambton, who ended up saying, 'If you have the cheek to apply for the job, you can have it. You can teach me things and I can teach you things.' They had big winners, and Lambton and his friends landed some massive gambles with horses like Compensation in the Ayr Gold Cup and David Jack in the Magnet Cup. But too many plans came unstuck and when Paddy found he was getting as friendly with the debt collector as any of the owners, he began to wonder how he would put bread on the table for his dance teacher wife and their two children.

'It must have got out that I wasn't happy,' said Paddy, 'and then one day Henry came up out of the blue and asked if I would like to join him. I had got to know him on the Heath when we would both be watching our horses. He was very chatty, no snob or anything, not too grand to talk to a mere head man. I actually started in the last months of the old man. I got on well with the Captain but it was obvious that when Henry started things were going to be different.'

The year 1969 began with frost in all quarters and ended with the string dispersed to the four winds. In between there was anger, despair, triumph and confusion, and the very first winner, Celestial Cloud, probably didn't win at all. Anyway, he should have been banned as a danger to his fellow quadrupeds.

That's probably a bit harsh on the three-year-old colt who not only earned his place in history as the first of the more than 3,000 winners to have 'trained H. Cecil' after their name but went on to score twice more in that crucial opening season, which ended with a highly respectable 27 winners and over £60,000 in prize money compared with the poor old Captain's 11 winners and just £15,600 in his farewell year. Yet the quirks surrounding that opening success by Celestial Cloud, in a 25-runner amateur riders' race at Ripon on 17 May 1969, are worth pondering because they reveal the fires that so often spit and crackle beneath the surface of the thoroughbred athlete. Not all the lines in Henry Cecil's face are down to illness or high living.

Celestial Cloud had a lump on the top of his spine and it made him, to put it mildly, 'very touchy'. George Winsor looked after and rode the colt, as he did the five-year-old Wolver Hollow who in July was to put Henry in the headlines by landing the Eclipse Stakes at Sandown. 'He knew me,' said George of Celestial Cloud. 'He was fine when I was grooming his neck and shoulder but when you went on down his flanks and arse he would keep eyeing you and going "rrrrr" as if to say "don't you dare".'

No doubt that lump was responsible for Celestial Cloud's hang-ups but, as with all delinquents, it's no fun if you are on the receiving end of their behaviour. Out at exercise, for which he needed a special cut-away saddle, he was that rare but always alarming breed of equine psychopath, a horse with a tendency not just to kick but with an intent, once started, to kick and maim. On one occasion as a two-year-old he split open the shin of a rider who had got too close, and on another he did much worse to one of his own kind.

'He nearly killed a loose horse down by Mark Prescott's [at the bottom of Warren Hill],' remembered George. 'The loose horse tried to get between him and the wall and he roared and hollered and kicked and kicked. I shouted like hell and when I looked round he had kicked the other horse down and was kicking it on the ground. Somehow I got him away and got the hell out of there. I am afraid I never did find out what happened to the other horse.'

It is to George's and to the rest of the team's credit that they managed to avoid any repetition of this attempted equicide, although when amateur jockey Bill O'Gorman came to ride him in preparation for the race at Ripon he was alarmed to find Celestial Cloud grabbing the neck of the horse working beside him at full gallop. It is also no coincidence that in the subsequent 40 years there have been few repetitions of anything resembling this behaviour in a stable where shouting is actively discouraged and any gratuitous use of a whip is a sackable offence.

But Celestial Cloud's moment in history's heaven did not come until early summer, and by then his young trainer was in despair from the deep chill he had faced from both frost and family.

It had been a brutally cold winter. The snow had come in January and hung around for weeks. Freemason Lodge had no covered trotting rings like the one Noel Murless had built at Warren Place, so the only way the horses could be exercised was to trot them round a circle of deep laid straw in the stable paddock. It is a tedious and often precarious process as ultra-fresh horses suddenly go from a reasonably controlled trot into a passable imitation of a bucking bronco. I was a professional jump jockey back then and what hangs worse in the memory is the moment when the bucking horse goes off the comparative grip of the straw ring into the rock-hard, ice-packed paddock alongside. When a car skids it does at least go in the same collective direction; the sprawling horse has no balance at all and the shivering creature in the saddle curses it and his or her luck and their employer in unison.

Henry was making the best of it, as was his ten-minute-younger brother David, who had set up his own stable at Stork House in Lambourn after assisting trainer Peter Nelson nearby. There is a wonderfully evocative magazine article featuring the snowbound pair of them as the first set of twins to have training licences. Both of

'A brutally cold winter': Julie Cecil leads the string on the straw ring in the snow.

them look impossibly young, dressy and serious: David in polo neck and neat leather jacket elegantly mounted on a white hack; Henry with his dark hair slicked down above a smart coat and narrow trousers looking out rather soulfully as a head-scarfed Julie glances across from the front of the string. David had just 12 horses, most of them two-year-olds, in a stable he was starting from scratch, but Henry had an inherited team of 41, and for all the set-faced bravado in the picture he was beginning to realise just how apt the article's phrase 'daunting assignment' could prove.

For he and his stepfather were barely on speaking terms. No one can quite remember what triggered it. Julie thinks it was about the Captain insisting on a jockey Henry did not like. However it happened, that prophecy about 'two dogs in the same kennel' was proving unhappily accurate. Instead of being able to wish each other well every morning the pair studiously avoided each other to the extent that Henry and Julie would dip down below eye level to avoid the Captain's disapproving gaze as they came past his study on the way to the stables. Since their wedding they had lived half a mile away in a house on the Beech Stud loaned them by Lady Sassoon, whose husband had won the 1953 Derby with the Gordon Richards-ridden Pinza and the 1957 and 1960 races with Crepello and St Paddy, both trained by Noel Murless and ridden by Lester Piggott. Beech House gave them a home of their own but it was not meant to divorce them from the place which had been Henry's home for all his conscious life. 'It's all past now and everybody got over it and became friends again,' said Bow Cecil, 'but it was difficult at the time, and Mummy was very sad when Henry could hardly get himself to come in the house.'

For all his youth, the pictures of the time show a sort of pouting determination in Henry's face typical of the young man intent on doing things his own way rather than in the manner of his mighty forebear. For during the last four years he had lived with the experience of a great empire in decline. The key staff had either left or outlived their usefulness and the rest were, in Henry's words, 'on the whole pretty rough'. To try to clear the Edwardian cobwebs, he insisted on being called the less deferential 'guvnor' rather than the forelock-tugging 'sir'. The Captain was always 'sir'. After all, he was a man who never called a jockey by anything but his surname except in the case of the brothers Doug and Eph Smith, and even then it was always 'Douglas'. Henry even tried to ease the military inflexibility of the old regime by committing the heresy of abandoning, except for the visits of important owners, the hallowed routine of 'evening stables', where every horse and box and lad had to be standing up to gleaming attention while the trainer did his impersonation of a picky colonel inspecting the line.

However, just as it is for the young football manager who succeeds an old martinet at a famous club, the honeymoon of good wishes never outlives a set of poor results, and quite soon Henry's team only looked like losers. The middle of May is not that far into the Flat racing season, which starts at the end of March, but for a young trainer desperate to prove worthy of his fabled inheritance, the weeks without any success had become ordeals of increasing worry and self-doubt. Henry's position was one familiar to all professions, but it was always going to be trebly so in Newmarket, the place where his stepfather had been a legend for so long. It is a town where the very nature of your calling means the world watches your preparation in public, reads of your runners in the racing pages, and then chortles about your lack of results in the afternoon. As the winnerless drought continues you begin to imagine daggers even in the friendliest of 'bad luck' smiles. All Henry's later triumphs never quite healed the wound inflicted on his memory by the words drifting over, 'Don't back that, it's one of Henry Cecil's. He couldn't train ivy up a wall.'

The trouble, in those early months, was that the words as well as the results did not lie. For all its fame, Freemason Lodge's four-legged dowry was not, with a few exceptions, a glittering one. What's more, after the hold-ups with the frost Henry committed one of the two cardinal sins to which young trainers fall prey. They are either over-eager and gallop their horses too hard, or they are over-protective and work them too little. Henry Cecil fell into the latter camp, but as his self-doubt increased he sought advice from an acknowledged master of his profession. The natural place to find one would have been in the study under whose eyeline he ducked every morning, yet with his relationship with his stepfather in deep freeze he decided to reach across the marital tree. He asked Noel Murless to take a look.

There are many versions of this story but at least they all have the same conclusion. Murless, whose tall, weather-beaten, stolid shyness could make him look as aloof if not as Edwardian as CBR, was also a kindly man beneath it all. He watched his son-in-law's string as they cantered up the four-furlong climb of Warren Hill – the basic benchmark of Newmarket trainers even before John Wootton painted that iconic mid-eighteenth-century study which fetched £188,000 when sold at Christie's in 1998. The word 'canter' is used here in the racing not the normal equestrian sense, that is an already fairly swift preliminary gallop, not the gentle rocking motion of the 'canter' you see in the show ring. The horse is moving powerfully and swiftly beneath you as it tackles the collar of the incline. Your hand is hard on the rein to keep within the lower gears of the thoroughbred machine. But the horse should still be feeling a degree of effort. Henry Cecil's were not feeling enough.

'Your horses are galloping like a lot of old gentlemen,' Noel Murless opined. 'You must make them work.'

Henry Cecil may have been young, he may have always been in the academic slow lane, he may have been at loggerheads with his distinguished stepfather, but he was quick enough to accept a truth when it was presented to him. When his own fame climbed into the stratosphere and we outsiders would enquire of Newmarket regulars what was special about Henry's training routine they would always say, 'You should see his horses' first canter. It's quicker than any other trainer's. They really have to work.'

Improvement may have been under way, but it continued to keep its face hidden from the self-beleaguered young trainer as the spring of 1969 turned into summer. Forty horses was a substantial string for a racing stable at that time, surely not all of them could be talentless? Finally a heavily fancied, five-strong raiding party was despatched to Nottingham accompanied by three carloads of Henry's supporters and the young man himself. The least fancied of the five runners finished second, but the other four sank with the hopes and fortune of all concerned. The 'couldn't train ivy up a wall' whispers seemed to linger wherever he went. In despair, Henry didn't go anywhere at all.

He certainly did not go up to North Yorkshire's cathedral city of Ripon that third Saturday in May. The race was not on television and he did not listen to it in the betting shop or await the results on the radio; he only finally heard the news when he went over to Freemason Lodge that evening to be greeted by a 'Well done, guvnor, you've had your first winner'. Julie had been despatched to do the saddling since the horse ran in her colours after being bought as a cast-off from Lady Zia Wernher. Celestial Cloud behaved with almost church-going decorum as George Winsor led him round in the paddock, and in the race Bill O'Gorman reported no neck-biting criminality, only a bonny little horse doing his best to inch out a tight finish with a rival called Author's Correction. There was no photofinish, which meant the official verdict had to be done by the naked eye. To this day Julie Cecil thinks it ought to have been a case of 'Judge's Correction'.

'You could see it was very close,' she remembers, 'but I didn't think he had won and in the press photo, which still hangs in my loo, he certainly doesn't seem to have won. But it was a start. We were all absolutely chuffed to bits.'

For a rookie trainer, just as it is for a jockey, that first winner is something you never forget however many triumphs, disasters and other life experiences may follow. You have dreamt about and worked and prayed for your name one day to be written in the newspaper results, and when it finally happens you hoard all sorts of tiny extraneous fragments in the memory to guard against the dying of the light. But it wasn't Bill O'Gorman's first winner. 'I was making a bit of a go of it as an amateur,' he says, before adding laconically, 'They seemed to be pleased. Somebody said it was their first winner. But back then he was not "The" Henry Cecil. He was just another well-bred young trainer trying to get started. They come and they go. I didn't know it was to be the first of three thousand and counting. I thought it might have been the first of two.'

As it happened the second one came a week later when a horse called Pride Of Alcide won carrying the Alcide and Parthia colours of Sir Humphrey de Trafford, best man at CBR's wedding to Rohays a quarter of a century earlier. Going into Derby week David Cecil's few runners had yet to score and a newspaper ran a story under the banner 'Twin Henry Is Two Winners Ahead', which must rival 'Small Earthquake In Chile, Not Many Killed' in the annals of pointless headlines. That sibling imbalance was partially rectified on 17 June when a two-year-old called Tefcros won something called the Wolver Maiden Plate at Leicester in the colours of David's wife Fiona. She had racing connections in her own right, being the sister of trainer 'Atty' Corbett, and as Lord Rowallan's daughter she had the funds to help launch the stable. But after Wolver Hollow shocked everyone by winning the Eclipse Stakes a week into July, it was Henry who was suddenly heading for the stars.

Henry had not expected it. He admitted that after Wolver Hollow had previously finished last in the Lockinge after beating his stablemate and eventual second Tower Walk in a gallop, 'I felt absolutely useless and my confidence absolutely shattered'. Lester Piggott had not expected it either. In the days before the race he had been trying to manoeuvre himself into riding the favourite Park Top. And 101-year-old Hope Iselin could not be aware of it as she had slipped into a coma at her home in Long Island. When she finally died six months later it was without having heard tell of her greatest racing triumph.

The 1969 renewal of the Eclipse Stakes was some way from the most competitive running since that day in 1886 when a horse called Bendigo won its first running up those now familiar Sandown slopes with the spires of London on the north-eastern horizon. Only Park Top, of the eight runners, was of the class normally needed to win the race, and admirable though Wolver Hollow had shown

Wolver Hollow (Lester Piggott) at the start of the 1969 Eclipse Stakes.

himself in the previous year's Cambridgeshire and that Deauville victory which saw Henry 'dropped' £50 on the owner's behalf by his stepfather, he would need plenty of luck to win it. As the cards were dealt he got it in spades.

The card-playing metaphor is the best one for Flat race-riding. The ability of the horse beneath you is the hand you play. The better the hand the more careful you tend to be. At Sandown Geoff Lewis had, in Park Top, much the best hand; just about the only way he could lose was if he played too soon and Park Top's propensity to ease off when in front allowed others to trump her ace. Of course there is always another way to lose – by not playing your hand until far too late.

That's what happened in this Eclipse. While Geoff Lewis did and does get castigated for it, anyone who has ever ridden in a race can have sympathy for his predicament. For while Geoff appeared to have Park Top in the perfect position turning into the straight just behind the leaders, the gap on the inside and the opportunity to take the lead came fully two furlongs out, way before he thought it wise to put his mare's speed on the table. Not trusting a second gap to appear, he tacked left only to get blocked by others while Lester Piggott opportunistically launched Wolver Hollow up the inside, and in a trice the big black horse was home and hosed before Lewis could disentangle himself from the bunch and set off in hopeless pursuit.

In such circumstances public reaction focuses more on the vanquished than the victor. It was to happen to Cecil himself exactly 28 years later when Kieren Fallon lived a similar nightmare on another truly great racemare, Bosra Sham, and the trainer departed from his normal extremely sensible view of never publicly blaming his jockey. In 1969 the opportunity to praise the success of the young trainer as well as the Lester Piggott master class was not lost and John Lawrence (not ennobled to Lord Oaksey until his father's death the following year) was not going to miss it in *The Sunday Telegraph*.

'To see 26-year-old Henry Cecil standing for the first time in a big race winner's circle,' wrote John, 'within a few feet of his octogenarian mentor who had stood there so many times before, was to have the clearest of impressions of a new hand picking up a famous standard.' It was all characteristically eloquent and generous but John was not right about the closeness of master and pupil. Henry and the Captain were still not talking to each other. 'He stood by me and the horse,' said George Winsor, 'with the Captain back with his own friends. You could feel the atmosphere, but I didn't care.'

Despite that continuing but mercifully not-to-be-permanent unhappiness, Wolver Hollow's victory was as astonishing a boost as any self-doubting tyro in his mid-twenties could possibly wish for, as well as a supremely fitting closure to the long association between the Captain and Hope Iselin, all of whose horses bar Wolver Hollow went under the hammer four days after that Eclipse. In truth the old man had probably allowed his heart to rule his head a little ever since he wrote to Mrs Iselin in October 1965 saying, 'I bought you a colt for 4,000gns today, I hope you will not be angry with me for doing so. I was so taken with him I could not resist him.' For a colt who was by all accounts very tall and unfurnished it is really quite surprising to find that he was run first time out in the New Stakes at Royal Ascot as a two-year-old, and one has to wonder if this was not more to suit the ageing owner's annual trip than the long-term interests of the horse.

Indeed while Wolver Hollow had proved his mettle with that Deauville victory and those two top-weight second places in the Cambridgeshire, his poor run when last in the 1969 Lockinge at Newbury followed by a moderate second in the Prince of Wales's at Ascot were easier for outsiders to ascribe more to continued over-facing than to any of the trainer's self-flagellating concerns about his own competence.

But in racing it is the results that matter. Henry Cecil had now landed a big one, and the effect was obvious. 'He began to relax,' says Paddy Rudkin, 'the staff relaxed, the horses relaxed, and the results began to come.' Celestial Cloud won twice more to make up for his potential criminality, as did a little filly called Karen who was as cussed in temperament as she was odd-shaped in the leg department. The stable won four races with Karen despite her early refusal even to canter at home and having to be led down to the start backwards before winning her final race at Chepstow by a short head. She had been sent as a cast-off from Noel Murless, who hadn't the time to bother with such a little madam. She was thus the first horse Henry Cecil trained in the black jacket/scarlet cap silks of Mr Jim Joel. It was to be a Classic-winning association.

It seemed the same could be said, even at this first time of asking, of the green and scarlet Humphrey de Trafford's colours, which had so famously won CBR his first and only Derby in 1959 with Parthia. For in September 1969 Henry saddled a colt called Approval, who was a son of Sir Humphrey's greatest horse Alcide and was still thought to be too backward to be fully competitive. A highly promising second in that race at Ascot was followed by a real jackpot of a success a month later in the Observer Gold Cup at Doncaster when he swept through past horse after horse after being last and either unwilling or unable to go anywhere turning into the straight. Approval had beaten a favourite of Vincent O'Brien's. He was second only to that trainer's unbeaten Nijinsky in the betting for the next year's Derby. His young handler was on his way. Except that he did not have a home to go to.

He had always known Freemason Lodge was up for sale. He had managed to get the lease of the first of the new yards that the Jockey Club was building in the Hamilton Road on the edge of the Rowley Mile on the other side of town. What he had not calculated on was having to move out before what was to be called Marriott Stables was ready in the new year. But Uncle Cecil and his mother were off to Kilnahard Castle in Ireland's County Cavan and the diggers were coming in. 'It wasn't ideal,' Henry now says with what has to be shrugging understatement. 'Jeremy Hindley was very kind and let me board some horses at Kremlin Stables [where Michael Jarvis and Roger Varian have followed him]. I got permission from the Jockey Club to have 24 in the racecourse stables and we had another 20 or so in another yard at Exning. One lad and I used to go down there and do the whole lot every evening.'

To the outsider it had been a dream start to an opening season. In December Henry Cecil had the first of what were to become legendary Christmas parties for the stable, albeit that it had three bases and none of them secure. True, the new yard was emerging out of the winter rubble. But they were not to know its walls would be of the edible kind. This stable would start by being chewed by its own string.

3

THE ITALIAN CONNECTION

MARRIOTT STABLES was very much on the other side of town to Freemason Lodge, in style as well as location. No big, gloomy house glowering over the paddock, just a modern office and a head lad's bungalow for Paddy and Joy and their two children, while Henry and Julie continued at Beech House on the road to Cheveley. No high-ceilinged old units with difficult floors to drain but a set of big American-style barns with the boxes facing each other and much easier to clean. The trouble is that the horses also found them easier to eat.

Well, not exactly eat, more rasp their teeth on. As the walls of the breeze-block boxes were not entirely set, in the first few weeks they became quite disfigured, even if not quite in Henry's words 'like a giant Gorgonzola cheese'. With a string now 60 strong he had felt able to hire the astute and talented Greville Starkey as stable jockey. Henry Cecil may have been ambivalent about being a trainer only five years earlier but now that streak of often hidden determination was hungry to build on the successes of his first season. Secretary Anne Scriven, travelling head lad Arthur Simmons, deputy head lad 'Dodger' Hopper and box driver Sid Harris may have come over from the Boyd-Rochfort kingdom, but at Marriott Stables things were going to be run the Cecil way.

'He changed things a lot,' Paddy Rudkin recalls. 'He had begun to do it at Freemason Lodge but now he was at a new place and it all became very different. We would get everything done first and then walk through the town to do our canters on Warren Hill after the others. He didn't like to walk old style in military lines but to go in twos and threes. He would say, "I want them to be able to talk to each other." He loved going through the town. He would wear cowboy jackets with tassels on them. He would chat to people, sometimes he would stop and buy an ice cream. I had been brought up in the old school and sometimes I would come back and say to Joy, "I am working for a crazy man, but I like it."'

What emerges from this testimony, and the recollections of others, is rather more than a talented butterfly taking wing from the chrysalis of sluggish youth. The image of a clothes-loving, filly-petting dilettante gave Henry a persona that did more than tickle his vanity; it gave him distance. As his fame grew it gave him space with TV inquisitors like me. He would stroke the neck of something in the winner's circle and say, 'She is so sweet you would like to take her out on a date. You would, wouldn't you?' Or if some big colt had won impressively he would point out a large member of the press pack and say, 'I think he could have won on him, couldn't he?' But most of all it gave him space in the yard.

'He was amazing really,' says Paddy. 'In the mornings he would ride out three lots, wandering up and down chatting to the lads about their horses, and in the afternoons when I was doing my rounds he would just drift around from box to box. I can remember moaning sometimes, "The guvnor has done nothing this afternoon but just wander about the yard", yet I knew he trusted me to get the lads to run things properly so that he could get to know the horses, which he was incredible at. Within days of a yearling coming in he would be telling me all about it. His whole thing was getting to know them better and better.'

What's more, Henry had not just found time for himself, he was prepared to find time for his staff and his horses. Instead of each lad mucking out the horse he was due to ride and then joining the first lot to get to Warren Hill as early as possible, Henry turned the system on its head. On arriving at the yard each stable lad would first muck out all three of the horses in his charge and only then would he go and find the horse, if different, that he was due to ride. This meant the Cecil string arrived at Warren Hill after the other trainers had been up it. The ground might be a bit churned but the coast was clear. 'This was much better,' said George Winsor. 'We used to have so many rows with the old system. You came to do your horse in the evening and found the guy in the morning had left the box in a state. Now it was your responsibility. And when we got to Warren Hill there was no hanging about.' It might have seemed a little thing from the outside; inside it worked.

What is obvious is that the idea of Henry being a lucky puppet sustained by inheritance, wife and head lad is woefully short of the truth. 'Oh, he was in charge all right,' says Julie, 'and anyway I was having babies and things. But I loved being involved. I used to love riding out and going round with Paddy. I would drive Henry a lot. At least I could understand what he was talking about.' Katie Cecil was born in 1971 and her brother Noel two years later. Julie would be at Beech House with the children, so Henry's routine was to have his breakfast with Paddy and Joy. It all seemed casual but it actually set a pattern, which continues to this day. Whatever other conversations may appear to be happening in the morning, the main one Henry has is the one he has with his horses.

In all professions and especially when training racehorses, concentration is central, and Henry Cecil the hopeless, no-attention-span student had found his own way of becoming a scholar at the one subject his life equipped him to master. In a stable of any size the trainer's role is always more strategic than physical, so his actual input is often easier to measure in the breach than the observance. By the time a racehorse arrives at a yard the limits of its as yet unknown potential are already defined by its genes, construction, constitution and temperament. A good trainer will get closer to that potential more often than others, a bad one will just further limit the limitations. Henry Cecil was on his way to becoming a good trainer but to do it he would need talented horses to practise on and good staff to support him. He was already getting the first, he was beginning to get the second.

In those crucial first four seasons at Marriott Stables, 1970 to 1973, the great majority of the 182 wins (just seven at Group-race level) came from owners inherited from or recommended by stepfather or father-in-law. What's more, the most prestigious of them, Cloonagh's first Classic for the yard in the 1973 Irish 1,000 Guineas, was actually owned by his younger brother Arthur Boyd-Rochfort. In that sense they were indeed the fruits of privilege, most noticeably in that first season at Marriott Stables when both Approval and what was to be the Goodwood Stakes winner Pride Of Alcide belonged to Sir Humphrey de Trafford. Approval built on his 1969 season promise to win the Dante Stakes and, while he was then only seventh to Nijinsky in both the English and Irish Derbies, he had become a first runner for Henry in the Classics. The arrival of Sir Reginald Macdonald-Buchanan's Parthenon on the recommendation of Noel Murless gave the stable their first Royal Ascot success that June before going on to win the Goodwood Cup, which was a real headline-hitting double for the 27-year-old trainer.

With his good start and impeccable connections Henry Cecil's had turned out to be a suitable place for an establishment figure like Sir Reginald to have his horses when his trainer Sir Gordon Richards retired at the end of 1969, and a year later the same view was taken by Lord Howard de Walden when Jack Waugh also handed in his licence. So it was that a tall, nearly black colt called Falkland became the first of a glittering trail of Henry Cecil-trained winners to carry the famous all-apricot Howard de Walden silks when scoring first time out at Newmarket in April 1971. By the end of the year Falkland had won twice more and run third in a blanket finish in the St Leger. Marriott Stables' reputation as a good place to have a horse trained was reinforced by Affection, the two-year-old sprinter who won five races and was second three more times for Mrs George Lambton, the mother of Henry's father's old friend and first trainer Teddy Lambton. What's more, the winning range, from Affection's sprints to Parthenon's staying cups, suggested this might be more than silver spoon success. That's when more owners start looking up.

Charles St George was a giant of his day. A former Coldstream Guards officer and a wealthy Lloyds underwriter, he was a tall man who exuded power, charm and just a tiny hint of menace. He was Maltese-born and the snobby racing set loved to point out his father's full name was the Marquis Zimmerman-Barbaro St George. But trainers offered the chance of good horses don't mind if the owner is part Martian. In the past few years St George had won the Oaks for Ryan Price with Ginevra and the Champion Stakes for Noel Murless with Lorenzaccio. Murless's son-in-law looked like an interesting young man to follow.

In October 1971 a horse called Orosio became the first big winner to have the 'owned Charles St George, trained Henry Cecil' affix when taking the Cesarewitch, the two-and-a-quarter-mile first leg of Newmarket's 'Autumn Double', under jockey Geoff Lewis. The next year St George's grey colt Irvine won the prestigious Jockey Club Cup and Italy's Premio Roma – just the fifth and sixth Group-race winners for a stable that has now amassed more than 400. But significantly these were not ridden by stable jockey Greville Starkey but by St George's great friend and ally in the saddle, Lester Piggott. It was to be an association that could also have its complications.

But those are the problems of success, and they were only happening because the basis of what was to become one of the most formidable teams in racing history was getting more established year by year. With the stable lad's weekly return of £30 for a six-and-a-half-day week lower than the agricultural wage, a good yard in a large training centre could begin to pick and choose its applicants. That process was not always an easy one and the best results certainly owed something to good luck as well as good judgement.

For example, the start of Frank Storey's 27 years of high-input association as work rider and stable lad began when his diminutive frame was turned away only for Julie to call him back for something and Henry to say, 'Oh, I guess you had better come and join.' At around the same time the equally vertically challenged but at that stage less sober figure of Frank Conlon was also accepted, although he was apparently 'under a cloud' over his departure from his previous employer Bernard Van Cutsem. It was not Conlon's ability that was ever questioned – he had ridden Classic winners in their work – but his reliability. 'A couple of years after he took me on,' says Frank, 'Henry said he had been told "he will ride anything but he will always let you down".' Talent comes in many packages and it was becoming clear Henry could also pick the two-legged kind.

Choosing the right work for each horse and the right rider to do it is probably the one key judgement for a trainer to make. Many of the other jobs, from feeding to stable management and even race selection, can be delegated and discussed, but in the end how fast and far a horse should go in his gallop and who should ride him are the piano notes of the trainer's day, and they are best played by feel than from any existing song sheet. They certainly always have been by Henry Cecil. In the search for that something that will prove he is more than good horses, good staff and determination, it is on the extraordinary trouble he takes in the planning of his gallop schedule that you need to concentrate.

Henry never seems to get round to giving specific answers about how he operates, but in the spring of 2011 he suddenly opened up on how important it was to fit the right rider to each horse and to be prepared to change them if they didn't seem to gel. At the same time he revealed that on the days before his gallops mornings on Wednesday and Saturday he spends up to two and a half hours running the exact permutations through his mind. It has been ever thus. 'With quite a few things he would leave a lot to me,' says Paddy Rudkin, 'feeding, shoeing, even horses' legs, but who rode what and everything was all done by him. He would spend hours and hours on it as if to get a picture in his mind. There was certainly something special there.'

Yet hindsight should not impose too much grandeur on what was still little more than a fledgling operation with a trainer who'd only turned 30 in January 1973. This was still very much a family-dependent operation. How appropriate it was that their first Classic winner, Cloonagh, should have been owned and bred at what had been his aunt's Tally-Ho Stud in Westmeath by Arthur Boyd-Rochfort, and that in the same year the stable should win big races at Ascot, Deauville and York with a filly named after their daughter Katie Cecil.

They were not afraid to celebrate, and celebrations could get out of hand. Arthur remembers some revelry after Cloonagh's success at the Curragh but thinks Henry was not there. The trainer certainly was when Katie Cecil's Deauville glory was toasted at the Mirabelle and fellow diners had to enjoy (or otherwise) a well-wined Greville Starkey scuffling round on all fours barking like a dog. And back home at Beech House some celebrations could go decidedly beyond the permissible. Not many of the shenanigans do much credit to the perpetrators; you just have to plead different people, different times, and even different legislation, and thank heaven not many bones were broken. Back then it could seem a riot for Henry and Tote Cherry-Downes to do 'wheelies' around the grass acres called the Severals next to the Newmarket clock tower and then high-tail it back to Beech House with the siren-wailing police in pursuit. With the law as it stood then not allowing the constabulary over the threshold, the 'adventure' ended with the pair waving drunkenly at their frustrated pursuers from the 'Romeo and Juliet' balcony at the front of the house. Mind you, it must have been some party. The esteemed John Dunlop apparently fell backwards into the fire.

But the professional trajectory was ever upwards. In August Henry put an advert for a pupil assistant in the *Sporting Life*. At John Winter's stables in the Bury Road it was read by a young trainer's son over from Milan on a holiday job. When he was accepted an Italian connection was forged that would lift them to the big time.

Luca Cumani was meant to be a vet. Or at the very least he was supposed to be getting a veterinary science degree at Milan University to give him some qualifications to equip him for the brave new world in which he would find himself if Italy continued its move to the left. But he was a trainer's son and an Epsom amateur Derby-winning jockey. Opportunity knocked.

Not that his parents saw it that way. 'They were dead against it,' says Luca. 'It was not just that I was an only child and England with only two flights a week and moderate telephone connections seemed like the other side of the moon. My father said if communism comes and you don't have a degree, you will end up as a labourer. But I had the usual impetuosity of youth and they finally said, "You go, but without our blessing." I loved it at Henry's straight away, but sadly

I didn't talk to my parents for six months, not until my birthday in April.'

Luca was 25 by then, an able, educated, ambitious young man keen to hitch his wagon to a stable that was surely heading for the stars. 'They had more than 60 horses, which meant it was one of the largest yards in the town,' he observes. 'At the yearling sales Henry was paying more than £10,000 for a horse, which was the top bracket in those days, and you could sense this was a yard on the move. I started just doing my three horses and tried to do things for Paddy whenever possible. Henry was very much in charge. He had this cloak of being laid back but he was very ambitious. At heart he was not laid back at all.'

The cloak slipped a little in April 1974 when Greville Starkey got trapped behind the leaders in Newbury's John Porter Stakes before ending a fast-finishing third on a colt called Relay Race and found he was not stable jockey any more. In truth, as with most such things, the relationship had been souring for some time and had probably never recovered from Greville being beaten in similar circumstances when failing by a head to win the Dante Stakes at York a full 11 months earlier.

The elements are familiar. The horse, in this case a tall, black four-year-old with a tendency to shin soreness, is not entirely straightforward (as evidenced by him being tried in blinkers when disappointing in the Derby, his next race after the Dante). The jockey, proud of his position in the top flight, including in this case his first Classic in the Oaks ten years earlier, is not keen to take criticism from an up-and-coming trainer still his junior in age and experience. The split becomes inevitable and the best outcome is that both parties should flourish thereafter, which certainly happened in this case. Greville Starkey soon teamed up with a raft of great horses for the dynamic Guy Harwood while Henry resorted to the racing figure who cast the longest shadow of them all. Lester Piggott began to take his pick.

It is impossible to exaggerate how great an aura Lester had back then. He was coming up to 39 but had been a household name since riding his first winner in August 1948 as a chubby-faced 12-year-old. By the summer of 1974 he had won six Derbies, nine jockeys' championships and 20 English Classics, and eight years earlier had ended a 12-year association with champion trainer Noel Murless to take even better rides offered by the Irish maestro Vincent O'Brien. He was the most outrageous talent any of us had ever seen and he was a wolf that walked alone. Far from being impeded by partial deafness and muttered speech he made a virtue of selective hearing and a soft Brandoesque delivery that would make friends and employers, not to mention TV interviewers, strain to catch each mumbled word.

He could be both dazzling and disgraceful, and whenever racing folk gathered they swapped stories of the rides he had given or the tricks he had pulled. In August 1973, on the very morning of the Benson and Hedges Gold Cup at York, he abandoned a commitment to ride Harry Wragg's runner Moulton and instead replaced Yves Saint-Martin on the subsequently defeated Rheingold, a move that incensed the French legend who had flown in especially from Deauville. Vincent O'Brien was happy to be quoted by me in *The Sunday Times* as saying, 'I would like Lester Piggott to ride for me in all the big races but in none of the gallops. He just messes them up to find things out for himself.'

But for all his contrariness the racing world loved Lester, and the heartland at Newmarket loved him most of all. For he had racing deep in his genes. His father had been a ruthlessly tough jump jockey, his maternal grandmother was the sister of one champion Flat jockey and daughter of another, and his grandfather Ernie Piggott had landed three jump championships in England, one in

France, and had won three Grand Nationals, the last one in 1919 at the age of 41. Lester had always thought he would grow too heavy for the Flat and had not been afraid to risk riding big winners over hurdles. He wasn't afraid of anything. If he was on song, anything was possible. It certainly was when he came to ride Relay Race.

It shouldn't really be that fantastic. Relay Race was a good horse on his day and Lester won only two races on him, but that first time in Newmarket's Jockey Club Stakes, less than a month after the Greville Starkey row at Newbury, had to be seen to be believed. The horse was settled right at the back of the field with his bent-hairpin of a jockey so motionless that it seemed he was on any errand but a race-winning one. Then, without any apparent encouragement, Relay Race took wing and sped past his rivals to score by five lengths. No one has ever drawn or will ever draw the bow of a thoroughbred's mind back to loose it in an arrow of winning desire like Lester Piggott.

Despite a Spartan routine to keep himself two stone below his natural weight Lester was strong as well as brave, but the key to his genius – and he is the only jockey I have met to whom such a word could possibly apply – was his understanding of a racehorse's psyche. The partially deaf only child of riding parents often found horses, even the difficult ones, easier to communicate with than humans. In some cases the more difficult the better. Roussalka, the other star he rode for Henry Cecil that summer, was a case in point. She may have had a royal pedigree that fetched 21,000gns at the yearling sales and have had talent to burn but she was a madam. She was lethal with both her hooves and her teeth, as one of Henry's best cashmere sweaters found to its cost. With a less understanding environment, with a less equable rider than Billy Aldridge, who rode her bronco bucks of a morning, and without Lester Piggott's mastery in the saddle she could have been one of the many 'talented but wayward' footnotes that litter the racing story.

Roussalka won four races that year, seven in all over three seasons including Goodwood's Nassau Stakes two years running, but in 1974 it was a horse not from the yearling sales but from across the sea that made as great an impact on the Henry Cecil story as the ever-changing phenomenon that was Lester Piggott. Over in Italy a horse called New Model was showing speed that demanded more than local targets. He was owned by a big, powerful but courteous lawyer called Carlo d'Alessio and trained in Milan by Sergio Cumani. It seemed a good idea to go and join his son.

New Model was a success. He proved a decent sprinter, winning the 1974 Challenge Stakes and finishing second in the July Cup at Newmarket the same year. But it was what he brought in his wake in those red, white and green colours that made the difference. For d'Alessio so liked what he saw at Newmarket that he commissioned Sergio Cumani to go to the Keeneland Yearling Sales in Kentucky where Luca's father paid a then whopping 125,000gns for a good-looking bay colt by the famous sire Round Table. They called him Take Your Place and within 14 months he had won all three of his two-year-old races for Henry Cecil culminating in an ultra-game effort in the 1975 Observer Gold Cup, which made him a major prospect for the following year's Derby.

But by then there was another even more promising d'Alessio-owned colt in the pipeline. For in September 1974, a couple of months after Cumani Snr had signed the cheque in Kentucky for what was to become Take Your Place, Arthur Boyd-Rochfort had a disappointment. At the Newmarket Yearling Sales his Tally-Ho Stud was selling what he considered to be a beautifully athletic colt by Wolver Hollow. Henry Cecil had got Charles St George interested only for his vet to query the heartbeat. Such incidents do not improve your value, but Henry liked the horse and Arthur was insistent on his quality. Henry persuaded d'Alessio it was a good idea. If he was

78

taking a risk, at 7,000gns it was a comparatively cheap one. The horse turned out to be one of the best Henry would ever handle.

Yet Cecil's own 'Italian Job' only got better because while the juvenile Wollow and Take Your Place were having their nursery lessons at Marriott Stables, in the winter of 1974/75 Luca Cumani had been called back to Italy to help his father with the stable's horses sent down to Pisa. Among them was a muscular chestnut of d'Alessio's called Bolkonski, who had ended his season by winning one of Italy's most important two-year-old races by eight lengths. Where New Model had led, Bolkonski could follow. He and Luca came to Newmarket early in 1975 with the 2,000 Guineas as the target. Hitting it would be quite an achievement for all concerned.

For a start, Bolkonski was one of those heavy-framed athletes that carries plenty of surplus flesh until you pare them down to peak condition. When we race fans first clapped eyes on him in the Newmarket paddock we saw a pretty burly beast and, while impressed by his second-place finish, it can't have been all chauvinism that let him start as a 33-1 outsider in the 2,000 Guineas itself 18 days later. Not all chauvinism, but quite a bit of it. For Bolkonski had not only come over from Italy, so too, horror of horrors, had his jockey. How could an unknown Italian cope with the famously tricky Newmarket undulations as the huge Guineas field swept downhill into 'the dip'? They knew the jockey in Italy: he had already been six times a champion and he would top the list 13 times in all. A generation later his son would become a global star. Bolkonski's jockey was Gianfranco Dettori.

He was a sunny little guy, shorter and sturdier than Frankie but with an even bigger smile, a hard-as-nails glint to his eye, and not a word of English. Gianfranco had got into racing by the unlikely route of running away from mixing cement for his builder father in Sardinia to wash dishes in Rome. Mucking out trotters at the local racecourse offered better money than washing dishes, and he then climbed on board a supposedly unrideable horse and found such a tune that he was put in a race and duly won, to much amazement. There was something in that smile that suggested he had been through tougher things in life than riding big-race favourites. Which was correct.

When Gianfranco came to Marriott Stables to ride Bolkonski in a gallop he carried a whip almost as long as himself. The stable might not have known what to make of him, but he was going to ride Bolkonski in his races, Luca was there to do the translation, and Carlo d'Alessio was clearly an important new owner. Everyone would have to make the best of it. Which was going to be difficult for reasons beyond any navigation problems Signor Dettori might encounter in the Guineas. The stable lads were on strike.

Considering the outwardly feudal trappings – staff called 'lads', jockeys bowing and touching their caps in greeting, the blatant difference in lifestyle between those who lead a horse up in the paddock and those who pat it on the neck afterwards as its official 'owners' – some might think it surprising there wasn't a major strike before or since the one that flared up at Newmarket in the spring of 1975. But that didn't make it any less inconvenient for those who were trying to train horses at the time.

The basic issue was that the Transport and General Workers' Union, which represented around half of the 700 'lads' in the town, wanted another 12 per cent on the £33.83 for a six-and-a-half-day week which the trainers had settled for on 17 March. The trainers would not budge, the union called 'one out, all out', and over 200 followed, 16 of them from Marriott Stables, including 28-year-old Tom Dickie, who looked after Bolkonski. However justified the reasons and however sincere union leader Sam Horncastle might have been, the idea of downing tools in a racing stable and leaving a rump staff to look after the horses in your care was a completely different thing to a factory stoppage. For a start, a stable can't stop.

'We got the horses out every day,' Paddy Rudkin recalls. 'We hadn't the time to go all through the town but kept to the racecourse side. We were obviously very short of staff and all sorts of friends of Henry's and Julie's came to help out. In an odd way it was quite fun. Everyone mucked in, a bit of Dunkirk spirit. But some of the guys were quite heavy. I seem to remember there was a big farmer bloke who rode Wollow and gave him a sore back.'

The picket outside Marriott Stables never caused any trouble – Henry tethered a goat out there to amuse them – but the one on the racecourse did. The day before the Guineas some of the strikers dug a ditch where the race was due to start and when the 24 runners were finally assembled a group of stable lads ran on to the course and not only blocked the way but actually tried to pull Willie Carson off his horse. What followed was one of those scenes that are part gallant, part shameful, part sad, and only redeemed by so little damage actually being done. An understandably enraged Carson galloped back to the grandstand and summoned a posse of trilby-hatted racegoers to come down and 'sort things out'. For a while utter chaos reigned, but somehow the police cleared the course of strikers and trilbies alike and, with the stalls inoperable, the race was started by flag less than 20 minutes late. Because of the trench, it was also begun 50 yards further up the track – no disadvantage to Bolkonski, whose stamina was in no doubt.

Otherwise, anything less suited to Bolkonski would be hard to imagine. He was a highly strung, free-sweating individual at the best of times, and this was certainly not that. But Dettori was unflappable, before, during and after the race. Under instructions above all to keep his horse balanced on the downhill run into the dip, the little man fairly bowled Bolkonski into it. And while his short-legged, slightly pea-on-drum style had none of the silky rhythm his son now shows, there was no doubting the strength and determination as he smacked Bolkonski hard for the line ahead of the favourite Grundy, who went on to win the Derby. It was a great riding triumph and the press gathered round and asked if back home Gianfranco had ever experienced anything like the striking scenes of that afternoon. The little man from Sardinia flashed his sunniest smile and rattled out about 500 words in Italian which apparently meant 'all the time'.

For Henry Cecil, the sweetness of this first English Classic on his home course just six years into his training career was tempered with a bitter aftertaste. For after the race Bolkonski's lad Tom Dickie was chaired past the winning post on the shoulders of the strikers and the press immediately quizzed the trainer on what would happen to the more than £1,000 bonus Tom would be due as the lad responsible for the winner of the £36,000 prize. To his credit Henry managed to reply with a considerable degree of diplomacy, saying, 'For my part I want no victimisation over this strike. You could not normally have found a more reliable or conscientious lad than Tom Dickie.' He then added, more pointedly, 'Bolkonski has always been a nervous horse who tends to sweat up when excited yet his lad was one of those who delayed the start. How would you feel?'

The strike eventually petered out. The stable staff later formed their own association under the guidance of soccer pundit Jimmy Hill, who had fought for the ending of the minimum wage when he was a professional football player. Most of Henry's lads came back and normal service was resumed, but Tom Dickie was not among them. He did not go to Royal Ascot and see his colt toy with the opposition in the St James's Palace Stakes or even to Goodwood for 'The Sussex' when he would have realised how lucky connections had been at Newmarket. For this time Bolkonski was in such a muck sweat in the paddock and down at the start that some thought

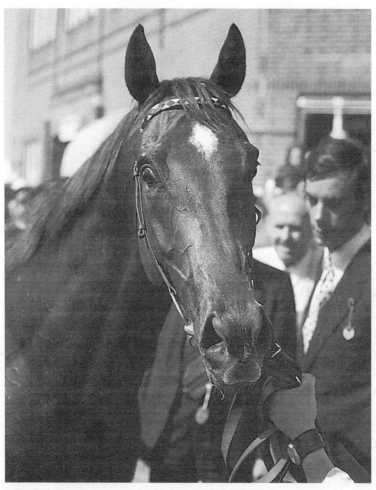

Bolkonski after winning the Sussex Stakes at Goodwood, 1975.

was given to withdrawing him. Despite that he and Dettori battled home gallantly, and in hindsight it was no surprise when he was well beaten on his final run.

For him and Tom Dickie it was over, but for Cecil and Dettori it had only just begun.

Wollow was soon carrying all before him as a two-year-old. He had won twice at Newmarket before taking the Champagne at Doncaster and then being so impressive in the Dewhurst Stakes that he was officially rated top of the juvenile tree. With those victories added on to Bolkonski's heroics, Take Your Place's Observer Gold Cup, Roussalka's Piggott-steered victories at Ascot and Goodwood and 82 successes overall, Henry Cecil was at 32 second in the trainers' table only to the champion Peter Walwyn. He gave an interview saying he was 'very ambitious but not ruthless' and blamed himself for Bolkonski's problems at Goodwood: 'I mistimed his preparation completely. It's a damned sight more difficult bringing a horse like this to its peak five times a year than, for example, to train a two-year-old.'

The season ahead would be even better, but he would be doing it without Luca Cumani. The success of the New Model and Bolkonski 'projects' had made Luca the 'go to' man for visiting Italians. Newmarket seemed a much firmer place for racing plans than communist-threatened Milan. They knew Luca had ambitions and encouraged him on. In the summer of 1975 he bought Bedford House Stables in the Bury Road. His days as assistant were numbered and not entirely trouble-free as tensions arose, as they always do when the hitherto supported pupil suddenly becomes a potential rival who might be taking the best owners and best staff with him. It was not a situation that lingered. None of Henry's top horses or staff got transferred and Luca quickly made a successful start to what has become a highly distinguished dual Derby-winning career. But there was at least one flare-up about which various reports differ, though all appear to include the impressive image of the former Canadian lumberjack's boot being applied firmly up the one-time Italian veterinary student's rear.

Luca Cumani was just beginning, but going into 1976 Henry Cecil was already on a roll. There is nothing like that feeling – and that's certainly what was happening with Wollow. He was a light-framed horse with a set of spots on his bottom, and that was the view his rivals saw in both the Greenham and then the Guineas once Dettori pulled him clear and pressed the pedal down. Acceleration is an exhilarating thing in a racehorse, as is the sharply upward curve of a progressive stable. I continue to treasure the hour spent at Marriott Stables on the Thursday evening when they were still celebrating Wollow's victory in the 2,000 Guineas, which, in the way of things then, had been run not as now on a crowd-friendly Saturday but on the Wednesday, 'as it always had been'.

When I got to the stables Henry and Julie were up at Beech House, no doubt trying to fish other trainers out of the fire. But down at the tack room there were empty champagne bottles lying about and Paddy and the team were still warming their hands on the memories of the day before. 'Wollow got in the mood all right,' said George Winsor. 'Normally he gets a bit funny with more than two people in the box but yesterday they were all over the place and he was as good as gold. It was the same at the races. Leading him across to the races he was playing the fool, rearing up and squealing. Once he got to the course he was quiet as a sheep – right until the parade ring where he wanted to get on with it.'

George had, of course, led up Wolver Hollow in the 1969 Eclipse to set his still-so-uncertain trainer on his now all-conquering way, and listening to him that evening seven years later was the best example I have ever had of how the interaction of staff and horses is at the very heart of how a stable works. 'This feller,' said George, looking at the light-framed three-year-old who had given him and his teammates their place in history, 'is perhaps a couple of inches shorter [just 16 hands, 5ft 4in at the shoulder] than Wolver Hollow but otherwise he's the spittin' image of his father right down to the way the top of his mane won't lay over the right side of his neck. Wolver Hollow was a great ride, but this feller's even better. You can sit behind anything in a gallop and when you want him you can go past like a Rolls-Royce. It's a tremendous feeling.'

George died in the summer of 2011 but the passion in his words lives on and the feeling in them is the core dynamic that can still lift working with racehorses from a physical chore to nothing less than a spiritual inspiration. They matter. It matters. It is what gets you out of your bed of a morning. Much more recently it is what has saved the life of Henry Cecil.

Back on Guineas day 1976 the excitement had been of the simpler, harsher, more nerve-racking kind. 'I was all right in the parade,' said George, 'because Dettori was so relaxed. Some jockeys get terribly nervous. But when I loosed them off I suddenly realised this was it and I could feel my heart going thump, thump, thump. It was the same when they first called Wollow's name in the race and I could feel the old ticker going hard against the shirt.' Passing the post, it was a triumph widely shared. It was the first back-to-back Guineas success for a trainer since 1886 and Carlo d'Alessio had the previous year become the first Italian to own a Classic winner since the romantic Neapolitan, Chevalier Ginistrelli, in 1908. That eccentric had saddled Signorinetta to win the Derby and Oaks, a mare he had bred from the vocally ardent but untalented stallion next door, relying not on the form book but 'on the boundless laws of sympathy and love'.

There were plenty such Italian-based giggles as we sat around at Marriott Stables, not the least of them Paddy's tale of what happened during Wollow's last gallop. 'Before a race,' he told us, 'Henry likes to give them a quick blowout, just three furlongs, letting them sprint along in your hands. Little Dettori comes into the yard as usual, big smile and even bigger whip. And then when he has gone a furlong he suddenly gives Wollow an enormous swat with that huge whip. Henry nearly choked, but I guess all's well that ends well.'

That season ended with the stable's first training championship and with two more major victories for Wollow, at Goodwood and York, and a later awarded Eclipse Stakes after the French winner Trepan was disqualified for failing a dope test. But first Wollow and Dettori would put their unbeaten record to the test over the horseshoe-shaped mile and a half helter-skelter that is the Epsom Derby. They would not pass it.

It's always easy to blame the jockey. Henry Cecil did not do it after Wollow finished only fifth in that Derby, and it is true that the furthest Wollow ran afterwards was only a mile and a quarter and that at Epsom he beat the sixth horse Vitiges by the same distance he had when that French colt was second in the Guineas. However it is also true that Epsom's unique slopes and cambers make it by far the most demanding of all the world's great racetracks and unfamiliarity can be a curse. It cursed Gianfranco Dettori earlier on Derby afternoon, when his first ride round the circuit got trapped on the inside on the final furlong, and it cursed him again when the 23 Classic colts were fired up that opening hill.

Everyone should walk the Derby course at least once in their lifetime. Every year I do it and each time I shake my head in wonder. That's what George Phillipeau and Gerard Rivasses did when I walked them round the weekend before that 1976 Derby. We had reached the seven-furlong marker, the highest point of the course, which we had got to by way of that opening 250ft right- and then left-handed climb, and were now looking across to where the ribbon of racetrack green snaked down round Tattenham Corner to finish below the great looming liner of a grandstand above. Gerard had been a tough, unfazed jump jockey in his youth but now he mopped his brow and muttered 'incroyable' in an uncanny echo of the French General Pierre Bosquet's words after witnessing the doomed Charge of the Light Brigade in the Crimean War – 'C'est magnifique, mais ce n'est pas la guerre. C'est de la folie.' ('It's magnificent, but it is not war. It is madness.')

Unsurprisingly Gianfranco did not have a happy time amid such madness. He got chopped off at the first turn, never got a settled position, was ninth turning into the straight and did not progress enough thereafter. Equally unsurprisingly the man who again had the happiest time was the one most familiar with the course. When Lester Piggott swept through poised and triumphant on the French colt Empery it was the seventh time he had taken the Derby since winning on the outsider Never Say Die as a still quite round-faced 18-year-old in 1954.

Experience always shows in Flat race-riding, where it's the horse that does the running and the rider needs to bring more mind than muscle to the party. It is therefore very hard for even the most talented of apprentices to step into the full jockey's role. In 1976 Henry had been trying it with the Epsom-based Alan Bond and, while Alan had already won the Dee Stakes for the stable on Great Idea and was to win the Ribblesdale on Catalpa at Royal Ascot two weeks later, the doubts were beginning to gnaw. What if a proven top-class Classic rider were to become available for 1977?

At that Derby meeting, Lord Porchester, the Queen's racing manager, called us together and with a troubled face gave us the shock news that Joe Mercer, the stable jockey for the royal West Ilsley Stable, would be replaced by Willie Carson. Now it was true that Willie, at 35, was eight years younger than Joe, but Mercer was only three years on from winning the English 1,000 Guineas and the French Oaks on Highclere for the Queen, and only five from completing 17 wins on Brigadier Gerard, the greatest miler any of us had ever seen. John Oaksey, the outstanding racing writer as well as amateur rider of his day, took to the airwaves in damning incredulity: 'The mind boggles if you are not satisfied with Joe Mercer.' But in Henry Cecil's head there was an obvious plan.

Hiring Joe Mercer as stable jockey for 1977 was the final step in the transformation. Back in 1968 Cecil Boyd-Rochfort had written to Hope Iselin to say he had given Henry £50 which would be hugely appreciated as he and Julie had no money of their own. Now the former 'Hopeless Henry' was on his way to becoming the youngest champion trainer in years and had amassed not just fame but fortune enough to buy, at admittedly family rates, the Warren Place training operation from his father-in-law Noel Murless, who was to retire at the end of the season.

In business terms, Henry had outgrown Marriott Stables. Now he would have a training palace all his own.

4

WARREN PLACE

IT WAS quite a palace, and quite a pair of boots to fill. Warren Place was as different from Marriott Stables in style and background as Henry was from his father-in-law, who had won the trainers' championship eight times in the last 20 years from that very special location.

Marriott Stables was a modern, Jockey Club-owned, American barn set-up of which Henry had been the very first occupant. Warren Place was an extended hill-top training operation a mile to the east of town originally built in 1926 on the gambling winnings of trainer Sam Darling. It ran to 15 acres, had several different yards, paddocks and staff cottages, and a large covered ride, not to mention a big mock Tudor mansion once occupied by the fun-loving Maharaja of Baroda.

While Henry was starting only his ninth season as a trainer having just taken his first championship, Noel Murless was stepping down after 42 years with a licence, the last quarter century of that at Warren Place, and the many contrasts between the two men emphasise the challenge the younger one now faced. Once settled in, Henry Cecil was to enter a 13-year period of dominance unequalled in modern times. Over those 13 seasons he would win 12 English Classics, top the training list eight times and retain three outstanding champion

Noel Murless with the Queen and Princess Margaret at Royal Ascot, 1955.

jockeys. It was a magnificent run of success, but don't doubt that one of the driving forces was the extraordinary career of the old father-in-law who for so many years had been a mounted icon of the Heath with those huge ten-to-two feet and that ancient, battered hat.

Following Noel Murless was very different from being a pupil of Cecil Boyd-Rochfort, quite apart from the fact that Julie had been a Murless student all her life. For while Noel at 25 had been even younger than Henry was when he first got a training licence, his start was anything but the strange drifting route his son-in-law had taken. Unlike Henry's immediate exposure to the very top of thoroughbred life, Noel was a farmer's son from Cheshire with only hunting and point-to-pointing in his background. But while Henry preferred to rag with his four brothers than spend extra time with his pony, Noel, with his mother on nursing duty and father serving in the First World War, spent most of his waking hours with a little Welsh mare called Mary Jane for company. 'I learned more about horses from Mary Jane,' he later said, 'than from anyone else in my life.' Even before Noel's father had carried him shoulder high to see their neighbour's horse Poethlyn win his second Grand National under the ageing (for a jump jockey) hands of Ernie Piggott in 1919, Noel Murless's course was set. 'I never had any other thought or ambition. I knew I had to be a trainer.'

To fulfil that destiny he had left home at 16 to work as a stable lad with the martinet Frank Hartigan at Weyhill in Hampshire, seven miles from Andover, to whose station he would lead a horse at dawn to entrain for the races and from where he would much later make the long return trek with an oil lamp on a pony gig as guide. He would risk those big feet over fences and would have won the Fox Hunters' Chase over the full Grand National course but for falling at the second last. His race-riding came to a wrenching halt when one of those stick-out feet caught itself in the wing of a hurdle at Leicester. Noel then completed his journey to his first training yard on the slopes of Sutton Bank in North Yorkshire with marriage to a magnificently down-to-earth Scottish girl called Gwen Carlow, who had herself just trained a winner at Kelso when she and Noel first met there on Jubilee Day (for George V) in May 1935.

In contrast to Henry, Julie Murless was an only child and had memories of wartime Yorkshire and post-war Beckhampton before moving to Newmarket. But it was at Warren Place with its sights and sounds and smells and daily rhythms that the lodestar of her life was set. For years she shared the stable's hopes and excitements as she rode out with the string. She was 14 when the controversial 18-year-old 'boy wonder' Lester Piggott was boldly appointed to succeed Sir Gordon Richards as first jockey. She was 17 when Lester gave her father his greatest week with Derby victory on Crepello followed by Carrozza winning the Oaks for the Queen – albeit in the owner's second colours as the first were down the field on a better-fancied filly trained by, ahem, Cecil Boyd-Rochfort. And when Henry was working for his stepfather in 1967, Julie was riding work of a morning on the stable's talented Eclipse Stakes winner Busted. Come the end of 1976, Julie Cecil was doing a lot more than just coming home.

Such situations can be as much trap as opportunity, and it says a lot for all parties that there was none of the awkwardness associated with Henry's succession at Freemason Lodge. Noel Murless was just 66 when he handed over, 14 years younger than CBR when he stood down. And while poor old Uncle Cecil was at that stage still marooned unhappily in the house and grumpily in the office, Noel and Gwen quickly moved across Newmarket to Woodditton Stud, content to busy themselves with their mares and foals and stallions rather than with the everyday hassle of a racing yard. Noel would stay interested but never intrusive. He was a much kindlier man than his rather strained public persona might suggest. I remember the shyness from a TV interview I did with him before he retired. For Henry Cecil, Noel Murless remained more than a support, he was an inspiration.

The move happened early in December 1976. It wasn't exactly The Great Trek but it must have been quite a day as the 70 horses of the Cecil string walked for the last time through the back of the town past St Mary's Church, out across the Severals and over the road to canter up to their new home on the hill. 'We had a big old van then,' says Frank Conlon, whose memory is pin sharp despite those being his drinking days. 'It took us up to Warren Place early and we got all our boxes ready and then came back to Marriott, rode the first lot up, loosed them down and fed them, and then did it all over again. Warren Place was a completely different layout from Marriott Stables, which had those four barns set up like Cell Block H. All the boxes close to the house were much bigger with high ceilings and then there was a fillies' yard 400 yards across the paddock and another little yard over in the far corner which we used to call the Hovels. But while the layout was different we didn't suddenly change our system – it was still the same relaxed way of doing things. Muck all your three horses out first and then pull out and walk in a posse up to ten abreast. Henry made us feel good about ourselves. In the old days we used to look up and say, "There are Murless's coming over the hill." Now we could sense the others saying, "Here come Henry's." It made you proud.'

With the horses retained from Murless the stable strength was up to 110, making it the largest string in Newmarket, and the principal parts of the core team soon fell into a smooth rhythm in their new surroundings. 'In some ways Marriott was easier to manage as everything was all close,' says Paddy Rudkin, 'but this was a whole community with flats and cottages, a decent hostel, a big paddock and best of all a covered ride. At Marriott in the winter we had to trot all around racecourse side sometimes as far as the Cesarewitch start. In the freezing cold you would all be feeling miserable and it became a nightmare if something got loose. You would not know where it would go. With the covered ride everyone was pretty secure however fresh the horses might be.'

Spending £10,000 to build the covered yard had been one of the best investments Noel Murless had ever made. Young horses on their winter break have energy to spare and any little thing can trigger them into a great bursting leap as the well-being surges through them. Out in the paddock, or worst of all on the openness of the Heath, your body tenses with the need to avoid the disaster of a horse getting loose and adding a series of explosive bucks and insultingly loud farts as it high-tails into the distance. In the walled confines of the covered ride the risk as well as the behaviour is contained and, while you hear plenty of mighty blows against the padded sides of the 300-metre circumference rideway, the ease of the banter as the horses trot by tells you fun has overcome the fear.

In one of the bad winters ahead the Cecil horses would be limited to trotting round the ride from New Year to almost the end of February. But by doing their full share of circuits they still built sufficient core fitness to win a clutch of races in early April at Newmarket's opening Craven meeting. And of course circling the horses in one place made it easier to concentrate on what they and those who rode them were made of. That concentration had been one of the keys to Henry's success to date and at Warren Place it only sharpened, especially on gallops mornings.

Of course nothing happens without having talented horses, but having men in the saddle of a morning whom you can trust to understand and report on what is beneath them is absolutely essential to the process. To his previous work-riding team of Frank Conlon, Stan Smith, Frank Storey and Raymond 'Woody' Woodrough, Henry could now add the big-hearted bantam-cock figure of ex-jockey Willie Snaith, who more than 20 years earlier had turned down the chance to succeed Gordon Richards as the Murless jockey but had been a lynchpin of the Warren Place squad in more recent times.

In years to come the sight of Henry's tall, angular figure using those great hands and that mobile, moody face to impress his gallop plans on the ring of Lilliputian pilots gazing up at him became as much a symbol of the Cecil method as that of the cowboy-saddled, leather-tassled trainer jesting along on his palomino as he shepherded his posse from their already historic headquarters. He had ideas in his head that he wanted to take shape on the turf. If the picture did not develop as he had hoped he needed to know what was lacking and why. Only those in the saddle could tell him. He and they needed each other. Even if other failings had sometimes to be reckoned with.

In particular, the prediction that Frank Conlon could 'ride anything but would always let you down' was proving too true to be amusing, certainly as far as Paddy Rudkin was concerned. While with everybody else Bolkonski would have already begun to sweat and yaw by the time they got to St Mary's Square, when tiny Frank was perched up behind his ears the nerves settled and they would hack away up Warren Hill together almost more like a hunter than a racehorse. And while other staff could be relied on to make some attempt at attending evening stables, Frank's drink-fuelled absences became so frequent that Cecil finally agreed to Rudkin's request to send him packing.

Sure enough, one Newmarket raceday Conlon's little porky face came hiccuping into the yard a full 50 minutes behind the rest. 'There he is, guvnor,' called Paddy, 'there he is. Sack him now.'

With thunderous colonel-like authority, Henry strode over to the swaying Frank and bawled, 'Where the bloody hell have you been?'

The diminutive drunk smiled dreamily and replied, 'I have just been to see JuJu after her race this afternoon. She ran so well and I think she is such a sweet thing, don't you?'

'Oh yes, Frank,' said Henry, taking him by the arm. 'Let's go over and look at her.'

Paddy Rudkin hurled his shovel at the wall.

Frank and Woody, who was equally thirsty and got by with a rule of never having a drink before nine o'clock in the morning, were tolerated because they had what Henry wanted from his gallops ingrained into their alcohol-soaked DNA. Joe Mercer was no drinker, but when he came to ride at one of his first 'work mornings' as Henry Cecil's new stable jockey a bystander might have thought it was he who was the tippler. For the instructions had been for him to allow Frank Conlon to lead for the first part of the seven-furlong journey and to then join up and pass the watching trainer together. Conlon duly set off at his normal tempo and sensing he was still alone after four furlongs looked round to see Mercer some 100 yards adrift.

On pulling up, Frank waited while Henry debriefed Joe before the jockey handed his horse back to its lad and sped off home.

Frank asked what had gone wrong. Had the animal hurt itself? What did Joe say? 'Nothing's wrong,' growled Henry. 'I've just given him a bollocking. He said, "That guy has gone much too fast in front, I can't be doing that." So I told him, "That guy has ridden a lot of good horses for me and he knows what I like to do. The next time he leads you, just lay up and do what I tell you, not what you think suits you."'

Henry Cecil's empire was not all built on easy charm.

Joe Mercer was far too good and experienced a jockey to need telling twice. He had already ridden some of the best horses in history. But ahead was something better yet.

The first time Mercer had met Henry Cecil, the future champion trainer was still a leery teenager begging a cigarette in the back of a car. That's what you had to do if you were CBR's stepson and the great man was bolt upright in the passenger seat, his kid-gloved hands folded atop a malacca cane, with the road stretching out to Yarmouth races. Driving the party was the chain-smoking figure of CBR's stable jockey Harry Carr, whom Uncle Cecil invariably referred to as 'Carr', as in asking 'Carr, what's his problem?' if another vehicle had the temerity to hoot at them during the journey. Joe Mercer was, in his old-fashioned phrase, 'courting' Harry's daughter Anne, the future mother of his three children. Henry and Arthur Boyd-Rochfort were just two teenagers 'dying for a smoke'. Obligingly Joe lit a cigarette, an act entirely unfazing to the Captain and one that enabled each of the two boys to take a desperate and unnoticed drag before passing it on. Mercer smiled. He'd seen it all before.

One of the great things about Joe as a professional ally rather than illicit supplier was that he had indeed seen so much water flow under the racing bridge. He had ridden his first Classic winner on a filly called Ambiguity in the 1953 Oaks for Jack Colling, who trained at West Ilsley where Joe had been based ever since with Jack Colling's successor Dick Hern. If the Bradford-born Mercer was loyal, he was also both talented and tough. In 1967 he would have beaten Lester Piggott to the jockeys' championship but for missing the last ten weeks of the season after breaking his back in a mid-August fall at Folkestone. In 1972 he rode the mighty Brigadier Gerard to win the Prince of Wales's at Royal Ascot just two days after heroically pulling trainer Bill Marshall from a blazing, about-to-explode plane that had crashed on take-off at Newbury racecourse.

But what mattered more to all at Warren Place was not so much what Joe brought as a courageous, golf-loving, pipe-smoking man, but what he could do in the saddle. For Joe Mercer was and remains the beau idéal of the orthodox English Flat jockey style: balanced, compact, ambidextrous, strong, sensitive, adaptable and superbly rhythmic, particularly in his finishing drive. Frenchie Nicholson was the greatest jockey mentor of the post-war era. I was one of his less distinguished wannabes who included top jockeys such as Paul

Cook, Tony Murray, Pat Eddery and Walter Swinburn. 'Watch Joe,' Frenchie would say. 'Keep the head still, hands and heels in rhythm, wave the stick as much as use it, that's the way to do it.' Greville Starkey had been a very fine rider. Joe Mercer was a master.

He took a flat in Newmarket and in February 1977 met up with a new employer tanned after a Caribbean holiday and fresh from giving an interview that outlined the three-pronged ambition of retaining the trainers' title, saddling 100 winners and amassing more than £300,000 in prize money. The interview ended with Henry gaily stating, 'I have got a real chance, haven't I?' After Joe had got to know some of the 110-strong string and appreciated a speed threshold somewhat higher than that at West Ilsley, he came very much to share his employer's sentiment.

'Henry was very relaxed but everyone knew their job,' remembers Joe, 'especially the horses. He would take great bunches of them and bounce them off at the bottom of the canter. One day we were over on Railway Land and I said to him, "We must have been doing 40mph." He just shrugged and said, "Only for the first furlong, it settles them down." It was not what I was used to, but it meant the horses were very fit and very focused. I had four fabulous years there and he was very straightforward. There was no agonising over the form and saying we had better dodge this animal or that. If he thought a horse was ready he would run it. He would sit down and go through the plans for the whole week and say "that runs there, it will win", and a hell of a lot of the time he was right. He was an extraordinary man to be around. After first lot he would suddenly take you out to see his roses or the asparagus he was growing – he had an amazing kitchen garden. He loved his food and his plants and above all he loved his horses. He had a great affinity for them.'

Joe Mercer was talking in the summer of 2011, looking out at lush green Berkshire countryside from a living room adorned with oil paintings of the champions of his past. Of course there was a rose-tinted glow to these first recollections, and anyone who has worked around the racing scene has to accept the old definition of training as 'a lifetime of worry for just moments of delight'. Henry Cecil's plans also went awry plenty of times, and never more vividly than when a bunch of two-year-olds were being asked to come up Railway Side close together, two after two, in a formation Henry used to describe as 'like a bar of chocolate'. After about a furlong's passable imitation of a slab of Cadbury's best, one of the youngsters shied off the gallop and the others scattered to the four winds in a chain reaction. Eventually the exasperated trainer caught up with the rider of the original offender only to find his 'what on earth were you up to?' remonstration crushed by the splendid rejoinder, 'Your chocolate bar just ****ing melted.'

Henry is more circumspect with his training these days. The string don't wander in the bunches of those earlier times; they certainly don't threaten 40mph in the early part of the canter. He explains that the two-year-olds he has are not as precocious as before and it is also true that in the British racing scene of today rather than of the late 1970s there is a logic in targeting the better rewards and enhanced value on offer for older horses. But some of the differences back then can be ascribed to the fearlessness of youth. During that first season at Warren Place Henry was just 34 and had already won a trainers' championship and back-to-back 2,000 Guineas. He had more than a hundred horses and both traditional and new owners knocking on his door. His equine academy set high standards and a higher tempo. To win prizes the pupils had to measure up.

Success is both an infectious and a coveted thing, especially in racing, where even the very act of controlling a hard-pulling thoroughbred depends totally on confidence spreading down the reins. A top stable with the winners flowing every week is a place of happy whistles and smiling whispers, of admiration and affection for the runners who earn your bread, of hopes and boasts of more to come. Warren Place was a happy spot, and as Joe Mercer booted the winners home it was only natural that other people should want to join. There may not have been a Wollow in 1977 but horses like Lucky Wednesday did more than just fly the flag. By riding the colt to beat his replacement Willie Carson on the Dick Hern-trained Relkino at Sandown, Joe showed up the absurdity of his sacking; and by then winning the Prince of Wales's Stakes at Royal Ascot he was demonstrating how much a master Henry Cecil had become of racing's biggest stage.

A year earlier at Haydock Joe had stepped in as a late replacement to win on a tough chestnut called Gunner B. The horse had won five of his ten races during that three-year-old season and his Beverley-based trainer Geoff Toft saddled him to win another three from nine in 1977. But despite all that Tom Barratt, who had bred Gunner B at his own Limestone Stud in Lincolnshire, thought his protégé could be even better. He remembered Joe punching Gunner B home at Haydock. He dreamt of him winning major races for Joe's new stable. At the time it seemed tough on Geoff Toft, but the results confirm that moving to Warren Place was not a faulty call.

Not that Gunner B appeared to appreciate it. He was a real thick-set man of a horse with a wide and handsome head, and he could be as stubborn as the most cantankerous Yorkshireman back at his Beverley base. He was reluctant to go anywhere in the string and in particular he would get to the bottom of the Warren Hill canter and refuse to budge. Henry Cecil has always needed guile as well as tempo in his training locker. He decided Gunner B should be Paddy Rudkin's hack, which would amuse and exercise the old horse as he cantered from one part of the Heath to another to check on different members of the stable. And as for refusing to go up the canter, this was one for Jim White.

Now here was a Warren Place institution. Jim White had first teamed up with Noel Murless when they were both at Frank Hartigan's in the 1930s. It was Jim who had the oil lamp on that pony gig to light Noel's way home as he trudged his horse those seven miles back to Weyhill. Jim went with him to Hambleton and Beckhampton and on to Newmarket. If you look at the pictures of the Murless glory years, Jim is the lean spare figure with the immaculate trilby, the paddock sheet over his arm and a big set of teeth in his smile. He was the travelling head lad through all those Murless championships, but now he was officially retired and making dolls' houses in his cottage at the back of Warren Place. There was still plenty he could turn his hand to, though. Especially when it came to old horses who thought they knew best.

Jim White had a battered white van and a well-used hunting crop. As Paddy walked Gunner B across to the bottom of the Warren Hill canter, Jim would get out of the van with the hunting crop. When Gunner B started his one-horse protest, Jim would lash the crop to give one of those pistol cracks cowboys make at rodeo shows. Gunner B did not like the sound of them. He would go up the canter like a shot. 'The old horse used to treat it like a game,' says Paddy. 'As you began to walk towards the canter he would look back at the road. If he could not see any sign of Jim he would stop and just refuse to budge. But the moment he saw the van he would know the game was up and hack away perfectly. I used to love riding him.'

Gunner B repaid the special treatment in spades. He won his first four races straight off: the Earl of Sefton at Newmarket, the Brigadier Gerard at Sandown, the Prince of Wales's at Royal Ascot and then the Eclipse Stakes up that Esher hill at Sandown. By then I was a main part of the 'ITV 7' team on World of Sport, and as Henry Cecil walked over to greet Joe Mercer and Gunner B with Arthur Simmons playing the 'travelling head lad' role, just as he did

Gunner B (Joe Mercer) wins the Prince of Wales's Stakes at Royal Ascot, 1978.

for Cecil Boyd-Rochfort with the Queen's Canisbay in 1965 and for Henry himself with Wolver Hollow in 1969, I remember thinking how brilliantly the trainer had picked up the gauntlet. More than that, for all Henry's long-haired, Gucci-shoed public whimsy there was absolutely no missing his pride and affection for the animal that had done the running for him. He and his team always kept the horses at the heart of it.

For horses like Gunner B are an inspiration. In the simplest but deepest way they symbolise the highest of athletic virtues, rock-solid mental strength linked to massive physical attributes. Joe Mercer's rhythmic, punching drive made the perfect accompaniment as Gunner B set his head and neck out and ran his rivals ragged up the last lung-busting climb. He could not quite do the same when second in the Benson and Hedges Gold Cup (now the Juddmonte International) and third in the Champion Stakes, but this final campaign was one of uplifting as well as much-improved endeavour however cunning he might have played it in the mornings.

It is always dangerous to get too anthropomorphic about horses but there is a bit of fun to be had with how such a bluff, tough north country character fared when he moved on to the sultan's life at stud.

After six honest years at his owner's operation in Lincolnshire, so few of what we might call the 'fashionable ladies' were seeking his favours that Gunner B was shipped off to slake his ardour in Germany. It was only when his son Royal Gait became Europe's champion stayer in 1988 before winning the 1992 Champion Hurdle that Gunner B was brought back to England, where he was in great demand as a National Hunt stallion. So much so that at the ripe old age of 29 he got 40 of his 45 mares in foal and his son Red Marauder won the 2001 Grand National. Indeed when Gunner B finally passed on in January 2003 he had long been Europe's oldest active stallion and was looking forward to his 25th year in what is known as the 'covering barn'. In human terms he would have been at least 150. It is thought he had a heart attack during the 'covering' process. Is it naughty to say 'what a way to go'?

In 1978 another, rather larger operator than Tom Barratt was thinking of changing his trainer, albeit in far more controversial circumstances. In many ways Daniel Wildenstein (opposite) was the most admirable of owners. A third generation of a famous art business family, he was also a serious scholar of Impressionism and had brought that application to his passion for thoroughbred breeding with notable success and the clearest of principles. His broodmares had to have real racecourse achievement as well as top-quality pedigrees. His runners should always have high and honest ambitions, and most of them, to the racegoer's pleasure, should carry what in those days were called Red Indian names. In 1976 Flying Water (1,000 Guineas), Pawneese (Oaks) and Crow (St Leger) had won him three English Classics. Those horses had been trained in France, so in 1977 when Crow and two dozen others came to join two-time champion trainer Peter Walwyn in Lambourn, it seemed like happy days.

The honeymoon lasted until the 1978 Gold Cup at Royal Ascot. Wildenstein's Buckskin was acknowledged as Europe's most talented stayer and was made favourite despite Walwyn making no secret of the fragility of the four-year-old's feet and legs. But when Buckskin trailed in a distant fourth the owner put the blame not on any physical ailment, or training error, but squarely on the shoulders of already four-times champion jockey Pat Eddery. 'He is too much of a boy to ride Buckskin,' declared the owner. 'With Piggott or Saint-Martin he would have won.'

Daniel Wildenstein

Such statements, however preposterous, are a trainer's nightmare but can often be passed off as heat-of-the-moment disappointment. Daniel Wildenstein's comments were different in that he stuck to them with the zeal that scholars in one subject bring to another, never mind their lesser understanding of it. 'Yes I do think that Eddery is too weak,' he insisted of the 25-year-old champion when we talked two days after the Gold Cup fiasco. 'He may be very talented but he is not man enough for Buckskin and will not ride that horse again. You see I have never had more than two pounds on any of my horses but if they are one of the favourites I am very conscious of all the public who are backing them and I am very disappointed if they are not in the first three. What is more, as I

The great stayer Buckskin.

employ the jockey when he is riding, if he does something wrong I am not afraid to say so afterwards in front of everyone.'

Such forthright opinions might have been good for journalists used to little more than 'he's a nice horse and we are very pleased with him' platitudes, but they didn't augur well for owner/trainer relations, especially not with Peter Walwyn. His own Royal Ascot reaction had been a blunt 'if someone else is to ride Buckskin, it will not be from my yard.'

A month later there was a further dispute, this time over the Wildenstein St Leger winner Crow's participation in Ascot's King George VI and Queen Elizabeth Stakes, and soon the next yard to house the Wildenstein string was to be Henry Cecil's. A decade earlier Henry had been the ingénue 25-year-old assistant for his octogenarian stepfather; now he was the sophisticated Classic-winning champion trainer flying off to meet a 60-year-old art tycoon in Paris and then giving the most measured of statements afterwards.

'My relationship with Mr Wildenstein will be exactly the same as with my other owners and my freedom of action is in no way impaired,' he told John McCririck, at that time an acute and award-winning news reporter unencumbered by the later excesses of his TV persona. 'I found him genuine and sincere and am determined to make the relationship work, and look forward to meeting the challenge which should benefit British racing.'

Such high-level meetings demand skills more usually bred at embassy tables than stable yards, yet though Henry Cecil has spent his entire working life in the parallel universe of the Newmarket soap opera, his charismatic charm, horse-focused determination and increasingly legendary status have often made him successful where even the finest of diplomats might have failed. However, his reputation has always depended first and foremost on his handling of horses, and when Buckskin arrived he and his team soon realised they were facing their greatest challenge yet. The four-year-old's feet and legs were all that Walwyn had warned they would be. His dropped soles required special shoes and the suspensory ligament in his off fore daily required hours of hosing to limit inflammation. Senior vet Bob Crowhurst pushed up his glasses and said, 'You will never train that.'

The gauntlet had been thrown down, and the way in which Cecil retrieved it was characteristically unusual. All Buckskin's previous successes had been on a soft surface, which in view of his foot and leg problems would presumably be one essential requirement in all future races. Henry saw it quite differently. 'If the ground was to Buckskin's liking,' he argued, 'I thought he would really let himself go and do almost too much. However, if it was on the hard side, I reasoned perhaps he would look after himself and do as little as necessary.' When Buckskin duly appeared on fastish ground at Doncaster and even firmer at Newmarket, many of us orthodox know-alls shook our heads at the trainer's vanity and muttered, 'Henry's done it this time.' As Buckskin drew further and further clear on each occasion, we shook those same heads in appreciation.

We were also witnessing Warren Place with an equine scholarship stream unequalled even in Murless's heyday. While Gunner B and Buckskin flourished, the two-year-old class of '78 were also sweeping all before them. In his 44th year Joe Mercer was to register a seasonal-best total of 115 winners and help Henry to a 110-winner £350,000 second championship title. The older horses had done him proud but it was the young guns who were giving him the thrill. They were that greatest of racing joys, hope on the hoof, giving one good season and following it with an even better one.

The good years usually begin early. There is sufficient talent and enthusiasm in the class for some of them to be ready to compete. When they do and win, a frisson of expectation ripples through the stable and the bite of the bunch's stride is just that fraction quicker. Lads talk. They always talk, but when there is a good bunch of two-year-olds their words become part of the shaping process. Of course there will always be a fair bit of unfulfilled wastage, but in 1978 at Warren Place there were at least five diamonds among the dross.

The first of them, a chunky chestnut two-year-old called Main Reef, was scoring first time out at Sandown before the end of May and in six weeks had also won the Chesham Stakes at Royal Ascot and the July Stakes at Newmarket before taking a break and winning (albeit subsequently disqualified) the Mill Reef Stakes at Newbury in

September. By the time Main Reef ended his season a disappointing fourth in the Middle Park Stakes at Newmarket he had long proved himself the sort of yardstick any stable would treasure. But even before he stormed home at Royal Ascot another chestnut two-year-old had worked beside him with even more potential. He was called Kris, and he duly winged in at Leicester before continuing on a 14-victory champion's career. After the Leicester debut Paddy Rudkin was quoted as saying 'we have got better ones at home', which was assumed to be teasing. The beauty, the thrill of that summer of '78 is that the teasing assumption was not entirely correct.

For a little earlier Joe Mercer had been legged up on one of the few sons of Brigadier Gerard who actually resembled his sire. This colt was owned by Charles St George and was named R B Chesne after the heart specialist who in the autumn of 1974 had upset Arthur Boyd-Rochfort by having 'spun' Wollow at the yearling sales. 'There was a great big bunch of two-year-olds,' says Joe. 'We set off at the back of them but by the finish we were in front. I rode up to Henry afterwards and said, "This is the real deal."' In his first two races R B Chesne looked like justifying that promise, a little less so in his third, and after that he, like so many others, while a decent winner, became best remembered as a talent unfulfilled.

By the nature of their calling, trainers have to be promiscuous in their equine affections. They fall in love with new talent and take the relationship onward and upward until reality intervenes. With a big bay colt called Lyphard's Wish it looked as if gravity would strike first because whenever he was fresh he would spend more time walking on two legs than four. Fortunately for the Cecil team among their number was a particularly fearless lad called Steve Dyble, who was the stable lads' boxing champion and then and now answers to the name of Yarmouth, for no better reason than that was the place of his birth. Yarmy might not always have passed a breathalyser test in those days, but his ability to ride Lyphard's Wish never seemed impaired. 'I was young and bold back then,' he says in the breathless conspiratorial rush he maintains to this day. 'I used to enjoy it when Lyphard's went up on his hind legs. There was a bit of "hey look at me". He was quite a boyo, and when he won his first three and broke the track record at Sandown we thought he could be anything. He didn't quite make it, but when he won the Craven and the Dante as a three-year-old I thought he might win the Derby for me. But after leading round Tattenham Corner he didn't stay.'

Such things are ever the stuff of racing dreams; the trainer's trick is to see the promise through the partiality of the physical partner on the horse's back. Henry Cecil's career has depended on this, but in 1978 one case took a fair bit of prompting. Among the two-year-old fillies was a tiny little thing with the hostage-to-fortune name of One In A Million. She was ridden every morning by a former champion apprentice called Robert Edmondson, whose great love outside horses was racing pigeons. To no avail he kept telling Henry that his diminutive conveyance was quick enough to catch one of his feathered friends. 'Just put me in with the good lot and she'll show them,' he implored. One morning the trainer consented and the pigeons were indeed under threat. Winning both her races that season and her first three the next, including the 1,000 Guineas, One In A Million lived up to her name. It pays to listen.

So it was little One In A Million who in 1979 won the stable its first English Classic from Warren Place, although to this day some of the team still can't understand how Kris got beaten in the 2,000 Guineas. Paddy still believes Joe Mercer made up too much ground too quickly; Joe thinks the colt had not quite recovered from rapping himself in a piece of work a week before the race; Henry shook his head at the time but could not find excuses. The truth is that there probably weren't any. Just because Kris had gone through his two-year-old season unbeaten and won all seven of his other races in 1979, he had no divine right to win the Guineas. After swooping through to challenge he was outrun to the line by the Barry Hills-trained Tap On Wood. The winner was ridden, on his 19th birthday, by the American phenomenon Steve Cauthen, who had arrived in England only three weeks earlier. Six years on, Steve would have a lot more to say in the Cecil story.

Belief in one's champions may lead to one-eyed reality in cases like this but it remains one of the uplifting characteristics of a major stable, and it starts from the top. One consistent theme of Henry Cecil then and now is his unreserved support, admiration and affection for the stars in his care. 'One of my best friends' was his famous definition of Twice Over, whose 2009 and 2010 Champion Stakes victories were central moments in Henry's reclaiming his right to the major stage. Traditionalists might have scoffed as much at the 'soppy language' as at the theatrical clothing but it was hard to pretend there was too much affectation in the trainer's affection. Especially not with Buckskin.

Some horses hit a chord with the public. Buckskin did. It was not that they saw that much of him. After his controversial transfer to Warren Place in the summer of 1978 he had only two races that autumn, and one more in May 1979 before his final pitch for the Gold Cup at Royal Ascot that June. True he was impressive enough on all three occasions, but it was more than just the power of his gallop that caught the imagination. Everyone around him was so open about the fragility which surrounded his talent and to which those white bandages on his forelegs were witness. Everyone also, and especially his trainer, was adamant Buckskin was not just liked for his ability and courage, he was really loved as a character. At Warren Place he would even wander around loose. The biggest danger for racing, especially Flat racing, is that it is seen merely as a betting game or a breeding business. It may be Henry Cecil's greatest service that he personalised horses like Buckskin.

He certainly did at Royal Ascot, for in that Gold Cup he wore his dilemma on his sleeve. Buckskin had looked sensational when he left a good field of stayers 15 lengths in his wake in that warm-up race at Sandown in May 1979 – at one stage Henry even described him as the best horse he'd ever trained. But the stable had another distance horse on its roster. Le Moss was an independent-minded chestnut who had won all four of his races as a three-year-old before finishing second in the St Leger. His comeback win had been nothing like as impressive as Buckskin's but he had very real claims to the Gold Cup. The trainer felt he had to run him against the stable favourite. Afterwards he wrote that what followed made him 'feel like Judas Iscariot'.

On the firmish ground Buckskin was never moving with the ease he had at Sandown but his great engine took him and Joe Mercer ahead before the final turn, and as they faced up to that deceptively testing final slope only Le Moss and Lester Piggott could go with them. At first it seemed Le Moss would not just go with them but go past easily. As Mercer drove, however, Buckskin dug so deep through the pain that for a full 300 yards we got the sort of neck-and-neck duel that sears itself into the memory. Then, well inside the final furlong, Buckskin cracked. The old wolf could no longer make his kill. Mercer conceded and Piggott and Le Moss swept away to a seven-length victory.

To win the Ascot Gold Cup is a major achievement in the Flat racing canon, but for Cecil and his team this was visibly bittersweet. In the unsaddling enclosure he went to tend his loser first and could hardly smile through the congratulations of the victory mêlée. He went on BBC TV, tossed that dishevelled mane of his and apologised to the horse he loved. It was a side of him many viewers would not have seen before, all furrowed brow and rapid, posh, polite sentences. 'I hardly dared look him in the eye,' he later said of Buckskin, 'for had his legs not needed all that cotton wool and bandaging he was a horse who could have won a King George and an Arc de Triomphe.'

Buckskin's final race may have been a setback, but for Warren Place in 1979 setbacks numbered precious few. By the end of the season they were breaking not just their own but everyone else's records. From a 1978 best of 15 Group races they took that victory score to 23, five of them at Group One level. The ultimate proof of the strength of the team came in the ratio of winners to runners: Cecil's third championship-winning total of 128 successes came from as few as 287 runners, giving him a scarcely believable and in fact unrepeatable success rate of 44.6 per cent. When assistant Willie Jardine, who had worked himself up from 'unpaid slave and general dogsbody' to an integral part of the team, says simply, 'If he didn't think they had a good chance of winning they didn't run,' he is stating nothing less than the truth.

Winning for Cecil was very much the thing. For a man so starved of success in his youth it was as if he wanted to gorge on it now in every field. At school he had never been the best in anything, now he wanted excellence in whatever he touched – the roses he was developing in the Warren Place garden, the vegetable beds that had so impressed Joe Mercer, the clothes that were his passion, the horses obviously, but his rider too. He wanted Joe Mercer to be champion jockey.

Since that fall at Folkestone had ended what had seemed a certain title win 12 years back, Joe had never been close to topping the list. But with his stable in such form he was setting a real pace in 1979. In July he rode 29 winners including seven at Glorious Goodwood, three of them – Kris, Le Moss and the talented filly Connaught

Bridge – for the Cecil team. At the end of the meeting he led with 86 winners to Willie Carson's 82 and Pat Eddery's 75. 'Henry really got into it,' Joe recalls. 'He was always encouraging me, saying I could win it. In fact I think part of the reason we had rather fewer winners in 1980 [84 compared with that record 128] was because he was prepared to run his maidens in 1979 who otherwise would have waited to score and probably run better next season. But it was great for me.' Mercer was to be 45 that October but he was not going to let this chance go begging. He booted home 31 winners in August, 29 in September and another 25 in October to finish with a total of 164, 24 clear of Carson, his junior by a decade, and with an admirable winning percentage of almost 27 per cent.

The Mercer/Cecil axis would last only one more season, in which the trainers' title would be ceded to Joe's former employer Dick Hern, but 1980 certainly had its stars. The most notable were the brilliant

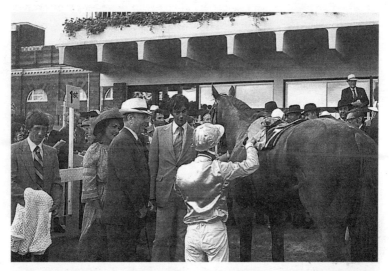

Joe Mercer unsaddles Kris after the Sussex Stakes at Goodwood, 1979 – with owner Lord Howard de Walden, Lady Howard de Walden and Henry Cecil.

two-year-old filly Pushy, who won five in a row including the Queen Mary at Royal Ascot; the stable's principal Classic contender Hello Gorgeous, who won the Dante Stakes and for a few moments looked as if he might win a Derby for Daniel Wildenstein before stamina failed him in the straight; the mighty Le Moss; and a big, upstanding bay with a long white streak down his face called Light Cavalry, who won the St Leger for Jim Joel and Julie Cecil.

The appendage of Julie's name is not because she had a share in the Brigadier Gerard colt which Mr Joel had bred at his Childwick Bury Stud, but because it was the horse she rode most mornings. There is a lovely picture of her accompanying an interview at this time: a slim and lively woman in her mid-thirties talking of the fun of juggling the roles of trainer's wife and mother to nine-year-old Katie and seven-year-old Noel. 'We just got on with it,' she said much later when her role at Warren Place was long gone. 'Of course summer holidays could be a bit of a nightmare because Henry liked me to drive him everywhere, and while Katie could go to the Pony Club, Noel was not keen on any of that, so it was tough on him. But I loved it all, especially the riding out. I had always done that with father, even horses like Busted. Light Cavalry was quite a big lump of a thing. We called him Francis and it was a great day when he won the St Leger.' Julie was talking with Noel by her side in the winter of 2011. Emphysema prevents her from being as mobile these days.

Noel's easy-going adaptability had seen him get jobs both as a restaurateur and an actor on his return from California earlier that year. 'I knew my father and the stable was famous,' he said without a trace of bitterness or self-pity, 'but it didn't really bother me. I am very proud of what he has done, but I like people for what they are, not for what they do. At that stage he and Mum were obviously a terrific team.'

It's a view echoed by assistant Willie Jardine. 'Julie was central to things in many ways, not just riding out,' he said. 'She used to go round the horses with Paddy in the evenings. Sometimes Paddy might suggest to Henry that a filly might need lighter exercise for a while and Henry would say no, because he wanted it for Royal Ascot or something. Julie would not say anything but you would see she had noticed and then a day or so later Henry would have taken the filly off the list. But the real thing she loved was riding out, and I do think that having all the major players riding out was a key part of our success. Paddy would ride out, often at the head of the string. Henry would wander up and down looking at horses, chatting to lads, often changing his plans. I would be riding out checking as well. And of course everyone loved Julie being there too.'

Light Cavalry's St Leger was one of the most popular victories they ever had at Warren Place.

It was also one of the most straightforward, Joe Mercer jumping him off in front and gradually winding up the tempo on that long Doncaster straight. I can see them now, Joe head down, arms and whip swinging in rhythm with his white-faced partner's long, relentless stride, with a persistence too implacable for the blinkered favourite Water Mill when Willie Carson drove him upsides. Light Cavalry was a giver both on the racecourse and at home, which is a lot more than can be said for the stable's biggest star in 1980.

Le Moss's three epic duels with the Irish stayer Ardross in the Ascot Gold Cup, the Goodwood Cup and the Doncaster Cup were among the most generous feats ever seen on a British racecourse, but at home he made Gunner B look like the school swot. Le Moss thought gallops were for the goofy. He wouldn't go near them, or if he did he might go 50 yards and then pull up. One day he stopped and started like that all the way up the Limekilns with Willie Jardine waving a hunting crop while the horse did his own version of 'Sulking Susan'.

In 1980 the position was made worse by Le Moss being confined to his box for six weeks in the spring with a pulled muscle. When

Henry says the horse's all-the-way victory first time out in the Gold Cup that June 'was probably the most satisfying I have ever had from a professional viewpoint', it almost smacks of understatement. He had to harness people and places and pleasure to get Le Moss to do his homework without the equine equivalent of sitting at his desk. He needed an experienced man, and preferably not too light, to play the tricks. Forty-six-year-old Alan Welbourn pulled a good ten stone on the scales and had done such stars as Proud Chieftain, Hethersett, Lorenzaccio and Welsh Pageant before handling Hello Gorgeous through that summer's campaign. If Le Moss wouldn't have any truck with gallops he could hack around the Heath. It was a big place. Some days Alan would take him right through the town and out to the far side of the Rowley Mile. If something ever lit the lazy sod up a bit, Alan would just let him run. In the evening Le Moss would be taken swimming. He liked that. Trips to empty Yarmouth and Kempton racecourses he didn't fancy so much. That looked like hard work. He wouldn't, in that splendid and never explained stable lad phrase, 'do a tap'.

Despite everything, the team got the five-year-old to the big days as hard and determined as any horse who ever looked through a bridle. Great duels need two great protagonists, and Le Moss had in Ardross a rival who that summer was almost every stride his match. Almost but not quite, for valiantly though Ardross and his partner Christy Roche battled there was no way Le Moss and his equally committed rider would let them past. Sometimes will-to-win can be an almost tangible thing. It was with Le Moss and Mercer. The three-quarters-of-a-length advantage they had at Ascot was shrunk to just a neck at Goodwood, and when Ardross closed hard again at Doncaster it felt that this time the prize was surely his. Le Moss and Mercer were not having it. In front all the way, they just would not allow their rival by. The pair flashed past us locked together, but you could see Le Moss's chestnut neck stretched ahead, and after seven and a half miles of those three cup races Roche must have felt that he would stay ahead till Doomsday.

It was one of Joe Mercer's finest hours, and next day he was at Goodwood to get Kris through a mental crisis at the starting stalls before the colt won his first race since pulling a muscle in May. But in between Joe was to shock us all with the news that he was resigning the Cecil job to go and ride for Peter Walwyn in Lambourn the following season. The official reasons were that Joe wanted to be closer to his family and that, in his mid-forties, the 240-mile commute to Newmarket was getting too much for him. But in fact it was not unrelated to other events.

On 4 September, exactly a week before Joe's announcement, the headlines had screamed 'Piggott Sacked'. Robert Sangster and Vincent O'Brien had decided to replace their long-standing but sometimes exasperating ally with Pat Eddery. It was Eddery's job that Joe Mercer was now taking. Which left a gaping hole at Henry Cecil's. No prizes as to who might be fishing for that.

Henry didn't get back from the Keeneland Sales in Kentucky until the day of the Doncaster Cup, and exactly who said what to whom is lost in the shrouds of the past. 'But I had heard talk in the wind,' says Joe Mercer. 'I felt it was time to move.' Within four days of Joe's announcement there was another one: Lester Piggott would be riding for Henry Cecil in 1981.

The ultimate talent would be back at Warren Place. As ever, it would prove an eventful ride.

5

THE PIGGOTT YEARS

LESTER PIGGOTT'S career should, by any even slightly normal standards, have been on the way down. Born in November 1935, only a year younger than Joe Mercer, he had won his first race way back in 1948, his first Derby in 1954, his first championship in 1960. There had been seven more Derbies and eight more championships, but as he returned to Warren Place in 1981 at the age of 45, the most one could surely hope for was the briefest of Indian summers. Instead there were more Derbies, more championships, and a prison cell.

Nothing except the last item should have come as a surprise. During 1980 he may have exasperated Vincent O'Brien and his big investor Robert Sangster once too often but he had still ridden over 150 winners, so he was hardly lacking support. Indeed one of his main backers during that season was the 35-year-old Barbados-born Michael Stoute, who had already trained a Classic winner and was emerging as Henry Cecil's greatest rival. Then and now Stoute knew the score about Cecil's new stable jockey. 'Look,' current champion jockey Willie Carson was to say during 1981, 'he may be getting on, but he is still Lester Piggott.'

Of course, up at Warren Place they knew him well already. An old hand like Jim White remembered him being signed up by Noel Murless as a slick-haired 18-year-old phenomenon in 1954, who in

1957 gave them their greatest ever week at Epsom. Crepello's Derby on the Wednesday was followed on the Saturday by the young Queen leading in Oaks winner Carrozza with Lester's leathers longer than jump jockeys use today. He landed them another Derby with St Paddy and another Oaks with the quirky-tempered Petite Etoile on whom his controlled, last-stride victories had all the nerveless wonder of a conjuring trick.

It was that extraordinary equine insight that the Cecil team remembered. After all, this was the man who had changed Henry's life by knifing up the inside to win that first Eclipse on Wolver Hollow. This was the jockey who had justified Henry replacing Greville Starkey on Relay Race by rolling that horse like he had never rolled before. This was the rider who seemed to be able to make even the oddest-tempered horse smile. 'He was uncanny,' remembers Willie Jardine. 'Roussalka could be really difficult to have anything to do with. When Frankie Durr came one morning she would not let him near her. With Lester, if she had been a dog, she would have wagged her tail.'

Trainer and jockey made a wonderfully contrasting pair. There is an illuminating Chris Smith picture taken on the Heath at this time. Henry looks rather younger than his 38 years, with a fashionable 1980s haircut and hands deep in the pockets of a snazzy windproof jacket. He grins rather boyishly down at Lester's inscrutable old chinaman's face glancing up from an opened *Sporting Life* where the real interest appears to lie. It was a foppish image that suited Henry once he got his confidence as a trainer. But it was not one that would mislead his jockey. 'He can give the impression of being casual and often appears as the court jester,' Piggott was to write about his new employer. 'His outward appearance however can be deceptive as underneath is an ambitious man determined to remain at the very top of his profession.'

It takes one to know one, and it was not long before the partnership made a very public statement of its intent. On the last day of the opening Craven meeting at Newmarket they had a brilliant treble with Long Legend, Ackermann and the 1,000 Guineas favourite Fairy Footsteps. It was but five months since Robert Sangster had made his annual trip to the Melbourne Cup to be bowled the blunt Aussie question, 'Did you sack Lester, or did he sack you?' It was also all of 24 years since Piggott had arrived at the Craven meeting struggling so desperately with his weight that the prospect loomed of returning to the heavier jump jockey world his father and grandfather had trodden. That year, like this of 1981, the winners had come and the doubts had fled. As he padded away from the weighing room in his Humphrey Bogart raincoat there was that familiar, wry, sardonic twinkle in his eye. He knew, we knew, and above all Henry Cecil knew, that even in this Indian summer of his greatness it was better to have Lester Piggott for you than against you.

That is provided he was in one piece, and one afternoon in April it looked as if he was in bits. Exactly one week before Jim Joel's filly Fairy Footsteps' tilt at the 1,000 Guineas the world had to witness what seemed little short of public dismemberment. Our ITV cameras were at Epsom that day and the last televised race was to be run on the sprint track, which has a world record time of 53.6 seconds for the five furlongs of the straight downhill chute with horses clocking well over 45mph in mid-race. Even for experienced horses and jockeys, the rattling bars and drumming hooves of the great steel cage that is the starting gates can be the tensest of places. That afternoon it was all too much for Piggott's mount Winsor Boy.

All seemed normal as he and his impassive partner were shoved into the narrow stall with its big, green-padded doors in front. Then suddenly something flipped in the thoroughbred's brain and he dived fatally forward to try to escape underneath. There was no room. 'One moment he was in, the next moment he was down,' said jockey Brian Rouse, who was in the adjoining stall. 'Nobody thinks or moves quicker than Lester but this one beat him and for a time I thought it might have killed him.' So, for much longer than all of us would have liked, did the million or so watching on ITV.

As we anguished over the airwaves about exactly what was happening to the ageing jockey clearly trapped between the writhing horse and the immovable starting gate, the deadline for the programme switchover came ever closer. In desperation I pleaded for extra minutes but finally had to wish viewers goodbye with the promise of news of what had happened to horse and man. The trick in these circumstances is to try to avoid any hostage-to-fortune speculation or too much worst-result worry in the voice. The first might have been achieved but I very much doubt we pulled off the second. Mind you, I wasn't alone. The entire racing world feared this was the last it would see of Lester Piggott. Imagine what it felt like for the trainer seven days before a crucial Classic tilt.

As so often in such circumstances Cecil was measured in his response – not something that was universally shared when what initially seemed like the mangled remains of Lester Piggott were finally cleared of the starting gate and the broken-backed Winsor Boy was destroyed. Lester's own back had been horribly wrenched and his right ear was hanging loose. As the ambulance took him to Roehampton Hospital the idea of him race-riding within a week seemed ridiculous in the extreme. Yet, incredibly, four days later he reported for duty at Ascot, with his ear sewn back and the bandages hidden by a woolly swathe beneath the riding helmet. He looked a wreck. He didn't look much better when he walked into the paddock to ride Fairy Footsteps at Newmarket. But Henry Cecil knew the implacability of the man and said if Lester felt up to it then Lester should ride. The repayment then and through the rest of the season was a classic one in every sense.

The mind has always been more important than the matter when it comes to making horses run. The trainer at home and the jockey in the race have to inspire their athletes' minds so that, in those famous John Masefield lines from his epic poem 'Right Royal', it is

> *Ready to race, though blown, though beat,*
> *As long as his will could lift his feet,*
> *Ready to burst his heart to pass*
> *Each gasping horse in that street of grass.*

That's what it was like when Lester Piggott sent Fairy Footsteps for the line in that 1,000 Guineas at Newmarket. He was in the black silks and scarlet cap of owner Jim Joel in which Joe Mercer had won the St Leger on the filly's half-brother Light Cavalry just seven months earlier. With stamina in her pedigree, Lester jumped her out in front to make the others hurt. He must have been hurting too as the advantage seemed to shrink and the winning post move back up the final climb. But the desire for victory was deep within the rider's psyche and his will as well as his whip would not allow Fairy Footsteps to brook any other result. The race had been first run in April 1814, a full year before the Battle of Waterloo. In all that time nothing as heroic had been seen up this historic Rowley Mile.

It was an astonishing day and is worth remembering for more than the race alone. For in these truly legendary moments lie the ultimate joy and in some senses deepest danger of inhabiting the extraordinary parallel universe of the galloping game. Something as inspirational as what Lester and Fairy Footsteps did up that Newmarket turf lifts us above all the negatives of what in other ways can be a limited and even dubious existence. As Lester and his filly were led back an actual tear showed above the sunny smile that broke across the frozen tundra of his face. It was one we all shared, perhaps Henry more than most. For all his wonders Mr Piggott could also be difficult, even devious to deal with, but when he did things like this you could forgive him anything. Well, we could. Others, tragically for him and for us but not perhaps for the sensible implementation of the law, would not take so generous a tack.

At Newmarket the abiding sentiment was one of thanks for the good fortune of being present when such a talent stalked our earth. It was something that stretched throughout the season as Piggott defied the years and the dangers to push on for his tenth riding championship. It was a year in which those dangers were tragically highlighted: apprentice Joe Blanks was buried two days before Lester and Light Cavalry battled in vain pursuit of superstar Shergar in Ascot's King George VI and Queen Elizabeth Stakes, and Willie Carson's title hopes ended when the filly Silken Knot snapped one foreleg and then the other before crashing him headlong into the ground at York. Such things were fully recognised by Lester himself when I spent a couple of days with him in the closing weeks of the season. 'I have been lucky,' he muttered, pulling on one of his big cigars, 'hardly had a fall. You have to make the best of it.'

His idea of filling Kipling's 'unforgiving minute' has always been a bit more ambitious than a mere 'sixty seconds' worth of distance run'. At that stage, although 70 winners clear in the jockeys' championship, there were no concessions whatever to any pretence of easing off at the end of the season. After six rides at Newmarket, Lester was Concording the Atlantic to ride in the Canadian International in Toronto, then returning to race at Leicester on the Monday and Tuesday before representing Britain in an international jockeys' tournament at Kempton on the Wednesday. Watching him that week you could only shake your head at his schedule and, while one could agree with Julie Cecil's verdict that 'he is much more relaxed these days', it still seemed unlikely that this defiant last throw of the dice should continue on quite so high a winning note.

Yet 12 months later there we were celebrating even better results both for him and for the Cecil stable, which had turned out a record 24 Group-race winners to take its own championship back after ceding it in 1981 to the Shergar-led battalion of Michael Stoute. We were in the long, low living room of Lester's ranch-style house just a quarter-mile down the Hamilton Road from where Henry had started at Marriott Stables. On the table, the form book, the telephone and the big blue diary were reminders of the obsessive planning behind the triumphs recorded around him. With its silver trophies and oil paintings, the room was in reality a shrine to his talent. As usual a big cigar was the only nourishment, but those famous nasal tones were soft, almost purring, like the black cat beside him on the sofa.

'Of course I enjoy it all,' he said. 'There wouldn't be any point in doing it otherwise.' The sentences were as lean and spare as the limbs beneath the fawn slacks and the grey check sweater. 'I still get a kick out of every ride, every winner. All horses, every race is different. The challenge is to get them right, but provided you enjoy it, it gets easier as you get older. It's experience. It all gets slower. You think quicker, see the problems earlier, so you have more time.'

So benign a Piggott was a surprise then; it would still be now to those who peer back through the years. We were so used to him in the eye of the storm, the body angled high above the saddle, the face lined and sinister behind the goggles, that we would forget the obvious: that for all his insatiable drive, Lester had more reasons at that time to feel satisfied than any man in the kingdom. Due to be 47 on Guy Fawkes Day, he needed only four winners to pass his best-ever total of 191 successes, even if the much-coveted 200 was now out of reach. 'It's much easier now that I am riding for Henry Cecil rather than Vincent O'Brien,' he said by way of explanation. 'It's got to be. All the horses are here. The plans are here, not 300 miles away in Tipperary. I couldn't manage that any more. Henry has given me five more years, really.'

The sense of satisfaction was warm in the cigar-scented air. You knew we were living in a parallel universe and that the years had to claim him some time soon. Yet it would still have taken the gloomiest pessimist to think that in the midst of all this wonder, the great man had already sown the seeds of his own destruction.

It may have been the ultimate of Indian summers for Lester Piggott, but the sun was also climbing ever higher in the Henry Cecil sky.

The trainer might still like to wear outrageous clothes and behave in tousle-haired and sometimes flirty ways, but he was now light years from the hopeless drunken youth of two decades before. He was a teetotaller, he was a big employer, and he was driven. He had not so much stepped into his father-in-law's shoes at Warren Place as laced them up and started to run in them. Henry was spreading his interests too. For fun he had started a shop in Newmarket high street called The Clothes Horse where he could indulge his love of fashion and make local ladies swoon as he said, 'Oh, you do look good in that.' For future development he was to take over the lease of Cliff Stud at Helmsley on the southern edge of the North York Moors from Noel Murless. It would have his brother David as manager and be run in partnership with Tote Cherry-Downes whom, you will remember, they had first met in those old car-crashing, greyhound-racing days as dodgy hands at Woodlands Stud. Henry Cecil was in business now.

But for all that, the real focus was always on what was happening with the horses at Warren Place. In 1981 Willie Jardine was joined as assistant by a 19-year-old Newmarket trainer's son called William Jarvis, who had ridden a winner for his father Ryan when still a 16-year-old schoolboy at Harrow. 'I thought I might be a great amateur like John Oaksey,' says Willie Jarvis, 'but Henry took one look at me and made me into a "car park jockey" – I was the sort of guy who rode the horses to the car park and then legged up the real jockeys for the gallops. But I had five of the happiest years of my life with him. Of course if things had gone wrong, there would be dark mornings when nothing would be said at the breakfast table, but they were very few. Every day I would have my boiled egg and toast with him and Willie Jardine at Paddy and Joy's bungalow on the edge of the stable paddock. It was a great feeling to be a small part of such a team. He was usually very relaxed and easy but they really knew their horses.'

The results did not lie. That utterly astonishing 44.6 per cent strike-rate in 1979 might not ever be repeated but it was back up to 37 per cent in 1981 and remained above 30 per cent for the rest of the decade. The winners were coming in all categories and in two very famous cases were, as with Gunner B, improving on what others had done before. In 1981 it happened with Ardross, that mighty Irish battler who had run Le Moss so close in those three titanic duels in the 'Stayers' Triple Crown' the year before. In January Henry Cecil and Charles St George had flown to Ireland to inspect Ardross at Kevin Prendergast's stables off the Curragh. The horse was already a hard-trained five-year-old but Henry thought he could find some improvement in him. And he did.

Who knows whether it came from a change of scenery and routine, from the daily care of his highly focused Scots lad Steven Kingstree, or from the stimulation of being in the equine scholarship company of 150 others. But improvement, even on Ardross's battling excellence of 1980, there most certainly was. In 1981 he won the

Ascot Gold Cup, four other good races, and finished fifth in the Arc de Triomphe, and in 1982 he took the Gold Cup, five other races, and closed his career with a best-ever performance when failing by a head to win that year's Arc. And that over a whole mile less than the Ascot stayers' showpiece he had made his own.

Ardross ran like a champion, looked like a champion and behaved like a champion. The same could most definitely not be said about Critique. He too came from Ireland, and from none other than Vincent O'Brien. The better the trainer the less chance someone else has of improving his horses. It is a fact that they rarely improved after leaving Henry Cecil's. So when Critique came over from Tipperary in the summer of 1981 he was the sort of challenge most people would want to avoid. The white-faced colt was good-looking and talented enough. He had won by six lengths on his debut the previous season and had been beaten only a neck in France's richest juvenile race, the Grand Criterium. But he had run off the course after winning that first time in Ireland, had worn blinkers in France, and hadn't been seen since. 'Oh you won't train him,' one of Vincent O'Brien's lads assured Steve 'Yarmy' Dyble at Royal Ascot the week before Critique was transferred, 'he's a real bastard. He won't go anywhere.' Now that was the sort of challenge Yarmy liked to meet.

After his exploits on the explosive Lyphard's Wish a few years earlier, Yarmy had become Cecil's 'go to' rider for tricky horses. He was not without his faults – he was so drunk one day at Newbury that Henry literally threw him out of the saddling stall and the box driver had to lead the horse round the paddock – but Yarmy thought nothing more fun than trying to get into the head of some stubborn mule of a thing that didn't want to go anywhere. Critique looked like a barrel of fun to him. He didn't to the rest of them.

'Critique was an absolute bugger to start with,' says Paddy Rudkin. 'He would hardly go anywhere and then only at a walk or trot. I had to lead him down to the canter and then, even though we would be only hacking, Yarmy would be flapping and shouting to keep him going.' Mr Dyble has rather happier memories. 'He was my baby,' he says. 'Henry always gave me quirky horses and told me to take him off on his own. I was younger then so I could vault on him any time and I would lead him out and then jump on him and hack him all over the Heath. We would go right down to racecourse side and I would take him swimming and for a pick of grass and a carrot. He sweetened up all right.'

It certainly showed on the racecourse, although Piggott had to apply quite a bit of his own equine psychology, waiting until Critique's mind was in its 'going' gear to ensure the colt did not down tools as he had done when he first arrived at Newmarket. Under the Cecil banner they won first time out at Kempton, did the trick again at Newmarket, landed the hat-trick in the important Cumberland Lodge Stakes at Ascot in September, and were even better in 1982. He was something to celebrate. The trouble was this was something Yarmy was apt to do rather too well.

If anyone doubts the accuracy of the 'soap opera-parallel universe' analogy for life at Newmarket they should time-travel back to Warren Place one particular afternoon in this era. In the early 1980s unsung Ipswich Town was being taken to football honours by a brilliant manager called Bobby Robson. Heroes of the side such as Mick Mills, Alan Brazil and Terry Butcher had become great fans of racing's capital and the feeling was mutual. Especially on this day for Yarmy, who thought Critique would appreciate a bit of Ipswich gold dust and so took him out for his pick of grass bedecked in a rosette, a football scarf and, for reasons unspecified, a Koala hat and a pair of motorcycle goggles. It has to be said that young Mr Dyble had also drunk something a lot stronger than tea for his lunch.

Not necessarily the scene with which a trainer wants to greet an important owner when he comes to visit. 'But we could not stop

Steve 'Yarmy' Dyble – with the enigmatic Critique dressed as an Ipswich Town fan.

it,' relates Willie Jarvis. 'We all knew Yarmy was pissed and had Critique in fancy dress out in the paddock but all of a sudden Henry comes round the corner with Mr Vanian and we could not divert him. Henry rolled his eyes and Mr Vanian just laughed. When it was over we all saw the funny side, and the next day we got Yarmy to do it again and the photographer John Crofts came in to record it. We did some amazing things in those days.'

Souren Vanian was pretty amazing in his own right. A Lebanese businessman with a fortune of unknown origins, he was a genial, square-necked, broad-smiling guy who resembled nothing so much as the prize bulls that were treasured favourites on the Derisley Wood Stud that housed his bloodstock. He had some good horses, and for Henry Cecil that rendered even the most unsuitable suitable. Critique was worth keeping.

Some wonderful cameos come back of him and of Ardross in 1982. Ardross standing triumphant at Royal Ascot after running in three consecutive Gold Cups and having been beaten only once in the last two seasons. His lad Steve Kingstree acting very much the forthright boxer's second rather than the mere hero-worshipping acolyte. 'He will have a bite and a kick at you sometimes,' said 34-year-old Steve in his straightforward Scottish way, 'and we have to keep him away from other horses in the evenings.' Steve had a job to do and his frantic whistling in the dope-test stall showed that Ardross was having the same trouble providing a urine sample as some of the World Cup footballers that summer in sunny Spain.

A day after that image the rains had come, but the scene following the Hardwicke Stakes was much the same. Critique, a Lester Piggott/Henry Cecil horse, had won, and as George Winsor (by now promoted to travelling head lad) and William Jarvis shuttled around to prepare the stable's next runner, there was a moment of told-you-so triumph from the man holding Critique's rein. 'This horse is such a character,' said Yarmy with his hair soaked and plastered to his head. 'He should be on This Is Your Life.'

Four months later the scene had shifted to Warren Place in the countdown to both Critique's and Ardross's final and personal showdown, at Longchamp for the Arc. Just as a boxing gym gets high on self-belief in the last few days before a fight, so in a racing yard the atmosphere becomes heady with the winner's dream as you approach a big race. Critique and Ardross were ready – Critique the old white-faced joker whose late, late finishes had made him the punters' nightmare, Ardross the super stayer nothing in the world could touch over two miles but who was now stepping down to the Arc's mile and a half.

Lester Piggott had chosen to ride Ardross – something he would not be allowed to forget by Yarmy if the joker Critique was to charge past that Sunday afternoon. But as Ardross banished us from his box, there was an arrogance about him that made one think Lester might have picked the right conveyance, and so it proved. Critique ran well enough to finish eighth, although needless to say Yarmy insisted that if Lester rather than Pat Eddery had been in the irons his partner in madness would have found an extra winning gear. But it was Ardross that was a revelation.

Six years old and with more than ten staying triumphs behind him, here he was out after the leaders, hunting down Europe's finest over a much less demanding trip. On and on he came like a hungry deerhound. There was something almost predatory about Ardross as he stretched out that hardened, unflinching neck with Lester's whip curling demonic in its demands. As the post flashed up it looked as if he might yet get a final leap on the leader. But as they passed us we could see his jaws had not quite closed on that victory bite.

Afterwards Ardross was being washed down just beyond the champagne and celebrities of the paddock-side Bar des Anglais. He had just been through the last and hardest race of a quite magnificent career and the weals of the Piggott whip could be seen across his quarters. But Ardross's eye was still bright, the great muscular body superb, and as Steven Kingstree led him away, it was a reminder that racing's greatest justification remains the majestic beauty of the horse itself.

There were plenty such reminders in these glory years, especially at Royal Ascot where all Henry's qualities, not to mention his relatives, shone brightest. 'All the brothers used to meet up at the same bar each year,' said Jamie, who made the pilgrimage down with his wife Fiona from his Clan Burnett duties as the laird of Crathes Castle. 'I even had a share in a couple of horses with him. They never did any good but you could see how much Henry loved the fashion, the excitement and the idea that he could be the best. We were very proud of him. We still are.'

Henry himself attached so much importance to Royal Ascot that he even insisted on his assistants attending every day 'to get themselves noticed'. Understandably this was not a view that got much sympathy from Paddy Rudkin. 'It used to drive him mad,' says William Jarvis. 'There he was beavering away in the yard while we were swanning off to Ascot in topper and tails. He made pretty sure that we made up for it later.' Whole forests have been felled to provide enough newspaper to hold the annual punditry on how the British Flat racing season should build towards its climax. Year after year Henry Cecil's team would recognise and conquer the reality that in British Flat racing the highest set of peaks come in June when the sun should know its duty and the monarch's carriage comes stately up the track for a week of racing still unsurpassed anywhere.

Hindsight usually highlights the sunshine, but even in this era far more hopes slipped away down the river than ever got netted and pulled on to the bank, even when the hook had seemed lodged deep in the mouth. By 1982 Henry Cecil's roll of honour still lacked either of Epsom's great Classics, but that spring the trainer was convinced that a Mill Reef colt of Daniel Wildenstein's called Simply Great could justify his name by bringing a Cecil-trained Derby winner back to Warren Place. Simply Great had long worked like a champion and when he powered home in the Dante Stakes at York in May the bookmakers and the press believed it too. But the trainer was well aware of how disaster can strike at any time, and when Lester Piggott came down to the Limekilns for one of his final pre-Derby workouts, Simply Great was great no more.

As so often at this distance there are different versions of how and why the injury occurred, but it was severe enough to end Simply Great's season and he was never the same again.

Other horses dropped out for separate reasons, but with the most difficult of them it was a case not of the bone breaking but the brain. The horse was Valiyar, another oddball colt bought by Souren Vanian, this time from the Aga Khan's distinguished trainer François Mathet in Chantilly. Once again the problem was confided to Yarmouth's skilful if not entirely sober hands. Valiyar had talent to burn and he won big races, but even with one look at him you could see the problem. He had little piggy ears and when they went back the brakes went on. He stopped dead on the gallop the day before he was to have his first run at Leicester.

'What do we do now?' asked Henry.

'Better run him, guvnor,' said Yarmy.

He did. Valiyar won by five lengths.

Subsequently Lester Piggott rode him at Epsom on the day the great man won his ninth and final Derby, on Teenoso. The magic did not transfer. Valiyar never tried a yard and finished last of three. Not surprisingly Lester chose to ride another Cecil horse, Ivano, when Valiyar next ran in the Queen Anne Stakes at Royal Ascot and didn't see the joke when Pat Eddery and old Piggy Ears came motoring past him. Valiyar seemed to, because he then refused to enter the unsaddling enclosure until Yarmy pushed him in backwards, and back at Warren Place he then gave a very clear indication, bordering on savage, that this was the end of any cooperation.

Not all winners needed quite such special handling, and now they were coming at a flood, 107 of them in 1981 and another 111 in 1982 when Piggott notched up that 188 total to take his 11th and final jockeys' championship. It was a time of hard work, fun and exciting competition. Henry was to win the trainers' title again in 1982 and repeated it in 1984, 1985, 1987 and 1988; Dick Hern took the trainers' title in 1980 and 1983, Michael Stoute in 1981, 1986 and 1989. But even that pair did not spark Cecil's sense of rivalry as much as Guy Harwood, whose whole modus of applying science and his business background to training seemed a direct challenge to the instinctive way in which Henry operated.

Harwood forsook an engineering apprenticeship with his father's business to train jumpers and build his own base on a dairy farm at Pulborough in Sussex. He was as direct and detailed as Henry was oblique and vague. I rode some winners for Guy over fences, and if the orders had been put down on paper they would have run to several pages. But he was a formidable organiser and when switched to the Flat he built a brilliantly balanced team. By the time he won his first Classic, in 1981 with To-Agori-Mou's 2,000 Guineas, he had deservedly won a reputation as the most open of all trainers. He even, horror of horrors, began to start the season with a 'media day'.

When To-Agori-Mou began his 1981 season by finishing only third in the Craven Stakes, Guy came on TV and told me the colt was still 15lb over his 1,090lb racing weight and that in a fortnight's time he would be back on it and take the Guineas. He did. If not quite a red rag to a bull it was a clear challenge to the 'art before science' approach that characterised Henry then and now. One day William Jarvis suggested Warren Place consider a 'media day'. It didn't go down too well.

But while Henry could afford to trust his instincts when it came to training, it was rather a different story in the changing world of international bloodstock where the advent of Robert Sangster and the rocketing price of stallion values had brought an entirely new attitude to ownership. It was one to which Henry Cecil would have to, and did, successfully adapt. But with that came a whole new set of dangers. As the old racing truism has it, owners can be a lot harder to train than horses.

The times were indeed a-changin'. In the wider world it was 15 years since Bob Dylan had first sung his great protest anthem, but the world didn't feel any safer. The Vietnam War was over but the

Cold War was heating up again, the Ayatollah was in Iran, oil prices had doubled and back home the Brixton riots were to be followed by three million unemployed, the Falklands War and the miners' strike. In British racing things were still tough at the bottom: the minimum wage was £63 a week and only 83 of the 370 trainers on the Flat managed ten winners for the 1980 season. But at the very top there were suddenly riches beyond the dreams of avarice. And when money and horses start to run, avarice is never far behind.

These were very different riches from Cecil Boyd-Rochfort's day, when wealthy owners were either pillars of the British establishment or anglophile Americans who came over for Ascot and whom he and Rohays would sail over to visit each winter. These establishment owners may well have had stud and breeding interests; indeed CBR had been integrally involved with the development of the Someries Stud where Lady Zia Wernher bred Meld and other stars at Newmarket, as well as Newsells Park near Royston where Sir Humphrey de Trafford produced the Classic winners Alcide and Parthia. But as the 1970s moved into the 1980s bloodstock became much more than an elegant diversion. It became an international business with a currency all of its own. Nothing would be the same again.

Henry had his traditional owners, of course. Few operations could be more establishment than Jim Joel's Childwick Bury or Lord Howard de Walden's Plantation Stud, and while Daniel Wildenstein might be a Paris-based outsider, his horses were very much raised and run on the original high-minded principle of breeding to race. True, Charles St George had always been quite nimble when there was some business to be done, especially if Lester had marked his card, Ardross being a supreme example. But when Robert Sangster teamed up with Vincent O'Brien and John Magnier in the mid-1970s, the concept was of a much bigger order. They would buy

Above: The Cecil twins (Henry second left) and younger brother Arthur with their stepfather Cecil Boyd-Rochfort and mother Rohays. *Below:* The young trainer sees his string out of Freemason Lodge.

Wollow and Gianfranco Dettori go to post for the 1976 2,000 Guineas at Newmarket.

Work day on the Newmarket gallops for (left to right) Frank Conlon, Woody Woodrough and Stan Smith.

Joe Mercer in the colours of owner Carlo d'Alessio …

… and winning the 1980 Goodwood Cup in those colours on Le Moss from another great stayer, Ardross.

The Lester Piggott years: *opposite*, Lester discussing the form with Henry Cecil on Warren Hill; *above*, going to post before winning the 1981 1,000 Guineas on Fairy Footsteps; *below*, at full stretch on Ardross at Newbury.

Henry Cecil at Royal Ascot with Lord and Lady Howard de Walden.

Henry Cecil (left) relaxing in the Caribbean with owner Henry Ponsonby,
trainer Paul Cole, and Julie Cecil.

The 1985 Derby: Slip Anchor and Steve Cauthen out on their own
at Tattenham Corner.

Steve Cauthen – *left*, winning the 1985 Oaks on Oh So Sharp; *below left*, winning the 1987 Derby on Reference Point, and (*below*) with Henry Cecil in the Ascot winner's enclosure.

Lester Piggott with Robert Sangster after The Minstrel's victory in the 1977 King George VI and Queen Elizabeth Diamond Stakes at Ascot.

well-bred American yearlings with the express aim of winning major European races and hitting the jackpot with seven- or even eight-figure stallion syndications.

The 1977 Derby hero The Minstrel was in their very first shopping basket along with the Arc de Triomphe winner Alleged. In 1975 the Sangster/Magnier/O'Brien team had gone to $200,000 to buy The

Minstrel at the Keeneland Yearling Sales in Kentucky, but after that colt had closed out his three-year-old season by also winning the Irish Derby and the King George VI and Queen Elizabeth Stakes at Ascot, they were able to syndicate him for a cool $9 million – job done. The idea of such massive bloodstock jackpots offered trainers both a new challenge and a huge extra set of potential rewards. They would not just campaign to win races, they would be incentivised to enhance value most of all. For if a trainer was offered a breeding right for any of his horses syndicated as stallions – a common practice – they would have their own jackpots to land as these rights ('nominations') rose dizzyingly to £10,000, £20,000, even £50,000 a time.

For someone like Henry Cecil the Sangster initiative was no immediate problem, as witnessed by the continued excellence of the Warren Place results. But a fresh and major force had entered into his field with hitherto unthinkable numbers and purchasing power. At Sangster's Isle of Man home in October 1980, I gave up the count at 279. And that figure was still less than halfway through the most extraordinary noticeboard in the racing world at the time. It was on the far wall of a shining new office on the lower ground floor of a large Victorian building which, in view of Sangster's sometime heroic bedtime reputation, carried the not entirely appropriate name of 'The Nunnery'. It listed every horse Robert owned or had shares in. Two hundred and seventy-nine was merely the number, over six countries and 36 trainers, of the racehorses in training; the other 400-odd name cards were of the mares, stallions, foals and yearlings that completed the Sangster portfolio, which in five years had developed into the most expensive in the history of the game. If it is true that the sun never sets over what used to be the British Empire, at that stage it could never complete a circuit without some little man in the green and blue Sangster silks flashing across one of the great racecourses of the world. The day before my visit they had won the Irish St Leger and been fourth in the Australian Guineas, a week earlier they had won the Arc de Triomphe in Paris with the filly Detroit, and five days later their two-year-old colt Storm Bird would land the Dewhurst Stakes at Newmarket and make his $1 million yearling cost look something of a bargain when he was later syndicated for an astonishing $30 million after running only once more.

Sangster was a rival rather than a patron of the Cecil stable but his operation was a benchmark to others, and by that summer he had already spawned a competitor who would soon be almost a Gulliver in Robert's Lilliput. At the Keeneland Sales in July 1982 the Sangster syndicate went to a record $4.25 million for a yearling by Nijinsky and spent a further $13.8 million on another nine. But someone else spent $12 million on 19 choicely bred yearlings. He had flown in on his own 727. He and his family already had 120 horses in training; by the following summer it would be 238 with three studs and a further 60 broodmares. Sheikh Mohammed was on his way.

He was in a hurry. He always has been. His first winner, a two-year-old filly called Hatta after a hilltop oasis in the Sheikh's native Dubai, had come as recently as 20 June 1977, just a fortnight after The Minstrel had landed Sangster his Derby jackpot. The Sheikh understood horses. He had stood on the back of one to canter past his wedding guests and then repeated the feat on a camel. He had a clear idea that an involvement in British horseracing could give him the profile and the contacts to deliver his father Sheikh Rashid's vision of using the newly gushing oil revenues to transform their tiny desert statelet into one of the great tourist and business hubs on the planet. Besides, Sheikh Mohammed very much liked what he saw in British racing. And what he liked he usually got.

In particular, that autumn of 1982, he liked a big bay Henry Cecil-trained colt called Dunbeath, who had won both the Royal Lodge Stakes at Ascot and the William Hill Futurity at Doncaster,

Best of friends: Sheikh Mohammed bin Rashid al Maktoum and Henry Cecil.

the two premier mile events for two-year-olds. A year earlier Tote Cherry-Downes and Henry Cecil had gone to $100,000 to buy Dunbeath for their Irish client Michael Riordan. Initially Michael and Dunbeath's breeder Lee Eaton, who retained a half share, were keen to stick. But when Sheikh Mohammed got to the six million mark they had no option but to twist. Dunbeath did not train on to be the hoped-for Derby winner but Sheikh Mohammed was on the roster and a set of those maroon and white silks hung in the Warren Place colours room. It was to prove one of the most momentous partnerships of Henry Cecil's whole career.

The Sheikh was not joining a sinking ship. When Dunbeath eased home in the Futurity he took the Warren Place stable's earnings to a new seasonal record of £872,614 despite not even having a runner in four of the five Classics and several other major races. The yard had won no fewer than 24 Pattern races, Ardross and Critique carried almost all before them, and in Diesis they had a colt who had landed an even more significant two-year-old double than Dunbeath and so would have fetched even more than that colt's £6 million if Lord Howard de Walden had ever opted to sell him outright.

For Diesis, being by the stallion Sharpen Up out of the mare Doubly Sure, was a full-brother to Kris, who had brought so much glory to those famous apricot silks in 1979. In what almost amounts to lightning striking thrice the youngest brother Keen was to prove nearly as good in the season ahead. Diesis's big two-year-old double of the Middle Park Stakes and the Dewhurst had made him favourite for the next year's 2,000 Guineas and was further proof to his trainer of the pleasure of training horses you have known not just from a foal but from the actual planning of the mating. When Henry focuses on someone he has always had a touch of almost oriental charm and he would have liked the words of the great *Dr Zhivago* and *Lawrence of Arabia* star Omar Sharif at the height of his powers: 'To select the mother and the father,' he said with a look that sent a large section of womanhood into meltdown, 'and for them to create a beautiful child – in its little way, it's a bit like playing at God.'

God, or at least success, had come to North Yorkshire – that's if full-blooded Yorkshiremen will ever admit that Jehovah might exist anywhere else. In 1940 a young vet called Alf Wight had journeyed down from Glasgow to join the Thirsk veterinary practice that served the local racecourse as well as the remote farmlands on the Hambleton Hills beyond the great shoulder of Sutton Bank. Students of Alf's future fame might note that the practice in the historic market town's cobbled Kirkgate was just seven doors along from the birthplace of Thirsk's most famous name, the eighteenth-century professional cricketer Thomas Lord, who was to found and be commemorated by the London ground which has become the temple of the game of cricket.

Alf was both able and popular as a vet. I remember a quiet, competent presence one problematic day at the races. But it was as a writer that he became an international sensation. He penned his first book in 1969, the same year as Henry Cecil started training. But neither that nor the next one caused anything like the impact Henry made with Wolver Hollow and Approval in that first Freemason Lodge season. However, the books made a big stir when they were put together and published under one title in America, a massive one when they were made into a film under the same name in 1975, and soon after the 1978 start of what was to become a 12-year, 90-episode, multi-million-viewer TV series there was not a household in the land that did not know its name. It was called *All Creatures Great and Small*, for the writing of which Alf had taken the pen-name James Herriot.

Alf began to cut back his veterinary work in 1980, at about the time Henry took over the Cliff Stud lease from Noel Murless, but for years he would have been driving up to those paddocks high above Helmsley just as he would have passed the training stables at Hambleton House where the mighty ridge of Sutton Bank looks down across the vale. It was from there that Noel Murless had become leading northern trainer in 1947 and 1948, and when his profession then took him southwards the Cliff Stud kept his Hambleton connection, providing a release for either resting racehorses or developing young stock like St Paddy, who went on to land the 1960 Derby under Lester Piggott.

Back in 1980 Henry planned to continue the same, as indeed he does to this day. Daniel Wildenstein liked the St Paddy precedent and sent his foals up to North Yorkshire, the future Breeders' Cup winner Steinlen being among the very first batch. But while Henry,

Tote Cherry-Downes and David might not be looking at Alf Wight's idea of bestsellers across the Atlantic, they were entitled to think they might get something from the bloodstock gold rush that was starting in Kentucky. Across the Vale of York, whole communities were facing extinction as mine closures climbed the government agenda. Up in Hambleton the old dreams had a new kick.

In his understated way, Tote Cherry-Downes had built an enviable reputation in the bloodstock business. After those first grafting, giggling days at Woodland with the Cecil twins he had gone to Ireland to manage Fort Union Stud for Lord Dunraven and the Barretstown Estates for the Canadian food tycoon Garfield Weston, before its castle was gifted to the Irish state and, among other things, it became an annual camp for actor Paul Newman's acclaimed youth groups the Hole in the Wall Gangs. Back in Newmarket, Tote's knowledge and contacts made him a natural ally for able trainers and his wish for value appealed to all but one client who complained when he only spent $20,000 of a $200,000 order.

In 1979 Tote bought a yearling colt in Kentucky which as Mattaboy was to win the next year's Middle Park Stakes for trainer Robert Armstrong. In 1980 he bought Robert another which, as Be My Native, went on to win the Coronation Cup under the trainer's brother-in-law Lester Piggott, not to mention becoming the most astonishingly libidinous of stallions, covering no fewer than 325 mares in 1994 alone. Tote was clearly the right sort of agent to have on your side in this fevered new boom in bloodstock. In 1980 he and Henry spent just 33,000gns on behalf of American owner James Stone for a colt that was to win the 1981 Middle Park Stakes under the name of Cajun. In the same month that Cajun won the Middle Park, Tote went to $62,000 at Keeneland for a filly to be called Bright Crocus, who was to win three races culminating in the prestigious May Hill Stakes at Doncaster in 1982.

Bright Crocus wore the colours of a Mrs Barbara Walters, wife of the English representative of what appeared to be a progressive art and bloodstock company called Alchemy International.

Alchemy were pleased. So much so that in November 1982 Tote Cherry-Downes was back at Keeneland for the Fasig-Tipton Fall Sale spending $95,000 on Alchemy's behalf for a handsome bay foal by Riverman, the star French stallion who had just moved to the legendary Gainesway Farm in Kentucky. The plan was to board the colt for a year at Cliff Stud and then reap the benefits of the Yorkshire air and limestone grassland by selling him at Tattersalls' prestigious Highflyer Yearling Sales the next autumn. When the Riverman colt finally came into the ring the atmosphere was right into the extremes of parallel-universe economics.

As the rest of the country braced itself for the cost of the Falklands War, the threatened miners' strike and the CND protests against the impending arrival of cruise missiles at the Greenham air base, we racing-philes watched in wonder as two yearlings passed the never-before-broken one-million-guinea mark with the most anticipated of all due in the ring immediately after the Riverman colt had taken his bow as lot 116. Not that the Cliff Stud colt didn't itself have bidders aplenty. That original $95,000 soon became a distant memory as a duel developed between an emissary of Sheikh Mohammed's Maktoum family and a youngish man standing with a companion at the back of the sales pavilion. When the hammer finally fell at 430,000gns, Henry and his team felt the good lord might indeed be up there above Helmsley. It was a false assumption.

It was only moments before the first trouble started. The man to whom senior auctioneer Captain Kenneth Watt had knocked down what would have been a whopping profit for Alchemy showed up to deny making the winning bid and then departed without leaving a name. Captain Watt, with the most anticipated lot of the whole sale now in the ring, stalled for time. He had three options: resubmit the colt immediately, contact the Maktoum family underbidder to see if their final 420,000gns nod would still hold, or wait until the dust cleared and put the colt in on Thursday, the final day of the sale. If he did the first there was a severe danger of anti-climax as the auditorium emptied following that biggest lot (the Hello Gorgeous colt went to Robert Sangster for a new record 1.8 million guineas). If he tried the second, he was likely to (and did) receive a deaf ear as the Maktoums had been stung by being 'run up' in the past. If he tried the third the fever would be over and the price would slump. He could be damned three ways. He would not be the only one.

Having been rebuffed by the underbidders, resubmitting on the Thursday was the only option, and the Riverman colt duly circled the ring a second time in front of a much less interested audience. The bidding was slow. The $95,000 purchase price was duly exceeded but by nothing like as much as on Tuesday evening. The hammer fell, to another Maktoum associate, at 200,000gns. Two days can be a long time, and a deep fall in the bloodstock business. Two hundred and thirty thousand guineas is a lot of profit to watch slip through your fingers.

The sellers were sore, Henry and Tote especially, as they were angered by Tattersalls asking if they knew the fugitive bidder with the (to them) clear implication that they might have been involved in some scheme to 'run up' the price once the Maktoums showed interest. Their view was that if Tattersalls had thought there was a problem they should have put the horse straight back in the ring, not wait two days until the sale was 'dead'. They believed that when such an experienced auctioneer's hammer had fallen at 430,000gns, the horse was then the company's responsibility and the money indicated on the hammer should have been immediately due to their clients, Alchemy International. The subsequent loss due to the bidding irregularity should be met by Tattersalls, not borne by Alchemy, who had watched what appeared to be a straightforward auction in good faith.

Tattersalls denied responsibility. They said these were exceptional circumstances. That to put the horse back into the ring immediately after a sales topper was a far less desirable option than contacting Mr Omar Assi, the Maktoum associate, whose 420,000gns bid was undisputed. At the time they were also entitled to see if they could get any sense, or sight, of the apparently successful bidder – he later turned out to be an Irish chancer called Jimmy Flood, whose motives, however dubious, were never fully proven. Captain Watt testified that he had never seen anything like it in 40 years. Melvyn Waters, Alchemy's man in England, had never seen anything like it either, and this was his first time. He was new to the scene and he sensed a stitch-up. He did not just want, he needed the money to finance what, given an earlier spell in jail and gambling debts, could be described as a somewhat irregular lifestyle. He wanted to sue. He wanted to make it public all the way to the High Court. The matter would not be settled until June 1985, after Henry Cecil had won his first Derby.

But by then trainer and owner would not be on speaking terms because of something else Waters had done: he had offered Cecil's correspondence to the tabloids. The plates were shifting under the Newmarket earth.

There was always going to be trouble when a miser and all this money met. Lester Piggott had long ago become a legend for his astonishing gifts in the saddle and his almost tangible will to win. It was as if his starvation-ration self-denial found outlets in an actual, physical hunger for success. But Lester was also famous for another hunger: he loved money. And he liked to acquire it and keep it, not spend it.

He was happy for the legend to spread and would smile

enigmatically while other jockeys complained of how he had tricked them into paying for the ice creams, the taxi, even the flight over. Once, after scooping three expensive T-shirts off the Arlington Park clothing desk, he nodded at Robert Sangster and muttered, 'He's paying.' On another day, his departure from the fabled Hotel George V for the Prix de l'Arc de Triomphe was delayed while he stuffed a monogrammed towel into his case. On a third, in the paddock before a big race in Italy, he refused to mount before the owners had rustled up the extra cash he had been promised for the ride, and when it was produced he promptly pushed it down his breeches and cantered off to the start as if this was normal.

Such behaviour was now deep in his being. For two privileged if blood-out-of-a-stone years I had ghosted his newspaper column in the *Evening Standard*. Among the pleasures associated with that role was the odd lunch at Scott's in Mayfair's Mount Street next to the Charles St George flat where he used to stay in London. He would have sole on the bone and a gin and tonic, both of which he would greatly enjoy but neither of which his disciplined appetite would ever allow him to finish. When I used to offer to pay, he would immediately accept with such touching gratitude you felt pleased to have helped him through. He was Lester Piggott. He marched to a different drum.

He always had. On a racetrack he had started as a daredevil young upstart who was not going to let older, more cautious jockeys prevent him from getting his due. When he felt the Noel Murless retainer was too restrictive he opted away for Vincent O'Brien. When the Sangster syndicates began to cash those millions, he wanted his cart piled high. He never consumed much of his provisions. When he was finally dragged to court in 1987 they had discovered an extra £3 million stacked away in 17 different accounts as if he was a squirrel storing up for winter. That's what misers do.

Everyone knew that Lester would want special arrangements if he rode for a stable. That's why the racing world affected relatively little surprise when his 'extra payments' letter from Henry Cecil was finally revealed by Melvyn Waters in 1985. Indeed the Jockey Club's response was merely to fine the trainer £2,000 for not informing Weatherbys, the racing secretariat, of the correct amount for the Piggott retainer. Henry Cecil obviously did not think it that extraordinary as he circulated it to his owners and most, if not all, did not protest. Neither had Waters as acting owner for Alchemy. It is the supreme irony that the only reason he hawked the letter that sparked the investigation around Fleet Street was to pressurise not the jockey but the trainer whom he did not think was supporting him enough in the battle with Tattersalls over the Riverman colt.

The letter had detailed the extra terms as a 'share', one-fortieth in any Group One-winning colt syndicated as a stallion, an extra 7.5 per cent slice of winning prize money and 10 per cent of place as well as an extra cash retainer of £45,000 on top of the registered £10,000. To help explain things, the letter added, 'Lester has asked that for the cash element of the retainer and for the extra percentages he be given a cheque made out to cash. It looks as if there will be 130 to 140 horses in training here next season so the cost of the retainer will work out at about £392 plus VAT.'

These were days of offshore accounts being used to avoid what was generally considered penal 80 per cent rates of income tax. To have Lester Piggott riding for you was bound to be expensive and what he did with his tax arrangements was really his affair. One or two owners, like Lord Howard de Walden and Louis Freedman, would not have anything to do with the letter but most shrugged their shoulders and looked forward to a new season even if one or two did raise an eyebrow at the postcript: 'perhaps it would be better to destroy it as soon as you have read it'.

The actual typing had been done by Tote's 26-year-old sister 'Jacko' Cherry-Downes, who was then helping out in the office a few days a week, and vet's wife Susie Greenwood even translated the letter into Italian for Carlo d'Alessio. 'No, we didn't really think about it at the time,' says Jacko, now married to trainer James Fanshawe and herself a public-spirited pillar of Newmarket life. 'There was all this money around, these arrangements had been made, and anyway Henry hated having to spend time in the office. We could see he just wanted to get on with it.'

While in hindsight this action might seem to be one of simple folly, it has to be placed in the context of our world where Lester Piggott did indeed march to a different drum, and had accounting arrangements rather more elaborate than the squirrel principle. Legend has it that as the Inland Revenue net was finally closing around him, Lester had just left some social gathering at Warren Place when he returned, poked his head round the door, and uttered the words, 'Henry – don't go writing any more letters about me – all right?' Typical Piggott gallows humour, but the fact remains that, while the publication of the famous letter sparked the process that led to Norwich jail, the only reason Lester ended up inside was that he somehow could not bring himself to reveal where he had squirrelled away his hoards. As you can imagine from the climate already described, he was a long way from being the only racing figure with dubious 'arrangements'. Yet when the inspectors swooped in February 1986, the others quickly and quietly came clean and paid up.

But while this book is not going to waste time splashing around the whitewash, neither has it any desire to crow from some purported moral high ground, whose population usually includes a lot of people with precious little right to be there. That's a maxim often quoted by Sir Mark Prescott, the only Newmarket trainer to have held a licence for almost as long as Sir Henry Cecil and certainly the only one to be able to discourse learnedly about the art and literature not just of racing, but of coursing, bull-fighting and cock-fighting too.

This writer should keep Prescott's maxim in mind as he looks back at some of the excesses of this bloodstock boom. They may not always have had a lot of art and literature about them but we revelled in the golden privilege of those early mornings, the rippling strides of the Classic hopefuls, the giddy excitement of the big days at the races, the gasping thrill of those driving finishes and, yes, the heady luxury of the high rollers. We wrote about the glories and did not think it was our business to worry about the excesses. We invited the viewers to share in the drama, not get bogged down in how exactly all the money added up. In 1984 when El Gran Señor beat Chief Singer, Rainbow Quest, Lear Fan and the Cecil horse Keen in just about the best 2,000 Guineas ever run, I remember saying during the TV replay, 'Don't let's go on about how many squillions he might be worth at stud, let's just wonder at the brilliance of the athlete and think that 300 years of selective breeding might not be in vain.'

Perhaps this should not be so much an attempt at special pleading as a 'mea culpa' for at times being a ringmaster to this madness. As the chief presenter for ITV and then for Channel 4 when they took over the racing slot in March 1984, it was me who brought the owners and trainers and jockeys to the microphone and invited them to share their special world with the viewers outside. It was me who would stand out in front of the grandstand and welcome you to York, and Epsom, and Sandown, and Newmarket, and all the rest. It was me who gave breathless accounts of a day on the prowl with Sangster, and from a first trip to what was then practically bungalow-sized Dubai in February 1983 there were reports from the desert as well.

Henry and the other trainers were invited too. We all stayed at the Hilton, which back then was where the dual carriageway turned to dust road a couple of miles out of town on the way to Abu Dhabi. It was flanked by the grandly named World Trade Centre, then Dubai's tallest building, all of 30 stories high. Sheikh Mohammed was very keen to indulge his guests. One well-fuelled night Guy Harwood danced on the restaurant table, but he and we paid for it when the Sheikh dragged us off on a 10km camel ride next morning. We shook our heads at his dreams but marvels started happening in the desert. Nothing seemed impossible. One year rumour had it that he was going to build a grass golf course out in the desert sand. We all laughed. Back then nobody had heard about desalinisation, so we were all dutifully chastened when Pakistan's General Zia ul-Haq thwacked off from the first tee less than two years later. Mind you, if General Zia did actually hit the ball that we soon saw bouncing far, far away in the middle of that greenest of fairways he should have been a golf pro, not a bloodthirsty dictator.

Dubai, 1983: Sheikh Mohammed explains the finer points of camel conformation to (from left) Michael Stoute, Henry Cecil, Luca Cumani and Julie Cecil.

But the real excitement about Sheikh Mohammed was that he appeared to bring unlimited enthusiasm as well as boundless wealth to the racing game. In very separate ways he was to offer both huge opportunities and massive complications to both Henry Cecil and Lester Piggott. Henry's problems would come some years down the river, but with Lester complications usually did not wait too long – especially when it came to keeping options open in upcoming big races. The trouble in the autumn of 1983 was that the other owner he was stringing along while he tried to hold a Sheikh Mohammed horse in play was the man who had made that Pat-Eddery-is-not-man-enough-for-Buckskin outburst back in 1978 – Mr Daniel Wildenstein.

Since Buckskin and his stablemates had been moved to Henry Cecil, the dark blue Wildenstein silks had seen plenty of success. Simply Great may not have proved the Derby winner, but Queen Anne Stakes winner Belmont Bay was among many good horses, Hello Gorgeous had been a champion and in 1983 the two-year-old Vacarme was showing real ability. When Lester Piggott switched him sharply across to the far rail to power home in the Richmond Stakes at Goodwood, veteran trainer and former Derby-winning jockey Harry Wragg said he thought it was one of the finest bits of race-riding he had ever seen. The trouble was that the stewards didn't. They disqualified him for interference. Mr Wildenstein was never a man to button his lip when it came to assessing jockeys. 'Piggott has lost a race that was unloseable,' said Wildenstein. Lester might have just won his ninth Derby and be the 11-times champion jockey but for Henry's biggest owner he was on borrowed time.

There was no Cecil runner in that year's Arc but there was both a Wildenstein and a Sheikh Mohammed one and, in his inimitable way, Lester Piggott had pledged himself to both. Wildenstein was convinced he had an assurance that Lester would ride his horse, but come the day Piggott took the ride and maybe even some 'extra arrangement' from Sheikh Mohammed. All Along was an impressive winner, but Daniel Wildenstein was not inclined to be magnanimous in victory. 'Piggott never rides for me again,' he said.

Cecil Boyd-Rochfort had died on 13 March 1983, aged 95. It was the year Ronald Reagan coined the phrase 'Evil Empire' and when the first cruise missiles were flown into Greenham Common – in November, at the precise moment a chaser of the same name was approaching the water jump at Newbury racecourse less than a mile away. For Henry Cecil the outlook was a lot better than for the world or even his jockey. At the beginning of 1984 he was talking of how he felt his 140-strong, 70-staff team was in better shape than the previous year when they had been only third in the table, how the winter had been mild and how Keen was better-looking and might even be as good as his full-brothers Kris and Diesis. But there was no avoiding the caveat. 'Ideally I would like the stable jockey riding all our horses,' said Henry. 'But I can't change anything and don't propose to do any more than I already have and just propose to book whoever is available on the day.'

Despite such reservations this last season together proved anything but a lame duck year for the Cecil/Piggott combination. The 100-winner total was passed again and the pair bowed out in fitting style when the Charles St George-owned Lanfranco won the Group One William Hill Futurity at the close of the season to guarantee a fifth trainers' title. Among the other horses Lester rode for Warren Place was a big bay two-year-old colt by the 1978 Derby winner Shirley Heights who did not impress him much when he wheeled around in apparent exhaustion after finishing third first time out at Newmarket. Then there was a lengthy, slightly plain-faced half-sister to his old ally Roussalka. 'This is an absolute aeroplane,' Lester muttered to George Winsor as he was led back after the Fillies' Mile.

'You could see he was choked not to be riding her the next year,' said George. Lester was right. She was called Oh So Sharp.

She was a chestnut like Kris, her Warren Place-trained sire. She had been bought in utero, when Sheikh Mohammed had taken her pregnant dam Oh So Fair as part of his purchase of the Phillips family's Dalham Hall Stud at Newmarket. She was a quite volatile talent, like her even more feisty half-sister, who had been so brilliant at Marriott Stables. She would become the best filly Sheikh Mohammed ever owned or Henry Cecil ever trained. Yet she would not be ridden by Lester Piggott but by the young American star who within three weeks of his English arrival had denied Kris in the 2,000 Guineas of 1979. It was as if all of Steve Cauthen's life had led to this.

6

THE CAUTHEN YEARS

STEVE CAUTHEN had turned 19 just four days before that 1979 2,000 Guineas. But at that stage the blacksmith's son from Walton, Kentucky had in racing terms lived one complete life already.

For in the previous two years he had conquered heights no jockey has ever reached before or since. His first full season was 1977 when, weighing under seven stone and standing just over five feet, he had outridden all America to land 487 victories and become the first jockey to win $6 million in a calendar year. He was called 'The Kid'. The nation went wild. He was on every TV show from *Good Morning America* to Johnny Carson. He was twice on the cover of *Newsweek* and three times on the front of *Sports Illustrated*, who named him Sportsman of the Year – the only racing person ever to be so honoured. There was even a record: 'And Steve Cauthen Sings Too!' (Actually, he couldn't.)

Even over in insular England – no Sky Sports, no rolling news channels then – we registered this new comet streaking Stateside. But not one in a million could have guessed that he would be on our shores within little more than 12 months and that even greater feats were ahead. In 1978, two months past his 18th birthday, he had become the youngest and last jockey to land the American

Triple Crown in three pulsating battles with his titanic rival Alydar, culminating in the greatest 'stretch duel' in history when Affirmed finally inched ahead on the post to nail 'The Belmont' and immortality.

What Steve Cauthen had done was beyond imagining, and suddenly he was here. To be exact, on 7 April 1979 he was in a rain-soaked paddock at Salisbury with all eyes and the World of Sport (no Channel 4 Racing until 1984) cameras upon him. He was a serious, bird-beaked man-child in long waterproof breeches. He could cope with bad weather but unfortunately Salisbury could not. In a scene guaranteed to reaffirm every foreign stereotype of the bungling English, I was left to fill for long empty minutes on the microphone while we showed pictures of the Salisbury stewards' car stuck in the mud. The clerk of the course's name – no joking – was 'Washy' Hibbert.

Steve was never going to be stuck. He had come over to ride for Robert Sangster and Barry Hills, and it was for Barry that he calmly brought through a horse called Marquee Universal to make our first view of him a winning one. It was a good start, so too was the unflurried and courteous way the young tyro handled the fevered post-race press conference. But in every sense we had seen nothing yet. Exactly four weeks later, on 5 May, Steve Cauthen stepped into the British Classic arena and promptly won that 2,000 Guineas on Tap On Wood.

By any standards it was a stunning performance. The unbeaten Kris was a red-hot favourite but there was a cool authority about Cauthen's long low back in the green-and-black striped silks as he got first run and held on by half a length. We media folk were almost tongue-tied with amazement. Steve Cauthen wasn't. For two years he had been asked every question on the planet by every person bearing a microphone who could get near him. Talking to stuttering

English questioners was like having tea with your granny. He had clear blue eyes and a deep Kentucky voice. We were in love.

The relationship never died, but to his and everyone's benefit it did at least cool a little after that tumultuous start. Under the wing of Barry and Penny Hills at Lambourn, Steve was able to both learn his craft and find his real self. After that first media flurry he was left alone and remained unrecognised off the racetrack. It was heaven compared to the goldfish bowl he had come from, where those who had hailed him as the new Messiah then revelled in rubbishing him when he got mired in what became a soul-destroying 117-ride losing streak from which only the Sangster move could bring salvation. He bought smart tweeds, went on royal shooting parties, dated county girls – and grew.

By the age of 21, the tiny 16-year-old had morphed into a five foot six athlete with the big hands of his father Tex Cauthen, the racetrack farrier. The battle with weight had begun. For the first few years Steve adopted something of a 'champagne and flip' approach which made him good company but would have hostesses complaining that a thief had raided the fridge at night. Steve was using the American 'heaver' system: he would gorge himself with goodies only to 'heave' or 'flip' before it could settle on the stomach. People tut-tutted, but Steve was so charming you could not complain, and anyway he was a star on the track.

Not the complete package yet, though. For once there was something healthy about the chauvinistic English refusal to be over-impressed. Punters would remain sceptical until the results became unanswerable and professionals didn't actually expect him to crack it straight away. At the York May meeting Harry Wragg booked him for a horse normally the ride of Lester Piggott. 'Well, he's good,' said Harry in response to the maestro's disgruntlement.

'Yes,' Lester conceded, 'he's good, but not that good.'

He was later. Accustomed to uniformly flat left-handed ovals, Steve took two or three years to get the hang of our different directions, cambers and gradients. He never complained at the time and won friends inside and outside the weighing room for the way he applied himself to the task ahead. It was only when he had solved it that he would admit how difficult he had found things. 'Goodwood, Epsom, Brighton and Salls-berry,' he recalled back home in Kentucky in the autumn of 2011. 'When I first rode there I seemed to be sliding all over the place.'

He laughed at the memory, a warm deep laugh that had been a feature of those early years. He loved to play golf and tennis, to go shooting in well-cut plus fours with the highest in the land. He was quite the dandy. 'Hey,' he said one morning when we walked down from Tattersalls with the burly master of the Sangster revels that was Charles Benson, 'we've got good horses, good friends and a good suit. Life's a beach!' He was sunshine, and we liked it.

After beating Kris in the 2,000 Guineas, Steve didn't ride another Group One winner in Britain until 1983. But by then he had developed his own method, a perfect blending of American toe-in-the-iron poise with English push and control, albeit retaining an element of the acey-deucey style (left stirrup deeper down than the right) of his formative years. To balance British horses on British courses he rode more upright than he had across the water, but the clock still worked in his head and, most memorably of all, there was a sweet, unhurried haste about his elbow-lifting finishing drive, like the slow swing a great golfer has. Just one glimpse and you knew it was him.

He was champion jockey in 1984 and by mid-summer had already signed, much to Barry Hills' understandable discomfort, to ride for Henry Cecil the following season. 'I think it's bad,' grumbled Barry. 'I will never make a young jockey again if this is what happens.'

The initial frisson didn't stop Barry supporting Steve right through to taking that first jockeys' title, or remaining a friend of a lifetime.

The Cecil contract, which had been part-negotiated by Lester Piggott's great friend Charles St George, had been announced on the Tuesday of what was a typically dramatic Derby week for Lester. On the Monday he got the ride on big-race second favourite Alphabatim, on the Tuesday he lost the Warren Place job, on Wednesday Alphabatim ran poorly, yet on the Saturday the 48-year-old maestro was winning the Oaks on Circus Plume with Cauthen back in third, thus equalling the 27-Classics record of seven-stone Frank Buckle, whose first winner was in 1783 when Steve's Kentucky homeland was being ravaged by a Cherokee chief rejoicing in the name of Dragging Canoe.

The Piggott canoe was never going to float gently away down the river. Three months after the Derby he took his Classics score to 28 when he and Commanche Run held off the Cauthen-ridden Baynoun in a sustained battle up the Doncaster straight. As so often Lester's drive was not the prettiest sight, and certainly not as rhythmic as the pumping finish of his 25-years-younger rival, but there was no mistaking the tangible will to win that set him apart. Lester was tough too. At Yarmouth in early August he got dragged beneath a two-year-old called Royal Octave and was so battered that rumours abounded it was curtains time. Yet just 23 days later there he was limping across the Sandown paddock to mount Oh So Sharp, the filly who was to so impress him there, and later at Ascot. That he did not equally rate a big, bay two-year-old, on whom he finished third in a maiden race at Newmarket before it later won a moderate event at Nottingham under Paul Eddery, could not be held against him. For no one else rated it either. The best that people could say about Slip Anchor was how well he was named. He was by Shirley Heights (the lookout above Admiral Nelson's Caribbean harbour in Antigua) out of a mare called Sayonara. As Steve Cauthen took over the reins at Warren Place, Lester was saying goodbye not to one Classic horse but two.

For all Barry Hills' understandable grumbles, Cauthen's move was a logical one. 'An opportunity came which I felt it right to take,' Steve said at York in August 1984, long after the dust had settled and on the day he had just won the prestigious Benson and Hedges Gold Cup for Barry on Cormorant Wood. 'I don't think,' he added with quiet understatement, 'that I owe anyone any more.' Lambourn had been a great beginning, but Newmarket, the wellspring of horseracing, remained the grandest stage and Steve Cauthen, harnessed to the Cecil operation still climbing towards the very zenith of its fortunes, was going to be at the centre of it. 'He was the best stable jockey we ever had,' says Paddy Rudkin. 'The moment he arrived he just wanted to muck in. He wanted to know all the horses and would be the same with everyone. He had such knowledge and good sense. And we sure had some good horses that year.'

Indeed there were no fewer than 62 promising three-year-olds under the Cecil banner at the start of 1985 and Slip Anchor would not have been the first choice even of his owner Lord Howard de Walden, who had a much higher-regarded colt in Presidium, or of his lad Dave Goodwin, who had a 2,000 Guineas hopeful in Heraldiste. What's more, as a two-year-old Slip Anchor had exhibited an oxygen deficiency that made him wobble in apparent exhaustion if he was not eased down slowly after work. On his first run at Newmarket Lester pulled him up sharply and didn't like it. 'Won't ride that again,' he muttered to Willie Jardine, 'nearly fell over with me.' In 16 seasons with a training licence, Henry Cecil had not yet even had a placed runner in either of the Epsom Classics. How the stable put that doubly right in 1985 with Slip Anchor and Oh So Sharp is a perfect cameo of a unique team at the height of its powers.

'It's hard,' says Cauthen, 'to really state strongly enough how everybody in that yard had their part to play. Paddy was way, way important, so was Willie Jardine. Julie was absolutely central, as were the work riders like Frank Conlon, Frank Storey, and Paul Eddery and Willie Ryan. Henry intrigued me. His mind was so animated all of the time that it was as if he suddenly needed to shut it down, and he would walk you out to look at the roses. But everyone was playing their part. Everyone was looking to see how we could get each horse right.' Slip Anchor may not have been high on their radar but how this first Derby winner was handled showed the team at their best.

In January 1984 the pair of eyes trotting behind the then two-year-old Slip Anchor in the covered ride belonged to 33-year-old Dave Goodwin, who had handled Dunbeath in the previous two seasons. Dave was a joiner's son from Largs in Scotland whose first equestrian job had been helping with the ponies on the beach and whose first visit to the races was at Ayr with an unlikely trio that included the future Scottish football star Lou Macari. Bitten by the racing bug, he went first to Ken Oliver at Hawick and then south to scratch away as a jump jockey before moving to Newmarket in 1978 to work for Michael Stoute and then on to Warren Place, where his partner Jean helped Julie look after the Cecil children Noel and Katie.

'This colt was obviously backward,' Dave recalls, 'but there was something I liked about the way he moved. Linda, the girl riding him, said he would soon be "spare" as her other horse was coming back from a break at the place in Herringswell where we used to send horses in those days. Then Slip Anchor went there himself, but when he came back Paddy said, "That big Shirley Heights colt you liked is over in the wooden boxes, have him if you want." I went across and Slip Anchor had scraped all his bedding into the centre of the floor and was standing on top of it. That was him. Always wanted to do something. He never liked to take a backward step.'

It was a characteristic that soon threatened the prospects of Slip Anchor ever making it to the racecourse. For at the end of his gallops the colt would reel round in circles like a drunken man. 'At the time there was much talk of oxygen deficiency,' says Warren Place vet Richard Greenwood, 'and I remember running around with an oxygen cylinder for him. But it was really like some sort of teenage fainting fit and we eventually cured it by making sure whoever rode him pulled up very gradually. I don't think Lester fancied that much when he rode him at Newmarket first time.'

This natural boldness still weighed against Slip Anchor on his opening run as a three-year-old. With Steve Cauthen on a more favoured Wildenstein-owned runner, Paul Eddery was given what proved to be self-defeating orders of trying to restrain Slip Anchor behind the others. Much wasted energy saw him finish only third, and when he returned to the course a month later Cauthen had no compunction in slipping Slip Anchor's anchor. The others only saw his tail.

The same thing happened at the Lingfield Derby Trial in which Henry later admitted he ran the colt only because it looked a soft way to win a Group race. But there was nothing soft about what Slip Anchor did to his rivals at Lingfield. He routed them by ten long lengths and when he was being led back Steve leant down to Willie Jardine and said, 'This will win the Derby.' It was a bold thing to say but the conviction was so deep in Steve that he insisted on riding Slip Anchor every day in the build-up. 'Steve was so bloody confident it almost became a nightmare,' says Paddy Rudkin, remembering how little luck the stable had seen at Epsom and echoing the feelings of Dave Goodwin. 'For some reason Steve came round on the Saturday night before the Derby on the Wednesday,' Goodwin recalls. 'He was not a jockey to talk big but he said to me, "Dave, this is a ****ing certainty." I remember that clear as a bell.'

Cauthen was right. Notwithstanding that the demands of Epsom's horseshoe-shaped helter-skelter of a track had seen no horse able to win the Derby by making all the running since 1926, he jumped never-take-a-backward-step Slip Anchor off in front and a mile and a half later his opponents were strung out as if they were in a three-mile steeplechase. A record 13 lengths separated the winner and third-placed Damister, who was six lengths adrift of the O'Brien-trained Law Society, yet Steve's had been a far more sophisticated ride than those fabled Irish tactics 'jump off in front and keep improving your position'. His American 'by the clock' training meant he always knew how fast he was going, his horseman's instinct appreciated how much energy Slip Anchor was using and his winner's flair saw him lure his pursuers into a comparatively slow pace (30.85s) for the first upward quarter-mile before loosing his colt so fast (23.13s) for the next two furlongs that by the time he rocketed round Tattenham

The Epsom winner's enclosure after Slip Anchor had won the 1985 Derby by seven lengths.

Corner he resembled nothing so much as an electric hare whizzing effortlessly clear of the straining greyhounds.

It was a brilliant, brilliant day. It was a first and magnificently won Derby for owner, trainer and jockey, and the Blue Riband of the turf was back at Warren Place. Great celebrations beckoned, but for Slip Anchor it was the box journey back to Newmarket. 'Slip Anchor still had a bit of winter coat on him at Lingfield, but in the last few weeks he has really bloomed,' said Goodwin, using an appropriate analogy for his garden-loving employer. When horse and groom reached the stables Paddy came across, put his four-fingered hand into Dave's and said, 'I have waited 20 years for that.' But they both knew there had been no fluke about it and that for more Classics there would not be much of a wait. Oh So Sharp was hot favourite for the Oaks on Saturday. This time Steve Cauthen didn't need to swear to make his point.

Oh So Sharp always had something of destiny as well as a touch of the devil about her. Racing, particularly Flat racing, has an extraordinary ability to pull the strands of people and pedigree together and create something which then paints golden memories into the timeless turf. It's hard to think of anything as multi-stranded as the filly Sheikh Mohammed had called Oh So Sharp.

She was one of the very first daughters of the former Warren Place star Kris yet the 12th foal of her dam Oh So Fair. As we have seen, the Cecil team remembered Oh So Fair all too vividly as the dam of Roussalka, who was as dangerous with her teeth for her trainer's cashmere sweaters as she was with her hind legs for anyone dumb enough to get within range. Oh So Sharp was the first and best filly officially bred by Sheikh Mohammed, albeit she had been purchased when inside Oh So Fair as part of the Dalham Hall job lot from the Phillips family. She was the first and only horse to win the Fillies'

The Oaks, 1985: Sheikh Mohammed leads in Oh So Sharp and Steve Cauthen.

Triple Crown (the 1,000 Guineas, Oaks and St Leger) for her trainer and jockey. She was the best with whom either of them ever dealt. And she could be high maintenance.

She did not always get the joke. That 'limping Piggott' victory at Sandown as a two-year-old came on Variety Club Day in September 1984, complete with its usual cast of ageing thespians and busty starlets. When Henry Cecil went to saddle Oh So Sharp she reared up and cracked her head on the ceiling and then kicked out so hard that both hind shoes went missing. When George Winsor was riding her next spring, she was so startled when the trainer

A pulsating finish to the 1985 1,000 Guineas: Oh So Sharp (Steve Cauthen, star on cap) just beats Al Bahathri (Tony Murray, centre) and Bella Colora (Lester Piggott).

cantered out from behind some trees that she stood straight on her hind legs and George berated his employer as harshly as an angry boss would an underling. In another yard, the racing world might have lost her.

But they didn't. She was just the sort of lean, slightly long-nosed young lady her trainer could put the charm on. She liked to work, she liked to race, because she was good at it. She was the most obvious of gifts for Steve Cauthen. 'She had a great attitude,' he says, 'and a wonderful stride. Straight away you could feel the power underneath her. She had a lot of talent and a lot of heart. I rode some great fillies – Cormorant Wood, Triptych, Indian Skimmer and Diminuendo – but, no question, she was the best.' Yet the tributes do not need to come in words, they are etched in the memory of what she did for us that first wondrous Cecil/Cauthen season of 1985.

In those days Newmarket's Craven meeting was very much the opening gambit of our TV 'Tale of the Classics' season. Channel 4 had taken over coverage from ITV the previous spring with a mandate for a brighter, fresher approach. What we needed was a new star, best of all a female one. When Steve Cauthen coasted Oh So Sharp clear in the Nell Gwyn Stakes we knew we had got it. Especially when he dismounted. For in the six years he had been with us Steve had shown he was the absolute best when it came to post-race briefing. He was clear, open, insightful, authoritative and humorous, and an uplifting contrast to Piggott's muttered asides or Eddery's limited vocabulary. Now Cauthen was linked with the best horses too, and he and Cecil became the finest jockey/trainer double act British racing has seen. We couldn't believe our luck. Still can't.

Back then, even being allowed to conduct a TV interview in the unsaddling enclosure was considered so daringly controversial that in May 1984 only a last-minute climbdown by the chairman prevented a public slanging match at York. Henry was never entirely at ease in the media scrum but had found an engaging, well-bred, clipped-voice way of turning the questions and the compliments back on the questioner. He was taller than the gaggle of hacks surrounding him and he would look down with a nervous toss of the head and lift of the mouth that meant you were never quite sure if he was serious. He would stroke a horse like Oh So Sharp adoringly and say something like 'you are a good girl, aren't you?' but that alone would have left us short. When Steve Cauthen came on, our cup was soon overflowing.

He would pick up what happened on the replay, explain what it felt like in the saddle and pay tribute both to the horse beneath him and to the trainer and his team that had got it there. It was as if Steve was throwing open the windows and letting the light flood in. For a TV programme commissioned to do just that, he was a

'A jewel beyond price': Steve Cauthen as interviewee for (a young) Brough Scott with microphone.

jewel beyond price. At the end of that Craven meeting, my producer Andrew Franklin said with slight concern that Cauthen had been interviewed six times in three days. I remember my reply: 'As far as the programme is concerned, we should have him on before and after every race!'

But good communications are nothing unless they disseminate good content and in Oh So Sharp we had a history maker, the first horse to win the Fillies' Triple Crown since Meld in 1955. Those Oh So Sharp races live on in the memory, particularly the first of them. For with a furlong to go in that 1985 1,000 Guineas, victory for Oh So Sharp looked impossible. Up in front the Michael Stoute-trained Bella Colora (ridden by who else but Lester Piggott) was holding off the attack of Al Bahathri, owned by Sheikh Mohammed's brother Sheikh Hamdan, and the likelihood of Oh So Sharp cutting them down by the winning post seemed remote.

But we had not reckoned on quite what an engine and a desire lay within the filly's long chestnut frame, nor with the galloping crescendo Cauthen could conduct. Man and horse gathered and seemed to hurl themselves up that final hill. The three fillies flashed past the post together. The photo showed there were only inches in it. But somehow this was always going to be the right result. Jockey and trainer had won a Classic at the very first time of asking. Lester made up for things by then riding Shadeed, another Michael Stoute horse, to win the 2,000 Guineas but he could not turn back the Cauthen/Cecil tide, which swept all three remaining Classics and even made the Piggott harbour at Epsom their own.

It was a golden time, but we all know one of the brutal truths of life is that when things look almost too good to be true, they very often are. So it was that for all the gilded success that saw 1985 bring Henry Cecil and Steve Cauthen record-breaking championships, both men also endured strains enough to have one man talking of quitting and the other ending the season in hospital. Training racehorses and riding them, done well with good horses, are two of the most enjoyable and fulfilling roles on this planet. It is what goes with them that can break you.

With Cecil it was the unfinished business dating back to that dispute with Tattersalls over the sale of the Riverman colt. As earlier related, Melvyn Waters, the London representative of Alchemy International, did not think he was getting enough help from Cecil in his attempts to recover the 230,000gns difference between the 430,000gns for which the colt had been knocked down to the disappearing bidder on the Tuesday and the 200,000gns that was finally collected on the Thursday. By now Waters was getting very disillusioned with his racing dream. His gambling debts were rising and he felt the establishment and Cecil were not fully on his side. In disgruntlement he had for some months been offering Fleet Street sight of the 'destroy this when you have read it' letter about Lester Piggott's Warren Place retainer, which he had received on behalf of the Alchemy-owned Bright Crocus in 1982. In February 1985 the *Sunday People* had published and an uncomfortable time was had by all.

Eventually, of course, it was Piggott who paid the ultimate price when his compulsive non-disclosure finally slipped the big dogs of the Inland Revenue on his trail. Henry Cecil's mistake – folly would hardly be too strong a word – was of a more obvious, in fact astonishingly open kind. For the letter had been sent to such luminaries as the Jockey Club's deputy steward Louis Freedman, who as mentioned earlier immediately declared he would have nothing to do with it. The publicity and the subsequent inquiry were absolutely not what was wanted in those crucial early months of the season when Henry liked to wrap his brain and time around his horses at Warren Place. It was not until early May that he appeared before the Jockey Club to receive a fine of £2,000 for the Rules of Racing offence of not registering a correct jockey's retainer. It was £1,000 less than the maximum penalty, but any relief the trainer might have felt as he went to Ascot to watch Steve Cauthen ride a winner was tempered by the knowledge that there was plenty more rubbish in the river.

Alchemy International's case against Tattersalls finally got to the High Court before Mr Justice Hirst on, of all dates for a Classic trainer, the day before the 1985 Derby. As it happened it was on that same day that Daniel Wildenstein told the trainer he would be moving all 16 of his Warren Place horses back to France. Cecil may have been in jovial mood when he returned to court as a Derby winner to receive congratulations from the judge himself, but the whole process was an extremely unwelcome strain at what for him is always the most intense part of the year. It took 13 days for the case to be finally resolved, with something of a judgement of Solomon. Alchemy were to pay Tattersalls' £70,000-odd legal costs but the disputed 230,000gns difference between the Tuesday price and the Thursday one was adjudged to be at the door of the mercurial 'mystery bidder' Mr Jimmy Flood, and the chances of his paying Alchemy looked remote.

Despite all this Henry Cecil was still riding the crest of the wave. He had never saddled a horse that had even been placed in an Epsom Classic, yet here he was after the Oaks, back in Flat racing's most coveted winner's circle with Oh So Sharp only days after taking the Derby honours with Slip Anchor. As he shook that then Beatle-like mop of hair, he said, 'After all that has been happening, if these two had not collected I would have given up and gone into landscape gardening.' Most people thought it just another piece of self-deprecating Cecil whimsy. As so often down the years, you could not quite be sure.

The 'day job' was certainly flying. Oh So Sharp's Oaks was Henry's 49th and Steve's 61st win of the season. Typically the potential doubts for a filly by the miler Kris to last the mile and a half were dismissed by a trainer's confidence and carried through by his jockey, who put Oh So Sharp in charge a full quarter-mile from home and left her field toiling six lengths in her wake. It was the performance of her life and one of the greatest days of both her trainer's and her jockey's careers. Yet, as so often in this strangely addictive world of racing, the very height of this success meant some downhill slopes were likely. Not for the season perhaps but certainly for the Classic winners. For Slip Anchor was never to win again and Oh So Sharp would lose her unbeaten record.

Even regular horsemen often think top Flat racing trainers are being precious when they talk of Classic horses 'just coming right on the day' and of how difficult it is to get everything right in the heat of Group One competition. Such 'rough neck' scepticism is especially easy with Henry Cecil, who is apt to cloak his thoughts with phrases of almost flower-sniffing silliness. But never doubt that Cecil is very aware of what he is putting his young athletes through and of the difficulty of bringing them to mental as well as physical concert pitch. Dave Goodwin doesn't. The man from Largs has always been more a champion cyclist than a blossom plucker. On the Sunday after the Derby he was pedalling away in the East Anglia divisional road race championship and remembers the effort Slip Anchor always put in.

'It was that "never take a backward step" thing,' he says. 'Slip Anchor would never take things easy and when he jarred himself at exercise after the Derby it was hard to get him back quietly. He didn't run bad when he was beaten on his return in September at Kempton or when second in the Champion Stakes afterwards but he was never the same as at Epsom. As I said at the time, the rose had really bloomed that day.'

Oh So Sharp had her setbacks, albeit honourable ones. At Ascot in the King George VI and Queen Elizabeth Stakes she got beaten a neck by Petoski, who finished fast and wide after the filly had been in front too long. At York a demonically Piggott-driven Commanche Run got first run in soft going and Oh So Sharp could not peg him back. 'In a fair world she would never have been beaten,' says Steve Cauthen. 'She had such terrific length and power when she was galloping. All her Classics were great, but it was special to win that Triple Crown.'

The St Leger success was Steve's 160th of what was to be a 195-winner season. Lanfranco and Lester Piggott cut for home early in the long Doncaster straight and, as always with Oh So Sharp and so often with Cauthen, there were no last-minute fancy tricks. Oh So Sharp's long, lifting stride was something that took time and compulsion to reach out to its optimum. Fully two furlongs out the Cauthen elbows pumped her into overdrive and she took this Classic by the throat. In the final furlong there was a moment of alarm when her head came up at the sight of the big, new, white marquees beside the winning post. 'She was dossing then,' said her rider, 'but she always had it under control. She was fantastic.'

The memory has a glow about it, and not only for the rider. Oh So Sharp's victory was not just the first Fillies' Triple Crown since Meld had done it for Henry's stepfather exactly 30 years earlier, a win that helped Cecil Boyd-Rochfort pass the million-pound mark for his career; her exploits were part of Henry Cecil's 132-winner score, which saw Warren Place pass the million-pound mark for a single season. Cecil and Cauthen seemed a partnership made in heaven.

But for the jockey, racing was playing its twisted games and taking him close to hell. To ride Oh So Sharp at Ascot he had boiled down to 8st 5lb. Now he was struggling to do a whole half-stone heavier. The champagne that provided temporary relief had become the prop that betrays. His father Tex had kicked the booze some years back. At the end of 1985 it was time for his son to do the same. At the close of this wonder year, the Christ Hospital in Cincinnati was the reality check.

In the English language 'sympathy' is too often used as a soppy, almost mournful word. The French *'sympathie'* has a more open, affectionate feel. It is one of the nicest parts of Henry Cecil.

It means he is both sensitive and supportive of human failings. His own mother and twin brother had long been entrapped by the demon drink and he himself had succumbed at times. Steve Cauthen's struggle was of a wider, more whole-appetite kind, but he was clear that Henry was all about praise not censure. 'He had this great ability to make you feel good,' says Steve. 'Of course there was all that outside clownish thing of the jokes and the funny clothes, but when we were on our own he could be right on the button. He would ask about horses, tell me what he thought, and as for tactics he would say, "You are the best in the world, do what you want." He could make you feel ten foot tall.'

This *sympathie* went deeper than the mere professional pragmatism of making the staff feel better. It had its roots in the vulnerability of a non-achieving childhood. It had showed itself in a distaste for the trappings of prefect-hood at Canford, as testified by a now South Africa-based fellow pupil still grateful for being spared the demeaning tasks normally associated with a prefect's 'fag'. It had an element of inverted snobbery: this most aristocratic and at times quite aloof-looking figure could often be at his happiest when joshing along with stable staff. Any morning at Warren Place is likely to include an apparently stray member of the public whom Henry has befriended on the Heath and brought back for no greater reason than to make them feel better for it.

As we've already seen, there can be a downside to such openness, an almost wilful naivety that could bring trouble in its wake. Julie Cecil's wistful 'I begged him not to have anything to do with Melvyn Waters' echoes back through the years. But it remains a remarkable characteristic and is central to how he wins the confidence not just of the humans but of the horses he works with. 'One evening stables,' says Willie Jarvis, recalling his days as a young assistant, 'I was very upset with the news that my mother had got cancer. Henry sensed it, stopped what he was doing, took me into the kitchen, sat me down and talked me through it and calmed me down. But he could do it with horses too. Another evening a filly got loose in the paddock and tore round and round bucking and kicking so hard she looked sure to injure herself. Henry walked out into the middle, called quietly to her, and she stopped and trotted over to him. You could not explain it.'

Trust was the key, and it was mutual. 'There were three or four of us who always used to put the horses through the stalls,' says Steven Kingstree, who had looked after Gunner B and Ardross and in 1986 had a promising three-year-old of Sheikh Mohammed's called Bonhomie, winner of the previous year's Royal Lodge Stakes at Ascot. 'He never used to come and watch. It was not that he didn't bother. It was because he trusted us.' Steve had joined Henry in 1970 at Marriott Stables after a stint with the contrasting but equally idiosyncratic training legend Arthur Stephenson. 'You got used to what he wanted,' adds Steve. 'Henry would say, "I've got a race for this horse in three months' time," and you would gradually build towards it. He wouldn't explain but he didn't need to. We were on the same wavelength and we trusted him.'

At times it could be a slightly confusing experience. As the late Louis Freedman and his son Philip followed Henry into the teeming paddock at Deauville in August 1986, the trainer turned to them and said, 'I think I will run that big Mill Reef colt of yours next week at Sandown.' At one level it might have seemed a rather casual way to talk of what, right from a foal, had been their Cliveden Stud's pride and joy and was to become the Derby winner Reference Point. On another, it meant that action was on the agenda, and with Henry in the 1980s success was likely to follow. The Freedmans had already learned better than to waste time trying to plumb the unfathomable.

'You felt it was all done on instinct and that he could not explain it,' says Philip Freedman. 'He had trained Reference Point's dam Home On The Range, who showed nothing as a two-year-old and when we were all disappointed after she had been unplaced in an ordinary maiden race in August Henry gaily said, "I'm going to put her away now because she will be a decent horse next year." She was. She was placed in three Group races and won the Sun Chariot. We just had to trust him completely.'

Not that all Henry Cecil's Reference Point judgements were infallible, however successful his system, or however well he might remember a horse's relatives. Back at the tall-tree delights of the former Astor stud at Cliveden, the groom Derek Powney insisted his hero had been a star from the very beginning. 'Of course you have plenty that don't work out,' said Derek, his long, flat Northumbrian vowels little shortened by years away from where he started down the Bardon Mill pit as a 14-year-old, 'but Reference Point was majestic from the start and if he and the other colts galloped round the paddock he would utterly humiliate them. He was big and strong. We called him Rambo. You had to believe he was special.'

There is no record of Henry Cecil having any mystical premonition as he had with the dam, Home On The Range – rather the reverse. One morning later in the summer of 1986 Frank Storey was assigned the now accepted luckless task of trying to stir Reference Point out of his apparent mediocrity. 'I was at the back of a big bunch of two-year-olds with Julie leading us on the Limekilns,' remembers Frank, who had long been a legend as a work rider and who had one or two discreet punters who backed his judgement. 'Once we had jumped off, Reference Point was struggling as usual, and at halfway I got really fed up and threw the lot at him. Suddenly he absolutely took off and finished right on top of the others. When we came back I told the guvnor, "This could be a proper horse." He just shrugged and said, "No, it's useless."'

Whatever Cecil's first reaction, the news of Reference Point's conversion from sluggard to potential superstar was soon off around the Newmarket grapevine and by the time he arrived at Sandown the week after the Freedmans' Deauville briefing the drums had been beaten enough to see him start odds-on favourite. Trouble was they were not beating very loud in dozy Rambo's head: he almost fell out of the stalls and could finish only third. When he returned to Sandown, Steve Cauthen decided to hire his own wake-up call. He paid one of the stall handlers to whack Reference Point on the bottom as the gates opened. Extreme measure maybe, but Reference Point rocketed off with the leaders and wasn't beaten until after the next year's Derby.

Mind you, it says much for the strength in depth of the Cecil string that another of their horses, Suhailie, was the preferred choice of both the punters and of Cauthen when Reference Point had his final two-year-old race in the William Hill Futurity at Doncaster and hung his rivals out to dry. 'They said he might not like the soft ground,' said Reference Point's jockey Pat Eddery, not a bad substitute considering he had logged over 200 winners Europe-wide that season and was three weeks on from riding the greatest waiting race in history with Dancing Brave in the Arc de Triomphe, 'but he has a great stride on him and just keeps going.'

Dancing Brave's trainer Guy Harwood and Derby winner Shahrastani's handler Michael Stoute might have taken some of the limelight away from Henry Cecil in 1986, but as 1987 developed they and the rest of us could do little more than shake our heads in wonder at what was happening at Warren Place. That was even when one of their best horses was in trouble and Cecil had to get in the habit of issuing veterinary bulletins on an almost media-friendly Harwood scale. In early March Reference Point, now long-time Derby favourite, had a hole drilled in his nose and for two weeks a tube was inserted to flush out the pus caused by a sinus infection. Any remaining chances, always against his trainer's thinking, of Louis Freedman's colt delivering his owner's dream of the Triple Crown were shelved as the stable raced against time to get Reference Point ready for the Dante Stakes three weeks before the Derby itself in early June.

'It was difficult,' muses the vet Richard Greenwood on one of his greatest tests in 25 years of tending Warren Place, 'but by draining the sinus every day we never had to stop his exercise completely. Up until about three weeks before the Dante I wasn't sure whether we would get there, and even afterwards there was a small cyst left where all the mucus had come down his nose. We had to treat that up until five days before the Derby. Henry would get pretty wound up before a race, he and Tote Cherry-Downes chain-smoking and pacing up and down, but he was very good with me. He would want to know what was happening and then say, "I leave it in your hands. You have never been wrong." That wasn't actually true but it made me feel good.'

When we look back at the mighty performances put up by Reference Point at Epsom and subsequently at Ascot and Doncaster it's important to realise that beforehand the doubts extended beyond any sinus syringing. Some judges even considered the Cecil stable's Lingfield Derby Trial winner Legal Bid a more likely Epsom candidate, and certainly the climbs and descents and cambers of the Classic course were going to set the big, rolling stride of Reference Point very much his biggest test. How he passed it said much for his own power and determination, but even more clearly stated what a transatlantic maestro British racing had in Steve Cauthen.

Remember nothing else of the Cecil/Cauthen years but recall that Derby week of 1987. Treasure no other ride of Steve Cauthen's English conquest but take what he did when the gates whacked open that Wednesday. For a start he had to confront the real worries for Reference Point. We had all banged on so much about his sinus problems that it was a bit of a disappointment not to see him with 17 tubes up his nose. We all knew that such a big, heavy colt would have a job handling Epsom's famous helter-skelter of a track. But what we hadn't truly faced was that the most likely place for Reference Point to lose that Derby was in the very first furlong.

The jockeys knew all right. That's why this was the fastest recorded opening burst in Derby history. The other riders had heard that Reference Point could lose interest if he got behind other horses. In boxing terms, his opponents had to go for an early knockout. Cauthen was drawn 10, in the middle of the 19 runners, and was classically vulnerable to being 'swallowed up' if he started slowly. Even for the young champion who won the Kentucky Derby as an 18-year-old there must have been pressure in those stalls. And when they sprang open the big horse missed his kick. Not by much, a length perhaps, but the next eight strides were absolutely vital.

Cauthen punched Reference Point forward. After 50 yards he was in front, yet there were horses motoring all around him. Something called Water Boatman was driven up the inside to challenge and lead. Steve kept the button pressed, and as they completed that steepest quarter-mile he was back ahead, in command of his field.

Let no one ever say Reference Point lacked pace, for from a standing start he covered those first two uphill furlongs in 24.60 seconds compared with 29.16s by the winner of the 1986 Derby and 30.8s in Slip Anchor's year. In that race Cauthen then spun through the next quarter-mile in 23.13s compared to Reference Point's 28.00s to show both the contrast in style between the free-running Slip Anchor and the idling Reference Point, and the precision of the clock that ticked away in Cauthen's American-trained head.

Indeed it is possible to look on the 1987 ride as the fulfilment of the brilliant but still hazardous journey he had embarked upon since his first winner at unsung River Downs, Ohio, 11 years earlier. That opening Kentucky chapter had given him a judgement of pace essential for anyone trying to set an all-the-way gallop in the Derby. But it was in the second vital phase of the race that we saw just how much Steve had learned from his eight full seasons among us.

For Reference Point was a big horse that needed balancing as he continually 'changed his legs' (switched his leading leg at the gallop). For him Epsom's gradients and sharply cambered straight were uniquely unsuitable; eight years earlier Cauthen, accustomed only to flat American tracks, would not have had a prayer. Now, as he stoked the colt up to maximum effort, we could see a perfect blending of balance and drive. The whip first came out fully a quarter of a mile from home. The first crack came at the two-furlong pole. Three times Steve had to put both hands back down on the reins to re-gather his partner before continuing the drive. Two hundred metres out Reference Point changed legs for the final time and Cauthen rolled him on with a rhythm and a stride that brooked no answer.

Yes, it was a masterpiece right enough, but there was also something in that week which had a hint of sadness about it. For even then we knew that, with stallion shed beckoning, Reference Point would have only one season, if that, back with us in the arena. We had noticed too that on Derby eve Steve had been unable to ride at under 8st 10lb, and the fear was growing that his constant battle with the scales was more and more likely to be a losing one. Then, that Saturday, the Cecil stable faced racing's swiftest sadness. One moment their Oaks candidate Scimitarra was in front and in sight of another Epsom double to rival that of Slip Anchor and Oh So Sharp in 1985, the next she was a hobbling wreck with fears that the friendly bullet might be the kindest answer. These are horrible images if you are a broadcaster trying to steer your way between foolish optimism and darkest fate. It helps hugely if a large, calming, charismatic presence appears at the horse's head. In what seemed a few seconds Henry was beside Scimitarra and the position felt more secure. Swathes of bandages were applied, the filly finally made it into the horse ambulance, and she was off to Newmarket and recovery for motherhood at stud.

It was a dark shadow across a summer which was mostly record sunshine. Warren Place sent out 35 winners in the four weeks through Epsom alone. A week after the Oaks, Cauthen won the Prix de Diane, the French equivalent, on Indian Skimmer for Sheikh Mohammed. During the four days of Royal Ascot the stable logged seven winners including the Gold Cup with Paean for Lord Howard de Walden, the

Ribblesdale Stakes with Queen Midas for the Freedmans and the Jersey Stakes with Midyan and the Hardwicke with Orban, both for Prince Faisal of Saudi Arabia. At the Ascot Heath meeting on the Saturday there were three more winners but also a reminder of how hard as well as historic a hoofbeat can be. As stable girl Diane Wilder went to loose Steve Cauthen and the two-year-old Sanquirrco to canter down the straight, the colt swivelled nervously away from her and lashed out flush into her chest. As Steve coasted home on what was to be the start of Sanquirico's top-class juvenile career, Diane lay groaning in the ambulance with the limited compensation that she had not been kicked somewhere even worse.

Reference Point got outsprinted by Mtoto when dropped back to a mile and a quarter for the Eclipse but was marvellous in his all-the-way dominance when he returned to Ascot for the King George VI and Queen Elizabeth Stakes on a rain-soaked day that started with Princess Anne winning on a 9-1 shot called Ten No Trumps. This greatest of all years was to close with the stable taking more than £2 million in prize money, 27 Group successes and a new record 180 winners for a strike-rate of an astonishing 40 per cent, but nothing summed it up better than when Reference Point ground down his St Leger rivals at Doncaster to take his second Classic.

It was Henry's 147th winner of the campaign, a figure that took him past the previous record set by the crooked, secretive John Day, who trained at Danebury in Hampshire, way back in 1867. Three weeks after the St Leger Reference Point was to end his career with a weary and foot-abscess-troubled defeat in the Prix de l'Arc de Triomphe. Almost a month later a tired but triumphant Cauthen would be back at Doncaster to best an exhausted Eddery 197-196 for the jockeys' crown. But it was on St Leger day that we most had to reflect on the genius of the flop-haired 44-year-old trainer who that afternoon was away at the yearling sales in America.

Paddy Rudkin's tribute was both direct and insightful. 'He always decides who rides what in the mornings,' he said of Henry. 'He doesn't clutter his brain up with other responsibilities, but all the decisions on how much work a horse should do and who should ride what, he takes. He's gifted.' Paddy has never felt the need for gushing overstatement and he was blunt in assessing what gave him and his employer the edge. 'He gets ahead because he is a greedy, ambitious man. We always get our horses very fit, they canter faster, work faster than others at Newmarket. We always think we are going to win.'

The sun was as high as it could ever be in the Warren Place sky, but we already knew that for them and for racing the thunder clouds were rolling in. In February 1986 customs officers had swooped on Warren Place, on Lester Piggott's stables and on several other leading figures in the Newmarket area. As previously related, everyone else with any irregularities came clean and paid up. Tragically, both then and in another lengthy interview in April that year, Lester Piggott did not. On Friday, 24 October 1987, two full weeks before the Flat racing season was over, Mr Justice Hirst passed sentence at Ipswich Crown Court. Henry Cecil and Charles St George had each originally put up £250,000 worth of bail. Now it would not be needed as the cell door slammed shut. For all the directness of the case, the overwhelming feeling was one of sadness.

The sentence was no doubt correct because we live in a tamed, interdependent world where non-acceptance of laws can lead to anarchy. Lester Piggott's fault as well as his great lasting attraction was that, at heart, he was a wild animal, answerable to no one. Now we had locked him up. It was sad because while it was proven how much he took, no one could ever assess how much he gave.

For all of us, not least for the man whose stable had played so central a part in both Lester's fortune and misfortune, a question hung in the air. Was this soap opera or morality tale?

7

A DOWNWARD SLOPE

SOMETIMES THE worst thing for people with inexplicable gifts to do is to try to explain them. In his direct Glasgow way, soccer legend Kenny Dalglish once said about his goal-scoring talent, 'If I have to talk about it, I might not be able to do it any more.' Henry Cecil has not always been much more expansive, but studying two wonderful interviews he gave during this absolute peak of his career give important clues both to his success and indeed to his later demise.

Both interviews, one TV and one newspaper, were conducted in something very different to that grudging Dalglish spirit. In his own way Henry was on a bit of a mission to open and cast light on racing's dowdier and more secretive corners. He may have stopped sporting spotted trousers at the races so outrageous that on seeing one pair George Winsor said, 'Guvnor, if you wear them again, I will have to disown you.' But he was ready to say things to cameras and microphones alike that other trainers would find odd or even embarrassing. He was champion trainer, he was breaking records, he revelled in his good fortune. Why shouldn't he say what he wanted, even if he had to overcome that innate, slightly self-mocking shyness which he also used as a cloak to avoid more difficult situations?

For those of us in the media Henry's attitude was an opportunity as well as a relief. In 1987 I was involved in a project about Sheikh Mohammed and the horses in his heritage. Henry, happy to humour his numerically biggest owner, was also keen to talk about how he played the racing game. So late in the summer he and Julie sat side by side in the Warren Place garden and hit away at some fairly innocuous serves from across the net. Paxmanesque the questioning was not, but he, and indeed Julie, have never been as revealing.

Take Henry's handling of Classic success. 'The first thing after a big race,' he said, 'is to see the horse and have a chat with the horse and say well done. The owner and the press can come later. I am sure horses know when they have won. It's in their breeding. They are competitive animals who are bred to race. A lot of horses also know when they have lost and they can sulk when they have lost. Yes, really, literally sulk. I remember Oh So Sharp was really down after she got beaten at Ascot. And when they have won, they can be as pleased as punch, all cocky and up with themselves.'

Just how much Julie's sharply added 'like some people' owed to archness or to mere affectionate humour is hard to tell. But inevitably there is poignancy in seeing them together less than two years before their union would be so irrevocably split asunder. On the screen they appear as a slightly awkward-looking couple in their mid-forties wearing a pair of contrastingly coloured sweaters, Henry's white, Julie's blue, with oddly matching jockey logos on the front. They both speak with elaborate, well-bred, rather nervous politeness and look tired, as people are at the end of a long morning that begins before dawn. Henry is long-haired and slightly puffy-faced; Julie, dieting for race-riding, almost shockingly thin. But she is full enough when it comes to the skills of training.

'To train a horse,' Henry begins, 'you have got to programme it rather like a human. I believe they only come to their peak once or twice in a year and I think you will find an athlete is the same if you talk to someone like Sebastian Coe.' To this articulation of the very nub of Classic race training Julie adds, 'Herb Elliott [the great Australian miler] said the same. He told my father [Noel Murless] that he would reach his maximum peak just once in two years. My father said he would have a horse at its absolute maximum peak only once in its career, and of course for a Classic horse a career is two years. The rest of the horse's form may be very good, but it won't be the peak. The challenge for us is to get it right on the given day.'

We are looking up slopes few can tackle but at which Henry can glance with the confidence of a conqueror. 'You can absolutely tell when a horse is right,' he continues, 'but it's the getting there.' Quite how the process of gradually increasing exercise gets the equine athlete to mental and physical optimum at a required date is left to drift in the metaphorical mountain air. But as the interview moves off into pretty pictures and rose-growing discussion – 'we don't actually dig the beds and do all the pruning but like to plan it all' – another and closer metaphor emerges. Henry is keen to divert into tales of his vegetable garden prowess and the oft-told story of the Boyd-Rochfort relative who was in on Lord Carnarvon's famous Tutankhamun discovery and plucked some pea pods from the mummy's tomb which now flourish at Warren Place, the fruit of pharaonic times, triple the size of a modern-day pea. Yet a shaft of intuition still shines through.

Asked about parallels between gardening and training, Cecil allows we visitors in. 'What I am doing is not like buying a plant in a hothouse,' he explains. 'But it is about having a picture of what you want and of trying to let it develop and grow to perfection at a time you want.' As so often there is a sense of the collective about what he says which takes in more than Julie beside him, and the one theme he likes to return to is the determination that is needed to drive ever onwards.

'When you have won a Derby, it is a marvellous feeling. I always said it wasn't my ambition as I never seemed to have any luck in it. But once you have won it, then you have got to win it again otherwise there is no point in going on. My stepfather and Julie's father were two great trainers, they had won the championship 12 times between them, but they were also great rivals. You have got to be competitive. Unless you are competitive you will never reach the top.

'Training is a bit like a game of bagatelle. I was born in the days of no television and in the evening we would play bagatelle, which was a wooden board with a spring that would hit out these silver balls and they would all roll up and back into little holes with numbers on. Then you added up your score before pressing the button and the balls would go back to the beginning again. Our season is the same as bagatelle. You can be champion trainer and break every record, but at the end of the season you go back to the beginning. We all return to square one, zero. It's just a question of how much stamina I have got, or' – he adds this with a slightly nervous little laugh and a sideways look at Julie – 'that we have got.'

He was speaking before urging Steve Cauthen on to that title-winning 197-winner score. ('I really admire the way he took the bull by the horns and pulled himself together,' he said of his jockey. 'It was really very important to us that he should win the championship.') He was also talking before the exhausting drive to his own seventh title and record winners total. But once again, after he and Julie had taken an Antigua holiday in the then accustomed company of Paul Cole and his wife Vanessa, Henry was back at the bagatelle board. With the spring at the ready.

'Look,' he told the *Sporting Life*'s Sue Montgomery a week before the opening of the Flat racing season in March 1988, 'I'm not champion trainer any more. I was last year, yes, but that's gone. I'm at the bottom now and I've got to start again with everyone else.

But I like to beat people. I like to be champion trainer. I liked going for the record last year and this year we'll try for something else to keep us amused. I've got to think like that to have some motivation, otherwise I would get bored. I've got to be able to say "I've never won the Arc, so this year I will do that". If you just sit there and relax, and say you have done enough, there's nothing to look forward to, is there? It's very important to me that I am ambitious.'

Whatever happened to that useless youth who sipped coffee at the Mad Hatter and whose only ambition at Cirencester was which secretarial college girl to chat up?

A roving eye could still change Henry's life for ever, but as he spoke to Sue Montgomery that March he expounded better than before or since on the one relationship to have truly fulfilled him. It is central to a life where he does not so much live for his work, he is only now alive because of it. At the core is an uninhibited, to an outsider almost naive, affection for the thoroughbred. 'It's lovely to have a good horse,' he said, 'but I don't treat them like machines. I go out and chat to them in the evenings.'

Most racing people, maybe even most horse people, will instinctively scoff a little at what they see as Henry's anthropomorphic whimsy. But the hard taskmaster on whose behalf Paddy Rudkin had proclaimed 'we always get our horses very fit, they canter faster, work faster than others at Newmarket' continued almost provocatively in his insistence on the priority of the relationship with his horses. 'Basically, they are my friends, and they help me. I think it's terribly important that you have a feeling towards them. There must be a rapport, an empathy between man and beast. If you are dealing with something then you must understand it. A lot of people actually don't understand. There's nothing between them and the horse, and if they do terribly well, then there's a lot of luck involved.

'I think it's the horse's nobility I like. There is no doubt they are far more noble than the average human. There's no jealousy or greed. They may have determination and they may be competitive, and if they lose and they're intelligent then they sulk. Oh So Sharp was miserable that day at Ascot [when she was beaten by Petoski in the King George VI and Queen Elizabeth Stakes]. But they are not going to take it out on anyone. There are some very nice humans, don't get me wrong, but there are an awful lot of people I resent, the way they behave, their attitude towards things. Whereas if a horse gets pleased with himself, then he gets pleased in a nice, happy way. He doesn't go around like a lot of people, thinking he is better than everyone else, saying "I did this, I did that".

'If a horse does something and proves he's good, he doesn't get snobby with other horses. He's happy and has a squeal and a buck, but it doesn't mean he's showing off to all the other animals in the string who aren't as good. They still talk to them. Diminuendo loves to chat away to all the crocks at the back of the string, but if she were human she wouldn't be seen with them.'

These words may be from March 1988 but they echo Henry's attitude down the years, bringing to the fore as they do the best and perhaps the slightly odder side of Henry's character. For all that flirtatious charm he can be difficult and indeed petulant with people. At times it is as if he resents those years of dismissal in early life and even now bridles at people who talk down to him on subjects of which he knows nothing (of which there are plenty). With horses he can be as simple and as silly as he likes. And since his approach has proved unbelievably successful it is worth trying to suspend normal scepticism when so great a trainer tells of the way he sees it.

At this stage I have to submit a personal confession. Coming from the school of professional jockeys I have always been rather distrustful of all this 'best friend' business. 'No they are not my friends,' the great jockey John Francome once said in his dry and teasing way. 'Can't afford to have them as friends, just business partners.' By and large professional jockeys tend to believe that trainers like Henry Cecil, who have never performed at any level, can't understand a horse the way a rider does. Trying to support the conceit inherent in this concept was hard enough for me during those fortnightly trips to see the master and his wonder horse Frankel in 2011, but then I got a message from beyond the grave.

It was from my grandfather General Jack Seely, who left us in 1947 at the age of 79 but who has made something of a comeback through the interest created by the Steven Spielberg film *War Horse* in Grandpa's own astonishing thoroughbred charger Warrior. This four-legged paragon survived every horror of 1914–18, came back to win the local point-to-point and was still trotting along in 1938 when their combined ages (man 70, horse 30) reached a century. In anticipation of this interest Jack Seely's own Alfred Munnings-illustrated memoir about Warrior was republished and sold over 40,000 copies in hardback. Re-reading the book in 2011 I came across a paragraph that almost exactly chimed with Henry Cecil, even down to the exclamation marks. At the end you can almost see Henry tossing his head and asking, 'What do you think?' Here is my grandfather writing about the arrival of a young ADC rejoicing in the name of Prince Antoine d'Orleans Braganza:

If you happen to be a General, you will note with what immense interest your horse will eye the newcomer. He knows very well that much of his comfort and well-being depends on this mysterious man who always goes with his master and seems able to order people who are much older than himself! Horses are even quicker than dogs at noticing these things although, unlike dogs, they are not snobs. The unattached dog will always attach himself to the senior man of any party. I have seen a dog join up with a private soldier, then in a day or two transfer his attentions to the sergeant. Within a week he is walking along with the company commander with a proud air of proprietorship and only an occasional look for the private and the sergeant. Horses, on the other hand, are no respecters of persons, or at least of rank. Warrior was just as fond of my servant, Smith, as he was of me, and so I think he is still.

That last line speaks of the sort of warm, unapologetic noblesse oblige that is part of Henry Cecil, who in March 1988 was back from the luxuries of his Antigua holiday to greet the dawn alongside stable lads who could never dream of such trappings. He and his 200-horse army were going into battle for winners, not the future of the world, but to be successful he was adamant the horse should come first. 'There has been a lot of trial and error over the years,' he explained about his methods, 'and you go on learning things. There's a lot I still don't know about, but on the whole now I think we don't over-face things. We feel our way with the horses. You like to think you know your horses, but if you start organising them, telling them to be ready for this race or that race, then it can go wrong. What you say to them is, "It would be lovely if you could go for the Guineas – and I'll go with you if you do." You go with them rather than make them come with you. They tell you when they are ready.'

At that stage he had three colts and two fillies under requests for their respective Guineas and, as proof of racing's enduring insistence that failure always heavily outnumbers success, only Diminuendo's third in the 1,000 came up with anything like a positive answer. Time was when this might have made a younger Cecil doubt himself, but this was a seven-times champion trainer set to take an eighth title by the season's close. 'I am more relaxed than I used to be,' he explained.

'But I do get uptight about things. When everything is going well it is easy. Winning everything is easy. But when things are going badly in the yard, if the horses are not running as they should, or there's something wrong with the hay or oats, I hate it.

'But that's the time I'm probably at my best,' he added revealingly. 'Because I have got to sit down and work it out and get things back up again. That's the time when the challenge really comes.'

The challenge was answered soon enough that summer. Little Diminuendo won impressively when moved up to a mile and a quarter for the Musidora Stakes at York. She destroyed the Oaks field before an almost serene Henry Cecil – 'I was very calm because I was very sure. I knew she was well, and I knew she would stay.' She only dead-heated in the Irish Oaks but could be excused as she was, to use that strangely euphemistic term for the equine breeding heat, 'in season'. But it was what Diminuendo did in the Yorkshire Oaks that was truly unforgettable.

Yorkshire Oaks, 1988: Diminuendo (Steve Cauthen) out on her own.

You have to remember that she was tiny. At barely 15 hands she was, quite literally, pony-sized, and there is always something stirring about the pocket warrior doing battle. York racecourse was at its most glorious and sun-spangled, mixing as only it can a smiling dash of Yorkshire earthiness with three long centuries of high-soaring thoroughbred tradition. Steve Cauthen's long legs and wide lifting elbows wrapped themselves into centaur mode as they urged the little filly into giant strides beneath him. As the pair winged past the post we hardly needed the clock to tell us something record-breaking had happened.

Two hundred years earlier they used to hang people before racing on the Knavesmire. After watching this you felt they should bring back the gallows for anyone present who did not rejoice to be alive. Henry Cecil did. He was able to use the York trip to stay to drink in the moorland delights of the Cliff Stud at Helmsley. All seemed good in his world. Many more winners were surely in the stream.

Indian Skimmer (Michael Roberts) wins the Champion Stakes at Newmarket, 1988.

A week later, High Estate, the best two-year-old ever to honour the black silks and scarlet cap of the now nonagenarian Jim Joel, continued what was already a Royal Ascot winning run by taking the Solario Stakes under Steve Cauthen. But for the jockey the river would become a waterfall and survival would be suddenly much more important than success. A filly called Preziosa came down with him in a minor race at Goodwood and after she and the following horse had rolled over him, he was unconscious in Chichester Hospital with a broken neck. As he battled for recovery back home in Kentucky the stable bandwagon rolled on. If Steve had been of a less God-fearing mode he might have worried over one of racing's gloomiest couplets:

The water closes over your head.
It always does. It's like being dead.

Some time later that same jingle would come to haunt Henry at Newmarket, but as he moved into the last year of the 1980s he had every reason to be proud of delivering one of racing's most magnificent decades. High Estate swept on to win the Royal Lodge at Ascot in a newly instituted Festival of British Racing where Tessla's victory in the Fillies' Mile meant the stable went into 1989 with the favourites for both the Derby and the Oaks. Another trainers' championship was long assured and when Indian Skimmer powered home across a rain-sodden Newmarket turf in the Champion Stakes we had to believe we were seeing yet another new high in the Cecil saga.

For not only had he been typically hands-on before that race, when Indian Skimmer contrarily planted all four legs in protest at the top of the track, it was the tall figure of the trainer who walked out to put those big lumberjack hands soothingly on her neck and cooed the silly captivating words that have cleared the knots out

At the Breeders' Cup at Churchill Downs, Kentucky, in 1988.

of so many fillies' brains. Afterwards he stood in the unsaddling enclosure stroking the grey lady's face and delivered the ultimate in tributes: 'When she is right in herself, and when she has the ground conditions like this, she is the best filly I have ever trained.'

So what if a trip to a dark-skied Churchill Downs for the Breeders' Cup Turf proved a failure? The American press were overcome with both delight and bafflement as they tried to work out this strange, exotically clad Brit who kept answering their questions with such awfully polite ones of his own. We could have told them they should not bother trying. What none of us knew was that he was little more than six months short of crisis time.

Who would have thought it? Who would have guessed there could be anything but temporary clouds on the Warren Place horizon as Henry gave his usual 'I have got some nice horses but we won't be rushing them' interviews at the start of 1989? When he closed out that season with another five Classics, 25 Group races and an overall tally of 124 winners, his 20-year career seemed to be going better than ever. But if what followed was not, mercifully, to be quite as theatrically tragic as the aftermath of that ominous 'something is rotten in the state of Denmark' line in Hamlet, something tumultuous had indeed happened to Henry Cecil. He had fallen in love.

So what? Racehorse trainers do that all the time, especially Flat racing ones, where every dishy, well-bred filly entering the yard might be an Oaks winner. The fact that almost all such horses end in disappointment merely has to be ascribed to racing's daily battle of hope against experience. In truth Henry's naturally flirtatious way around ladies, be they on two legs or four, had already got him into a few scrapes. Occasionally the big Mercedes had been seen parked in some surprising places. So what again? Newmarket was renowned for that. One trainer famously exited a forbidden bedroom in such haste that he left his wooden leg behind. Horse-lover and best-selling 'bonkbuster' author Jilly Cooper had a theory. 'Racing is so sexy,' she said in a TV interview at Sandown. 'All that sweat and hot leather.'

But whatever passing excitements there might have been, Henry Cecil's abiding passion had always been for the horses that fired his energy and imagination every morning, and for the team and the family that bound them to him at Warren Place. It appeared nothing had changed when he gave an eve-of-1989-season interview looking forward to how Tessla might shape up for the Oaks, how well Derby hope High Estate had recovered from the split pastern discovered after the Royal Lodge, how high a lovely unraced colt called Brush Aside might climb, and how well the garden would look for its charity opening in June: 'It will be round about Ascot time when the roses are out. The money will pay for handicapped children to visit Disneyland in Florida.'

And it seemed business as usual two months later when Henry talked to the *Racing Post*'s Simon Crisford, then a young Newmarket correspondent before distinguished later service as Sheikh Mohammed's racing manager. The article was written to mark 20 years since the Cecils' first so-longed-for winner at Ripon in 1969, and to preview what was to prove an unsuccessful reappearance for High Estate at York on the actual anniversary, 17 May. 'I think you must be able to delegate and if you have first-class staff there is no reason why you should not be able to train 200 horses,' Henry said. 'I am very lucky in this aspect as I have a marvellous wife in Julie, a first-rate headman in Paddy Rudkin and a loyal and extremely capable assistant in Willie Jardine. Between us we manage to get by.'

They were the words of a confident man with plenty to be confident about. They also sounded like those of a settled and grateful one, if you listened to his response when asked what had given him the most satisfaction in his life. 'Being in a position to be able to buy Warren Place at an extremely reasonable price from Sir Noel Murless,' Henry replied. 'Warren Place was the first thing that Julie and I ever owned and I could not wish for anything more than to be up here happily married with two children.'

By then Steve Cauthen was back with his neck mended and his winning genius intact. So too was Indian Skimmer, whom Steve had nursed home at Sandown on the same card on which a big lazy colt called Old Vic had powered up the hill in the Classic Trial but still had me damning him in *The Sunday Times* with the faint praise of 'looking more a St Leger than a Derby horse'. By then, too, an apparently backward two-year-old called Be My Chief had returned from Chris and Vicky Coldrey's boarding yard at Herringswell, five miles from Newmarket, so improved that he was able to win first time out at Doncaster before continuing on his six-race unbeaten road to become the season's top juvenile. And by then Henry and Julie had been back at Herringswell for Chris and Vicky's staff party. And a girl called Natalie Payne had asked him to dance.

During the evening a spark was struck and in the weeks to come Natalie began to ride out with the Cecil string. The relationship was

Natalie Cecil.

under way and so too was the season – in flood, in fact. Old Vic missed Epsom but the sight of him under full sail in both the French and Irish Derbies was to witness some of the finest examples of Steve Cauthen at his front-running best. Be My Chief won the Chesham Stakes to become what we were not to know was Henry Cecil's last two-year-old winner at Royal Ascot. A filly called Chimes Of Freedom won her first four races and in the Group One Moyglare Stud Stakes in Ireland became the biggest winner yet trained by Henry for the Greek shipping tycoon Stavros Niarchos.

Another young lady was also making progress. The riding-out had not gone too well for a girl used to event horses out hunting rather than thoroughbreds on the gallops, but the assignations had. In July Henry took Natalie with him to the Keeneland Yearling Sales, as 'an assistant'. One day Tote Cherry-Downes came up and warned, 'I know what you are. There have been hundreds before and hundreds to come. It doesn't mean anything.' Tote was wrong.

It happens. It doesn't make it any easier, but it happens, and it always will. Henry was not the first nor will he be the last middle-aged man to fly too close to the sun and start crashing towards earth as the wax melts – Icarus wings in the male menopausal heat. There were passionate rows between family and friends. Natalie got the sack from Herringswell but stayed in Newmarket working as a chambermaid at the White Hart, unbeknownst to prying reporters in pursuit of the 'Top Trainer and Stable Girl' story. The rumour mill went into overdrive but most people thought it would pass. 'Of course I could see what was going on,' says Paddy Rudkin. 'About 20 of the Charles St George horses were kept at Sefton Lodge in the Bury Road and she would be down there and on the Heath sometimes. But Henry was still doing his job. I had great respect for him as a trainer and all we cared about was having winners. To be honest we had seen a bit of this sort of thing before and we thought it would just blow over.'

Despite the easy newspaper tags, Natalie Payne was a lot more than a 'stable girl' or 'chambermaid'. She had been brought up in a well-to-do expatriate family in Nigeria, where her grandfather was a leading lawyer and her father also had a successful business. It had been a life of country clubs and polo and parties. No surprise, then, that a return to Britain and to being one of only three girls in a boys' boarding school was something of a culture shock. One of the few redeeming features of the moderate girls' schools that followed had been escaping to the hunting field and to the horses at her grandmother's. It was the pursuit of those interests that had brought her to Herringswell. She had, to put it mildly, never met anyone like Henry Cecil.

But the 100-strong staff at Warren Place thought they, and particularly he, had met many people like Natalie Payne, and the dynamics of their reaction say much about the central motor of their success. For, although they were devoted to 'madam', as Julie was called, they did not mind the 'guvnor' having a bit of a fling as long as the 100-winner seasons continued to roll. Many of the staff had come to rely on quite a bit more than their £60-a-week wages and two per cent of stable prize money bonus. They needed the winners for others to back them. They needed to keep their 'punters' happy.

The now strictly outlawed practice of stable staff, and in particular of work riders, being paid for giving 'information' to outsiders was officially against the rules in this era, but at a yard like Warren Place it was recognised almost more in the breach than in the observance. 'We all had punters,' says Paddy Rudkin. 'You couldn't survive on stable wages alone and anyway it kept us all sharp. What we wanted were winners. Henry must have known but he didn't mind. He was never interested in betting, and as far as he was concerned, if it was helping us concentrate that was fine by him.'

So it was that there was quite a bit more to those 'work mornings' than the trainer's admittedly crucial overall take on things as the gallops unfolded on the Limekilns and on 'racecourse side'. As the likes of Frank Storey, Nobby Clarke and Frank Conlon and former jockey Sandy Barclay were switched from one promising prospect to another, a questioning 'How did that go?' frisson would run through the string. Was this the one they should tell their men to have their money on? It was never huge money. Perhaps the odds to a tenner, or £50 a winner. But every one counted. Crikey, in 1987 there had been 183 of them. The staff loved the jokey way Henry shared their obsessive daily addiction, but driving them were more basic reasons than the slightly airy views about fulfilment and success which Henry had given to that *Arena* documentary. They loved him most because he gave them the chance to make some bread. They didn't care how many reporters puffed around after this new girl problem as long as Henry was out with the string every morning and the winners were still up ahead.

And they were. While Doncaster messed up its racetrack by allowing old drains to form horse-tripping holes three furlongs from the finish line, Warren Place seemed to be running as efficiently as ever. Doncaster's Classic was moved to Ayr, where Michelozzo gave the stable its fourth St Leger of the decade, and a month later the Yorkshire course's final big two-year-old race, the Racing Post Trophy, moved to Newcastle, went to Be My Chief on whom Steve Cauthen had dictated front-running tactics in trademark fashion. This was what Henry Cecil was good at. I remember at this time he and Julie and owner Peter Burrell joining us for lunch. Rumour had it that the extra-curricular romance had cooled. We all hoped so, but the truth was that we were more interested in Henry saying something more meaningful than 'What do you think?' when asked on TV about Be My Chief's future. We media guys went off to the jumping season imagining peace might be restored by springtime. We were wrong.

For come the end of January 1990 everything was back in the headlines, and more. Henry and Natalie were pictured in Venice beside an article whose first sentence had a sad predictability about it: 'Top racing trainer Henry Cecil and the 22-year-old stable girl he left home for, talked last night about their love for each other.' Here was the classic price for being busted by the tabloids: Henry coming clean to buy a bit of space. The fact that the phrases were familiar ones did not make the situation any less irrevocable. Henry told of how he had moved out of Warren Place before Christmas – 'I decided to leave. I have been fighting against it, trying to carry on with my life, but it was a losing battle.' He admitted there was 'a slight sadness, resentment and bitterness – although none on my part', and you didn't know whether to laugh or cry at the wistful defiance of his conclusion.

'I am hoping this will go away when everybody accepts the situation,' he said, 'and that we will all be very good friends. Life is too short to be unhappy. I think I have made the right choice and I do not worry about the age difference. If you want to grow old, put on your whites, drink your port and talk about the fish you have caught, that's up to you. I'm not saying I am going to the funfair to eat toffee apple all the time, but when your mind is straining in two directions, you have to make a decision. My main thoughts now are on having a very good season and putting all this sadness behind me.'

Come the spring that was certainly happening professionally. Four Steve Cauthen-ridden Saturday winners on 21 April at Newbury put Henry on the top of the trainers' list and already through the £100,000 barrier. Those successes had included two promising three-year-olds in Razeen and Belmez, and the previous year's injured Derby hopeful Brush Aside, whose eight-length destruction of the John Porter Stakes field after a 352-day layoff is considered by no less an authority than Steve Dyble to be Henry Cecil's greatest training achievement. 'He had such patience,' said Yarmy. 'He would have me trotting and hacking all the way round racecourse side. You couldn't gallop the horse, so we did a lot of swimming and hill work, and by the time I led Steve Cauthen out at Newbury I could tell him, "You will p*** up." When Steve came in he gave that

A Cecil one-two in the Prix de Diane at Chantilly, 1990: Rafha (Willie Carson, near side) beats Moon Cactus (Steve Cauthen) by half a length.

big Kentucky laugh and said, "You were right, Yarmy." As for all the other stuff, well I was in one of Henry's cottages and while "Madam will always be Madam" I did not want to take sides. When he talked to me I said, "I don't care about your marriage problems, I have got enough marriage problems of my own.'"

A week after the Newbury bonanza Henry was interviewed by Marcus Armytage, who had succeeded Simon Crisford as the *Racing Post*'s Newmarket man but whose Grand National triumph on Mr Frisk would soon pluck him away for higher things with the *Daily Telegraph*. During the course of Simon's handover the previous autumn Marcus had to be party to Crisford's 'no win' manoeuvring as a 'cover' for bringing Natalie on to the Heath as a 'gallops watcher'. In April 1990 Armytage was too discreet to discuss the then arrangement whereby Henry and Julie were working together daily at Warren Place before the trainer returned every evening to Natalie in a house on the Bury Road. It was called The Gables and, in Newmarket's soap opera way of things, had been lent them by Ivan Allan, whose St Leger winner Commanche Run had lowered Oh So Sharp's colours in the 1985 Benson and Hedges Gold Cup. Yet informed readers would have read the runes as Armytage reported that Henry's 'ambition for the season is not, as you might expect, to add another couple of Derbies to his tally, but purely to "survive"'.

It was to be a bittersweet irony that in yet another title-topping season Henry did rather more than 'survive'. Be My Chief did not perform as a three-year-old but Razeen did, becoming Derby favourite and prompting *The Times* to despatch Olympic legend Sebastian Coe to sit with Henry and Julie and discuss comparisons between the equine and the human athlete: 'I went to Warren Place to talk about science; Henry Cecil convinced me his is an art.' Belmez won the Chester Vase, then went so lame that his 'retirement' was announced, only to recover and run third in the Irish Derby. Razeen was only 14th in the Derby but pony-sized Rafha won the French Oaks (Prix de Diane) under Willie Carson with Steve Cauthen on 'stable selected' Moon Cactus in second (promoted from third). Royal Ascot saw four big Cauthen-steered winners for four different owners: Shavian for Lord Howard de Walden in the St James's Palace Stakes; Private Tender for Louis Freedman in the King Edward VII; River God for Sheikh Mohammed in the Queen's Vase; and Chimes Of Freedom for Stavros Niarchos in the Coronation Stakes. Yes, a bit more than 'survival'.

The pace rarely slackened all the way to when the Charles St George-owned Peter Davies became another Racing Post Trophy winner at the end of October, although there had been the added irony that Belmez, the biggest victor of all in Ascot's King George VI and Queen Elizabeth Stakes, was actually saddled by Julie, as Rafha

King George VI and Queen Elizabeth Stakes, Ascot, 1990: Belmez (Mick Kinane, right) heads Old Vic (Steve Cauthen).

had been in the Prix de Diane. For Belmez, like the filly, was the stable's second choice; Steve Cauthen had opted for Old Vic only to lose out in a final-furlong duel with Mick Kinane and Belmez after making most of the running. By the end of the season the Cecil divorce had gone through and Julie was no longer at Warren Place but at a new yard of her own in the Hamilton Road next to where she and Henry had begun at Marriott Stables two decades earlier. Willie Jardine and George Winsor went with Julie, as did her closest ally Alma Wigmore, the red-wellied, ski-goggled eccentric who had ridden beside her most mornings right back to those Marriott days.

The teams were changing, then, but one much-liked member was now in the great stable in the sky.

After riding a promising three-year-old in a gallop on the racecourse side Nobby Clarke came back to the car park where Paddy Rudkin had another for him to work past the trainer. Fifty-six-year-old Nobby knew what a good horse felt like, as he had sat on many of the top Warren Place stars, with Noel Murless as well as with Henry. Most recently he had looked after Diminuendo through her glory days, and he, like the other work riders, lived for the feel of another future winner that would do him and his punters a favour. Imagine the warmth in the words as he dismounted: 'Tell you what, Paddy, we'll have a right touch on this one.' They were the last words he spoke. Four strides after being legged up on his next horse, Nobby keeled over from a heart attack and not even Steve Cauthen's instant efforts at mouth-to-mouth resuscitation could revive him. It was a tragically premature exit for one of the most popular and enthusiastic of stablemen – but would he have wanted it any other way?

Steve wasn't removing himself quite so completely from the scene, yet after signing as first jockey for Sheikh Mohammed he would no longer be the pivotal figure of the Slip Anchor and Reference Point years. What with Indian Skimmer's partner Carol Litton also leaving the stable she had first ridden with at Marriott as a 12-year-old schoolgirl, and with the injuries that prevented Old Vic going for the Arc de Triomphe, which was then won by the three-year-old Saumarez, who had been sold out of the Cecil stable in the summer, no wonder there was a downbeat feel to the interview Henry gave to *The Sunday Times* in November. 'I really don't know how I managed to be champion again,' he told John Karter. 'So much has gone wrong for me this year, and to add to my professional worries I have faced enormous pressures over the break-up of my marriage.'

There was a realisation that changing circumstances might need a change of attitude, especially with regard to finding owners. With the likelihood of his stable strength being reduced from 210 to 140 as several of his major patrons supported Julie, Henry remarked, 'You need an army not a battalion to succeed at the highest level, it is so competitive nowadays. I have always sat back and waited for owners to come to me. Now I will have to go out and tout around a bit more.' The words struck an odd, slightly discordant note, but it wasn't long before he returned to a more familiar refrain.

'I would like to do it all over again,' he said, 'to win the big races again, which of course means the Derby. But if I can just keep Warren Place running at a high standard that is all I can ask. Nineteen ninety-one could be a hard year for me; I might need a year to get myself straight. But I'll get back up there, if not next season, then the following one.'

Which is precisely, despite much disapproval of his family arrangements and many dire predictions about his professional ones, what Henry Cecil did.

8

PRINCE KHALID ABDULLA

NO ONE, not even Henry, was to know it at the time, but the key step had already been taken. In 1990 he had broken the habit of a lifetime and written to an owner soliciting horses. The response was the beginning of the most supportive arrangement of his whole career. Henry Cecil was to become a trainer for Prince Khalid Abdulla.

He had trained just one horse for him, in 1982, a colt with the Old Testament name of Adonijah. The owner had sold it to the Prince, but while that horse remained in the stable, nothing more came of the connection. With Abdulla's principal trainer Jeremy Tree retiring in 1989, this Cecil letter could not have come at a more appropriate time. At the end of 1990 a draft of ten yearlings and three unraced two-year-old fillies were allocated to Warren Place. One of the fillies was no good, another won the second of her only two races, but the third, Peplum, won the Oh So Sharp Stakes at Nottingham and then went on to land the Cheshire Oaks. A major racing marriage was down the aisle.

In just 13 years, Prince Khalid, the shy, quiet businessman cousin and brother-in-law of King Abdullah of Saudi Arabia, had built the best-run racing operation of them all. Originally attracted to the game during a Paris stay back in 1956, he had not got involved until buying four yearlings in the autumn of 1977. There had been a year's wait for the first winner, but by the end of 1990 his green and pink silks had seen victory in eight Classics and he had established an international six-stud, 150-broodmare operation with the express aim of breeding, not buying, success. If Sheikh Mohammed's racing activity had the feel of a man trying to launch a whole nation with it – which was exactly the situation – Prince Khalid's had the sense of a carefully studied hobby where only the rigid pursuit of excellence could justify the expense. Here was a racing union made to last.

Henry and Natalie did not become man and wife for another year, and it has to be said that much of Newmarket had closed ranks against them. Julie was a popular figure, Natalie was depicted as a brazen young hussy. Even best friends like Tote Cherry-Downes cut themselves off from Warren Place. It was a situation of considerable unhappiness and one from which the daily challenge of the racing stable was a dawn-to-dusk relief. 'The horses were always what fulfilled him,' said second jockey Willie Ryan, who had joined in 1986 from Reg Hollinshead's small Staffordshire stable and apprentice academy in a move Willie described as 'with due respect, like going from Preston North End to Arsenal. It was not just what the horses were like, but the staff, and especially Henry, knew all their breeding too. They would be saying things like "this was the sister to that", or "so like her half-brother", or "it could be an Oaks filly, will probably go Pretty Polly Stakes, Musidora and Epsom". It was like a code at first but you soon got used to it. Because everything was geared to producing Group horses, if they weren't likely to be good enough he just wouldn't run them. It helped when you knew how the families had shaped up.' It was exactly the sort of assistance that Prince Khalid liked best.

The tabloids still hung around for titbits but the racing press didn't. Not for any hugely worthy reasons but because, in our own little world, actual racing issues trumped the titillations of even a leading trainer's private life. Like at the end of October when Lester Piggott crowned the most astonishing comeback in sporting history. Nine days short of his 55th birthday he emerged from a near five-year retirement (which had included 12 months in a prison cell) and came from last to first to land the Breeders' Cup Mile in Belmont, New York. Like two months later at Kempton Park when an old grey warrior called Desert Orchid won his fourth King George VI Chase to a crowd reception that the fleeting world of Flat racing can never emulate – that is until 20 years later when a certain trainer was to do an even more improbable impersonation of Lazarus than Lester himself.

Desert Orchid was trained by David Elsworth, who in 1990 had also saddled the filly In The Groove to win the Champion Stakes, under Steve Cauthen no less, and so had the unique distinction of handling the highest-rated Flat-race filly in Europe as well as the world's most charismatic steeplechaser. David's father, like Henry's, was killed in the war before he was born, but this parent was an unmarried farm boy not an aristocrat, and his son's upbringing had to be self-help of the most basic country kind. D. Elsworth did ride a 66-1 winner at Cheltenham as a 17-year-old, but it was two years before he rode another one and not many more followed. At 30 he found success as a trainer under someone else's name, only for that man, Colonel Ricky Vallance, to get warned off. David was reduced to running a clothes stall at Romsey market. Mind you, Henry would have loved that.

David Elsworth was 39 by the time he finally got restarted with the aptly named Fortune Cookie in a hurdle race at Exeter in March 1979. His own gifts had at last been given the chance to prosper and his recent achievements had included the 1988 Grand National with Rhyme 'N' Reason and the matching, a year later, of Desert

Orchid's Cheltenham Gold Cup over 22 fences and three and a quarter miles with Indian Ridge's five-furlong sprint triumph in the King's Stand Stakes at Royal Ascot. David's dear old mother never revealed his father's identity beyond telling me he was a 'sweet young lad'. She also denied, with a smile, the idea that the third of her son's Christian names, Cecil, had any link with the great family of Burghley and Hatfield. Perhaps you can see why for racing fans there were more interesting things than H. Cecil's private life.

The lure of beautiful young horses of infinite potential has a strength that is centuries old. It is what is best about the thoroughbred racehorse, the fastest weight-carrying creature the world has ever seen, and Britain's greatest gift to the animal kingdom. It is a lure that is strongest at Newmarket, and for three full decades Warren Place had been its temple. Personal difficulties notwithstanding, Henry Cecil had a call to answer, and 119 winners were saddled in 1991. On 1 October a white-faced chestnut called All At Sea cantered up in a little race at Wolverhampton and what she and another Abdulla runner did the following season suggested their trainer's ship was a long way from the rocks just yet.

By the spring of 1992 it seemed like full steam ahead. At Newbury, on the Friday before the Craven meeting, Musicale won the Fred Darling Stakes impressively enough to be made favourite for the 1,000 Guineas. She carried the green and blue silks of former arch rival Robert Sangster, as she had done through her unbeaten five-race two-year-old season. On the Monday of Craven week the Abdulla colours were the focus as All At Sea cruised home in the Oh So Sharp Stakes at Nottingham, and she followed that with wins in two other races, the Pretty Polly at Newmarket and the Musidora at York, both also named after Oaks winners. Little wonder that she was soon hot favourite to become an Oaks heroine too.

No surprise either that the Sheikh Mohammed-owned three-year-old Twist And Turn got a big call in the Derby betting when winning on the Craven Thursday before taking the Chester Vase under Steve Cauthen in his new role as contracted rider to runners under the Sheikh's maroon and white. So it was a confident as well as candid Henry Cecil who gave his traditional pre-Derby briefing that year.

'I've got masses of incentive at the moment and I'm really enjoying training,' he told the *Independent*'s Richard Edmondson, before adding significantly, 'I'm enjoying working with the Abdulla horses. The whole set-up interests me an awful lot, the organisation required to be the best. I have been training the Abdulla horses for only a couple of years and the families are new to me. I like to think I will be even more effective when I have got to know them better. I am enjoying training far more than I have done for the last few years. I'm still hungry and I think I am working better. The year before last I was champion when I wasn't even living on the place. I was in the Bury Road just coming up here in the daytime. My private life hasn't been very easy and the media don't always take things the right way. I've had a bad press, and though it's my own personal life everybody still seemed to want to get involved in it.'

Epsom did not see him land his highest hopes, just as Musicale had failed in her Classic bid at Newmarket. All At Sea started 11/10 favourite in the Oaks but could finish only second to User Friendly, the final quarter-mile proving beyond her stamina. In the Derby, Twist And Turn led into the final furlong before fading to fifth behind the chunky chestnut Dr Devious, whose previous race, uniquely, had been in the Kentucky Derby at Churchill Downs. The big talking point that year at Epsom was the favourite, Dr Devious's stable companion Rodrigo De Triano, being ridden by Lester Piggott, as he had when winning the 2,000 Guineas in one of the most outrageous snooks ever cocked at Father Time. As the old bent hairpin of Lester's body curled over the young legs below it, 38 years had passed since his first Classic on what now seems the aptly named

Never Say Die. For a jockey, whose physical powers are bound to be waning, to do such things at the pipe-and-slippers age of 56 was little short of a miracle. For a trainer, however, the fifties can be the best of years. That was certainly the impression Henry was giving John Oaksey when they sat down together before Royal Ascot.

In the summer of 1992 Henry was a mere 49, not 56, and Bolkonski, his first British Classic winner, had not come until 1975. But 13 Classics had already followed as well as no fewer than 53 successes at Royal Ascot; two more would be added a week later when the colts Perpendicular and Gondolier won in the apricot silks of Lord Howard de Walden. John Oaksey was 14 years Henry's senior; his insightful columns in *The Telegraph* had chronicled the Cecil career from the very beginning. He was a wonderfully kind man but would have had an easier rapport with Julie than with her enigmatic husband, and when he wrote about 'the divorce which so distressed Henry and Julie's many friends' it was not hard to see where his sympathies lay.

But John was also something of a hero-worshipping traditionalist and there is no mistaking his admiration, or his eloquence, as he tackled the secret of the trainer's success. 'I asked Henry Cecil,' John wrote, 'how much he has changed his methods down the years. The answer offers his rivals no obvious encouragement. "Not at all," he said firmly – adding with that laid-back modesty which, even if partly assumed, is one of his most engaging qualities: "Maybe it would be better if I had. But there is only so much you can be taught. In the end you learn, and if you have any sense, go on learning from your mistakes – your own and other people's."'

John Oaksey left Warren Place once again impressed with the permanence of the trainer's dominance, albeit with a cryptic reference to the specially ordered interior refurnishing that Henry and Natalie had carried out: 'tables, chairs, sofas, chest of drawers and carpets, all made to Henry's order by local craftsmen, or found, painted and woven by his friends. I don't know what Sam Darling, who built the place, or the Maharajah of Baroda, who modernised it, would think but suspect that they would be delighted. In any case, as even the present owner's critics would admit, the result is typical of the man – relaxed, comfortable and stylish.'

But unbeknownst to John and to most of us, not everyone around the yard was comfortable or convinced that Henry had changed 'not at all'. Paddy Rudkin, for one, was coming to the end of his tether.

Looking back it seems inevitable, but then life is never lived in hindsight. One of the things that attracted Henry to Natalie was that she was a young, fresh pair of eyes also fascinated by the horses on which his whole being depended. She may not have had any experience with thoroughbreds but throughout her teens and early twenties she had hunted, evented and show-jumped whenever she was able. Henry had a new and enthusiastic ear into which to talk. And Natalie loved to listen. The trouble started when she began to talk a bit too.

'People say I interfere, but I don't,' she said later, with some exasperation. 'Having been a horsey person married to a horsey husband I couldn't spend my time in the house, could I? In racing,' she continued, referring to her plan of reducing the standard size of the Warren Place bits from five and a half to four and a half inches to cope with the smaller more 'araby' mouths of the current horses rather than the larger ones of the original Murless era, 'it is the same old story. You have been doing it for 50 years so it must be right. A horse should have a piece of metal in its mouth that is comfortable.'

Her husband was giving her a receptive hearing, and I remember Henry telling me at the time how Natalie's ideas were 'bucking him up', of how 'we all get stuck in our ways and it's good for us to have a rethink, isn't it, isn't it?'

The smile of recognition that tends to spread at the thought of all those H. Cecil rhetorical questions was not, sadly, one that Paddy Rudkin shared. For the first time in his professional partnership he began to find some of his central judgements being queried. 'It was not any one thing,' he says now, 'and Joy and I had 24 unbelievably happy and successful years with the man. We were the very best of friends, so I am not going to start saying any rubbish. But the main reason we had lasted such a long time was that, while he was very much in charge and did all the training, the yard was mine. He would never question any of the normal decisions I was making. If someone came to him and complained he would say, "Paddy runs the yard." When Natalie came, it began to be different. It's understandable perhaps, but he started to listen to her. It became difficult.'

Just because it is one of life's more familiar scenarios doesn't make it any less painful for all concerned. One day in the summer of 1992, Paddy snapped. When he got back to his bungalow, he rang Anthony Stroud, Sheikh Mohammed's racing manager, to ask whether there would ever be a job on the team. When the Sheikh was next in Newmarket, Paddy was asked up to Dalham Hall. When the Dubai season started that winter Paddy Rudkin was installed as trainer of the 'Blue Stable' where he continued for 14 happy and successful years. The leaving had not been easy. On the last morning Henry could not face coming into the yard, so Paddy went into the kitchen to say goodbye. It was a civilised exchange, but no words have since been spoken. Parting can sometimes be the saddest thing.

Yet with or without the Rudkins, the trainer's own joy had, as always, to be taken from the promise of those early mornings. In 1992 this most of all meant the two-year-olds, and most especially the second batch from Khalid Abdulla's Juddmonte Farms breeding operation. At Craven meeting time Henry was already flagging up a son of Storm Bird called Wharf, who duly collected first time at Newmarket before taking the July Stakes on his only other outing. Although Wharf was then sidelined with sore shins, he had already done enough to ensure Prince Khalid had a fancied contender in the next year's 2,000 Guineas. But his exploits in the Abdulla colours were to be superseded long before then by three colts who took unbeaten records into the winter and whose season had culminated in an October beyond the dreams of almost any owner.

The third of October was Arc de Triomphe day. One of the great supporting acts is the Grand Criterium, France's top race for two-year-olds. In it Henry ran a little, round Caerleon colt of Prince Khalid's called Tenby, who had already won at Goodwood and Newbury. We could perhaps forgive Cecil a smirk of satisfaction as Tenby pulled clear of Steve Cauthen in the Sheikh Mohammed silks on the Michael Stoute-trained Blush Rambler. It had been a tremendous performance. Tenby was small but he looked powerful and tenacious and every inch a worthy Derby favourite. Two weeks later Prince Khalid had an equally impressive 2,000 Guineas favourite when the Andre Fabre-trained Zafonic rocketed clear of the Dewhurst field at Newmarket.

Two top colts with Wharf in the wings was a good hand for anyone. Only a week later at Doncaster another Warren Place-based Abdulla colt went and topped the lot. Armiger had run just once before, winning easily at Newmarket, but as this son of Prince Khalid's Arc winner Rainbow Quest set his chestnut neck forward and left the Racing Post Trophy field toiling further and further adrift, it was clear that he too would be atop the rankings. Not that it mattered to the owner. When the international ratings came out, Armiger was first, Tenby second and Zafonic fourth. No owner, the erudite men from Timeform told us, had collected such a cornucopia of two-year-old talent since the old Aga Khan had four of the top six back in 1934. No one therefore could possibly have guessed that back at Warren Place there lurked an even better Abdulla prospect than all the others. And this one had yet to race.

One afternoon the previous autumn Henry Cecil had come into the yard with a printed sheet. It was the Warren Place allocation of the Abdulla yearlings. With no names yet given, each was listed just by the names of its sire and dam. Seeing Dave Goodwin, he walked over and said, 'Quite a few have been taken already, but see if there is anything you would like to do.' Dave ran his eye briefly down the unmarked ones on the list until he reached a colt by Dancing Brave. 'The dam Slightly Dangerous rang a bell,' he recalls. 'I remembered her being second in the Oaks to Time Charter, so I said to Henry I would like to have him. He told me it was a nice colt but a very late foal and big and backward so would not be coming to us until the New Year. I wasn't worried. Somehow with that horse I never was.' The colt was to be the dual Derby winner Commander In Chief.

It says plenty for the staff as well as for the trainer that this new influx of talent was handled with much the same aplomb as in the singing success of those glory days with Julie, George Winsor, Steve Cauthen and Willie Jardine. 'Henry was the captain of the ship and Paddy had been an incredible first mate,' says Willie Ryan. 'Of course it was different when the others left and Natalie came and Frank Conlon was head lad. But the same old principles applied. We had good horses, we made sure they were very fit, and it was winners that we wanted.'

In 1990 Commander In Chief had not been foaled until 18 May, compared to Tenby on 21 January, Armiger on 15 February and Zafonic on 1 April. At birth the younger colt was, at 60kg compared to 48kg, 25 per cent heavier than Tenby with whom he would eventually line up at Epsom. By the September version of the monthly report in which Juddmonte scrupulously logs everything from horse size to

Henry Cecil with Indian Skimmer at Churchill Downs for the 1988 Breeders' Cup.

Old Vic and Steve Cauthen in glorious isolation on the way to winning the 1989 Prix du Jockey-Club at Chantilly.

Steve Cauthen at work
– with Paddy Rudkin
on the Newmarket
gallops – and at home.

Henry Cecil with owner Charles St George on the gallops.

Commander In Chief and Mick Kinane led in after the 1993 Derby.

On the Newmarket gallops: (*above*) with fellow knighted trainer Sir Michael Stoute; (*below*) Tony McGlone puts Bosra Sham through her paces.

After Lady Carla's victory in the 1996 Oaks: (left to right) winning owner Wafic Said, winning trainer Henry Cecil, and winning rider Pat Eddery.

Post-race banter with Sheikh Mohammed after Bosra Sham's victory in the 1996 Champion Stakes.

Henry Cecil introduces Princess Ramruma, daughter of owner Prince Fahd Salman, to her equine namesake Ramruma, winner of the 1999 Oaks.

Sleepytime and Kieren Fallon land the 1997 1,000 Guineas at Newmarket.

The 2000 Oaks: Love Divine and Richard Quinn go to post.

At York with twin brother David (right).

grass quality, Commander In Chief was still at 12 hands 3 inches (4ft 3in), some two inches shorter than Tenby; by the June of Derby Day he was a towering 16.3 to Tenby's diminutive 15.1.

Such details came (in those days via fax rather than the as yet uninvented email) courtesy of Prince Khalid's principal stud manager Philip Mitchell, but most of all thanks to his employer whom I had first met some 12 years earlier on a train returning from York. Prince Khalid was a small, quiet, spare, grey-suited figure sitting with his aide in the corner seat by the sliding door. The aide came with a message inviting me to swap places with him and went to get some coffee, which eventually appeared in two of British Rail's most unpleasant plastic cups. There was no fuss about the beverage, any more than there was preening when his butler brought us another coffee in rather more elegant style at the Abdulla London base in Belgravia the week before that Derby of 1993.

The normally retiring Prince was going on the record only because of a convincingly written but wildly exaggerated newspaper report, which, besides such howlers as dubbing the stallion Caerleon's mating with Tenby's dam Shining Water in Tipperary as 'a coupling in a Surrey barn', had given machines more importance than people in the Juddmonte success story. 'Across our operation we have top-class committed professionals,' Prince Khalid said. 'The success, the satisfactions are all for them. They collect and use the best advice and keep me in touch by phone and fax all the time. I like to be involved in decisions, but if the professionals feel very strongly about something, I would not normally disagree.'

That summer he had not disagreed that the big Dancing Brave colt who had looked so good when he won his first two races at Newmarket in the spring should accompany Tenby to the Derby while Armiger, who was actually injured, should aim for the French version, the Prix du Jockey Club. That was despite Commander In

Chief looking much less effective at York where, after winning by only a neck, Pat Eddery had leant down to Dave Goodwin and said, 'Sorry, Dave, but I don't think he's a Derby horse.'

That day in 1993 Prince Khalid was talking in his office with a huge canvas of some sixteenth-century Italian naval battle hanging behind him. A week later Dave Goodwin was speaking in the slightly less refined trappings of the lads' canteen at Epsom. But his sense of ownership, not to mention his confidence, was more than a match for the self-effacing Saudi royal. 'I have always liked my horse,' said Dave, whose twin claims to fame in Newmarket are having done Derby winner Slip Anchor and being a seriously good road cyclist. 'He was big and unfurnished when he came to us but he was very calm and sensible. It was never on the cards to run him as a two-year-old. He would go out third lot and Tom, Dick and Harry would ride him. Henry was never going to hurry him, but this year, once we started, you could see he had something. I rode him work myself before he ran first time and Henry came up smiling and said, "You ought to be able to get a new bike out of him."'

Tenby had won both his warm-up races before that Derby and, not discouraged by the trainer, we had all fallen so completely for the thought he was a class apart that we allowed him to start odds-on favourite at Epsom despite the evidence of our eyes that he had not grown an inch and had needed to work hard enough for both of his victories. No such myopia affected Dave Goodwin. 'My horse didn't look great at York,' he explained, 'but it was a sprint finish after a slow pace and was the first time he had ever been asked a proper question. The race has really woken him up and he has been working better and better. Michael Kinane came down to ride him last week and I said, "I promise you will beat Tenby."'

So it proved, Tenby compounding quickly after leading into the straight and Commander In Chief picking up so well that Mick

After Commander In Chief's Derby, 1993: owner Khalid Abdulla, trainer Henry Cecil, jockey Mick Kinane.

Kinane said he had come too soon. As Dave Goodwin led him back to the same treasured winner's circle into which he had walked Steve Cauthen on Slip Anchor in 1985, his eyes caught Pat Eddery looking despondently over at the Derby winner that should have been.

'There was nothing I could say to him,' says Dave, 'but when I led him out on Commander In Chief for the Irish Derby it was the only time I ever remember him being a bit nervous. Pat was normally the calmest of all the jockeys. But he had called it wrong at Epsom and he so wanted to get it right in Ireland. I think that's why he was in front a bit soon at the Curragh too. I'm not complaining. Everybody did a great job on the horse.'

In Ireland, Commander In Chief had beaten the French Derby winner Hernando in a perfect mid-season showdown. In just three seasons Henry Cecil had given Prince Khalid every reason to be pleased he answered that 1990 letter. For the Irish Derby Henry and Natalie took a cottage at the K Club which they shared with Prince Khalid Abdulla's racing manager Grant Pritchard-Gordon and his wife Sandy. With no connection to Warren Place's previous regime Grant is one of the few people who will stand up for what the new wife brought to the party.

'I could see what Henry loved about Natalie,' he says. 'She was enthusiastic and loved animals and clothes. Henry was lit up by her and was relaxed in that situation. The four of us went holidaying in Antigua a couple of times. Whatever anyone may say, those were happy days.'

The Abdulla pink and green would now be at Warren Place for ever. But you would not be able to say the same about Sheikh Mohammed's maroon and white. As so often in life, and especially in racing, the good times were too good to last.

9

SHEIKH MOHAMMED

SHEIKH MOHAMMED was a very different sort of owner, and by 1995 he was looking at things very differently from when he and Henry Cecil first got together to win the Fillies' Triple Crown with Oh So Sharp just ten years earlier. Considering what he and his brothers had invested in the last decade it was hardly surprising. In American terms they had all but 'bought the farm'.

Between 1985 and 1988 their average spend at the yearling sales was more than £10 million a year in Britain and over $50 million in America. At the end of 1988 Sheikh Mohammed topped the UK owners' table with more than twice the winners and double the prize money of the next two in the table (Prince Khalid and the Aga Khan), with the Sheikh's younger brother Ahmed fourth. And while the senior sibling Sheikh Maktoum was only ninth, his impact, with 25 winners and £185,000 of prize money, was hardly trifling. Over 30 per cent of that season's Group Two and Group Three races were won by horses sporting the brothers' livery; in Group One races the numbers reached almost 40 per cent, headed by the brilliant fillies Indian Skimmer and Diminuendo. The pair had been trained, of course, by Henry Cecil.

These figures all come from a massive three-broadsheet 'Special Report' that the *Sporting Life* ran in November 1988 under the headline 'Racing's Gulf Crisis' complete with an unsmiling headshot montage of the four brothers led by a dark-glassed and heavily bearded Sheikh Mohammed glaring rather sinisterly from the page. The report didn't shilly-shally. 'After eight short years,' it said, 'the Maktoum family factor is in danger of dominating and destroying the very fabric of the greatest racing in the world,' and it quoted Robert Sangster after winning the long-distance Cesarewitch: 'I don't usually go in for slow horses – but these days they are the only races the Arabs will let us win.'

It was all quite embarrassing for the many top owners and breeders whose fortunes had been transformed by Maktoum offers they could not refuse, and indeed quite difficult for me who in 1985 had talked myself and Sheikh Mohammed into starting the *Racing Post* as a replacement for what had seemed a terminally sick *Sporting Life*. Having at our launch put out the hostage-to-fortune statement 'we will not be the Maktoums' poodle', I could hardly set the *Racing Post* on heavy Maktoum counter-attack and any public agreement with the sensible points underlying the more sensational aspects of the *Sporting Life* report were a bit close to biting the hand that fed us.

In private I had counselled Sheikh Mohammed about being more selective, only to receive the disarming answer, 'But you must understand we like buying horses and people like us buying horses from them.' I had also encouraged him, as a hands-on horseman, to develop the idea of his own operations in both Britain and in Dubai. By 1992 the first advice had been ignored to the extent of another doom-predicting newspaper report, this time in the *Independent on Sunday*, counting 713 horses with 61 trainers for Sheikh Mohammed alone long before it came to detailing countless more foals, stallions and broodmares in studs across Europe, America, Australia and Japan. But the second thought, which in truth never needed much input from me, was growing ever stronger in his mind. And as the world, let alone racing, was coming to realise, what Sheikh Mohammed thought quite soon became what Sheikh Mohammed did.

You may remember that back in March 1988 Henry had been among the spectators as General Zia ul-Haq hit that opening drive on what was to be the first of so many grass golf courses in Dubai. The khaki-suited President was to meet a sticky end alongside five of his generals and the US ambassador in a plane crash in the Punjab that August, and by then it was clear that the Sheikh Mohammed momentum for rather more than golf courses was an unstoppable stream, and that racing would be part of it. A new racecourse had been opened at Nad Al Sheba in what was then an out-of-town desert location next to the camel track. All-weather gallops and modern air-conditioned training stables had been built beside it and the likes of Paddy Rudkin recruited to run them. But Sheikh Mohammed was restless. However great, or controversial, his success in British and indeed in world racing, he did not want to wait to put Dubai and its horses on the map.

He was a very physical man. There is a great photo of him on a camel smiling back at a rather uncomfortable-looking Henry Cecil on another. But at the beginning of 1993 he inveigled his trainer and me into an even more bottom-bleeding event. Somewhere deep in the desert between Dubai and Abu Dhabi he got up the most remarkable four-legged race ever staged – 402 camels against 28 horses going 25 miles towards the three o'clock sun with £400,000 in prize money.

'You want to ride?' said Sheikh Mohammed. 'Ride that one.'

At least it wasn't a camel. It was a rather elegant little chestnut called Cyprus II, who earlier in life had won in the show ring at New York's Madison Square Garden. This was much harsher stuff. For me, unprepared and unequipped, the unthinkable was about to begin. Within minutes Sheikh Mohammed reappeared on a

Sheikh Mohammed bin Rashid al Maktoum (centre).

magnificent big chestnut, flanked by his two daughters, their faces completely hidden by the niqab veil. With his black beard and dark glasses beneath the white wrap-around Arab headdress, this was a figure like Saladin.

'We go,' the Sheikh said.

He may have been in control but not many of us were, and certainly not the kids on the camels. Half an hour earlier they had launched off into a false start and it had taken a couple of miles to catch them. Now Henry was among us somewhere on a massive bay called Coachman, whose purple, gold-embroidered saddle cloth was a happy match for Henry's socks. He had looked remarkably calm beforehand, but Coachman went off at far too great a rate of knots in what had become something between Lawrence of Arabia's attack on Aqaba, that land rush scene in *Far and Away* and a crazy modern motor rally. It was a mad swirling mix of horses, hovering helicopters, sandstorms and shouting; it seemed every four-wheel vehicle in the Gulf was churning up the dust, honking horns and yelling encouragement. Any chance of Coachman getting the trip or my slowing Cyprus II to a pace steady enough to last the 25 miles was dreamtime.

My silly chump pulled as if he was a car with the choke out, and after a few miles he gradually wound down, like a fading clockwork toy, to a slower and slower canter, then to a trot – and then even that was too much effort. His rider dismounted. The day looked like being a long one. Cyprus's breath came back but it was going to be a question of walking and jogging to make the finish before nightfall, while up front a mad mass of car-borne spectators were witnessing what must rank high in the annals of horse achievement. Over the scrubland, rock and sand dune, Sheikh Mohammed's 12-year-old daughter Hassa and her eight-year-old horse Al Naes kept up such a pace that she finally completed the 25 miles with an all-the-way victory in just one hour and 11 minutes.

Her father was hardly a minute behind her, and his horse was almost more of a hero. A six-year-old from Florida, he had won four races over just six furlongs under the unromantic name of Sample Copy. Now called Abyan Al Ashqar, he not only carried Sheikh Mohammed rather than his sylph-like daughter, but was having to put up with the sort of mobile mobbing normally confined to the maillot jaune on the steepest mountain climbs in the Tour de France.

'Over the last two miles the scene was quite unbelievable,' said Bill Smith, who had swapped a 500-winner career as the Queen Mother's jump jockey for a role masterminding Sheikh Mohammed's schedule and endurance horses. 'There must have been 20 cars around us, all cheering them on. We only stopped three times, but Sheikh Mohammed must have poured 40 bottles of water over his horse and going to the finish it was still fresh enough to be cantering 25mph on our speedometer. Afterwards the animal was pretty weary but we gave him electrolytes and a saline drip and he was fine.'

To those present the winning ceremony was equally remarkable. Sheikh Mohammed, in urging his nation's womanhood to take up horse riding, said the race 'symbolised Arab customs and traditions' and duly presented the winning horse to the UAE's President Zayed, a gesture then repeated by Prince Abdulaziz bin Fahd al-Saud, owner of the first camel, which finished sixth. They were all far, far ahead of where Cyprus and I were wearily marching on. Despite a comprehensive hosing down from a passing water tanker, our walks were getting longer and our jogs fewer. On one of them I was passed by a plodding camel ridden by a Bedouin boy little more than six years old. He pointed his stick in mockery. It was my most humiliating moment since I ran in a marathon and was overtaken by a walker.

Worse was to come. With the sun lowering in the evening sky and barely a mile from the finish, a friendly Range Rover drew up with the news that there was nobody left up ahead and no horse boxes as they had all, including Henry and Coachman's, got stuck in the sand dunes. Walking the reverse journey was the only way home. There was a full moon that night. We waited beneath it for help to come. Trucks and lights eventually got through. Hotels and comfort beckoned, and soon only the sores were to remain.

If you think the above a gratuitous self-indulgent diversion from the Henry Cecil story you are only partly right. Because five months before that desert drama something other than Paddy Rudkin had moved from Warren Place to Dubai. In 1992 Sheikh Mohammed owned a talented chestnut filly called Dayflower, who had refused to start when odds-on favourite for her debut at Doncaster in midsummer before making amends very easily three weeks later at Newmarket. She had not run again in Britain, but Sheikh Mohammed had shipped her back home, and at the time of Henry's desert gallop (he sensibly pulled up long before me) she was in the care of trainer Satish Seemar in Dubai. It was Satish and Sheikh Mohammed who were in charge of Dayflower's conditioning when she returned to England and won the Middleton Stakes at York on 12 May 1993.

In the racing scheme of things it was not an important event, but in the range of Sheikh Mohammed's attitude to racing and most particularly to Henry Cecil it was to prove momentous. It was a mere coincidence that the easy win at York was at the expense of one of the Sheikh's other horses, Helvellyn, that was actually trained at Warren Place. For Dayflower's British success after spending her winter in Dubai had changed the game. It had given Sheikh Mohammed a taste for doing it himself.

At the time Dayflower seemed more of a curiosity than anything else. After winning at York she finished way out of the numbers in both the Irish 1,000 Guineas and the French Oaks (Prix de Diane) and was never seen again. Satish Seemar, her official trainer, was a stylish, self-possessed guy from a business family who trained next to the Sheikh Mohammed palace in front of which was a 'Quadriga', a four-horses-and-an-angel statue like the one atop Wellington Arch at Hyde Park Corner. Back at Warren Place it was the year of Tenby and Armiger and Commander In Chief. That was plenty enough to get excited about.

Looking back, there is an utter inevitability about the collision course on which Henry Cecil and Sheikh Mohammed had now embarked. Ever since he was first champion trainer in 1976 Henry had publicly stated his craving for the most winners and the best horses every year. Not for nothing had Paddy Rudkin's tribute actually praised him for being 'a greedy, ambitious man'. Sheikh Mohammed had been happy to feed this continuing appetite and Oh So Sharp's 1985 Triple Crown had come in his very first Cecil year. In 1988 owner and trainer won 13 Group races together and in 1989 they won another 12 with horses like Old Vic, Alydaress and Indian Skimmer.

Yet the body language was subtly changing. At the start of the relationship Sheikh Mohammed was almost the supplicant, happy to laud and entertain; Henry the bestower from his eminence on the British turf. In the 1980s there was still a touch of the old colonial snobbery about us as we shuttled around Dubai's often still small and dusty outposts listening to Sheikh Mohammed spelling out his dreams. As we moved into the 1990s, his racing was taking off just as his country was. Henry Cecil had never been anything like his only trainer, and in 1989 Sheikh Mohammed brought John Gosden back from America to Newmarket and the spacious and historic trappings of Lord Derby's Stanley House operation between the Bury and Snailwell roads. In 1990 Belmez flew the Mohammed flag at the Cecil stable, but the Sheikh and the champion trainer had only three Group winners together in 1991, just one in 1992 and in 1993 none at all.

Maybe there had been straws as well as sand in the wind when Henry and I had set off with the cars and the camels in that mad desert stampede in January 1993 but we were soon all too busy, not to mention too sore, to notice. Besides, Henry was once again surfing the Classic tide and in the week before he despatched Armiger to Paris for the Arc in the autumn of 1993, he attended a celebration party for Prince Khalid at the Savoy. It was luxury with taste: tubs of caviar, an ice unicorn and MC Lord Charles Spencer Churchill standing with his back to what appeared to be an embroidered wall and gushing, 'Flown in by Concorde . . . a true megastar . . . Miss . . . Liza Minnelli!' The wall slid back and there she was – 'Cabaret' with a capital 'C'. For nearly an hour Liza held us until finally stopping the show with 'We can't give you anything but love, Khalid' to our shy but deliciously embarrassed host.

That season Henry's 95-winner total may have dropped below a hundred for the first time in ten years, but he had landed his tenth trainers' title and Sheikh Mohammed's colours were to be carried by the stable's Racing Post Trophy winner King's Theatre in the Classics of 1994. When the colt duly ran second in both the English and Irish Derbies and then landed Britain's richest prize, the King George VI and Queen Elizabeth Stakes at Ascot, you could be forgiven for thinking all was well with the owner/trainer relationship. But then you would not have appreciated the significance of the horse who had beaten King's Theatre in the Irish Derby four weeks before his Ascot triumph. She was called Balanchine and she had won the Oaks at Epsom earlier in June. For a filly to trounce the colts in a Derby is feat enough, but the big thing about Balanchine was that she had spent the winter with Sheikh Mohammed in Dubai. Her owner now had the classic taste in his mouth.

The filly had been bought from Robert Sangster after winning both her races in September 1993, trained by Peter Chapple-Hyam at Manton. In Dubai Balanchine had been based at Al Quoz in what was still open desert just off the Abu Dhabi road on the other route to the camel track. State-of-the-art new stables had been built, a seven-furlong sand training track laid down and John Gosden's bright young assistant Jeremy Noseda had joined Simon Crisford on a team that was officially headed by Hilal Ibrahim. We haven't yet mentioned his name but we should have done for he had trained both Al Naes and Abyan Al Ashqar, and you should remember them. They were the horses who had finished first and second in that crazy gallop against the camels towards the dying of the sun.

But no one had any doubt who was behind it all, and we certainly didn't that summer when Frankie Dettori punched Balanchine home through the driving Epsom rain to land a first Classic for himself and, even more significantly, for an operation Sheikh Mohammed had named Godolphin after one of the Arab-reared founding fathers of the thoroughbred. For all those years he had been telling us that horses as well as people would thrive in the winter sunshine of Dubai. Here seemed proof. He could not wait to do it again, and he might as well start with some of his own.

Three two-year-olds went from Warren Place that autumn of 1994. Out of 170 inmates, it did not seem too drastic a depletion, and anyway something much, much worse had happened in Newmarket in September: 34-year-old Alex Scott, already a Breeders' Cup winner, had been shot dead by an embittered employee. These were just horses. The big colt Classic Cliche had got home in one photofinish and been inched out in another. Vettori, another colt, had won handily enough on his final run at Newmarket, but the filly Moonshell was more of a problem. She had won her only race easily and was by champion sire Sadler's Wells out of Moon Cactus, who was that talented filly Steve Cauthen had preferred over little Rafha in the 1990 Prix de Diane. Moonshell looked like she might be a big loss. They would all be.

In May 1995 Vettori and Dettori won the French 2,000 Guineas. In the first week of June Frankie powered Moonshell home in the Oaks on the Friday, and just as he thought he was going to win the next day's Derby on the John Gosden-trained, Sheikh Mohammed-owned Tamure, he was swept aside by Godolphin's own runner Lammtarra under an inspired Walter Swinburn. Lammtarra had won his only other race when trained by poor Alex Scott the previous season. There was sadness among the smiles that day at Epsom but no hiding from the statement Godolphin was making.

A week later Henry was putting a brave face on things. 'I'm not whingeing,' he told the *Guardian*. 'You've got to take a long-term view of everything. Every year Sheikh Mohammed sends me more than 20 yearlings, really nice young horses, and if he wants to take three to

Dubai during the winter I certainly have no complaints.' It was the sensible line to take, but as the season progressed with him only eighth in the trainers' list, some of his own thoughts and of those around him would be rather more extreme. Especially after Classic Cliche made it three lost Classics for Warren Place by winning the St Leger in September. Even more especially when their top-rated two-year-old Mark Of Esteem was given his ticket for a Gulf sunshine winter. Things could get messy.

No one could say they hadn't been warned. Back at Al Quoz as early as January, Sheikh Mohammed had been drooling over Moonshell as the dawn came up in the Emirates sky. The previous year he had in his own right been leading owner in England, Ireland and France, winning 230 races and over £5 million in prize money, but it was obvious Godolphin was his racing pride and joy. The licence was now held by a lean, shy and smiling former policeman called Saeed bin Suroor, whose 1995 statistics would read 19 winners from just 52 runners and a cool £1,970,000 in money won. In March 1995 Sheikh Mohammed had introduced him to us on the eve of the Dubai International Jockeys Challenge, which had brought the likes of Chris McCarron and Pat Day from America, Yukio Okabe from Japan and Mick 'The Enforcer' Dittman from Australia to link up with Dettori and company – 23,000 successes and 350 Group One winners between them. This was only the beginning.

We were gathered in a galleon-sized and much-carpeted tent next to the Al Quoz stables. There was a wind outside and two huge lanterns swung off the tent beams as on a ship at sea. Sheikh Mohammed sat against a row of cushions, cross-legged in his dishdash, and for 40 minutes the greatest investor in racing history extolled his still unbridled enthusiasm for the game that fires him. They were uplifting words, but there were warnings within them. Ten days earlier Dubai had seen its first rain in two years and now its ruler was stating that he would dampen the dreams of anyone bold enough to take him on.

'My trainers must remember that I am the owner,' he said. 'These are my horses and when you own something and see it every day you always appreciate it more. I am a horseman and I like to see my horses. I can come over to Al Quoz in the morning or in the afternoon, and if I'm tied up through business I can ring my trainer and tell him to delay work until I get there. I get annoyed when a trainer tells me I should run my horse at Newmarket rather than Longchamp and I know it is just because he wants to be champion trainer.' There was plenty for me to do that weekend what with the TV transmission of the Jockeys Challenge linked into the opening of the British Flat-race season at Doncaster. But Sheikh Mohammed's remark about the trainer kept gnawing in the soul. Who could he mean?

The collision between the opposed Cecil and Maktoum ambitions may have been inevitable, but another factor precipitated it. Sheikh Mohammed may have championed the cause of girls and horses when his daughter won that horses versus camels race, but he had his limits. In all our trips to Dubai we never saw women doing business by his side. English culture was of course different, but it was also noticeable that his racing team was very much an all-male crew. That was not true at Warren Place. Paddy Rudkin was not the only one to have a problem with what we will call the 'Natalie factor'. Now Sheikh Mohammed did too.

It was difficult for Henry, for everyone. He was happy to listen to his young wife's fresh ideas but not so happy about overruling the less appropriate ones. Natalie would take opposition to her suggestions as proof of staff being old and in need of a shake-up. Resentment was easily stoked on either side. This was not the 'happy, happy ship' of the glory days. The sad thing is that Natalie's energies were aimed at making things better, and she was certainly responsible for smartening up both the house and yard to fine effect. It was the other things that were becoming a Warren Place version of 'the road to hell is paved with good intentions'.

Specifically, Natalie was keen to apply wider equestrian truths to the narrower Flat racing discipline. The show-jumping and dressage worlds focus on exercise and equipment in order to physically and mentally optimise the abilities of the individual horse. In racing and in particular in high-mettle, big-number Flat racing the method is to let the young athletes progress collectively in groups of matching ability. Right from Noel Murless's time, the way at Warren Place was to keep it as simple as possible. The thoroughbred was a 300-year-old genetically programmed galloping machine; you needed to keep its head calm and allow its legs and body to develop without ever losing sight of the fact that it was there to race. Watch the pace of Henry Cecil's string on their first 'canter'. His father-in-law's words in that doubt-ridden first season – 'your horses are galloping like a lot of old gentlemen' – still echoed across the Heath.

It was, of course, 'the way we have always done it'. That's a phrase which has proved challenging for young people down the centuries. It challenged the young wife at Warren Place, and while the theory of fitting bridles with smaller bits might not have caused too much upset, some of the other ideas did, particularly because many of them were founded on principles which either the rider or the horse itself could not satisfy in the racing context. For instance, it's a well-established maxim that if you can get a horse to bend in its head it will in consequence arch its back and lengthen its stride. Indeed the record-breaking French trainer Guillaume Macaire operates a version of this at his base down in Bordeaux: his horses do all their preliminary canters with their head held in by a rubber 'draw rein' running from the bridle to the girth. But Macaire is working with much mentally cooler, jumping-bred horses which don't come to him until well into their two-year-old summer. Trying to do the same with a volatile yearling can be quite a different matter. And it was.

'The trouble was,' says Frank Conlon, who was head lad right through until the beginning of 2006, 'that the guvnor found it very difficult to overrule her. He did one day when Bosra Sham threw herself on the ground after Natalie had put on a standing martingale, and another time when he realised that almost every horse in the string was suddenly wearing bandages. We got on with things, but people found it difficult to speak out.'

One who didn't was Dave Goodwin. He was loyal and hard-working but he had not done the Derby winners Slip Anchor and Commander In Chief without having very clear views of what was possible with a young thoroughbred and what was not. At one stage Natalie tried to tackle the perennial problem of ensuring sufficient padding beneath each saddle at exercise. Sore backs can sour horses and all stables benefit from reviewing their process on a regular basis. You can argue that the padding can hardly be too deep. But Dave didn't like it, and he said so.

'It was not easy to have a showdown,' says the quiet and able Tony McGlone, who had originally joined as jockey and work rider in 1989. 'Natalie produced these great big eventer-style saddle pads. You could see the idea, but if you were riding short for a gallop it meant your legs were right out from the horse. And, worse than that, the padding was so thick that the saddle would shift around on top and the only way to feel secure was to pull the girths up desperately tight. We tried to say something but got overruled. Then one day Dave had to use one and he came into the office, threw it down and said, "I am not ****ing using that again." It did the trick.'

Such stories no doubt filtered back to Sheikh Mohammed and to those thought to have his ear with derogatory gossip. But with his hands-on style, he could see for himself. And so, at least on the racecourse, could we. At the Chester May meeting in 1995 my TV position was in a glass-fronted hutch set above the weighing room overlooking the paddock. Next to it was a similar construction occupied by the West Merseyside Constabulary with a long lens and a notebook. 'This is where the Manchester crime families come out to play,' they confided. 'Look, there's old Joe the Fence. Didn't know he was out. And look who he's with.' I was studying form not 'The Fancy', but looking down that day the strongest memory remains the completely integrated not to say assertive way in which Natalie gelled with her husband Henry.

He was stylish and hatless as usual, with the Gucci shoes, pink socks, dark narrow slacks and elegant blue cashmere jackets which have become his trademark. She was looking young and snappily smart in an outfit recently enhanced after a trip to Chester's extensive boutiques which the two shopaholics so favoured. But it was her proximity to her man that was so noticeable. All trainers' wives have a difficult row to hoe at the races as part hostess, part saddling assistant, part translator of their husbands' reactions (or lack of them) to triumph and disaster. Natalie had come to play her job as not so much on hand as right under her husband's right shoulder.

Chester's 'Roodee' racetrack is famed for the tightness of its circuit packed in between the city's ancient Roman walls and the eternal beauty of the River Dee. The paddock and saddling area is equally cramped, and down there trainer and wife moved from saddle collection across to saddling boxes, to paddock to owner greeting, jockey briefing, race watching, winner's or loser's circle and happy or worried post-race conference before starting the same process all over again. My position was too far away to hear what was said but it was clear that Natalie did plenty of talking. She was unlikely to stay silent for anyone.

It all kicked off in September after Classic Cliche, in Warren Place terms, rubbed their noses in it by winning the St Leger. In the next week Sheikh Mohammed returned to claim some more horses as his own. By 21 September it was too much for Peter Robinson, a retired bookkeeper whose Newmarket home is piled high with every sort of Henry Cecil record and quite a few of Cecil Boyd-Rochfort's. Dog-loving Peter would be on the extreme wing of the Warren Place fan club, but his letter to the *Sporting Life* spoke for a much wider constituency:

Henry Cecil must be on the point of despair, and who can blame him? Last year the Godolphin operation took three of his best two-year-olds, Classic Cliche, Moonshell and Vettori, to Dubai, and this year they have all become Classic winners. Now in the space of five days the Master of Warren Place has also lost Allied Forces, the fifth Group-winning two-year-old to have run for Cecil this year. As a long-time supporter and fan of the yard, I not only feel despair but feel very angry as well. All five of these horses were broken, nurtured and made as two-year-olds at Warren Place only for the glory to go to Dubai.

Allied Forces had not been seen since Goodwood in July, but Mark Of Esteem had been due to appear in Ascot's Royal Lodge Stakes on the Saturday after Peter Robinson's letter. 'Mark Of Esteem has been working very well but I've been told not to run him at Ascot as he is going to Dubai,' Henry said, before continuing, 'I am very disheartened and disappointed, especially as this is the fourth Group-class two-year-old I have lost to Dubai in the last two years. It is also very disheartening for the staff who work so hard on these horses only to lose them before their three-year-old careers.'

Henry's reaction had been fairly circumspect, but Natalie's was reported as rather less so, roundly condemning Sheikh Mohammed on behalf of her husband and his staff. The Sheikh was not used to being challenged by women, and come Saturday at Ascot the hack pack had another summons, this time to his plush private box overlooking the racecourse where a much more brutal point was made than the one to those gathered beneath the swinging lanterns back in Dubai six months earlier.

'Henry Cecil is a great trainer,' said the Sheikh in his deceptively soft, deep, very clear although still quite accented English, 'but when he allows people who hardly know anything about thoroughbred horses to interfere, that is a bad thing. He knows about it. Everyone in Newmarket does.'

It was a breathtaking public rebuke, and the defence came in the next morning's *Sunday Telegraph*. 'Not only is she knowledgeable,' Henry said about his consort, 'but she is very streetwise and a perfectionist. Women play a very important part in the life of a trainer, you know. My wife Julie was a tremendous help and Natalie is as well. This is not a one-man show.'

This was very obviously unfinished business. On the Sunday afternoon the Wafic Said-owned Bosra Sham did the Warren Place talking by sprinting to favouritism for the following year's 1,000 Guineas by winning Ascot's Fillies' Mile with the Godolphin-trained Bint Shadayid three long lengths adrift. On the Tuesday at Newmarket a two-year-old called Helicon became what was to be the last Henry Cecil-trained winner for Sheikh Mohammed. In the unsaddling enclosure the two men shook hands rather formally, but any suggestion that this was a rapprochement ended when Warren Place received a fax on the Friday afternoon instructing that Sheikh Mohammed's two runners Kalabo and Marocco should be withdrawn from their respective races next day. 'It's a pity they did not tell us earlier,' the trainer commented tersely.

The final bombshell did not come until the following Tuesday, and it erupted into the massive *Racing Post* headline 'Henry Cecil Sacked'. Allegations were made that when Mark Of Esteem reached Dubai he was found to be suffering from a degenerative knee injury and would not have been able to run at Ascot anyway. In consequence all Sheikh Mohammed's horses were to leave Warren Place as soon as possible. Henry and Natalie were at Goffs Yearling Sales in Ireland. Over the phone it was suggested that the departure should be staged over the next few weeks. Harsh words were spoken. On Wednesday a fleet of boxes shuttled all 35 horses away down Warren Hill. Frank Conlon wept as he saw them go.

'I'll just say one thing,' Henry Cecil concluded. 'After the last two weeks of what has been written and read, his decision to take his horses away is probably the best thing.'

Six months on, the trainer would be saying something else. He would be thanking Sheikh Mohammed for giving him a 'kick up the butt'. Mind you, with the filly Bosra Sham he now had at his disposal one of the most powerful and graceful butts of his whole career.

10

THE FALLON YEARS

BOSRA SHAM was big enough to be almost buxom, and she was certainly beautiful and brilliant from the start. She was a blonde, not too pale and flashy a chestnut but a perfect mid-tan with long, often pricked ears and an open face with a lengthy white blaze down the front and matching white socks on her hind legs. She was as attractive as chestnut fillies come. She may not have been quite what Raymond Chandler had in mind when he wrote 'she was the sort of blonde that would make a bishop kick in a stained-glass window' but she was the type of horse for which people would raid the bank.

For she was also 'bred in the purple'. Her half-brother, Shanghai, had won the French 2,000 Guineas, as had her full-brother Hector Protector, whose nine victories in 1990 and 1991 made him the outstanding two-year-old and then three-year-old miler in Europe. Little wonder that there was an expectant hush when Bosra Sham, announced as merely the unnamed 'chestnut filly by Woodman, a full-sister to Hector Protector', was led into the Tattersalls sales ring one October night in 1994. Even a bishop might have held his breath.

Wafic Said didn't. The Syrian businessman and philanthropist had originally made his money in banking and construction through

239

his close links to the Saudi royal family and had helped Margaret Thatcher land the controversial multi-billion-pound Al-Yamamah arms and fighter plane deal in 1985. Married to an Englishwoman, Wafic was an anglophile whose lasting legacies will be the Said Business School at Oxford University and Tusmore Park, the award-winning neo-Georgian mansion he had built 15 miles north of the city. It was in the 1990s that he made his impact on the turf. He first had connections with Henry Cecil in 1993 when his racing manager Tim Bulwer-Long spent more than £300,000 for a colt and a filly at the Newmarket October yearling sales. A year later neither of them had yet run, although the colt, called Balliol Boy, was to win first time out at Nottingham three weeks after Bosra Sham had been through the sale ring.

The sales watchers were expecting fireworks and they got them. As the filly circled the ring the normally genial 'Captain' Tim Bulwer-Long was a stony-faced figure, staring at the auctioneer from under his tilted-back trilby with just the occasional, seemingly random nod to take the bidding higher. When he reached 530,000gns all opposition was over and Wafic Said was the owner of the most expensive yearling sold in England or Ireland that season. Such prices have never been any guarantee of success, of course. Back in 1983 Sheikh Mohammed had spent no less than $10.2 million on a Northern Dancer yearling who was to be called Snaafi Dancer. Although well made and nicely mannered, Snaafi Dancer proved too slow to race and so infertile that he could father only four foals. Bosra Sham was to be a shining, gliding, gleaming chestnut exception.

'It might sound silly,' says jockey Tony McGlone, 'but when you were riding her, you would keep getting a smile on your face. She was so sweet and attractive and you could feel she was good straight away. She wasn't that tall, but she was quite beautifully balanced and she had this lovely round, powerful backside on her. She wasn't nearly as big, nor as hard pulling, as Indian Skimmer, and she didn't have anything like the long-eared ranginess of Oh So Sharp. But whatever you worked her with, however fast you went, she could just coast in behind them. When she was a two-year-old, I rode her with Mark Of Esteem before she won the Fillies' Mile and I was sure I went the better. That's how good she was, and she knew it. She was not all sweetness. She had a ruthless streak in her. I think all good fillies do. She would walk along with her ears pricked and then something would get too close and she would turn her arse and go "whack" with both barrels. She liked to assert herself.'

So of course did her trainer, and in the spring of 1996 Henry Cecil was doing just that. Predictors of doom after the previous autumn's debacle were being met with a head-on energy that took even his admirers by surprise. 'I have never talked about my split with Sheikh Mohammed,' he told the *Daily Mail*'s Colin Mackenzie in March, 'except to say that as an owner he is entitled to do what he wants to. But now I must thank him for kicking me up the butt and giving me renewed ambition. I have lost a stone and a half in weight, I haven't smoked for 16 months and I haven't had a drink for two years now. In fact this whole business has given me a new lease of life. The yard is buzzing and, frankly, it's quite exciting. It's a challenge for all of us and the stable is very united from the head lad right through to the newest lad.'

Henry Cecil may have lost Sheikh Mohammed six months earlier, and his core group of friends when Natalie replaced Julie at Warren Place in 1991, but there was detail in the defiance of the old lion's roar as he looked forward to the summer of 1996. 'I have been very fortunate that my existing owners have been very supportive,' he said to Colin, 'and it was not necessary to make any lads redundant when Sheikh Mohammed's horses left. I have been particularly well supported by the Saudi royal family: Prince Khalid Abdulla has 40 horses in the yard, Prince Fahd Salman has ten horses, Prince Faisal six and Prince Ahmed Salman four. I have 175 horses in training, which is plenty. I had 200 last year but I am very happy with what I've got. As you get older you have got to pace yourself, but the adrenalin is coursing again thanks to this fresh challenge. It is my ambition to be champion trainer again.'

A month later, on the Wednesday afternoon of the Newmarket Craven meeting, Henry was putting that ambition into winning effect, but at 7.15 that morning he had summoned a whole gaggle of us for coffee at Warren Place to celebrate his new marriage – to Saab. This was Henry Cecil post-Maktoum, Britain's most famous racing stable apparently in a full embrace with the business world. Here was the sponsor's managing director, marketing director, media adviser and enough assorted consultants, hacks and cameras for a major product launch. But it was still vintage Cecil from the very first, for in the world of big business you don't normally find too many people clad in suede leather leggings with blue tassels down the side. Not many of them get loaded on to a dashing white charger before eight in the morning, and certainly none of them can ever have done so sporting a mauve velvet hat while proclaiming their love of Saab to the waiting minions.

Our motley crew giggled and goggled as some of the most coveted quadrupeds in the kingdom filed out of the yard towards Warren Hill, but you noticed outsiders turning to each other and asking, 'Can this man really be serious?' For in some ways this seemed like pantomime time, with all of us streaming across the lawns and the gravel to scramble into cars and career down the road before then straggling over to the side of the Polytrack gallop to await the master's briefing on the four-legged pupils thundering past. But even Cecil's feyest phrases could not disguise the pride, almost menace, in his voice. 'Dushyantor,' he said, indicating a big bay horse storming by, 'Sadler's Wells half-brother to Commander In Chief. Mile and a half horse. Had some foot problems but is fine now. Will run in one of the Derby trials. Love the family.'

On the horses came, and on and on went a litany to send any punter off to prayer. Only snatches stick in the memory. 'Silver Dome, he goes for the Thresher Classic Trial' – he did, finished down the field, and was never seen again. 'Lady Carla, she's an Oaks filly' – she proved to be just that, and how. But the simplest statement came as a beautiful chestnut filly swung past, ears cocked, neck erect, shoulders flowing with class in every line. 'There's Bosra Sham,' said Henry. 'She should need no introduction.'

He had two runners that afternoon. One was third, the other came good in the last race. So far in 1996 he had saddled 11 runners, four of which had been winners, six placed and only one out of the first three. He had long been a giant, but this looked like a giant dangerously refreshed.

Yet it is not modesty but the truth when Henry Cecil, and any other racehorse trainer with an ounce of sense, stresses that his is a team game. Never was this more obvious than in Bosra Sham's crowning achievements that season. For while her body was brilliant her feet were fragile. They were shallow with thin soles and were terribly liable to bruising. As a two-year-old, problems with her near fore had forced her to miss Doncaster's May Hill Stakes in early September 1995, and after skating up in her Newbury 'prep' in April 1996, trouble with the same foot threatened her participation in the 1,000 Guineas right up till the very last minute. Two days before the race she was lame enough for the farrier to have to treat the foot by building it up with padding and putting a shoe over it. On the eve of the race the little filly was still partly lame and only poultices got her to the racetrack sound.

The trainer lost plenty of sleep, but not as much as Nick Curtis the farrier, Richard Greenwood the vet, or John Scott, the Freddie

Mercury-moustached stable lad who tended her throughout this time. 'It was a nightmare for everyone,' said Barnsley-born Stewart Broadhead, travelling head lad since 1993, having joined the stable in 1980. He had come to Newmarket as an apprentice to trainer John Waugh to escape going down the pit like his dad. 'She was brilliant but her feet were terrible. Even walking her off the box was dangerous and we always had her led round on the grass in the paddock lest she get even the tiniest stone in her hoof.'

All the attention paid off, but Bosra Sham's Classic victory came at a price. Her feet were not just sore but bleeding after that 1,000 Guineas and the Warren Place team were not able to get her back on to the racecourse until the autumn, and they had to do so without the help of Nick Curtis. For at the height of the drama a dissatisfied Natalie had another farrier helicoptered in from the New Forest. 'He came in one evening,' says Richard Greenwood. 'It was like a scene

Bosra Sham with owner Wafic Said and Henry after winning the 1,000 Guineas, 1996.

from a Vietnam movie.' For Curtis, a war with the boss's wife was one he could not win.

Bosra Sham was the star, yet with 113 winners in total this was anything but a one-horse season. Godolphin were again big players of course: Mark Of Esteem returned from his desert winter to land the 2,000 Guineas and Henry's first winnerless Royal Ascot since 1973 also included the salt-in-the-wound sight of his Godolphin-trained ex-pupils Charnwood Forest and Classic Cliche winning the Queen Anne Stakes and the Gold Cup respectively. But some people were already publicly querying the idea that the Godolphin operation was doing no more than making an elite band out of its owner's outspread resources. The claim was that the warm-weather training undergone by the Dubai-based runners was giving them a specific advantage in early season. Some trainers were even saying despondently, 'We can't compete.'

How come, we countered, that Balanchine, so impressive in the 1994 Oaks when fully acclimatised, had a month earlier failed to beat the Irish filly Las Meninas, who had spent the colder months splashing through the mud during one of Tipperary's wettest winters? Were people really suggesting that Moonshell and Lammtarra, who had both shown such promise in 1994, would not have won the Oaks and Derby if they had remained trained at Newmarket in 1995? And before anyone danced on Henry Cecil's grave in celebration of Mark Of Esteem's admirably game 2,000 Guineas triumph in 1996, perhaps they could check out the winter routines of two horses whom he probably only bested in that tightest of three-way photofinishes because an inspired Frankie Dettori got a run up against the inside rail. Second-placed Even Top, beaten by about a millimetre, had spent his winter in Newmarket; equally close third Bijou D'Inde had been prepared in the cold and snowy heights of Middleham in North Yorkshire. Neither had run before the Guineas and neither ran much better later in the season, while Mark Of Esteem was almost a stone superior come the autumn. His coat was certainly much shinier, but that was because it had been in the sunshine. The argument that he had gained some sort of 'advantage' by converting what would have been a Newmarket 'home' match into an 'away' fixture was standing logic on its head.

The new 'Maktoum-less' Henry Cecil could let his horses do the talking. The Godolphin filly Bint Shadayid had toiled in third behind Bosra Sham in the Guineas at Newmarket and things went even better at Epsom when Bosra Sham's little stablemate Lady Carla drew nine lengths clear of the Godolphin favourite Pricket, who had spent her previous summer, guess where – at Warren Place! The diminutive Lady Carla ran in the same white and green Wafic Said colours as Bosra Sham, and as she had cost 'only' 220,000gns on that same night at the yearling sales the 'Captain' (Tim Bulwer-Long) can claim to have landed bargain buys, even more so when the two fillies went to stud and their progeny were sold for millions more. Other stars came in more familiar silks, the Khalid Abdulla-owned Dushyantor winning the Great Voltigeur and coming second in both the Derby and the St Leger, and Eva Luna winning the fillies' St Leger, the Park Hill Stakes. Among the Prince Khalid two-year-olds, Reams Of Verse took the Fillies' Mile at Ascot and Yashmak only just failed in the French equivalent, the Prix Marcel Boussac at Longchamp. Considering Henry also trained Sleepytime, who was favourite and an unlucky third behind Reams Of Verse at Ascot, the trainer was not just having a good season, these three top two-year-olds were setting targets for the next.

Yet the highlight of 1996 was always going to be Bosra Sham. The stable knew how good she was but it was hard to win the battle with her feet. Royal Ascot, Goodwood and York came and went but finally she was sound enough to have a public gallop at the Doncaster

St Leger meeting before turning out at the big Ascot 'Festival of Racing' on 28 September. This was to prove a historic racing day, and Bosra Sham had only a bit part. This was the day of Frankie Dettori's unforgettable, impossible, through-the-card 'Magnificent Seven', and Mark Of Esteem's brilliant acceleration to apparently toy with Bosra Sham in the Queen Elizabeth II Stakes was seen by many as the highlight. But Henry Cecil and his team knew how well their filly had done to finish so close after such a long absence. They were not to dream that she could have a history day of her own.

The 1996 Champion Stakes had just about everything you could ask for in terms of all three Classic phases that make up a great horse race: anticipation, realisation and appreciation. The frisson began in the billing. For this was now the 'Dubai' Champion Stakes and victory for Bosra Sham would see Sheikh Mohammed handing Henry Cecil the trophy as an ultimate symbol of the trainer's return from the previous year's personal rebuff. To do that she would have to beat the very best horses around: Even Top was back on the track where he had run Mark Of Esteem to that millimetre verdict in the spring, the Irish filly Timarida was on a unique roll of top-class victories in Munich, Chicago and Leopardstown, and Godolphin fielded the five-year-old Halling, who started hot favourite after going undefeated in Europe that season. But as ever, the biggest challenge for Bosra Sham was her own feet.

Vet and farrier and lad and trainer worked incessantly to hold those hooves together, knowing that above the legs Bosra Sham was better than ever. 'She was tough as old boots at the heart of it,' remembers Tony McGlone. 'In one of her first pieces of work on the way back she was going rather lazy on me and I had to give her a smack. I never had to do that again. She was very willing and very, very good. At the end of a gallop Henry always used to come up and ask how your horse had worked. But she went so brilliantly in her last piece before the Champion Stakes that he didn't say anything. It had only ever happened one other time and that was after Commander In Chief's last bit of work before the Irish Derby. He just smiled and I smiled. He knew and I knew.'

But the world knew how difficult it would be to get Bosra Sham to the start in one piece. Stewart Broadhead had a strip of coconut laid down on the ramp of the horse box to cushion the descent. John Scott religiously kept the filly on the grass in the Newmarket paddock, and as the stalls opened Pat Eddery's strong but calm fingers had the best filly in the world at the end of the rein. He was far too great a jockey to be anything but clinical in his execution. Frankie Dettori and Halling took over from the pace-making Even Top three furlongs out, but Bosra Sham was always moving deadly behind her. Coming to the bottom of the dip in this longest of all straight runs in racing, Pat asked his filly to strike and in an instant Bosra Sham brushed aside the also-challenging Timarida and cut clear of Halling all the way to the line. At the finish she had two and a half lengths over Halling, with Timarida another length away third and Even Top beaten only a head in fourth. Bosra Sham had taken herself to the top of the European rankings and Henry Cecil above Godolphin in the trainers' table. But she had done more than all this. She had reduced that Newmarket crowd to something close to a religious outpouring of happiness.

I was standing in the centre with the TV cameras and it was an astonishing place to be as the feeling hooked into both those closest and those afar. In the saddle, the normally restrained Pat Eddery was almost ecstatic as he said, 'She's a great filly, that was electrifying.' Beside him John Scott and Stewart Broadhead were wreathed in smiles, and vet Richard Greenwood just couldn't believe the pleasure. 'After all we had been through with her,' he remarked. 'That was my best moment ever on a racecourse.'

But the ultimate focus went beyond the horse to its trainer. The crowd were welcoming Henry back as their own. Suggestions that he would never again train at the level of the glory days, most of all the thoughts that he could not recover from the Sheikh Mohammed blow 12 months earlier, were now scattered to the winds as 'three cheers' were called and then were roared upwards to the Suffolk sky. And as Henry walked forward to collect the trophy there was the Sheikh himself, his face all smiles, to present it.

By perfect chance the trophy was a large, ancient, perhaps ornamental but still fairly lethal-looking Arabian dagger. With considerable style Sheikh Mohammed handed it to Henry handle first and then cowered back in mock terror at the prospect of the trainer taking retribution. It didn't just defuse the situation, it lifted it high into the memory, and any scribbler worth his salt had to dip the pen in purple. The *Racing Post*'s Paul Haigh did not let us down:

Sometimes in sport you get a moment in which triumph is so complete, vindication so unarguable, that you just have to think to yourself, 'I wonder how that feels.' You only get it a few times and the crucial ingredient is a triumphant comeback after what had appeared to be a crippling blow. Muhammad Ali's defeat of George Foreman is the perfect example. Sebastian Coe's 1500m gold medal after he had lost the one he was supposed to win is another. Nobody with an interest in British racing could have failed to wonder how Henry Cecil felt when he saw Bosra Sham bursting away from two animals who, as Pat Eddery pointed out afterwards (his voice rising to a squeak in his excitement), were 'the best turf horses in the world'. Nobody could have failed to wonder what was going through Cecil's mind as he made his way through the crowd to receive the trophy from the sponsor's hands. There will have been a lot of people looking very carefully at that moment, looking for

*any sign of churlishness or animosity. They wouldn't have seen it
even in their own imaginations. Cecil was as gracious and elegant
a winner as he would have been a loser if things had gone the
other way. Sheikh Mohammed will have won friends too in his
demonstration of both generosity and humour in defeat.*

It had been the most spectacular of days, and it gave an unexpected
lift to what is often the dull fag end of the Flat racing season, as a
duel then developed between Henry Cecil and Godolphin's Saeed bin
Suroor for the trainers' title. For a while it looked as if Cecil would hold
on to his advantage. Simon Crisford even asked Sheikh Mohammed
if he 'felt like a lame duck', only to receive the prophetic answer, 'No,
Simon, I am a lion who has a pine needle in its paw.' But while victory
for Medaaly in the Racing Post Trophy clinched that trainers' title
for Suroor and Godolphin, Bosra Sham was voted ahead of Mark Of
Esteem as Horse of the Year and Henry Cecil was honoured as Flat
Trainer of the Year at the Horserace Writers Awards.

But nothing in that season ever bettered that reception at
Newmarket. 'Big moments don't come any bigger,' Paul Haigh
concluded. 'Triumph doesn't come any better than total. If Mr Cecil
is ever going to surpass this one, you'd want to be writing his scripts.'

The wonder of this book is that surpassing the Bosra Sham
moment is exactly what the Henry Cecil saga would one day do.

Instinct can be an irritating thing, especially to those who don't
understand it and who then see it turn the irrational into the rational
when applied by someone else. It had been like that with Henry Cecil,
and we subscribers to the orthodox had long agreed that he couldn't
be the fool he sometimes pretended to be. But the news he announced
in August 1996 once again raised the eyebrows – and the possibility of
the later irritation of him proving us all wrong.

For up to then few people had placed any significance on the jockey booking for the Henry Cecil-trained stayer Corradini when it beat stable companion Prussian Blue in a four-runner race at Doncaster on 30 June. But the trainer obviously did because he booked the same rider when the horse next ran and finished third in the Ebor Handicap at York. By then he had also taken a perceptive but ultimately fateful decision. He had signed Kieren Fallon as his jockey.

Kieren was a talent and a coming man all right. That year at Royal Ascot he had won the Hunt Cup for Lester Piggott's son-in-law William Haggas and the Windsor Castle Stakes (first time out) on Michael Stoute's top two-year-old filly Dazzle, on whom he had doubled up in the Cherry Hinton Stakes at the Newmarket July meeting. But to most of us, particularly those away from the north where Kieren had been based since moving from Ireland as a heavy and not very successful apprentice in 1988, he seemed a long way from the elite mould of the champions Mercer, Piggott, Cauthen and Eddery to whom the Cecil horses had hitherto been entrusted.

A plasterer's son from County Clare, Kieren Fallon was already 31 years old when he took Henry's call. By the same age Pat Eddery, whom he was in effect replacing, had won the Derby, the Oaks, the King George and the Prix de l'Arc de Triomphe. Fallon's biggest success before Royal Ascot had been winning the Lincoln Handicap, Gimcrack and Chester Cup for his extremely astute retaining stable of Lynda and Jack Ramsden just outside Thirsk, that little North Yorkshire town where Alf Wight (James Herriot) had worked as a vet for Noel Murless. Indeed the controversy surrounding that Chester Cup victory in May 1995, allied to the far greater furore the previous September when Kieren earned himself a six-month suspension for pulling fellow jockey Stuart Webster off his mount after a race at Beverley, had blinded most of us to something hugely significant linking the two events. For Fallon had spent his exile riding track work in America and had used his time alongside the likes of Chris McCarron, Gary Stevens, Jerry Bailey, Laffit Pincay and Eddie Delahoussaye to make a quantum leap in his development as a jockey.

'In America,' he told Marcus Armytage at the start of 1997, 'my confidence increased. I feel much better balanced now, much more comfortable on a horse, and I tightened up. British jockeys tend to push and shove and jump around on a horse. In America they teach you to get down behind a horse like Bill Shoemaker did. It was the best six months of my life. It taught me to ride a race to suit a horse, not the horse to suit the race.'

But most of us hadn't logged much of this except to note that in 1995, the year after his return, Kieren Fallon had scored a career-best 91 winners in the 11th season since he had ridden his first success on a horse called Piccadilly Lord at Navan in County Kildare. What we had done is get quite overexcited when he brought the already seasoned stayer Top Cees slicing through to land the Chester Cup for the Ramsdens. For on their previous run, horse and jockey had been beaten in controversial circumstances when favourite at Newmarket. In all the brouhaha – the *Sporting Life* was eventually taken to court and had to pay libel damages for their race report – few mentioned what a masterly race Kieren had ridden at Chester.

Fifteen months later the press and therefore the public reaction was much the same when news came through of the Henry Cecil contract. No matter that Kieren Fallon had that same week achieved his first century of winners in a season; there was much more emphasis on his temper, his many suspensions, the Stuart Webster incident and the Top Cees controversy than on the possibility of what actually happened – that Kieren would develop into one of the great riders of his generation. As so often we did not give Henry much credit for it at the time. He was quoted as saying all the right things. That Pat Eddery 'had been a great friend and a great help to me' and how he would help him to be champion jockey, as indeed Pat would be for an 11th and final time that season at the vintage age of 44; that Kieren was 'the most exciting I have seen' of the emerging jockey talent and that 'I wanted somebody young as you've got to be thinking of the future'. But most of us just thought Henry had gone for Kieren because rumours were racing around that Fallon was about to sign for arch rival Michael Stoute. Such is the grudginess of life.

Naturally there was a bit of truth in that, but there were other factors at work. Prince Khalid's camp had decided they were not going to have a retained jockey for all their horses regardless of who trained them as they had in the past with Pat Eddery. But obviously Henry could not make any appointment without first running it past Prince Khalid and his racing manager Grant Pritchard-Gordon.

Henry Cecil flanked by stable stalwart Willie Ryan (left) and new stable jockey Kieren Fallon.

Normally neither the Prince nor Pritchard-Gordon would have had a view on a northern-based jockey. But enquiries made after Fallon's high-profile Michael Stoute-trained successes on Dazzle at Ascot and Newmarket would have elicited the information that Kieren had made a big impression on Abdulla's American trainer Bobby Frankel when riding work in California.

So there were likely to be few difficulties in getting the Fallon appointment ratified by Prince Khalid, Henry's greatest supporter numerically and owner of five of the top ten highest-rated Warren Place horses in 1996. What was not such an easy 'sell' was persuading Wafic Said, owner of Bosra Sham and Lady Carla, the two highest-rated of all. 'Wafic was not happy,' says Tim Bulwer-Long. 'He wanted to keep Pat Eddery on Bosra Sham in particular. But Henry was insistent and we agreed, but only with the proviso that if there were any "mistakes" Eddery would be reinstated.' Jockeys know the guillotine is always poised neatly above their neck. But in Kieren Fallon's case with Bosra Sham it was on nearly as light a catch as the notoriously sceptical southern press were making it out to be.

Yet Kieren had already been through too much to be fazed by adverse publicity. 'Because it's a job everyone wants,' he told his northern confidant Tom O'Ryan at the turn of the year, 'I know that some people will be hoping I fall flat on my face. I've even heard they have been betting on how long I will last, but I am going into this job full of confidence. People say to me there will be a lot of pressure but I don't see it like that. When you are riding good horses, it makes the whole job easier. I haven't a worry in the world. What I call pressure is riding a fancied one for the Ramsdens that you have been told to hold up and trying to find your way through 15 horses from the home turn at Beverley. That's pressure!'

It was an attitude that served him well when he moved south and started riding out at Warren Place in February 1997. 'We took to Kieren straight away,' said Frank Conlon. 'He loved riding out and spending time with the horses. The lads liked him because he was very open with them and didn't just want to come in and ride work and leave. He would always hack home with everyone and talk about how the gallops had gone.'

Willie Ryan also did not need much convincing despite having more reason than most for not entirely welcoming Fallon's arrival. Willie had been on the Warren Place team for ten years and had been the stable's principal jockey outside Pat Eddery. Indeed when Willie finally retired from the saddle in 2004 his record of 380 winners was second only to Steve Cauthen's 418 in terms of successes for Henry Cecil.

'When I first heard the news of his appointment I did feel a bit put out,' says Willie, 'a touch of "what does this northern kid know about it?" But I had a job and I got on with it. Kieren was fine. He enjoyed riding out and mucked in with everyone, although he was a bit raw in his knowledge. If you said a filly was from one of the Howard de Walden families he wouldn't know what you were talking about. I remember telling him that one was the right sort for the Musidora [the Musidora Stakes, the principal Oaks trial at York in May] and he went all Irish and said, "What's the Mewsey-Dooorah?"'

Fallon's crash course in the snakes and ladders of the Classic season started perfectly with the Derby hope Street General winning the opening race of the Craven meeting followed by the Stavros Niarchos-owned Dokos, a full-brother to the dual Breeders' Cup winner Miesque, winning the Wood Ditton Stakes. But the critics were soon on his back when he and 1,000 Guineas favourite Sleepytime were badly blocked on the inside before finishing only fourth in Newbury's Fred Darling Stakes two days later. Fallon was unfamiliar and they didn't fancy him. They didn't like his default option of taking his time, and even the normally charitable John Francome wondered about the apparent loose-rein untidiness of his finishing style. Three furlongs out in the 1,000 itself and the sceptics had their man. 'Sleepytime behind a wall of horses,' called the commentator.

But then she wasn't. With the neatest of symmetry a gap came inside the filly Dazzle, on whom Kieren had made his name the previous summer. Sleepytime stormed through it and left Fallon's first Classic field four lengths adrift. Cecil was all smiles. 'He really loves his horses,' he said in tribute to his jockey, who returned the compliment by saying about his trainer, 'It was great for him. He had put his head on the chopping block by hiring me. Today I needed to repay him.' Kieren's smile might never be as wide again. It split his face so much from ear to ear that his eyes bulged to accommodate it. Fourteen years into the racing game, but in fewer than 14 weeks as Henry Cecil's jockey, he had come to the Classic big-time and not been found wanting. Vindication doesn't come much sweeter than this.

For two glorious months the tide rolled on; it even washed over a ten-day riding ban by the Italian authorities that would have meant Kieren missing Epsom and Ascot had it not been deferred on appeal. On Guineas day Fallon had taken the next two races to log a treble. At York he found out exactly what the 'Mewsey-Dooorah' was by winning it on the Cecil Oaks hope Reams Of Verse by an official 11 lengths which might soon have been 20. At Epsom he and she took the Oaks itself after getting out of a typical Derby-course bumping match in the last quarter-mile. And so on to Royal Ascot. The Oaks fourth Yashmak won the Ribblesdale by nine lengths in the driving rain on the Thursday, but the greatest memory was what happened on the Wednesday when Fallon asked Bosra Sham to really run in the Prince of Wales's.

One moment she was fourth and not going much better than the others. The next she had swept up and past them, her ever suspect hooves getting such a bite out of that green, green Ascot grass that you realised you were seeing something special. On and on she came. Up, up went the cheers. By the time she passed the post there was acclamation. At 4-11 she cannot have earned many punters much profit, and Wafic Said didn't need the money, but a huge roar went up as John Scott and Stewart Broadhead led Bosra Sham into the winner's corner.

There was such a crush that the man behind us was clapping her with his hands trapped down by his thighs. As he came through you could see it was Henry Cecil. He was weepily overjoyed. As ever he went first to her and then to John and Stewart. When we closed in on him he said she was the best filly he had ever trained and how proud they all were to have her.

It was Ascot in high summer and for a few moments all the world owned Bosra Sham. Then, in one of those lovely public-to-private moves that are easily missed at the races, ownership passed back not to the theatrically dressed mastermind of a trainer or even to the sleek munificence of Wafic Said, but to the drooping Freddie Mercury moustache of John Scott who took 'his' filly off to the washdown.

'I have done some good fillies, like All At Sea and Moonshell, but this is the best by miles,' said John, whose mother died in childbirth and whose lot was Barnardo's and a foster home before he ended up with David Cecil in Lambourn. 'She likes to do things her own way but that trouble with her foot has completely cleared up. What she does is take her work and her food and never leaves an oat. She just loves this life.' Bosra Sham's chestnut coat darkened under the water and the strength of her muscle pattern showed hard along her flanks and across those powerful hindquarters. As she was led out to dry, a little girl stepped in for a photo. The filly's pose was nothing short of regal. All seemed well in the world. It would only take another race to change it.

The 1997 Eclipse Stakes was neither the jockey's nor the trainer's greatest moment. And just to make the mix worse it wasn't the horse's either. The Bosra Sham of the Prince of Wales's or the Champion Stakes would surely have won whatever the tactics. Perhaps everything had gone too well at Ascot. Even Henry, certainly several us on the Channel 4 team, had lost a bit of perspective. Bosra Sham was only a racehorse, not a jet plane, and a major Group One race always needs plenty of winning. This one did – especially for Kieren Fallon as the five-runner field swung right-handed and headed up the Sandown hill with three long furlongs ahead of them.

For while he had only four opponents three of them, Benny The Dip, Pilsudski and Sasuru, were ahead or close to the left of him. And while Bosra Sham was going well beneath him, the pace set by Willie Ryan (no less) on Benny The Dip had been steady enough that the others had plenty to sprint with too. Two and a half furlongs out at Sandown the inside rail is taken back to widen the course. With his path blocked to the left Fallon launched Bosra Sham into this opening only to find that Ryan was quite legitimately planning to move across and take the space himself. There are only black-or-white judgements for manoeuvres like Kieren's: if your horse has the speed to get through in time you are a hero; if she doesn't you will be hung from the highest hook. Within an instant we and he knew that Kieren was ceiling bound.

There was no animosity in what Willie Ryan did. He may have smarted a little when Fallon was appointed but in July 1997 he was having his best ever season, in and out of the Cecil yard. Indeed his career highlight had come just a month earlier when his enterprise and determination on this same Benny The Dip had won him the Derby for trainer John Gosden. Willie was a professional, and the professional thing to do was to make that inside rail his own.

There was a collective groan from the stands as they saw Bosra Sham's passage blocked and the green colours having to pull back and round to the outside in hopeless pursuit of the powerful Pilsudski, whose rider Mick Kinane had sent him past Benny The Dip just as Kieren had vainly opted for the inside.

It hardly helped that Kinane had some recent history with the Cecil stable. Notwithstanding Mick's triumphs for them on Commander In Chief and Belmez, or his fourth on Yashmak to Reams Of Verse in that 1997 Oaks, Henry had been convinced (although the stewards were not) that the 13-times Irish champion jockey had blatantly interfered with both Lady Carla and Canon Can in their respective races (the Hardwicke Stakes and the Queen Alexandra Stakes) at Royal Ascot. In a most uncharacteristic outburst on the Sunday of the Royal meeting Henry said about Kinane, 'I think he wants to seriously watch himself. I don't know what he's doing but a jockey of his class should not be banging into my horses and bumping them around.' Kinane did no more than say he was 'surprised and disappointed' at the remarks, adding with a lift of those famous ginger eyebrows, 'these sort of incidents happen in races all the time. They're in the nature of the game.' As Mick drove his mount forward, such thoughts were well behind him. For Henry, they would only make Bosra Sham's unavailing pursuit of Pilsudski even harder to swallow.

In the stand Wafic Said was so angry that he refused to come down to the unsaddling enclosure. But his manager did. 'The moment I got there,' relates Tim Bulwer-Long, 'Henry said, "All right, all right, Eddery rides her next time." He was so wound up he could hardly speak. When the press surrounded him you could see he was at snapping point.'

Ah, the press; the bane and the beauty of a trainer's life. The pack they all want to crow to after they have had a winner, the people they would most like to avoid if it has all gone wrong – particularly when it is as glaring as Bosra Sham that day. The trainers try to hold their tongues, we press men or women wear all sorts of weasel smiles to try to get them loosened. And all in search of some juicy 'quote' if an Alex Ferguson-style 'red mist' has suddenly descended.

As a matter of fact I have sat in on a couple of Ferguson post-match conferences and have to tell racehorse trainers that they have fawning dogs in front of them compared to the more Rottweiler approach of several football hacks. But with a 90-minute match there is usually more than one flashpoint to be covered, whereas for a trainer after a two-minute race like the Eclipse there can only be one issue on which to focus. What went wrong? Why did the jockey go there? Will he be sacked in the morning?

Annoying as it is to us media folk, the best policy for a trainer is to say as little as possible. On that Saturday Henry managed to hold his tongue, but on the Sunday he let it slip. 'I think the whole thing was appalling,' he told the Press Association before reaching for a rather 1930s metaphor: 'If people do not have eyes to see they should not go racing but go to the theatre or something else instead. They went a crawl and she likes a good gallop. She has been beaten a length and a quarter and if she had dictated it she would have won six lengths.'

That hit the papers on Monday. Tuesday saw the start of the Newmarket July meeting, and before we got there an official statement had been issued by the master of Warren Place: 'I have decided, having talked to connections and in the best interest of the filly, that Kieren Fallon will be replaced in future races.'

If Henry ever thought that would defuse matters he soon knew different. Kieren Fallon had ridden three winners on the Monday and here he was winging home on another one for Cecil in Newmarket's first. As the two-year-old Craigsteel was led into the notoriously cramped unsaddling enclosure all Henry had to do was give Kieren a public vote of confidence for everything but the Wafic Said horses and make the best of it for the rest of the season.

It may sound easy, but that day it most certainly wasn't. Henry's arm was stiff and electric with tension. I touched it, trying to turn him for the TV interview. There was a mumbled refusal and he tried to beat it across to the comparative safety of the weighing room. Some hope. A pack of some 20 hacks pinned him against the fence and asked him to elaborate on the now famous jock-off statement. One even read it to Henry off his notebook. But this was no Neville Chamberlain with a piece of paper and a 'peace in our time' declaration. This was a trainer. A trainer whose temper was running short. 'If you could not understand it, you were stupid,' he said. 'Why don't you leave things alone? You're a bloody nuisance, all of you.' Natalie Cecil stepped in, a supporting she-wolf at his side. 'He's not talking to anyone,' she snarled, 'because you keep asking nosey questions.' The trouble was that he was angry and most of us were not. 'You think it's funny,' he said to one chortling scribe.

One or two journos complained, and that week David Walsh took Cecil to task rather magisterially in *The Sunday Times*. But in reality it was all pretty tame compared to what happens when the real 'red mist' descends on Sir Alex. A jockey risked the inside when he would have been better going out. Strikers miss open goals. Owners, trainers and 'talk-through-our-pocket punters' get frightfully cross. But it happens. It will always happen. If this was a storm, the Newmarket unsaddling enclosure is not too large a teacup and next day Henry was out to make amends.

'I think Kieren did make a mistake,' he said, 'but it doesn't mean you cut someone's throat. He hasn't the experience of the Pat Edderys, Mick Kinanes and Frankie Dettoris of this world. But he is a very good jockey and he will improve. He is first jockey at Warren

Place this year and there was never any question that he'll be stable jockey next year.'

That statement was made at the beginning of the afternoon. It was hardly necessary by the end of it. Kieren Fallon had won the first race for Henry Cecil and Prince Khalid in a photo and then came up with three more. He had quietly kept his head when, in the Kipling line, 'all men doubt you'. He may have had to answer all sorts of questions about his conduct in the future, but this, in behavioural terms, was his finest hour. Prince Khalid had a sore throat and was not originally going to come. He was glad he did. Another winner trained by John Gosden made it five for the afternoon. 'It is going to spoil me,' he said in that careful English of his. 'When I come to the races again and have a winner I will not think it enough.' Next morning many in the racing world joined half a million in London on the march for the Countryside Alliance. At Newmarket, another alliance had now been forged in the fire.

Mercer, Piggott and Eddery had all become champion jockeys in their first year of association with Warren Place and it was soon clear that Kieren Fallon was on course to repeat the trick. At Goodwood Ali-Royal won the Sussex Stakes for the stable under a brilliant Fallon ride and when I spent a day with him a week later his 111 winners for the season, including 42 of the 53 then logged by the Cecil stable, were 14 clear of the pursuing Eddery and Dettori. He was living in what seemed like happy chaos in a converted Methodist chapel five miles out of Newmarket. His adored three-year-old daughter with the unwittingly significant name of Natalie (and his wife is called Julie) was eating cornflakes beside her half-opened tea set on the table. But in his riding Fallon was the hungry one.

That meant he was still ready to try anything, and that watching him could be a nerve-racking process – hadn't both Sleepytime's Guineas and Reams Of Verse's Oaks been 'escapes from jail'? But at that stage Kieren was touchingly aware of what he wanted. 'I need to calm down, to ride smoother,' he said with a brooding intensity. 'I went to America six years after Frankie Dettori and I will never get the beautiful poise that he has. But I am working at it. I always dreamed of making horses run even when it was just hitting the spokes of the cycle back home. I promise I can get better.' He was anxious to explain that there was method in what some saw as loose-rein untidiness, how he liked to wrap his body round a horse to urge it forward. After he rode a winner at York a week later he came running up and said, 'That's the way I do it. I am shifting my weight with them. People don't really understand but it does work.'

By the end of the season there were 202 winners and a first championship as proof. There was also the telling statistic that he was the only jockey in the top ten who would have shown a profit if you had put £1 on each of the 947 horses he had ridden during the term. That meant just one thing: that bookies as well as punters hadn't tumbled quite what a star had come south. It was Henry Cecil who had brought him here. The trainer may have had his own stages of irritation but his instinct had once again proved spot on.

At season's close I tried to assess what had happened. 'Most of the negative predictions have proved way wide of the mark,' I wrote in the *Racing Post*. 'But something of an outsider Kieren remains. He still doesn't quite fit into the rather smart suburbia of Newmarket life. The hurling stick in the back of his car is a very physical symbol of where his roots remain. But a lack of cosiness is no bad thing. For the real thrill of watching Kieren Fallon is the thought that if the rest of his life holds together, the best is yet to come.'

The tragedy both for him and for Henry Cecil was that while the best did come, the rest did not.

As the racing circus trotted its zany way towards the end of the century Warren Place remained a magical and even a daunting spot for a new arrival. At the start of 1997 it was not just Kieren Fallon who had trekked south to join Henry Cecil. Former 'Cock of the North' (leading northern-based jockey) John Lowe had decided to return to Newmarket in the confident hope that it would be a rather happier and longer stay than his first one some 30 years earlier. 'After three weeks, three kids in the yard had died,' said John in his chirpy Scouse tones. 'One lad hung himself, one got run away with and hit a tree, and the third was fooling around when someone threw a pitchfork that hit him in the head and killed him. I was just 15 and only there because I had bet a mate I could get a job. I went home to Liverpool double quick.'

The next year the little lad from Sefton Park was back at another stable, that of veteran trainer Jack Watts who put him on a horse called Pally's Double to win the then much-coveted Great Jubilee Handicap at Easter in 1968 on only John's fourth ride in public. When Jack retired the Lowe apprenticeship was transferred to his son Bill Watts up on the North Yorkshire moors at Middleham and more than a thousand winners had followed by the time John returned south to be closer to his wife Gayle's family and to look to the future. His successes had mainly been in big handicaps where his light weight (he could ride at under eight stone, at least seven pounds less than most leading jockeys) made him much in demand. But he had also won France's premier fillies' race, the Prix Marcel Boussac, ridden a double at Royal Ascot, and in 1979 had finished second on a filly called Abbeydale to Cecil's One In A Million in the 1,000 Guineas. Two years before that Lowe had posted his best-ever score of 86 winners, and if by the spring of 1997 the success rate was down to single figures it was clearly anything but an inexperienced pair of eyes or hands that came to Warren Place.

'Yes, it was a little bit daunting when I first started,' John remembers, 'lots of banter about "Cock of the North" and "how many other races would you have won if you hadn't been hooking them up in handicaps?" But when they realised I was not just coming for work mornings and would ride anything, I think I was accepted all right. One cold morning I was put on [future Sussex Stakes winner] Ali-Royal, who could sweat for England. He kept dry that day and Henry said, "You get on with him, you had better stay on him." When the press surrounded him after Ali-Royal won the Earl of Sefton at Newmarket he saw me in the corner and said, "You had better talk to Johnny." He was very good at involving everyone. I loved riding out there. After the horses I was used to riding, these were like a different breed.'

Of all the things in a work rider's life the purest pleasure is to sit on a good horse in the morning. And the harshest of class divides is between those who have the opportunity and those who don't. For the high-quality horse has the power and the movement that you associate with a really good car; the ordinary animal can be an old banger by comparison. In 1996, his last year in the north, the highest Racing Post Rating (RPR) for any horse John rode was 68. At Henry Cecil's in 1997, Ali-Royal was rated 123, Bosra Sham 130; anything as lowly as 68 did not spend much time at the stable. Lowe was used to making any sort of a purse from the sow's ears of horses that were put beneath him. But at Warren Place there was always the possibility of stitching together the real silken article. His experience that first year with a two-year-old called Fleetwood is symptomatic of the way Henry Cecil's operation allowed talent to develop.

Fleetwood was the sort of ride that stable lads hate. He was reluctant to go anywhere, and if he did was liable to stop with you. John Lowe was the victim of his own expertise and Henry took to sending the pair off on their own just as he had done so famously with the likes of Le Moss and Critique years before. What might have been a chore for the former 'Cock of the North' quickly became a project as John realised that not only was Fleetwood the 'real deal' but that because J. Lowe was riding him no one else would appreciate the horse's talent. 'My dream scenario,' says John with a chuckle in his voice, 'was that he would run in one of those big Newmarket maidens, that Henry would keep me on him, and because I was riding him as apparently the third string he would be 20-1 and we could all back him and clean up. For I will always say this was the best horse I ever sat on among all the good ones at Henry's.'

The trouble with Lowe's little plot is that it depended on him persuading the trainer to run Fleetwood without actually putting him in among others for a gallop where it would be impossible for his scheming rider to keep the colt's ability hidden. 'For a time Henry went along with me,' recalls John, 'but then he said, "I've got a race for him next week at Haydock, we must work him on the Limekilns." Fleetwood was an absolute bastard to get started. He would only do it if you could hack him in a circle to join the others. I wished he had not done it that morning on the Limekilns, because once he did he was cruising all over them and they included Dr Fong [to be the star miler of 1998]. Now everyone had seen it. Fleetwood started odds-on at Haydock, won by eight lengths, and Kieren took six furlongs to pull him up.'

John's postscript to that cameo is even more revealing. 'A few weeks later I was riding him back after ordinary exercise when Henry came up and said, "There's something wrong with him." I assured him the horse was fine but he was insistent that there was something wrong with his knees. Sure enough, it showed on the X-rays. He had treatment over the winter, worked well in the spring, but in the end never ran again. How did Henry see that? It is something like a sixth sense.'

Those training gifts were bringing new relationships and rekindling old ones, even, at least in the professional sense, with Tote Cherry-

Downes, who had found the Natalie saga so hard to forgive. For Tote was the racing manager for Sleepytime and Ali-Royal, whose exploits were not to be matched in the future, much to the disappointment of those of us who enjoyed the Dickensian schoolmaster name of the rather nice American owner, Charles H. Wacker III. Most outgoing of the new intake was the King of Saudi Arabia's California-educated nephew Prince Ahmed Salman. In his twenties he had owned the crack miler Lear Fan, who was third in the 1984 2,000 Guineas for Guy Harwood. The now American-based Prince was returning under the banner of The Thoroughbred Corporation, which he had formed with his old college friend Richard Mulhall, and adopted the rather daring idea (for Britain) of insisting that all his horses ran with white reins and bridles. He was a big, smiling man who if he liked you was apt to put his arm around you and say you were the best in the world. I know because he did it to me when I made a film for him about Lear Fan. Imagine what he felt when he started getting big winners from Henry Cecil.

In 1996 he had just two runners from Warren Place, both ex-American three-year-olds. Both won a race, but it was the class of '97 and '98 that put those trademark white bridles into the public consciousness. This batch included Dr Fong and Royal Anthem, who were both to win at Royal Ascot in 1998 and prove themselves to be among the very best in Europe over their respective distances of a mile and a mile and a quarter. At the very highest, Group One level, Dr Fong won the St James's Palace Stakes, and Royal Anthem flew to Toronto to make all the running in the Canadian International, which at that stage was Henry's greatest success in North America.

But even more exciting for Prince Ahmed, Warren Place and for a quickly fevered public was a 1998 two-year-old with the evocative name of Killer Instinct. Even as a yearling he was whizzing up Warren Hill as if he was an old horse, by the spring he was already on every shortlist including Henry's usually reticent stable tour, and he duly started at odds-on for his only run as a two-year-old. His defeat that day did not deter us: 'Killer Instinct Heads Classic Challenge' was the headline on the *Racing Post* stable tour of Warren Place three days before he started his season with another odds-on defeat at Newbury.

Over the years Henry Cecil has been fiercely protective but rarely deluded about the reputations of his horses. Killer Instinct proved to be one that got away. Although the colt duly cantered up at 1-7 in a little race at Nottingham, he was favourite and beaten again when more highly tried at Kempton, yet Henry was not ready to condemn. 'He's still working fantastic,' said the trainer, 'but his brain isn't working as fast as his legs. We've got to get him to do it, but I don't rule out the St James's Palace Stakes. I might put a visor on him. He's not ungenuine, he's just not doing it on the racecourse. At home he's fantastic.'

The St James's Palace Stakes brought another failure, as did an apparently simple option at York a month later, which led to an exasperated 'I thought he was getting his act together but he couldn't even lay up with the pace here' from Henry. We did not see the horse again. The truth was that Killer Instinct did not have what his name suggested. Happily, events surrounding the horse's failure at Kempton proved that the same was not true of the trainer.

The half-hour it would have taken for that race to prepare and unroll would have been the only time Henry Cecil could have laid eyes on Kalanisi, the Luca Cumani-trained winner who was to be a Breeders' Cup hero the next season under the care of Michael Stoute. Yet a fortnight after Kempton Henry recognised the horse straight away when Kalanisi escaped riderless from the Cumani string pursued by Henry's former assistant Simon Sweeting. 'Kalanisi was a dark but not that distinctive bay,' said Simon. 'We must have had more than 80 colts all wearing the same exercise sheets. Henry can only have seen him in passing yet he knew it was him.' He concluded by echoing John Lowe's words about Fleetwood's knees: 'How do you explain that?'

Henry's gifts were still there, and so was the drive, as witnessed by the traditional interview re-pledging himself at the start of each season. In 1997 it was that he had given up smoking as well as drink. In 1998, 'I enjoy working with my staff and I love my work. It's not a job really, it's a way of life, and I love every minute of it, riding out in the morning and wandering around evening stables.' In 1999 he was talking of 87 two-year-olds in a 190-strong string with all kinds of hopefuls. That season marked his 30 years as a trainer and one in which he was to win three of the first four Classics and only be beaten a neck in the fourth; and how those Classic winners – Wince in the 1,000 Guineas, Oath in the Derby and Ramruma in the Oaks – were highlighted speaks of a trainer and a team on top of their game.

One morning after breakfast the previous September, Henry had said to Tony McGlone: 'That horse you ride this afternoon. Look after her because I think she's nice. She could be my Oaks filly next season.' The jockey could not wait to get out to the yard to see Willie Ryan and the others. 'He didn't often talk like that,' says McGlone, 'and none of us had ever heard of Ramruma. Eventually we found the lad that rode her and he just said she was still very green. She was only third that afternoon but I could feel the potential. Henry had seen it before any of us.'

Next spring there was nearly as much talk on the fillies front about a bay called Bionic as there was about Killer Instinct by the same sire, Zafonic. But even before Bionic got injured Henry had been making encouraging noises about Prince Khalid's other filly Wince, an opinion that was more than endorsed one morning when she was ridden by John Lowe on the racecourse side. 'There were four of us in the gallop,' John recalls. 'Frank Conlon was on something and Willie Ryan was on Enrique, who won the Greenham and was beaten only a neck in the 2,000. As Willie went clear, Frank shouted across to me, "Just look at that go!" and I yelled back, "Just look at what I've got here!" Wince was going so well I was absolutely swinging off her.'

A couple of weeks earlier Tony McGlone had been asked to get up on a little colt called Oath that nobody either rated or liked very much. 'None of us knew he was there,' recalls Willie Ryan. 'He was a tiny weasel of a horse that would jig jog all the way to the gallops and all the way back. He used to be ridden by a little old boy called Smiler, who was about 70 years old. But somehow the horse must have caught Henry's eye because one morning he said to Tony, "You get on Oath and go with those," to which Tony said, "What am I getting on this for?" He knew why after the gallop. Henry had a big smile and said, "I think I have found one." After that it was gallops Wednesday and Saturday and harder and harder. Oath stood it and won the Dee Stakes, but after the Derby it was the end of him.'

If there was ever a horse trained to the minute it was Oath for that Derby Day at Epsom. He and Fallon were 11th of the 16-long file of horses parading in front of the Queen and the 40,000 of her subjects in the stands. At the head of affairs two top-hatted, black-veiled ladies rode their white horses grandly forward to carry the flag. One of these animals was called Hooray Henry. Back on board Oath, that was not the 'Henry' Kieren was thinking of. For beneath him all of his Henry's plans were on the melt.

The sweat scalded out on Oath's neck and flanks in steaming, creamy flecks – a speckled match for the whiteness of his bridle. His lad Steve da Costa tugged desperately at the bridle as 500kg of hard-trained muscle pawed and lurched and strained to answer the surging energy now raging in his brain. Oath could see the long, green carpet of the Epsom course ahead of him. He had not read about it or heard about it, but something in him sensed this was the place where he was born to run.

Fallon's three previous Derby rides had all been long-priced outsiders. This was different. This was a big, big contender, and it was boiling over. Trainer and jockey had discussed this happening, so Fallon took the law into his own hands. He broke the parade and cantered off up the hill to release the fury steaming between those big bay ears. He would be fined £1,000 afterwards, and it should have been the easiest 'grand' Kieren would ever pay.

What followed was one of the greatest fulfilments of the Fallon-Cecil relationship, and it remains an ultimate irony that we watched it fewer than two months before their partnership was severed in the unhappiest of circumstances. It's not how Kieren and Henry react as people but how they inspire horses that has made them special, and at Epsom that day Oath was a little boiling masterpiece of conditioning with a master in the saddle.

Oath was calm by the time he entered the stalls. From the number one draw Fallon quickly had him up in position. You could see from the arch of the jockey's green and white back that the horse was on the muscle. What you did not know was how much energy had already been sweated away. But as they swung down through Tattenham Corner there was little change in the Fallon stance as he stalked the three leaders, and when Gerald Mosse cut for home on Daliapour, Kieren and Oath immediately countered in pursuit.

A terrible fall which was to all but sever his arm at Ascot the following summer meant Kieren Fallon can never be physically as complete as he was then, when he clamped his body on the horse beneath him and compelled him up those last three furlongs of the straight. His whole life, his whole style could have been meant for this, for no course so tests the balance, strength, courage and tactical daring as the extraordinary contours of the Derby track, and few jockeys have been as blessed as Fallon in all four departments. No Flat race-rider in my experience has used his body so compellingly around his horse as Kieren does. Twenty-four hours earlier he had driven Ramruma clear to take the Oaks; the next day Epsom and Oath were made for him.

It was a triumph for horse, jockey and especially for the trainer who had now saddled four Derby and 22 English Classic winners, and whose public response to the congratulations was 'at least people won't think me completely useless'. Four days later I went to see him at Newmarket, and for a man at the top he looked terrible. He had been up since five o'clock and all morning had been spent on the Heath with his horses. Now, back at his desk, there was a list to get through and a long, chain-smoking afternoon loomed ahead. In the week between Epsom triumph and Royal Ascot challenge,

Oath (Kieren Fallon) goes clear to win the 1999 Derby from Daliapour.

Henry Cecil was not into feet-up time. But with a 28-strong raiding party out to improve on his 65 previous Royal Ascot successes, more than twice the number of any other trainer, it seemed as good an opportunity as any to ask him about his trick.

He lit another cigarette (whatever happened to that resolution?) and came across to sit on the sofa. He was 56 then, and the mannerisms, like the bags under the eyes, were well set. He gave a characteristic shake of the head and said, 'Honestly, I think of myself as lucky. I really do. I have been well supported. I have nice horses to train. You try to understand the animal and let them tell you when they're ready. It's sort of common sense really.'

It was not that clear an explanation for the most sought-after gift in racing. Yet sitting in the elegance of the tartan-curtained study with its Burnett coat of arms on one wall, a cabinet of toy soldiers across another and moose antlers above the door, the clues were all there for the gathering. Henry has indeed been lucky. His voice and manners signal an aristocratic heritage, which becomes almost plutocratic in racing terms when you think of those Boyd-Rochfort and Murless connections, and any recollection of his winning the Eclipse with the Boyd-Rochfort 'hand down' Wolver Hollow in his very first season would prompt many to think his is another tale of the silver spoon.

Yet it is also the parable of the talents. For the central law of racehorse training, and in particular with fragile three-year-olds coming up to the Classics, is that you cannot make your athlete any quicker, but you can mess them up. One failure to heed a warning sign, one gallop too many, one race at the wrong time or distance, and the flower never fully blooms. Cecil, whose other passion was on display in the garden outside, had become the master of 'horticulture on the hoof'.

Yet this still begs the question about what exactly is a trainer's role. Bar PR duty with the owner in the paddock and reminding the jockey of a previously discussed strategy, the trainer's only duty on the day is the act of tying the saddle on. His impact has come earlier. To switch metaphors, the best analogy is probably that of the headmaster. A top stable like Cecil's would be sent the equivalent of a string of talented kids from wealthy and achieving parents, but there are two massive problems: the 'kids' are very young (in 1999 Ramruma was not three until February, and Oath's birthday was as late as 22 April) and above all else they cannot talk. Well, not to you and me they can't. They talk to Henry, though. That day it was very noticeable that, while he paid all the usual 'teamwork' compliments to his staff, from head lad Frank Conlon and Willie Ryan ('part of the family') to Natalie (for 'modernising' him about his approach to feeding and to tack), the one time Henry got truly animated was when he spoke about 'understanding the animal'.

'The most important thing,' he said, 'is to be able to assess them. It is more difficult now because a lot of them don't come to me as yearlings as they used to [Ramruma had come in the autumn but Oath had arrived as a once-raced two-year-old as late as the previous June]. You can teach an animal an awful lot and find out a lot about it before Christmas. Then you feel your way. I watch them, see if they are getting well in themselves, and I never move them up a gear unless they are telling me they want it.'

At that stage I had known him for more than 30 years and the image returned of him out with his string on a thousand early mornings. The panache of the 'actorish' suede chaps and the white-maned Arab hack can deceive you about the seriousness of what is happening.

'This is my life,' he said, suddenly intent. 'I get up at five. I ride out three lots every morning. I never work a horse unless I am here. I watch them. I change the riders around. Different people are good for different horses at different times. I do all my lists myself.

Even if I come back late from evening racing at 11pm, I sit down and do the list. I am doing it now. Of course I am wound up,' he concluded, looking ahead to the challenge of Royal Ascot, 'but I am very ambitious. I am not stale or bored with the thing at all.' And then the great giveaway line – the five am fulfilment. 'I love it,' he said.

There is a poignancy as well as a strength in that summer of 1999 memory. For despite some sniping personal rumours that go with the territory, Henry Cecil really did seem to have realigned this third stage of his professional life for the better. When two more winners came at Royal Ascot, and when Ramruma slaughtered her rivals in the Irish Oaks that July, it only seemed to confirm that opinion.

Then, on the Saturday before Goodwood, the call came through. The sort of call no one ever wants to hear and anyone in the public eye with a private secret is right to dread. It was from the *News of the World* asking for comments on a story they were going to splash across the nation's breakfast tables next morning claiming that Natalie Cecil had been 'romping', to use the tabloid argot, with a famous married jockey on the Ramruma trip to Ireland. The jockey was not named, but the clear suggestion was that it was Kieren Fallon.

Excreta was about to hit the fan.

The next week, year and decade were to test, break, seemingly destroy but ultimately revive and define what was Henry Cecil. Its start was so messy that it remains a wonder and a tribute to the man that the end has been so heroic.

For the victims, there are no redeeming features of a big newspaper 'bust'. By the time the call comes through the headlines are written, the pictures chosen, the libel checked, and however specious the story, the one guarantee is that it will be pitched so full of shock-horror, nudge-nudge innuendo that millions will be sniggering at you over their cornflakes and later in the day millions more will be saying 'Did you read that?' as if it were absolute fact. Well, the only undeniable fact, then and now, in that original *News of the World* story was that Natalie Cecil had told 'a friend' she was having trouble with her marriage and that on a recent trip to Ireland she had 'erred' with a married jockey in a hotel. More specifically she had said that part of that 'erring' had been in a shower, so that forever after the encounter could be shortened to the catchy 'Romp in Shower'.

Since there were no witnesses to the soaping, no actual names ever mentioned, and that the only one, Kieren Fallon, ever linked to it in print immediately and adamantly denied any involvement, you could argue that the best course for Henry Cecil was merely to say something about his wife being unwell and to press on with life as usual. But it was, and was to become, rather more complicated than that. For a start, Natalie was indeed unwell. She was in The Priory trying to overcome an addiction to diet pills and Prozac, the anti-depressant and her mood swings had led to plenty of gossip about Henry's public and professional life.

That was the background when Henry called Frank Conlon in some disarray that Saturday evening. 'He was in terrible shape,' remembers Frank about his employer of more than 30 years. 'There were bottles of red wine everywhere and he was in despair. I poured it away and eventually got him to bed, but he had to tell me the story. To be fair most of us did not get on that well with Natalie, so we thought this would at least be the end of things. But when he said, "Poor dear, you know she is not well," I realised it could get even more difficult.' It did. And with a vengeance. In hindsight, the only two saving graces in the week that followed was that their five-year-old son Jake flew off to Greece on a pre-arranged holiday that Sunday morning and that in 1999 we were not yet into internet chatrooms and 24-hour rolling news, which can spread any piece of gossipy roadkill to the four winds within minutes. Nonetheless there was little short of a feeding frenzy in the British papers. Here were all the ingredients they crave – sex, fame, money, whips, sweat and silks – and all at the start of the Silly Season. They couldn't believe their luck.

It was the beginning of Glorious Goodwood, and for the tabloids that was another 'Hurrah!' It meant there could be a thousand body-language photos and dodgy puns as Cecil and Fallon went through the necessary paddock routine in the public theatre of a major race meeting. On the Tuesday evening Henry released a brief two-paragraph statement saying that after Kieren had ridden the somewhat inappropriately named Endorsement in France that coming Sunday, 'our association will be permanently terminated and next season Richard Quinn [then second to Fallon in the jockeys' table] will be first jockey to Warren Place'. Notwithstanding there being no actual evidence, along with Fallon's insistent denials of any 'romp in shower' involvement, the papers now gorged at the story like a ravenous pack.

On the Thursday *The Sun* ran a two-page spread under the headline 'Have A Good Ride' featuring a 'better days' photo of Henry and Natalie looking down at a smiling Fallon and an opening paragraph that was a model of the ever-suggestive kind. 'Racing trainer Henry Cecil, still reeling from his wife's alleged fling with a top rider,' it began with suitable breathlessness, 'helped his jockey get his leg over yesterday despite sacking him after the scandal.' There was much, much more of this sort of thing, and if you had thought it could not get worse, you would have been wrong. Next day the papers could feast on a brief statement from Natalie about becoming 'close to a married man who appeared to show me kindness and companionship. This was no more than a strong friendship but unfortunately on one occasion it went beyond friendship.' The *Daily Mail* could gather up all their best Jilly Cooper allusions, including the iconic skin-tight jodhpur-bottom cover picture of her book *Riders*, under the headline 'Blazing Saddles (Or Why Horsey People and Sex are Utterly Inseparable)'.

That Friday Henry went back to his hotel in Brighton and got caught out by a tabloid sting. A 20-year-old 'vice girl' spent the night in his room and got herself pictured on the bedroom balcony in the morning. For the second week running the *News of the World* could run amok. The outside world could snigger and tut-tut, but on the inside the mood changed to one more of sympathy. 'We just felt sorry for him,' says Tony McGlone. 'He would look so tired and vulnerable when we came into the office first thing in the morning. You would not wish what he went through on anyone, especially not on someone trying to run a yard as big as Warren Place.'

Training might have been an extra strain but, as throughout his life, it was a lifeline for Henry Cecil. He may have had his private world strewn around the newspapers but 180 horses and 70 people needed his professional attention every day and he could ask for results to be his judge. York's Ebor meeting comes three weeks after Goodwood. For many of us, Henry included, these are the most enjoyable four days of the racing year with their northern jollity added to thoroughbred style in a unique location not half a mile from the ancient minster and set on historic public land called the Knavesmire for two very good reasons: it can indeed become a mire after heavy rain, and in the 'bad old days' they used to hang a knave or two before racing at the edge of the course.

Whatever else was going on, at least Henry and his supporters had something to cheer at York that August. Ramruma, ridden by Pat Eddery, won her third 'Oaks' in a row by taking the Yorkshire Oaks decisively to ready herself for what was to prove a game second place in the following month's St Leger at Doncaster. Ramruma was splendid enough, but the day before her 'Oaks', Royal Anthem had been a revelation.

He, of course, was one of those 'white bridle' horses of Prince Ahmed's Thoroughbred Corporation and had swept through the previous season with those brilliant wins in the King Edward VII Stakes at Royal Ascot and the Canadian International at Woodbine. The dice had not really rolled for him at either Epsom or Ascot in 1999, but as the field for the Juddmonte International swung into the long, flat Knavesmire straight they rolled for him like few have ever rolled before. If you watch a lot of racing it takes a lot to impress you. By 1999 I had covered that Ebor meeting every year since first watching Derby winner Roberto give the mighty Brigadier Gerard his only career defeat in the 1972 equivalent of the Juddmonte. I had images seared into the brain of Steve Cauthen and little Diminuendo on the wing in the Yorkshire Oaks of 1988, and of Willie Carson and the flying Dayjur scorching up the five furlongs of the 1990 Nunthorpe

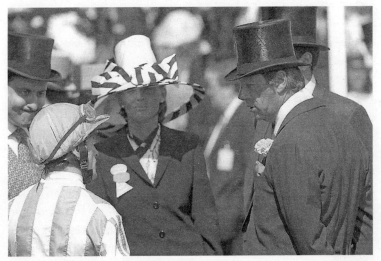

At Royal Ascot: Ahmed Salman, Kieren Fallon, Natalie Cecil and Henry Cecil.

Stakes in an astonishing 56.16 seconds. The moment Royal Anthem cut loose in 1999 I knew I was seeing something among that number.

The performance was only enhanced by its context. This was Henry Cecil drawing attention in the way he craved, but it was also the ultimate fulfilment for 36-year-old American jockey Gary Stevens of what must be the most successful 12-week stay in British racing history. In 1998, Idaho-born Gary had topped the USA lists with winnings of $19 million – more than four times the £2.7 million of our champion Kieren Fallon. He had won all the American Classics, six Breeders' Cup races and major events in Tokyo, Dubai and Hong Kong. On his right shoulder was tattooed an eagle with three small drops of blood dripping from its talons to mark his three winners of the Kentucky Derby. In the three months since he had flown in to join Michael Stoute and ride Beat All to finish third to Oath in the Derby, Gary had won 45 of his 207 races and logged £1.4 million in prize money. Ever restless, he was returning to America the week after York to become a head honcho for Prince Ahmed. It had been an astonishing trip, but not all watchers were convinced. He rode two other winners that day at York but some grumbled when he got beat on the favourite in the fifth. They didn't know where to look.

Not that Stevens didn't have some problems trying to adapt, particularly going to the start, where he was sometimes precious close to out of control. 'The technique of holding a horse in Britain is totally different to what we do in America,' he explained. 'Over there we take a horse tight by the reins and start them off at the trot. Over here you have a long rein and go straight into a canter. I was giving them completely the wrong message.' Such equitation details aside, the critics felt his quieter, less powerful-looking finishing drive would get outgunned by the likes of Fallon or Dettori. Whatever they thought, the results were the answer. So, most of all, was the sight of Royal Anthem at York.

He was a tall, dark bay with a pointed white star on his forehead, and at full stretch that day he was the very beau idéal of the thoroughbred in glorious, flowing 25-foot stride. Gary Stevens had a particularly low, crouching style and as Royal Anthem came towards us the jockey was tucked in so tight behind the mane it was almost as if the colt was loose as he strode majestically up that famous turf. Four, five, six, seven, eight extraordinary lengths he had forged clear by the time he hit the line. Watching him you felt you might never see anything to equal it on the Knavesmire and that it would be best if the horse's career stopped at this peak of excellence, which could surely never be scaled again.

So it proved, with an abject defeat on Royal Anthem's next run in the Irish Champion Stakes, a decent second in the Breeders' Cup Turf and one other minor victory in two American starts under the care of new trainer Bill Mott before retirement beckoned. Such an option was neither open to nor contemplated by Henry Cecil, and while his number of winners (65) was some way below his previous season's 100, he had amassed £2.4 million in prize money at the season's close to be second, for the third time in four years, to Godolphin's Saeed bin Suroor in the trainers' table.

On the face of it he had recovered well from the public madness of midsummer, as indeed had Kieren Fallon, who was champion again after taking over the Michael Stoute post from Gary Stevens. But back at Warren Place this was an unhappy and uncertain period for Henry Cecil. Natalie was living in London, and despite her being quoted as saying 'he's the most talented, unbelievable person, you could not have a bigger gentleman. Whatever happens, Henry and I will never, never fall out,' a permanent return to Newmarket never really seemed possible. Which meant he would be seeing less of his adored Jake and that some unwanted chickens were coming home to roost.

Looking back, it's easy, if painful, to see there was a doomed inevitability about what happened to Henry and Natalie's relationship.

HENRY CECIL

A middle-aged man fell madly in love with a much younger girl and installed her as first lady of his world-famous establishment in place of his wife of 20 years to whose father that establishment had first belonged. Once there his encouragement of her 'fresh thinking' alienated many of his staff, and that was only aggravated by his sometimes seemingly besotted indulgence of what came to be her excesses.

For Natalie the situation was equally difficult. Virtually to a man and woman Newmarket sided with Julie, yet every morning Natalie would have to brazen things out with the knowledge that eyes were against her in every corner. Strong-willed she may have been, high-handed she might have become, but there was hurt as well as acceptance when we lunched early in 2012 and she told me, 'There wasn't a single day in ten years when someone didn't say something that made me cry.' She has a new life now, and Jake is a big, handsome young man set to study art after showing real promise at the Surrey school in whose annexe this book has been written. There's little to be gained from raking over the embers of past unhappiness, although it has to be said there remain plenty in Newmarket ever ready to poke that particular fire.

A racing stable has to push on regardless of what is happening in the house, although by that autumn events had clearly taken some toll on the operation. 'It did feel a slightly strange place at first,' said Harry Dunlop, Henry's godson, who arrived as an assistant in October 1999. Harry is the son of trainer John Dunlop and after working at Nicky Henderson's top jumping yard in Lambourn had been pointed to Warren Place by his father 'because Henry has something extra'. What was difficult to begin with was locating that 'extra' through some of the complications that had built up over previous seasons. 'We had an assistant who didn't know what distance the Derby was and was trying to use some of Natalie's dressage and eventing principles,' remembers Harry. 'Frank [Conlon] and the others were dead against it and didn't feel that it belonged in a racing stable. Coming from Nicky's with people like Corky [Browne, Henderson's legendary head man] very much in charge of the standard way of doing things, it felt a bit strange. But we still had some good horses, the lads were great, and Henry was very kind, although he did look very lonely at times.'

There was a double and twisted irony that autumn for Henry Cecil. For after many years of failure, alcoholism, broken marriages and despair, his twin David had finally got his life together. Two years earlier he had at last kicked the bottle and met and married a bright young TV producer called Joanna Howes, 20 years his junior and herself also an identical twin. Their first child was due before Christmas and meanwhile the *Daily Mail* magazine was running an impressive feature picturing him at his Poissonerie restaurant in Hungerford with which he was enjoying a success much celebrated by the many friends even his worst dramas had not seen off.

'Henry has been through an awful time,' David said of the twin at whose hip he had been joined in those earlier years. 'Of course at the moment I am happier than him. But I have been through bad times too.'

For David there was the serenity of seeming to have reached some peaceful sunlit upland where he could at last lead his life with pride. The bitterest of ironies for him, and an unhealable wound for Henry, was that he had only one more year on this planet.

11

THE DEPTHS

THERE HAD been plenty of times in Henry's training career when the stars seemed almost unfairly aligned in his favour. But any study of what happened to him in the year 2000 has to make you think there was something malign in the arrangement of the constellations. Within 12 months he had lost his wife, the custody of his son, his sobriety, his driving licence, his health and that of his horses, and all that while his beloved twin was being struck and then taken by terminal cancer. For Henry Cecil, this first year of the century became in every sense an annus miserabilis.

Not that you would have dreamt of this as he sauntered into spring apparently intent on dismissing all that 1999 unpleasantness as a passing nightmare. With those mauve breeches, brown-suede bomber jacket and matching leather-tassled chaps he looked as elegant as ever as he rode out with the string on Snowy, his huge, white, handsome former show-jumper, chatting to new stable jockey Richard Quinn. He had 170 horses and more than 80 two-year-olds. At the Craven meeting a handsome Danzig three-year-old of Khalid Abdulla's called Shibboleth won by five impressive lengths first time out and looked a major player for big mile races in the season ahead. Two days earlier another three-year-old, a Sadler's Wells colt of Lord

Howard de Walden's widow Gilly called Wellbeing, won his maiden impressively enough to give him a Derby place alongside the stable's Beat Hollow, whose victory a fortnight later at the Guineas meeting had that Abdulla colt confirmed as favourite at Epsom. With a newcomer called Subtle Power scoring well at Newbury in mid-May for the Thoroughbred Corporation and the Niarchos star mare Shiva taking the Group Three Brigadier Gerard Stakes at Sandown ten days later, an outsider could reasonably assume all was once again well in the House of Cecil.

In reality the poisoned rot of ill fortune was already taking hold. In February David Cecil had been diagnosed with the rarely beatable cancer of the pancreas. The brothers kept it quiet until Epsom, but before then insiders could see the toll it was taking on the trainer. With Natalie away and Jake set to join her, Henry was alone and at times was resorting to drink for company. His despair was made more acute when some of his horses, including Beat Hollow, were found to be suffering from a low-grade infection. By the time Shiva was due to run and win that big race at Sandown, Henry was so low that it took some persuading from Frank Conlon and Harry Dunlop to get him to accept a lift to the races rather than another swig from the bottle.

In the face of all this Henry still arrived at Epsom with major chances in both Classics. The stable sickness meant that neither Beat Hollow nor Wellbeing had been able to run since winning at Newmarket's Guineas meeting, but the way Beat Hollow moved with his stablemate in a gallop at Yarmouth racecourse a week before the Derby meant he would be the big-race favourite on the Saturday. On the Friday, the filly Love Divine would also start favourite for the Oaks after looking all class when she won the Lupe Stakes at Goodwood. But on the Thursday, Colin Mackenzie's column in the *Daily Mail* carried the news the brothers now felt should be made public. It told of how Henry had been making twice-weekly round trips to see David in Lambourn and of the anguish he was enduring as his twin battled through chemotherapy. 'This has been the most worrying time in the whole of Henry's life,' Colin quoted the trainer's friend Henry Ponsonby as saying.

He and David are incredibly close and supportive. This isn't like a close friend having cancer or even a blood brother. Twins are two halves of the same person. They not only look alike, they dream alike, and they even have the same aspirations. They even suffer alike, as you can see with David's admitted alcoholism, which has made Henry very wary of taking a drink himself.

Henry, who rarely drinks these days, is so concerned about David's unhappiness that he spends every waking hour worrying about him. He has always been there for David, sorting out his drinking problems in the past and helping him financially. In turn David is tremendously proud of Henry and what he has achieved – there is no envy at all. The fact that his own training career failed made him all the prouder of Henry's enormous success.

Henry Ponsonby is one of those rather splendid, ever optimistic, sometimes not entirely pecunious, independent-minded coves with which racing abounds. His speciality was corralling friends and connections into budget-priced ownership syndicates, which he would run with trainers he knew, specifically Paul Cole and Henry Cecil. The first horse he had at Warren Place was called Halston Prince, which in 1990 had won the appropriately named (for its clothes-loving trainer) Moss Bros Handicap at Ascot under Steve Cauthen. Two years later Ponsonby had been a witness at Henry's wedding to Natalie. His home near Newbury has remained a treasured sanctuary from the Newmarket glare. In the summer of 2000 he was the conduit for David as well as Henry to speak. 'Henry had great difficulty in accepting it [the cancer],' the *Daily Mail* was able to quote David as saying. 'In the end I got the doctor to call him. But he could not talk about it for days. It's really hit him hard. People have always tried to set up this rivalry between us, but I don't want anything he's got, although I am very proud of him. Since the cancer he has been wonderful. I see him two or three times a week. If the worst comes to the worst he has told me he will always look after Joanna [David's third wife], Sebastian [his stepson] and Jemima [their baby daughter]. He has told me he will educate the children and said to me just the other day, "Where do you want to go? Eton? I'll send him anywhere you want."'

Such public tributes were given added poignancy when Love Divine came clear in the Oaks and Beat Hollow ran a good third to the future Prix de l'Arc de Triomphe winner Sinndar in the Derby. At Royal Ascot Shibboleth was a decent fourth in the St James's Palace Stakes and Prince Ahmed was a characteristically over-the-top winning owner after Subtle Power took the King Edward VII Stakes. Two days later Beat Hollow went to Longchamp to land the prestigious Grand Prix de Paris, and when a Khalid Abdulla two-year-old called Vacamonte won with stunning brilliance at Newmarket's July meeting, you could think that Henry also had the 2001 season secured.

But the brutal rules of life often dictate that if your grip slips on one thing, so it does on others. On the Sunday after Vacamonte's dazzling debut, Henry had Jake for one last day before returning him to his mother. He and a friend took their two boys to a jolly lunch in Ashley. It was coming up to 5.30pm when they set off back to allow the two children to play at Warren Place. Henry was in a better mood but, when later tested, was twice over the limit. As they came into Newmarket there were two pensioners in the road, and as the big Mercedes passed them it did not allow enough clearance. Seventy-eight-year-old Len Hurrell received cuts to his fingers and elbow, his wife Joan had her right arm broken. This could be criminal disaster.

Matters could hardly have been worse – Henry had a previous drink-driving conviction from 1991, the first post-Julie year. This time, when the police first arrived there were suggestions that his friend, not he, was the driver. The gathering that evening at Warren Place was a battered and sombre one. It included the late Leslie Harrison, the long-standing friend who ran the Plantation Stud for Lord Howard de Walden, and Willie Ryan who, as 'part of the family', had been summoned by his distraught employer. 'It was obviously a terrible mess,' recalls Willie. 'Henry had taken another drink and was in a bad way. I remember Leslie insisting that the only way forward was to be completely open and tell the police everything. Then Julie came in. Henry did and does still depend on her but she was never that soft with him. When she saw him she paused for a moment and then said, "You twit [actually something rather stronger]." He looked up rather woozily and replied, "Oh don't call me that, darling." It was not a good time.'

And that was anything but the end of it. The court case would not be heard until November, but before then the problems would come crowding in. The infection seemed to return to affect some of the horses. Shibboleth injured himself on the gallops and could not run again that season, Beat Hollow started breaking blood vessels and never ran again in Britain, Vacamonte blew out when fifth of seven at no less than 1-4 at Sandown, and three days later Subtle Power was last of five in the Great Voltigeur Stakes at York. 'I remember thinking "This can't get any worse,"' recalls Harry Dunlop. Oh yes it could.

At the end of August the normally so reliable Snowy jinked left and threw Henry when hacking up beside the Al Bahathri gallop. It was one of those falls that land you flat and jarringly on your back. Henry already had trouble with his vertebrae. It was something that soon required the ministrations of London's Wellington Hospital, which is located within a couple of overthrows of the Test pitch at Lord's. But for Henry this was absolutely not cricket. He spent most of September watching the Sydney Olympics through sleepless nights racked with pain and fraternal foreboding.

Although the Derby fifth Wellbeing won at Newmarket on Henry's first full day out of hospital it was little compensation for having been out of commission during the crucial yearling sales time and absolutely no sweetener for two bitter events to come. On 2 November the drink-driving case was finally heard at Ely Magistrates' Court. Although the charge was not 'dangerous driving', the presiding magistrate Mrs Sue Thompson initially said the offence 'was too serious to be dealt with by financial penalty' before settling for a £3,000 fine and a five-year ban. Henry expressed regret and disappointment but he knew there was much worse ahead. Exactly a week later, on 9 November, his twin brother died at the John Radcliffe Hospital in Oxford.

When I went to discuss this book with David's widow Joanna she at first preferred not to speak but to hand me eight typed pages in a script large enough to be legible without bothering with glasses. After I had finished reading it I cried, and she cried. It was the address Henry had given at his brother's funeral at Lambourn's church of St Michael and All Angels on 16 November. It outlined a life of his own David battling against the Goliath of alcoholism and losing again and again until at last, although much too late, conquering and slaying the monster. He spoke of David's final happiness and then, from the church's wooden lectern, took his listeners into the closing days.

Henry recalled how, only a month before his death, David had made a surprise visit to his brother at the Wellington Hospital bearing presents of a coat and sweater. The following day David had been admitted to the Churchill Hospital in Oxford, critically ill with double pneumonia. Henry regularly telephoned his twin, and when David sounded particularly depressed would visit him in the middle of the night – when he would be greeted by David, cigarette in hand, dressed in yellow sweater and bright red trousers. Hospital staff and patients had named David 'The Iron Man', for although he was desperately ill he just refused to submit.

Then Henry told of what was to prove the second last time he saw David, whose body was wired with countless tubes and who was having great trouble breathing. When David saw Henry come into the ward, he had raised an arm in frail greeting and immediately asked about the mixed fortunes of Henry's runners the previous day.

By this stage of the address many in the congregation were weeping, and before Henry signed off with his farewell to such a wonderful twin, he insisted that those who claimed that David had followed in his shadow were wrong: Henry knew David better than anyone, and knew that in truth, David was the better half.

There had indeed been winners in 2000, 61 of them, just five fewer than the previous campaign, although some way short of the 100 of 1998; and Love Divine's efforts had lifted the winnings to just ahead of the £1 million mark. But imagining the mournful figure delivering so devastatingly sad and eloquent an address, and knowing the confusion and difficulty beginning to build in his yard, the words echoed back to me of Hugh McIlvanney after he had listened to Muhammad Ali talking up that ill-fated 1980 comeback against Larry Holmes when the old fires had gone out. 'However one may hope for something different,' wrote Hugh, 'it's hard to escape the conclusion that we are now on the downward journey to where the bad times are.'

It took five years to get to the bottom of the pit, and once there not one outsider in 10,000 would have given Henry Cecil any chance of climbing out. The stable that had been in the top ten since 1973 and had been first ten times and second six, most recently in 1999, now skidded to 12th, 37th, 41st, 66th and, in 2005, to a nadir of 97th in the table. By then the 100-winner seasonal totals had fallen to a paltry 12. The stables that once needed overflow yards to house more than 200 horses could in 2005 muster fewer than 40 individual runners under the Henry Cecil name. From the years 2000 to 2006 there was just a single Group One winner, and even then the flag did not fly. For that winner, Tidal Fury in November 2005, was in France's Champion Three Year Old Hurdle at Auteuil in Paris and was saddled by Jonathan Jay, one of three trainers lodging at Warren Place to provide the rent to keep the Cecil team afloat. Yes, it had come to that.

There was something of an unhappy self-fulfilment in this downward spiral. It was as if Henry's career was some giant 'Slinky' toy that had coiled its springs at the top of the staircase and was curling and uncurling itself, step by step, all the way to the bottom. Every time there were sprigs of hope or enthusiasm, events would snip them off and newer but inevitably more tender shoots would come to replace them. How soon would it all be over? The rumours of retirement began to grow, and to think that he'd started the first ones himself.

In January 2001 the *Racing Post* carried the headline 'I don't think I should retire yet, do you?' Henry had intended it to be one of those typically jokey rhetorical questions he puts out in TV interviews. He was commenting on the news that the size of his stable, the lowest since 1984, had 'shrunk' to the not exactly career-ending number of 157 – two and a half times the strength he and Julie originally had at Marriott Stables. He was actually putting out a rallying call –

'there's plenty of ammunition, I'm still competitive and I feel really good' – but he was unwittingly echoing a growing scepticism about his prospects, which the horrors of 2000 had naturally bred. Such feelings were only reinforced a month later when the *Mail on Sunday* ran a big feature under the headline 'The Sad and Lonely World of Henry Cecil'. It pictured him looking gaunt and miserable on not Snowy but his other hack, the brown and white American 'Paint Horse' Bug, and the wall-eyed ghostliness of Bug's face only added to the gloomy feel. So did the accompanying quote: 'It sounds pompous but to win races just for myself presents a kind of emptiness.'

No matter that Henry also reiterated 'I am as competitive and determined as ever. If I started to be an also-ran, it would be time to go.' Millions of *Mail* readers, and of course the whole of gossipy Newmarket, still winced at the sadness of the message. 'I hate being alone,' Henry had told the *Mail*'s Malcolm Folley with that engaging if sometimes unwise candour with which he often spoke to strangers. 'It's a big house and I don't like being by myself. I don't think I am the sort of person to spend the rest of my life alone whatever happens.' Harry Dunlop, who stayed as assistant until going to help his invalided father at Arundel in November 2002, found rumour-crushing among his tasks. 'People were always on to me with stories,' he recalls. 'It got worse at the end of each year. I remember my brother Ed [who had succeeded poor murdered Alex Scott at Sheikh Maktoum's stable in 1994] asking me, "What happens if he retires? Will you take over?"'

Horses like Khalid Abdulla's colt Shibboleth would show promise but the promise would wither. Daniel Wildenstein had returned to the owners' roster with a talented filly called Rolly Polly, who looked good in the 2001 Fred Darling but blew out in the French 1,000 Guineas. Sandmason won at the Royal meeting in the Howard de Walden apricot livery before succumbing to injury. For the first time in 25 years Warren Place fielded no runners in the Derby, Oaks or either Guineas. At the end of Royal Ascot Henry was depressed enough to wonder aloud if it was worth carrying on.

By the 2001 July meeting he was in better form having won the Lancashire Oaks the previous Saturday for the fifth time in ten years with a Niarchos filly called Sacred Song, who would later play an even more crucial role in her trainer's career. In the *Daily Mail* there was a jolly Henry Cecil tipping column saying how this meeting was one of his favourites, and a feature by Colin Mackenzie trying to look on the bright side in which Cecil dismissed any idea of an impending abdication:

Some of the horses who had problems last year are still not quite right. They were ill for a long time and there are five or six "bleeders" who still are. Last year's virus was damaging and some of the horses were ill for a long time. It weakens their lungs and then they get things like pulled muscles.

It does get you down a bit, but I am absolutely fine now. I have got no intention of retiring – for one thing I can't afford to. What happened at Ascot was that I heard on the telephone that my best two-year-old filly had jarred her knees and then that Beat Hollow, who I was hoping to run in the Eclipse, had also temporarily gone wrong. It was very disappointing and followed a couple of poor runs by my horses. I have a few nice ones but not the numbers I had in past years. One of the reasons is that I was too ill to go to the sales last year. You work hard all your life and then something comes along to knock you on the head. But you have to learn to deal with it and I will be all right. There is no way that I am going to retire.

They were brave words, and while at the close of the year he could talk about having 'a very good end of the season', that was only partly true and most of the horses he mentioned for 2002 would prove unable to deliver. For instance, the three highly awaited Abdulla fillies Half Glance, Protectress and Revealing mustered only one win between them and that, Half Glance's odds-on success in a lowly event at Yarmouth in July, came only after four failed attempts at the target. The highlight of 2001 had been four successive wins for High Pitched, whose breeding and ownership details were symptomatic of the changing trends. For this three-year-old colt by Indian Ridge had been bought as a yearling for a 'bargain' 38,000gns by the Greek tycoon Leonidas Marinopoulos, who had joined Warren Place in 1991 when he had also been best man at Henry and Natalie's wedding. But High Pitched's vendor, Cliveden Stud, had a rather longer Cecil connection, as did the colt's dam Place de l'Opera and grand-dam Madame Dubois, who had both won races for the trainer, the latter crowning a five-victory season in 1990 with the Park Hill Stakes under Steve Cauthen.

Louis Freedman, whose yellow silks with black spots had won immortality for Reference Point in the 1987 Derby, had died in 1998, as had Lord Howard a year later. Louis' son Philip continued with the colours in a more modest way, as did Gilly Howard de Walden with the likes of Sandmason, who won the 2001 Hardwicke Stakes at Royal Ascot under the 'Plantation Stud' banner. Indeed Sandmason had his own long-standing link to Warren Place being a son of Sandy Island, who had won the Lancashire Oaks for the stable under Lester Piggott back in 1984. But this string of well-connected families which had been such a central part of Henry's intake and of the very way he handled his training regime was shortening all the time.

How helpful, then, to have Madame Dubois' grandson return to the yard. How unhappy the news that Prince Fahd died of a heart attack in 2001 followed by his brother, the 'white bridle' Prince Ahmed, a year later. How career-savingly crucial it would be that the Niarchos and in particular Abdulla teams kept sending some of their talented offspring to the Henry Cecil academy.

Because most of the others didn't. Success governs almost everything in racing, always has done, always will. The only place I have been where they played it any different was Hoppegarten in what used to be East Germany, just on the edge of Berlin. There, under the everyone-should-be-equal communist system, Hoppegarten, the other four racecourses, the five national studs, their staff, jockeys and trainers were all paid out of a central financial pool. 'It's no good just blaming Honecker [Erich Honecker, the East German 'First Secretary'] and the other comrades,' said chief executive Artur Bohlke, standing in front of the shabby old grandstand in March 1990. Artur, who had never been a party member and, surprise, surprise, didn't get his title until the week after the Berlin Wall came down, had a cool view about the merits of equine socialism. 'Racing itself has a lot to answer for over here,' he said. 'It always resisted restructuring, had far too many people employed and didn't make success a criterion.'

For Henry Cecil the wind of success with which he had sailed on a seemingly ever favourable sea was suddenly becoming more difficult to find, and as he and his crew struggled they faced a tide that had been on the ebb for some while. Owning a racehorse is an extreme example of a 'discretionary spend'. If an owner doesn't see their or any other of the stable's horses among the winners, they tend either to cut down their commitments or change their allegiance. Once again, they always have done, always will. Of the owners of the top ten highest-rated Warren Place horses in 2001, only Khalid Abdulla and the Niarchos family were still there in 2005; of all the stable's long-standing patrons, only Plantation Stud, Cliveden Stud and the Wills family also had horses with

Henry in 2005. But by that year the winner count had skidded down from 47 to 12, and where there had been 16 horses with a Racing Post Rating (RPR) of 100 or more in 2001, there were only three in 2005. That's not much wind with which to sail your boat.

These were tough times, but it should be stressed quite a bit less straitened than for our friends in Berlin 15 years earlier. The deal there had been that stable lads got 700 marks a month, trainers and jockeys were on 800 marks plus four per cent of winnings, and Artur Bohlke, the head of the whole shooting match, was on just 1,600 marks a month. That last monthly figure equated to £650 on the official exchange rate, although the reality was even worse. Henry Cecil would not have got many Caribbean holidays out of that. Yet as the weather blew him closer and closer to shore, it became hard to see how he could avoid the rocks let alone change tack to sail the highest seas anew.

It was not just his own morale and at times concentration that dipped. The truth is that for all his energy and intuitive gifts he had never fully replicated the personnel balance of the years when the rest of Newmarket practically bowed as the Cecil battalions came marching over the hill of a morning. You could not take lynchpins like Julie, Paddy Rudkin, George Winsor and Willie Jardine out of a crew and expect things to proceed as efficiently as before. Some key players, like ace work rider Frank Storey, retired. Others, like dual Derby-winning lad Dave Goodwin, had decided to move on to other yards. Natalie's interventions had not always been helpful, and in a place which had thrived by being almost myopically racing-focused there could be confusion, not to say resentment, when the centre of the covered ride was converted into a full-scale dressage arena and two dressage horses made demands even on the veterinary staff. 'One day she told me I wouldn't understand why one of them was lame unless I got up and rode it,' says Richard Greenwood's successor Charlie

Light Shift (Ted Durcan, white cap) holds off Peeping Fawn (Martin Dwyer) to register an emotional victory in the 2007 Oaks, and (*below left*) is greeted by her trainer and owner Maria Niarchos in the winner's enclosure. *Below right*: Richard Hughes on Passage Of Time.

Henry Cecil in his study at Warren Place.

Frankel and Shane Fetherstonhaugh burn up the Newmarket gallops.

Frankel as a foal, 2008.

Midday and Tom Queally after winning the Breeders' Cup Filly and Mare Turf at Santa Anita in 2009.

Henry Cecil (*above*) shows his appreciation after Twice Over's second victory in the Champion Stakes, October 2010; and (*below*) on Newmarket Heath with Jane Cecil.

The mighty Frankel: *above*, going gently to the start of the 2011 2,000 Guineas under Tom Queally; *below*, after his sensational eleven-length win in the Queen Anne Stakes, Royal Ascot 2012.

Formal and less formal meetings with Her Majesty the Queen: (*left*) receiving his knighthood in November 2011; and (*below*) after Frankel had won the Queen Elizabeth II Stakes on British Champions Day at Ascot, October 2011.

Team Cecil – *above*, at Warren Place, and *below*, coming down Warren Hill.

Sir Henry Cecil by Johnny Jonas, 2012.

Smith, who had been linked with the stable since 1993. 'Luckily the lads never saw me or they would have pulled my leg to pieces.'

A great stable always depends on much more than just the drive and insight of its principal. Over many fortunate years I have been able to look closely at men such as Vincent O'Brien in Ireland, François Boutin in France, Charlie Whittingham in America and Colin Hayes in Australia, and when they were going well it was always noticeable how secure were all the links in their working chain, and how high was the quality of those who manned them. At the turn of the millennium, quite apart from personal problems that would have sunk a lesser character, it is fair to say the links were not as good for Henry Cecil. And that, as night follows day, meant more problems would affect the horses than in better times, and when lesser horses arrived they would suffer by not being equipped for the rigours of the elite regime around which Henry had always geared his system.

'He didn't really know how to train bad horses,' Willie Ryan observes. 'I always used to say that if he learned to fiddle around with the lesser ones he would have had not a hundred but two hundred winners each season.' The facts of Henry's later resurgence mean it is now possible for those involved to remember with relief in their smiles. 'We used to laugh about handicaps,' says Harry Dunlop. 'He really did not know how they worked. Didn't like what they did. Remember he had once famously said they were "a licence to cheat".' More seriously, Richard Greenwood, who moved into more of a veterinary 'consultant' role when Charlie Smith took on Warren Place as first call in 1998, felt the downward trend had multiple causes. 'In my experience,' he says, 'it's never just one thing, one particular virus. But there were overall health issues just as there were overall staff issues. You can't lose that many key personnel and it not make a difference. And of course what follows is that you get sent inferior horses, which are more likely to succumb to the demands of training. I used to talk a lot to Charlie about it and there was obviously going to be no quick way through.'

Sure enough, ill fortune would not easily loosen its grip. In 2002 Burning Sun won at Royal Ascot as no other Cecil runner would for another seven years, but despite then scoring handsomely in France he ended the season finishing last in the Champion Stakes. High Pitched won a decent race at Newbury but failed in two brave efforts at higher grade. Catherine Wills' filly Succinct showed promise in early summer but ended her three-race career finishing last in the Ribblesdale. Henrietta Tavistock's Oval Office won her only two races on the track but her time was also cut short. The days seemed ever more distant of her dam Pushy and other Tavistock horses such as Precocious carrying those purple and white striped Bloomsbury Stud silks to glory. Henry's seasonal total slipped to just 30 for 2002 and the strike-rate, which in 2001 had dipped below 20 per cent for the first time in 25 years, slid further to 15 per cent of winners to runners. However much he would have it otherwise, it seemed that the only way was down.

As always, troubles rarely come unaccompanied. A plan for 'Henry Cecil Corporate Hospitality' failed to work, as did an unwise involvement with a tipping line and an internet scheme using his name for selling cashmere knitwear. It only needed a foreign nest egg for his children to get scuppered by a massive tax bill to confirm that off-track ideas had never been his forte. On the track in 2003 the Abdulla colt Tuning Fork was the stable's highest-rated performer, but after winning first time out and being second in the Dante he was last at Newmarket, sixth at Ascot and never won again. Similarly the same owner's Midsummer, a half-sister to Oaks winner Reams Of Verse, won promisingly first time but got beaten at Lingfield and Goodwood and was never seen again. The Abdulla filly Singleton

THE DEPTHS

ran second at Royal Ascot but four subsequent efforts could not hit the winner's frame. That year only 25 Warren Place runners could.

Something rather terrible was now happening. While to the wider world the trainer was still a figure of fascination, within the racing circus the cognoscenti had written him off and would raise a slightly condescending eyebrow when they read interviews like Andrew Longmore's mid-2004 piece in *The Sunday Times* quoting Henry as saying, 'I haven't had many people ringing me up recently. When you have had two or three moderate years, you're not in great demand, are you? But we try to be positive. There will be light at the end of the tunnel. It's a long tunnel; a sort of Channel Tunnel.' By the time Clare Balding went to see him on the eve of what was to be another winnerless Royal Ascot in 2005, he had saddled just four winners that season and was to have only another eight by the close. When she had last visited in the days of plenty Henry had had on his desk a grid of over a hundred boxes which he was colouring in a winner at a time. It was not a very big grid now. There is sympathy as she quotes him as saying, 'Things don't always go right and you can't change them. Nowadays I am quite hardened to racing – I accept things much better. I used to get very upset if I was beaten but you can't always win. In some ways my priorities have changed. I know now that this is not the end of the world so just enjoy it. You have to sit down, work it out, and it's a challenge for next time.'

With her own background as the daughter of Derby-winning trainer Ian Balding as well as being in the very first flight of broadcasting and journalism, Clare was too professional to let her own views protrude, but now admits how difficult she found the situation. 'I had always admired him and he had been very kind to me,' she says. 'I felt how harsh the racing game must be for him to drop down so quickly and that he was just pleased to have someone to give him his say when most of Newmarket had turned their backs on him.' But despite wishing it otherwise she still found it hard to think there would be anything but a bad outcome for Henry's final remarks: 'I'll keep at it for as long as I can. I think I will be retired by others rather than retire myself.'

Quite a few had already been trying to do just that. One day in 2005 Henry was walking back from watching a couple of his horses make their unpromising way up the Al Bahathri gallop when he passed a young trainer holding forth to an owner. His words drifted over to Henry on the wind: 'That's Henry Cecil, he should have retired years ago.' The scar that remark was to leave in his memory would be placed alongside the original 'could not train ivy up a wall' he had overheard while yearning for that very first winner way back in 1969. What neither the young trainer by the Al Bahathri nor any of us was to know was that Henry had already equipped himself for the changing of the tide, and that in the autumn two horses would emerge to surf the waves.

Not that his days of swimming valiantly against the tide were over yet. Far from it.

Dick Hern died in May 2002. He was one of the trainers Henry Cecil had most admired, albeit cut from very different cloth, the older man having no racing background and deriving his horsemanship from his own excellence in the eventing saddle rather than from any family exposure to a training stable.

Dick had taken the first of his four championships back in 1962, trained the legendary Brigadier Gerard and saddled the winners of 16 English Classics including three Derby winners. That last Derby, in 1989, was with Nashwan, four years after Dick had broken his back when his horse Badger swerved in mid-air while out hunting with the Cottesmore and threw him into the side of an iron water trough. Dick's favourite thoughts to keep his spirits up came from another horseman, Adam Lindsay Gordon, one-time student at Cheltenham College and poet, adventurer and even politician in Australia as well as one-time rider of a treble over jumps in Melbourne in 1868. You may remember the verse, because at this stage Henry needed every line:

Life is mainly froth and bubble,
Two things stand like stone:
Kindness in another's trouble,
Courage in your own.

In these first few years of the twenty-first century Henry Cecil had undoubtedly visited some pretty dark places but he never seems to have reached the depths plumbed by the dashing Lindsay Gordon. Depressed after a bad head injury at Flemington racecourse in March 1870, the jockey poet walked out into the garden and shot himself. However, in the spring of 2006 even Henry must have been tempted when the tests came back for what had seemed chronic indigestion. For now he had cancer too.

'He was incredible about it,' recalls David Lanigan, Cecil's assistant at Warren Place from 2002. 'He told me at the end of one morning and said we would keep it quiet because it would put off one or two new owners we were getting. It was and is in his stomach, but he said that with regular chemotherapy he should be able to keep going, and he did. Sometimes the treatment would hit him much harder than others. I had to look at the calendar to make sure we made space for him around those times but he just would not miss a day. Obviously he did get weaker in some ways and eventually he had to give up riding. But Snowy was getting very creaky too and Henry was terribly, terribly upset when we finally had to put the old horse down.'

The illness might not have been official but the effects of it began to be all too apparent as what had, for the stable, been a much more hopeful 2006 moved into 2007. 'What with holidays and things I had not seen Henry for quite a few weeks after Christmas,' says Khalid Abdulla's racing manager Teddy Grimthorpe, 'and when I did I was really shocked at the sight of him. I remember clearly coming back and ringing Prince Khalid and telling him I did not think Henry would be alive at the end of the summer. What has happened since is so unbelievable that I have to keep checking to see I am not dreaming it. Forget about racing, hardly anyone, anywhere, has come back from where Henry was headed.'

Teddy was speaking at the end of 2011, the year Henry won the 2,000 Guineas and ruled the roost with Frankel. He was in his office at the top of the handsome Georgian house at Banstead Manor Stud, which is the operational centre of the Abdulla racing empire, some five miles

from Newmarket. It's a place where, as with all that Prince Khalid does, absolute efficiency has to bed down with, but never usurp, a sense of taste and decorum. Suitably, perhaps, Teddy takes his name and title as the fifth Lord Grimthorpe from the first Baron, Edmund Beckett, who was ennobled for his architectural and horological work, which in 1861 saw the creation of the clock tower at Westminster. Teddy's forebear was responsible for the chimes of Big Ben.

The current peer was just plain bloodstock agent Teddy Beckett until he succeeded his father Christy in July 2003. His racing connections extend

Teddy Grimthorpe with Henry Cecil.

to his grandfather (the third Baron),

who won the 1947 Cheltenham Gold Cup with Fortina, the only 'full horse' to do so and therefore able to spend his retirement happily fathering future winners. But Christy Grimthorpe was bitten all too deep by the racing bug. For in 1975 financial demands forced him to sell 11 mares, foals and yearlings in a job lot from his Westow Hall Stud in North Yorkshire to local trainer Mick Easterby, who promptly passed on a filly to be called Mrs McArdy. She then won the 1977 1,000 Guineas two years before Henry Cecil took it for the first time with One In A Million.

Teddy was 18 when Mrs McArdy won the Guineas, so he was all too familiar with how racing fortunes could ebb, as Henry's appeared to once (although to be fair not immediately) the new manager had succeeded Grant Pritchard-Gordon on 1 February 1999. 'We had 30 runners without a sniff of a winner,' says Teddy in his dry, bespectacled way, 'then Wince came along and won the Fred Darling and the 1,000 and saved the day. We did have some nice horses like Beat Hollow and Burning Sun but it was difficult because I was conscious that the whole thing was beginning to unravel. My father had been a great friend of Noel and Gwen Murless and Julie had always been very kind to me, which made it all the more difficult.

'The trouble is that when you have been as successful as Henry had been the expectations are so much higher,' he continued as we revisited the days when the magician at Warren Place seemed finally to have lost his wand. 'After all we were only a few years on from Ahmed Salman saying "the secret of the Classics is to buy a horse and send it to Henry Cecil". But so many of ours would promise and now not deliver. I remember Henry saying "this could be another Oh So Sharp" after a chestnut filly called Revealing won at Newmarket in September 2001. Yet she was never able to run again. There was something wrong. There were a lot of bleeders. It just wouldn't seem to get better.'

The phrase 'burst blood vessel' is common enough parlance in racing circles for 90 per cent of people to consider it no more than a comparatively minor glitch in the pulmonary system that affects a horse's breathing if it happens in a race. Indeed, while this is later reported and the 'b.b.v.' affix added to the form book, any traces of blood often don't transpire until the horse puts its head down in the box afterwards. But a severe burst blood vessel can be a horrendous thing, the actual burst exploding out of the horse's nostrils and soaking the rider in blood. Improved medication makes these worst cases a rarity nowadays, but I still remember it happening to me one day down the back straight at Wincanton some time late in the sixties, and Cecil stable jockey Richard Quinn recalls an even more shocking occasion at Newmarket during the lean years. 'Frank Conlon was breezing a three-year-old up Warren Hill when it burst so bad that it came down and collapsed on its side with blood gushing out of it. Frank was no chicken then, it must have been very traumatic. Nothing burst quite as bad as that again, but almost the worst thing about the situation was the inconsistency between what happened on the gallops and on the track. One horse would work much better than another at home but on the racecourse it would be quite different. Henry was great to work for, a real gentleman. But it was difficult for everyone.'

Quinn had joined the stable in 2000 in the confident hope that the Warren Place support could put him in with a shot at the jockeys' championship, just as it had for Joe Mercer, Lester Piggott, Pat Eddery and Kieren Fallon before him. In fact, while Richard was second to Kevin Darley (with Fallon injured) in 2000, that score of 141 was to prove the highest of his career; 2003, his final season with the stable, saw his total slip below the 100 mark not least because Warren Place could provide only one horse in Quinn's top ten and that, Bagan, was a 50-1 outsider when it won a big handicap at York.

Richard was not the only one to feel the numbers on the ebb. In 1992 the Racing Post Trophy-winning exploits of the two-year-old Armiger meant that a Henry Cecil-trained colt was the most successful of the Abdulla horses in England. That situation had been repeated five times, most recently in 1998 (in 1999 Wince was actually second to Distant Music, the Barry Hills-trained winner of the Dewhurst). But by 2003 the most successful horse in the Abdulla rankings from the Cecil stable was the filly Ithaca at a lowly 17th. 'I remember,' says Harry Dunlop, 'Henry saying rather wistfully to me "we are no longer getting the crème de la crème",' to which Charlie Smith adds, 'You only had to look at some of the horses coming in from Juddmonte [the collective name for the Abdulla studs] to see these were not the most impressive of individuals.'

Teddy Grimthorpe denies there was any specific downgrading, pointing out that while Henry was still getting a fair allocation of yearlings, unsuccessful two- and three-year-olds meant both that his numbers dipped and that few if any older horses would be kept on to fly the flag. There is no clearer proof of the trainer's comeback than the Abdulla picture in 2011. Among the Prince's most successful horses in Britain that year the first four were all trained by Henry Cecil: Frankel, who was a three-year-old, Timepiece (four), Midday (five) and the dual Champion Stakes winner Twice Over, an evergreen six summers gone. Teddy insists that, while he and stud manager Philip Mitchell might add details of where the dams of the individual yearlings had been trained or what ground they or their progeny seemed to prefer, the final decision would be left to Prince Khalid. 'He takes all the papers,' says Teddy, 'and goes off into almost papal conclave with himself. When he is finished we may not get the white smoke but he will hand the papers back with the yearling allocated to each trainer. Would Henry have got better quality if he had been flying? Probably.'

It was a situation that would have depressed even the sunniest soul, and there is no doubt that at times it affected Henry Cecil. 'My memory,' says Grimthorpe, 'is that he got as near to the brink as is possible both professionally, physically and in every way. Another year like 2005 and it would have been hard for him to stay in business.' Yet while statistically this was the absolute nadir of the Cecil fortunes, the most dangerous time for Henry as a person had actually been three years earlier when the slide first gathered momentum.

Before Royal Ascot in 2002 he was forced to deny a Sunday newspaper piece quoting one Warren Place worker as saying 'the place is falling apart' and another remarking that 'no one thinks he has the stomach for it any more'. During an Attheraces interview at Doncaster that autumn Frank Conlon was suddenly flummoxed by an unwittingly penetrating question. 'Where's Henry?' asked Derek Thompson. Frank flannelled, an activity to which his friends know he is well suited, but suddenly realised that the answer was 'I don't know'.

Yet for all that, for all the afternoons when Henry would just go to bed after third lot and hope the world would go away, he was a man back in focus when David Lanigan came up to see him in November 2002 with a view to taking over from Harry Dunlop as assistant. 'Henry asked me up to lunch at Warren Place during the Houghton Yearling Sales,' remembers David, whose parents Bob and Deirdre owned and ran the highly successful Tullamaine Castle Stud near Fethard in Tipperary and who himself had ridden out for Vincent O'Brien during his school holidays before getting a degree in agriculture at Cirencester and then doing rather more serious racing postgraduate work for five years with Johnny Jones' stud and racing stable in Kentucky. 'We had sausages and mustard and he said there had been some problems but that he was determined to overcome them. Maybe I was young and naive, but I believed we could do it, and even though it got very difficult at times we just kept at it. Through all this what really kept us going was the way in which Henry was insistent that we should not falter. Even though the results were going down he kept being positive.'

Nonetheless, running the operation had to be a matter of handling the siege while working double time to find a way to defeat the enemy, and when extra help was needed it came from across the sea. As the inconsistency of the horses continued, and in consequence the winner count dwindled, the vet Charlie Smith got Lanigan to call on his friends at the Irish Equine Centre, where Professor Tom Buckley's microbiology department had developed a specialist unit under Alan Creighton for testing the environment in racing yards. What has now become an international service for stables as far away as Japan was formed after helping Irish trainer Dessie Hughes out of something of a slump a couple of years earlier. Bringing Alan over turned out to be a crucial move in the drive to end the vicious circle that seemed to have Warren Place in its grip.

The situation at Dessie Hughes's yard had been turned around not just by the identification of a fungus called aspergillus in all parts of the stable from hay to feedstuff to bedding and the covered ride, but by systematically altering the practices that had allowed what is essentially a form of mould to develop. Dessie's son Richard Hughes had become the retained rider for Khalid Abdulla, but not necessarily on the Cecil horses. After Dessie watched one run as poorly at Newmarket as his own had in Ireland he related his own case to Teddy Grimthorpe. All hands were coming to the pump.

But it's one thing to identify a problem, another to solve it. 'We located aspergillus in feed, bedding and other places,' says Creighton, who is affectionately known as 'Fungus Paddy' this side of the water. 'The presence of aspergillus can lead to aspergillosis, which is an infection of the air passage so crucial to a racehorse. So it was a question of clearing the whole environment and changing some of the practices that had brought the problem in the first place. Charlie and I and David worked together but there was never going to be a quick fix, and to be honest it took time for all the staff to buy into what we were trying to do.'

There were some obvious things like moving the chaff cutter, which could fill the feed house with little particles of hay, and ending the use of replacing brooms with blowers to clean the yard and all too often blowing dirty bits of muck back into the atmosphere of the boxes where the horses were feeding. From 2004 Creighton came over every six weeks. His tests were a reinforcement of the changes Smith and Lanigan were encouraging, and bit by bit the results improved until finally in early 2008 he could be sure the yard was clear. Even now, if Charlie or Mike Marshall (Lanigan's successor as assistant) are not happy with something they call Alan over. They did when concerned about one or two bad performances in the summer of 2011, but everything was still clear.

Anyone doubting the absolute necessity of keeping a racehorse's narrow air passage entirely infection-free should ponder the thought that at full gallop no fewer than 2,000 litres of air are being pumped down it to provide enough oxygen to propel 500kg of athlete at up to 40mph. Then study a diagram of how much lengthier is the air's nostril-to-lungs journey than in the human athlete, who inhales through the mouth and eventually generates hardly a third of the speed with a more than eight times lighter body mass. Take Charlie Smith's helpful layman's analogy of horses with one of these viral complaints being inflicted 'by a form of asthma' and you can understand how so often through these fallow years a Henry Cecil runner would move up promisingly in a race only to drop away when extra effort and therefore air intake was needed.

Watching these races must have been dispiriting work, but the key players persevered and, best of all, the trainer kept his spirits up.

David Lanigan remembers the kick they got out of winning three little handicaps with a filly called Portrait Of A Lady in 2004 – a Cecil horse would not have stooped to that in the golden days. Better still he recalls the trainer's reaction that same year when confronted by an old lady in a wheelchair on the way to saddle the much-awaited Camacho on the two-year-old's debut at Newmarket. 'We felt this was the sort of horse that could put us back on the map, so we were all very wound up,' says David, 'then Henry sees this old girl asking for an autograph and he stops, signs the racecard, and then kneels down beside the chair and puts her hat on his head for the photograph. The horse won all right, but I remember thinking what style it was to bother about the old lady at that crucial time.'

For Henry Cecil, 'kindness in another's trouble, courage in your own' was being put very firmly to the test. Dee Deacon is a Northampton girl who had joined the yard in 1998 and who by 2012 had progressed to being head lass in charge of the equine temple – that part of Warren Place which housed the deity that is Frankel. As the horse and therefore staff numbers slid she was one of the few, along with Billy Aldridge, Peter Emmerson, John Fletcher, Billy Brown and John Scott, who stayed the course. 'Of course there were times when we got pretty low,' says Dee. 'It's hard to come out with the same vim and vigour when horses are running badly and the numbers are down. But he always kept incredibly positive. He would gather us together and tell us not to believe any rumours of retirement, that we could get through this, that there was no way he was packing up. We thought that if he's going to battle, we will too.'

Still, in 2005, as we know, it was getting precious close to the end game. Indeed but for a strong-swimming lifeguard Henry would not have started any season ever again. While on holiday in South Africa with Henry Ponsonby and his wife in January, Henry and his then companion Angela Scott got caught by the currents at Plettenberg

Bay near Port Elizabeth and for a while it looked like he was heading not for the racing heights but for Davy Jones' locker.

Back home there was almost as strong a wake-up call from Henry's accountant with the stark assessment that without further drastic pruning of staff and an increase in tenant income Warren Place would be completely unviable. 'I remember Henry sitting me down and being very professional about it,' says David Lanigan. 'We planned what staff we would let go and how we would keep the main yard by the house and let out all the rest. We would continue with our clean-up systems, and most of all we would keep on believing.' Lanigan's own belief would be tested when a tempting offer came from America, which Henry then insisted he went over to explore. Only much later, when the tide had clearly turned, did he tease David about having the 'wisdom' to turn it down.

Not many would have thought Lanigan wise at the time. The Cecil 'first lot' would be little more than a dozen strong as it trailed down from Warren Place, and except for the always Classic-bred yearlings still coming from the Niarchos and Abdulla camps there could surely be no hope of climbing back from this blackest of holes. In early 2005 even that slim chance was diminished when a promising Niarchos two-year-old called Multidimensional was hospitalised with pneumonia. But he survived, and the spirits of those in the pit were further revived when among the yearlings that autumn was a Niarchos filly, who was to be called Light Shift, and an Abdulla one out of Clepsydra, who had taken a little race on the full Derby course at Epsom in August 2000. She was named Passage Of Time. They were young members of famous families. Along with Multidimensional they were soon to make fame of their own.

By the time they did their trainer would have shocked the world with the evidence of his professional comeback all too easily echoed by the outward signs of his personal battle against cancer. Much of

Henry Cecil's earlier life may indeed have had plenty of 'froth and bubble', but what happened as he battled the 'Big C' finally altered any doubts about his standing as a man.

The curse of cancer had not yet appeared as Henry Cecil set off into 2006. But once it did he faced it down as stoically as the other mishaps inflicted by an apparently vengeful fortune. He and those closest to him came to realise another depth to the easy phrase that 'training was his life'. For Henry Cecil did not so much live for his work as now only stay alive because of it.

He did not make his illness public until February 2007 when, after first telling his staff, he issued a brief statement. 'I didn't want to discuss it,' he said, 'but I have been having treatment for non-Hodgkin's lymphoma for the last nine months. The treatment has been going well, I'm on the mend, and it hasn't affected my work in any way. I've been carrying on as normal throughout, and enjoying it.' If you talked to him he would add little beyond the need to keep positive, but on occasions he could be quite passionate in his credo. 'I really do believe,' he said to me one day, 'that you can help yourself by having thoughts about the things you like and want to do in the future. If people ever ask me for advice I say to them, "Think of things that you enjoy, that make you feel good." If you can keep your mind happy, your body must have a chance too, don't you think?'

Much is made of the 24/7 stresses of training racehorses but no one should forget the early-morning inspiration of your very own hopes on the hoof. The gardener in Henry that delighted in thoughts of blooms to come would be even more exercised by the dreams of what his horses might become as the season progressed, or, better still, as the next one did. He became a living symbol of that rather grisly racing adage 'no trainer ever committed suicide with a couple of promising two-year-olds yet to run'.

In 2006 at least a couple of his two-year-olds did indeed seem 'promising'. Even more importantly, Henry now had someone with whom to share the dream. Jane McKeown had returned to his life and it was to her every bit as much as to his positive attitude that he could ascribe his improved position, both physically and financially. Jane, as the daughter of jockey Charlie Guest, sister of trainers Richard and Rae, and former wife of jockey Terry McKeown, had long been locked into the pulse and the perils of the racing calling. As Henry's secretary in the late nineties she was also familiar with the demands of Warren Place, and as the person who drove him away from court at the end of his driving case in 2000, when their relationship first become public, she knew how demanding he could be.

So much so that for 18 months she had left for a job in Dubai with Sheikh Mohammed's Godolphin team. But she was back in 2005 when the accountant read the riot act. And she was there a year later when the doctors produced even unhappier news. As such her role has sometimes been as much that of nurse or business partner as normal wifely duties, but all the more important for that. Inevitably there are those who roll their eyes when a third marriage comes round, as this one finally did in June 2008, but those who study the resurgence of Henry Cecil can be certain that one of the keys has been the presence of Jane at his side.

Warren Place would now be a very different stable from the unstoppable juggernaut of the eighties, but it would still be a stable. Jane Cecil stresses that for Henry, the stable was his life, and that had he gone bankrupt and stopped training, his life would have been over. So Warren Place had to be kept going. With the number of people working there having sunk to just ten or twelve, other staff houses could be rented out. Jonathan Jay had come into the Hovels – complete with Grade One-winning hurdler Tidal Fury – and stayed until August 2006. Ed Vaughan occupied the Fillies' Yard until the end of 2007, and Paul Howling's string occupied part of the stables from 2005 until the end of 2010. This was a highly unusual set-up for a major yard – never mind an establishment as iconic as Warren Place – but everyone involved was very positive, and got on with each other perfectly well.

Ed Vaughan had been assistant to Henry's friend and fellow trainer Alec Stewart, who lost his own battle with cancer in August 2004. 'I wanted to start up on my own,' says Ed, 'but had hardly a dozen horses and did not have a yard. Henry heard about this and said he had room. He could not have been more helpful in my time there. After a year in the Fillies' Yard I moved across to the Hovels and had a really good season there in 2007. That was the year Henry won the Oaks with Light Shift, so there was a good feeling all round. What I really admired about him was the way he never panicked. He may have been changing one or two things in the yard, but he never changed the way he trained. He still fed straight oats rather than nuts or special mixes, still felt his way with his horses. At that stage his numbers were down and he had lesser horses. But his comeback just shows that you cannot buy talent.'

By 2006 new signs of that talent were already beginning to appear. So too, although still kept private, were the effects of his illness. Reams Of Verse's half-sister Novellara won so impressively first time out that she went to the Ribblesdale Stakes as Henry's sole, albeit unsuccessful Royal Ascot contender. The trainer looked as resplendent as ever. The best help of all would come from the winner's circle and as that summer moved on towards autumn, that best of treatments began to take hold.

Multidimensional had got over the previous year's pneumonia. He was not as small as his mother Sacred Song and stood out in the paddock when he finally appeared at Newmarket in June. Patience and the knowledge of the equine Niarchos families paid off with a vengeance as the now three-year-old colt stormed home as if it were 'the good old days'. Much, much better than that, after repeating the trick at the same course a month later and then being hopelessly unsuited to the firm going at Goodwood, Multidimensional went over to Deauville to land the Group Two Prix Guillaume d'Ornano under the French jockey Christophe Lemaire. In the great scheme of things it was hardly the biggest event on the planet, but it was the main event of the day, it was Henry Cecil's first Group winner since Burning Sun won in France four years earlier, and it was in the distinctive dark blue, light blue cross belt colours of the Niarchos family, who had remained rock solid in their support.

Maria Niarchos was there, and Henry was touching in his tribute to her and to her father Stavros Niarchos, who had first been at Warren Place in the early eighties. He was also generous in his praise for the good sense of Ted Durcan, Multidimensional's jockey at Goodwood. The pair had been last of eight that day but on his return the rider told Henry that he had eased up because the colt was unhappy on the firm going. 'A less confident trainer might have quarrelled or gone back to the drawing board,' says Ted. 'But he understood what I was saying. He believed in the horse. The Deauville race was just two weeks later but he had the balls to go there. I knew then he had not lost it.'

Ted had been educated to be a solicitor like his Dublin-based father but his further studies had been of the racing kind and he had finally found champion jockey success during his winters in Dubai. In consequence Godolphin was his main summer employer, but when Willie Ryan retired at the end of 2004 he was able to fit the then not hugely extensive job of riding work for the Cecil stable with his other duties. It was now starting to pay off on the racetrack. A week before Deauville he had ridden Passage Of Time to her first victory at Newmarket. A month later, to use a unique-to-racing phrase, Durcan 'donned the Niarchos silks' to win on the two-year-old filly Light Shift on the same course. It was Light Shift's third and last race of the year. It did not leave her very highly rated but Ted liked her attitude. A year later, the world would too.

Meanwhile it was Passage Of Time who would put her shoulder to the climbing wheel and it was the Juddmonte stable jockey Richard Hughes who rode her. He did so to such impressive effect at Newmarket at the end of October that Teddy Grimthorpe put up the seemingly daring plan of running the filly against the colts in the Group One Criterium de Saint-Cloud in Paris a fortnight later. 'At the time Prince Khalid was neck and neck with the Aga Khan for the French owners' championship,' remembers Teddy, before adding with a smile, 'In the high days I am not sure how Henry would have reacted if I had suggested we took one of his best two-year-old fillies over to France in November. But at that stage he was very keen to take a chance.'

So, when the stalls opened, was Richard Hughes. 'I rode one of the most daring races of my whole career,' he says in his autobiography, admitting how, ignoring Henry's 'go with the flow' instructions, he held up Passage Of Time behind the leaders and then angled her through the narrowest of gaps in the final furlong to outgun the future Irish Derby winner Soldier Of Fortune before the line. Hughes is as long and pipe-cleaner thin as that famous willowy Spy cartoon of Fred Archer 130 years ago. Richard had the same jump-racing roots as Archer, who had won 13 consecutive Flat racing championships by the time he shot himself in a fit of depression at the age of 29. Like Fred, but without resort to spurs or 'cutting whip', Hughes specialised in the daring late challenge. When these fail, they fail disastrously. When they succeed, it can be the sweetest thing. There were few sweeter than this day when Henry Cecil saddled his first

Group One winner since Beat Hollow won the Grand Prix de Paris in 2000. The Burnett flag once again flew over Warren Place. Best of all, there was promise of even better to come. The next year would see the promise kept.

To the surprise of many, it was not Passage Of Time who did the keeping in 2007. Her performance at Saint-Cloud may have made her favourite for the Oaks throughout the winter and spring, but early in the year she got an infection that led to an abscess in her mouth. A tall, quite light-framed filly, she did not thrive and her trainer was not able to produce her until the Musidora Stakes. Although she won all right there was only a neck in it at the line. No matter that Richard Hughes reported that she was pulling up when in the lead and that the filly was found to be 'in season', not all of us were entirely convinced she was that much of a certainty for Epsom. Not everyone at Warren Place was either.

While Passage Of Time battled her problems, Light Shift positively bloomed. She and Ted Durcan powered home at Newbury, and then at tight-turning Chester she coursed down ten rivals like the little greyhound she was. 'Henry excels with this type of filly,' Ted observes. 'He has a plan in his head and he takes them slowly, slowly and lets them come to him. It's not just hindsight but by Oaks day I didn't think she was a second string and neither did Dave Lanigan.'

On the morning of the big race the *Racing Post* hedged its bets but caught the mood. 'It's All About Henry' the front page proclaimed, and in the afternoon the BBC coverage rightly followed suit. The greatest Classic trainer of our time had seemed lost but now was found again. The viewers had not seen him for a while and he was a lot greyer and older than they remembered, the thinning hair cut short, the sickness very evident. They wished him winners like they wished him health.

Since Passage Of Time was favourite, it was on her that the tightest focus fixed. Richard Hughes had her fast out of the stalls, his bent-hairpin of a body poised easily above as he settled in third or fourth place behind the leaders. At these moments the mind races ahead on a script for your runner to follow. But as that 2007 Oaks field came through Tattenham Corner the Hughes body lowered and the elbows began to move. The script could not be followed, the longed-for 'Henry Cecil comeback' would not be hailed. You wanted to look away in disappointment – until you remembered he had another runner.

At the top of Epsom's famous hill Light Shift had been in danger of being trapped at the back of the field before Ted Durcan moved her out wide, and she repaid him with a run round Tattenham Corner of the slingshot kind. As Hughes began to work, Durcan gathered his filly to strike. Passing over the road which (and it could only happen at Epsom) actually crosses the Classic track, All My Loving, the principal Aidan O'Brien hope, struck for home with three furlongs left to run. Light Shift was after her, and in a hundred brilliant yards had shot past and moved across to hug the rail. A quarter of a mile to run in the Oaks and the race was won if the breath and the legs and the heart would take her.

Light Shift had beaten those around her, but from way out of the pack there now came Peeping Fawn, the O'Brien second string. Only five days earlier she had been third in the Irish 1,000 Guineas; this was already her sixth race of the season and after this she would be unbeaten in four more. Racing towards the furlong pole it looked as if Peeping Fawn's momentum would win through unless Light Shift could dig very deep.

Light Shift was lean but her neck was set very straight, the white diamond on her forehead very steady as she strained every sinew to hold on. Ted Durcan used the old trick of changing his whip from his right hand to his left and as he did so the filly changed her foreleg lead, and grabbed a new rhythm and bite to her stride. Peeping Fawn had got to her quarters. It was as far as she would get.

'My filly was trying so hard,' said Durcan with the admiration reserved for the one who has shared that 'top-of-the-centaur' moment. 'She was so determined it was as if she was mirroring Henry. With Passage Of Time failing, the whole race might have been an anti-climax, like when the Queen's Carlton House was only third in the Derby. Henry needed her to rally and the little honey helped him out.'

As the horses hurtled over the line the cameras flashed back to the impact hitting Henry. With his face still frozen with tension he first kissed a cloche-hatted Jane to his right and then a frizzy-haired, dark-glassed little Jake to his left. With the realisation of victory running through him, he motor-memoried his way down to that famous winner's circle where he had walked seven times before. His mouth showed the strain as his arms reached out to well-wishing handshakes and his eyes struggled to hold back the flow. When he reached that little hallowed patch of green a voice called out, 'Three cheers for Henry Cecil!' As the crowd roared out in answer his lower lip jabbered and he had to wipe away a tear.

Only two years earlier Clare Balding had sat in his study and doubted if he would have any future at all. Now she was beside him and introducing 'the man of the moment'. Firmly but gently she coaxed out a few short, quick, clipped sentences so packed with emotion you felt that at any time Henry's lips or eyes would betray him. 'I thought the two fillies would go close,' he said, 'there's not much between them. Marvellous for Ted. He's a great friend. Helps a lot. Marvellous for the staff. Through all my illness . . . very supportive. Yes, it means a lot.' One last gulp, and then he said what we wanted to hear: 'It's lovely to be back.'

And it was lovely for the whole racing world to welcome Henry back. What he needed now was a supply of good horses and a guarantee of good health for himself. To the anguish of his supporters he would be granted the first but not the second.

12

RESURGENCE

WATCHING THE aftermath of that 2007 Oaks was an extraordinary experience, both uplifting and haunting at the same time. Light Shift's much-applauded victory was Henry Cecil's eighth in the Oaks and a modern-times-record 24th English Classic for him as a trainer. A day later Frankie Dettori made his own headlines by winning the Derby at the 15th attempt. But while Frankie did his trademark flying dismount like a very young 37-year-old with many glories to come, Henry seemed all of his 64 years as the emotion and the illness saw him stumble on to the winner's podium. He was back with another Classic, but there was a horrible sense that it might well be his last.

Yet good horses are fierce medicine. Neither Light Shift nor Passage Of Time won again that year but they still competed at the highest level, Light Shift coming second to her Oaks victim Peeping Fawn in the Irish Oaks at the Curragh and then third to her at Goodwood. Passage Of Time had the long-delayed operation for her throat abscess and then returned to run a good third in the Prix Vermeille at Longchamp before going to America for the Breeders' Cup Filly and Mare Turf only to be bogged down in the rain-swamped grass track at Monmouth, New Jersey. Henry was playing on the big stage again. Better still, he had more young hopefuls to carry the flag. He even had a potential Derby horse.

It was called Twice Over. He did not run until October but then won both his races so easily that Richard Hughes stated, 'He's as good a two-year-old as I have ridden in a while.' The bookmakers marked him up for Epsom next June. Twice Over did not make it to the Derby but by the end of 2011 he had become the highest prize-winning horse Henry had ever trained. Over three continents, four seasons and 27 races he would amass more than £2.4 million for Khalid Abdulla, winning the Eclipse, the Champion Stakes twice, the Juddmonte International and big races in France and Dubai, as well as running third in the Breeders' Cup Classic. He was a four-legged reminder of the lasting values of loyalty, patience and class. As Twice Over's career flourished Henry used to call him 'one of my best friends'. It didn't seem a silly thing to say.

Twice Over was a fine, big, if rather plain horse with a large, open, honest head. He was all Juddmonte breeding, by the Abdulla stallion Observatory out of the mare Double Crossed, with whom Henry had won the Lingfield Oaks Trial in 2001 and who herself was out of Quandary with whom Henry won three races back in 1995. Quandary was also, through her daughter Clepsydra, the grand-dam of Passage Of Time. That may be getting too detailed – I'll admit my own ears can glaze over when people start reciting pedigrees. Nonetheless, the importance of this family knowledge for Henry and for all who worked at Warren Place could hardly be overestimated.

When we sometimes regret Henry not being more explicit when it comes to explaining his training methods, perhaps we have not listened hard enough. 'I am like a schoolmaster,' he used to say when Warren Place was overflowing. 'Two hundred in a school is not really that many. I get to know all the pupils, I remember a lot of their families, I split them into matching groups and let them come along together. It's common sense really.' Common sense perhaps, but also something of the genius of simplicity. For while what is happening out there on the gallops and in the yard is not rocket science, it does need clear and

In stride: Henry Cecil with Mike Marshall at Warren Place.

understanding heads to take what are quite simple but young, fragile and volatile thoroughbreds through the rigours of physical preparation. Because of this a trainer cannot prosper without the right staff. To that end, Henry made a crucial appointment in the autumn of 2007, when Mike Marshall and his wife Aideen joined the team.

David Lanigan had done wonders to see the yard through and out of the aspergillus-ridden mire but was now leaving to train on his own, very much with Henry's blessing. 'At one of the worst stages,' says David, 'I remember his telling me that he was determined to make things better not just for him but for my future career. And when I had a press release ready to announce that I was setting up, he insisted on holding it back until he had called his contacts to make sure they supported me. Working for him was an incredible experience. He was boss enough to give you a bollocking but was also a friend. Some of my favourite times were sitting out on the terrace with him on Sunday morning going through the programme book for races ahead. He would ask me to find a little race for some filly and when I had at last got something he would trot out the exact programme. He can seem away with the fairies but he just knows so much.'

Lanigan, and Harry Dunlop before him, had been vital in holding the ship together as it edged perilously close to the rocks, the numbers dwindling, the winners and staff in decline. But now the wind and the currents were set fair again, and as more horses and new staff arrived, someone fresh was needed to instil order, to ensure that everything was ship-shape below decks, to leave Henry free to concentrate on the bridge where his real genius lay. After years of smiling service Frank Conlon had also left, at the end of 2005. Great work rider though he was, Frank was never quite the stickler for detail that Paddy Rudkin had been and that a newly resurgent Henry would now need. Mike Marshall would exactly fit that bill.

He was actually billed as 'assistant' rather than 'head lad' but still had plenty of ankle-snapping directness about him. His father 'Ginger' Marshall had been a stalwart of John Dunlop's Arundel team where the young Mike first worked before going to Ian Balding and becoming an apprentice and a successful enough jockey to have ridden a double on the same card on which Mtoto beat the Cecil star Indian Skimmer in the 1988 Eclipse. Following a spell with Dick Hern he went to work for Godolphin, where he became a head man before being recruited to Warren Place. In horseracing terms, Mike Marshall's education had been in the scholarship stream.

A health scare had stopped him riding out, so he and Henry made a happily contrasting pair as they watched the horses circle in the covered yard of a morning: the tall, languid figure of the trainer alongside the short, purposeful frame of the assistant. The image spoke of 'Elegance' and his 'Enforcer'. Warren Place would do what it said on the tin.

Mike did not come alone. He and Aideen had eloped from Ian Balding's long ago and she too had top-level racing experience; she also matched her husband in terms of a tireless attention to detail. At 4.30am even Henry Cecil is not up at Warren Place, but Aideen Marshall is, already feeding her stamping, softly whinnying students in the Fillies' Barn. The word at Newmarket had been that the best of Henry's staff had either left or were retiring. Mike and Aideen were soon setting new standards, and others were matching them.

The gaggle of British hacks who watched Passage Of Time canter on the track before her Breeders' Cup bid at Monmouth Park in October 2007 might have noticed something familiar about the rider. It was Shane Fetherstonhaugh, who had won deserved acclaim as the man who sat on the livewire Derby favourite Motivator in the much-publicised (a fair bit of it by me in a monthly series in the *Racing Post*) build-up to that colt winning at Epsom in 2005. By the Monmouth Park trip Shane had already been 18 months at Warren Place and had not regretted a minute of it. 'Some people told me I was joining a sinking ship when I went for a job there at the beginning of 2006,' remembers the man whose first racing experience was with his Irish journalist father, 'but I wanted a change, and when I went up and met Henry he was really upbeat. He said how things would improve, how better horses would be coming in. It was extraordinary. He talked like a young trainer starting out.' Shane was exactly the sort of quiet, skilful rider and stablehand Henry loved to have on his horses. At the beginning of 2008 he teamed up with a two-year-old filly called Midday who would prove Twice Over's globe-trotting counterpart, becoming the highest-winning female Henry had ever trained. Early in 2011 Shane was to ride an even more high-profile runner, called Frankel.

Back at the end of 2007, however, such highlights were still some way into dreamland, though the tide was noticeably on the turn. After the 12-winner pit of 2005, the figures had climbed to 25 in 2006 and 45 in 2007; the prize money too had rocketed from £144,000 to £732,000. And entering 2008 it was clear this was only a start. The only thing better for a trainer than two winners on the same day is another double on the next, and that is exactly what Henry Cecil did on the last day of the Craven and the first of the Newbury Greenham meeting in 2008. In the race after Twice Over won the Craven Stakes, Phoenix Tower beat Multidimensional in the Earl of Sefton; and when a filly called Burn The Breeze followed the Niarchos colt Unnefer to win consecutive races at Newbury the ever-reserved *Racing Post* Analysis quietly logged: 'Henry Cecil can do little wrong at the minute.'

Twice Over's Derby hopes ended when he was beaten in the Dante, but he ran well at Royal Ascot and a win in the Prix Eugene Adam at Maisons-Laffitte rightly suggested that bigger days lay ahead. So did the German-owned colt Kandahar Run's victory in the Newmarket Stakes, which earned him an Epsom ticket and brought the press to Henry's door to wonder if the magic of Light Shift's Oaks was still doing its work.

They found that, while the Warren Place horses were blooming, the trainer was not. In the early months of 2008 the chemotherapy hadn't been containing the cancer and with the doctors scratching their heads Prince Khalid had insisted that Henry went to the Mayo Clinic in Minnesota to see if they had anything not on offer over here. The clinic suggested a slightly different type of treatment that was also available in England, but although Henry went to a hospital in London, it hadn't really helped. The *Daily Telegraph*'s Paul Kelso was quite shocked when he went to Warren Place at the beginning of Derby week. 'I have been feeling pretty unwell,' Henry told him with that startling openness he often reserves for those he has just met. 'I've got to get the cancer under control and get rid of it. It hasn't spread and it is probably under control but Rome wasn't built in a day. I've had lots of chemotherapy. I'm not sure quite how much I've had, 15 or 16 maybe. These sorts of things are terrifying really, and the thing is you have to be very determined to beat it. The only way to do that is to be very positive and get on with things, and I think that helps a lot. When you are lying on the sofa worrying about the pain in your tummy, that doesn't do any good. So I look to the future.'

It was a stark assessment, as was his analysis of what had gone wrong. 'I think over the years getting to the top, it was exciting and I was lucky,' said Henry. 'I had very good support and good owners and horses, and probably year after year one took it for granted. It was easy, but I've always wanted to beat everyone else. Then I went through a period with the studs cutting down, a lot of my owner-breeders died, and my personal life and everything went to rock-bottom. Everything combined really. One just kept being knocked on the head, and you hadn't the horses to pick you up.'

As if mindful of the dangers of dwelling on the problem, Henry moved quickly to the positives, first giving credit to the lady he was to marry before Ascot. 'With Jane's help we've managed to pull things together,' he said, referring to the financial situation at the stable, which had been losing up to £180,000 a year, 'and now it's basically got its head above water and the business is secure rather than looking like it was going bankrupt. Jane is much more streetwise than me. I'm much more slapdash and I'm not very good with money. Basically I do everything through instinct. I'm not a financial brain, it's all instinct really. I am always picking on things which go into this very small brain. Sometimes I use it.'

All of this was a typical Cecil mix of charm, power and vulnerability, and as he discussed what had happened at Epsom a year earlier it was as if he was using it as a lever to crank up renewed ambition. 'Light Shift's Oaks didn't feel harder won, but it did feel fantastic,' he said. 'You think that if you can win an Oaks, perhaps that means you are capable of winning other Classics again, and hopefully it helps advertise that one is not a has-been and maybe to think about the future.'

It was an attitude backed not just by results but by people, some of them from the most unlikely of places. Best man at the June 2008 wedding (in best 'busman's holiday' tradition the honeymoon was at Royal Ascot) was Gerhard Schoeningh, a German financier whose interest in racing and Henry Cecil had been kindled as a member of Bristol University Turf Club, and who had since sold part of his London business to start transforming Berlin's Hoppegarten racecourse from that East German basket case I had visited in 1990. 'He was the hero of my racing youth,' admits Gerhard, who first had a Warren Place horse in the dog days of 2005. 'A lot of people said "you are crazy to go to him", but I sensed the hunger was still there and really came to like him as a person. What he has achieved in his fight against adversity is very admirable. He is also highly entertaining, although he can be pretty stubborn. We have had some good times.'

So has Shane Fetherstonhaugh. 'I have got a cracking new filly!' he called out in Newmarket High Street one summer day in 2008. 'She runs next week!' Midday did not win that first race but she promised plenty, if not quite the whole astonishing career which in 23 runs over four seasons would land £2.2 million for the Juddmonte operation, with nine races won, six of them at the highest Group One level including a Breeders' Cup victory at Santa Anita, California in November 2009. No doubt it was the likes of Midday that inspired

Henry before the 2008 Champion Stakes to say of training, 'I love it. In fact I've enjoyed it more in the last two years than ever before. For lots of reasons I went into a downward spiral for a while, but when that happens you've got to pick yourself up. I've always enjoyed a challenge and I've enjoyed trying to do this.'

He was trumpeting old themes again, but while there were indeed many greater glories ahead, cancer's claw would not back away any more than would the sort of instant disaster that any stable can suffer any morning. Early in December 2008 the top-rated two-year-old Wingwalker collapsed and died during a routine canter on Warren Hill. He was a grandson of Peplum, one of those very first Abdulla fillies to come to Henry's in the 1990s. Wingwalker's two victories had put him in the betting for the following year's 2,000 Guineas, but none of these connections counted any more. 'He was dead when he hit the ground,' said Shane Fetherstonhaugh, who had been in the saddle. 'A furlong from the end of the canter it felt to me as if he was trying to get under the rails. I was pulling his head up and then down he went. I thought he must have broken his leg at first but they said it was a heart attack. It was the strangest thing looking at him. He had gone from being this beautiful horse to just being a slab of meat. In his eye I could see the life going out of him.'

Black clouds do not often come alone. That same month they also loomed above the trainer with a very depressing meeting with the cancer specialist, who said that stem cell therapy would only be possible if they could reduce the tumour first. That involved two weeks of daily radiotherapy in early 2009, which by March had been effective enough for a stem cell transplant to be tried. Unhappily all the earlier chemotherapy meant there were not enough cells for a transplant, so from then on Henry had to survive on maintenance chemotherapy and his own indomitable spirit. No one could ever over-emphasize the importance of the latter.

For the world now knows that in the next three seasons Henry Cecil was to train 28 more Group winners, including 15 at Group One level. Major races would also be won in France, America and Dubai, and of course there was another Classic, taken by Frankel, whose 2011 performances would be so awesome that Henry would even be quoted calling him 'the best we have ever seen'. To say it was an Indian summer would be to give the subcontinent more than its due.

Charisma is hard to lose. Even in adversity that 'gift of grace' (its original definition in Greek) can come shining through. If the good times return the gleam is all the greater because it links the present with the past. That was what was now happening to Henry Cecil. We were beginning to realise not just that he could be a success again – in 2008 his winnings had passed the £1 million mark for the first time since 2000 – but quite what style he still had. Sometimes we had to pinch ourselves to believe it.

What's more he was the same but different. Not surprisingly his ill fortune and his ill health had changed him. He had needed to reshape the way he trained and he found that life had to an extent reshaped him. No longer able to ride out and so be alongside his horses during exercise, he had to redouble his observation of them in their boxes, in the covered ride, crossing the paths and at the canter. He had to use the eyes and ears of his fresh set of staff more than he ever had with their predecessors. And having been right to the bottom of both the professional and personal pit, he had to treasure the days and not allow even close defeat to feel like disaster.

As the charisma of Henry Cecil beamed out anew he remained competitive all right – black clouds could still darken the face when things went wrong on the racecourse or in the morning – and he was very obviously a man back in the game. Although Paul Howling was still at the Hovels during 2009, the Cecil string was up to 120, more than double the strength of 2005, and with the two-year-olds

Tom Queally with his new boss.

numbering over 50 he had also gone for youth with his new jockey. Tom Queally would not be 25 until October. That made him even younger than Steve Cauthen had been on arrival at Warren Place, and of course Steve had at that stage already been to the mountain top on both sides of the Atlantic.

Tom had also twice been a champion – apprentice champion. In 2000 he had topped the young riders' list in Ireland and in 2004 did the same in Britain, although each case also proved to be something of a poisoned chalice. He was just 15 and former Southern Area pony racing champion when he drove a hitherto unsuccessful four-year-old called Larifaari between horses to win his first ever race at Clonmel, in April 2000. It was to be almost too explosive a start. For while the boy was keen to do anything trainer Pat Flynn said en route to landing the Irish apprentice title, his parents were insistent that schooling at the Christian Brothers in Dungarvan must come first. By February 2001 Declan Queally had unsuccessfully applied to the Turf Club to have his son's indentures transferred to his own small yard in Waterford, and by October it had become a very public dispute finally resolved by the Turf Club ruling that the Flynn/Queally contract should be terminated a year early as 'relationships between the parties had irretrievably broken down'.

Tom does not like revisiting the issue, except to say how much he now appreciates his parents' pressure, which saw him gain a Leaving Certificate (the Irish equivalent of A-levels) with better grades than many fellow pupils not encumbered by another life on the track. 'My mum would pick me up at 12 o'clock,' he says, 'and I would study my school work as well as form on the way to the races and be back in school next morning.'

After the split with Pat Flynn, his weekends were spent riding out with Aidan O'Brien, to whom Tom went full time in 2003. But while the Ballydoyle experience was invaluable and even provided a shock first Group winner when the pacemaker Balestrini slipped the field in the Ballysax Stakes, it did not fuel a winner increase or a change in the perception that the young man from Clappagh had something of a tip for himself. At the end of 2003, with just 11 successes on the board, Queally told O'Brien that he needed to try his luck overseas.

'Aidan was very good about it,' says Tom with the self-possession some have taken as conceit or even idleness, 'and if I had ridden three more winners that year I would probably still be in Ireland. Hand on heart, I was not cocky, but when you are an early success and handle yourself with a degree of confidence, the papers can take against you. I felt sorry for my mum and dad and knew it was time to try somewhere different.'

The road to the Cecil saddle was not a direct one. In January 2003 Queally spent several weeks with David Elsworth at Whitsbury and rode the winner of a seller at Lingfield. The next winter he had a spell work riding at the Fair Grounds in New Orleans and then travelled to New Zealand, where he rode a winner and so impressed experienced owner Doug Rawnsley that he immediately predicted a classy future. 'He possessed brains, good manners, beautiful hands, flair and balance,' Doug wrote to me. 'It was obvious that he had great potential but he told me he had nothing lined up and was about to accept a job as a work rider in Lambourn.'

A father figure was needed and, as it did for a string of jockeys including Jamie Spencer and Frankie Dettori, it appeared in the slow-talking, hard-smoking, cryptic but benign shape of Barney Curley. The once would-be monk has over the years been a stewards' challenge and a bookmakers' nightmare with the betting coups he has engineered. On his beat Barney cost Tom a 21-day suspension for 'not making sufficient effort' on the quirky Zabeel Palace in 2007 and also involved both Tom and his younger Limerick University student brother Declan with winners in a successful £5 million accumulator in May 2010. But when it comes to caring for young men's futures no one doubts Barney's credentials, nor the hurt he still feels over the tragic death of his own son in a car accident.

For in his other life he is a humanitarian of quite touching distinction. Linking up with some of his fellow hopefuls who stayed the course as Jesuit Novices at Mungret College, Limerick, Barney has cut through bureaucratic red tape and corruption to create his own charity, Direct Aid For Africa (DAFA), which does inspirational work among sick and impoverished children in Zambia. My visit in 2001 was one of the most moving weeks I've ever experienced, even if the architect insisted at the outset, 'Don't make me out as a saint or anything. This is just a bit of fire insurance.' In 2008, with a British apprentice title won and his links with Henry Cecil developing, it was Tom Queally's turn. 'Barney said to me, "You have a big season up ahead. I am now going to take you to Zambia to make sure you realise how lucky you are." What I saw down there of the work he is doing with DAFA stops you ever feeling sorry for yourself if you are in a traffic jam after riding three beaten favourites at Sandown.'

Queally's first ride for Henry Cecil had come at Lingfield on 9 November 2006. The horse involved was Moonshadow, a full-sister to the Oaks winner Love Divine. She was beautifully bred but desperately slow and on this seventh and final attempt duly finished a fading sixth of 12 and had her targets changed from the parade ring to the breeding paddocks. Yet for the 22-year-old Queally it had been an opportunity to die for. 'I was really thrilled,' he says, 'and although I could not get hold of Henry on the telephone, when I saw him in the street at Newmarket to say thank you he asked me to ride work for him the next season. He's a genius to work for and I now know what he wants from me and I think he understands what I can do for him. He has this way with his horses, is so at one with them. It is as if he has something extra. I could stand here and talk about him for an hour and not do him justice.'

In 2007 most of the Cecil/Queally connection was on the gallops, but Tom did ride one Warren Place winner, Lady Lily at Pontefract, from 14 rides, and 2008's 18 winners from 90 rides included an Earl of Sefton victory on Phoenix Tower, beating Ted Durcan on the stable's better-fancied Multidimensional back in fourth. Durcan is far too sensible a character to hold any grudges about his eventual replacement, emphasising that he never had a formal connection with the Cecil stable and that his original loyalties were with Godolphin, for whom in 2009 he won the St Leger on Mastery. Looking back, Ted merely remarks 'there were too many seconds' without bothering to elaborate that four of them were in consecutive Group One races with Phoenix Tower on whom Tom had struck lucky at Newmarket. That's the way it crumbles. By the early summer of 2012 another neat turn of fortune's wheel would see Ted Durcan associated with Derby second Main Sequence, trained in Lambourn by Henry Cecil's former assistant David Lanigan and carrying the same Niarchos silks Ted had worn on Light Shift in the 2007 Oaks.

As 2009 warmed up so too did Midday, that Shane Fetherstonhaugh-tended daughter of the mare Midsummer who in the Abdulla/Cecil way of things had herself won a race for Warren Place and been second in the Lingfield Oaks Trial of 2003. In April Midday had run a good third on the last mile and a quarter of the Oaks course and then bettered her mother with a handsome victory in that Lingfield trial. Midday's progress had Henry reflecting on his relationship with the female of the species. 'I've been lucky over the years,' he told the *Racing Post*'s Steve Dennis as they sat in the Warren Place garden talking of these fleeting flowers he loved to bring to bloom. 'I've trained for some very good owner-breeders who have sent me some very good fillies. Good animals make good trainers and jockeys. If I'd had fillies who were capable of winning only Pontefract maidens you wouldn't bring up the subject. Women are different from men, aren't they, so why wouldn't fillies be different from colts? They're not as straightforward as colts, they're more delicate. You have to let them come to themselves; they'll tell you when they're ready. They mustn't be rushed. They need confidence, time, understanding. I think Midday will stay the mile and a half. She's by a sprinter, but I believe most of a horse's stamina comes from the dam's side and there's plenty of staying blood there. She's out of a half-sister to Reams Of Verse, who won me an Oaks a few years ago.'

Midday got to within a head and a stewards' inquiry of winning Henry a ninth Oaks, coming through bravely in the straight but being done no favours by the winner Sariska as that filly squeezed up those on her inside. It was already Midday's seventh race; her mother had run only three. But this lady was definitely not for turning: there were 16 more races to come over the next two and a half years, four at the highest level in 2009 alone. She was third in the Irish Oaks to Sariska on unsuitably heavy ground. She was a splendid winner of the Nassau Stakes in extremely un-Glorious Goodwood weather. After a break she returned to run a good third at Longchamp, ready to fly out west to California and give Henry Cecil the crowning moment of a first win at the Breeders' Cup.

With the San Gabriel Mountains as a backdrop and the desert palms as extra scenery, Santa Anita is one of the finest theatres on the racing globe. It had been 21 years but only five unsuccessful tries since Indian Skimmer had spun wide round the turns at a dark and dank Churchill Downs Breeders' Cup. This time Tom Queally drove Midday daringly up the inside to get first run in the Filly and Mare Turf and America's media could look and listen in both delight and bafflement as this (in one scribbler's words) 'deliciously posh Englander' thanked them for their congratulations and asked them what they thought. The *Daily Racing Form*'s Jay Hovdey is too good a writer to scrabble in the scrum, and besides he is married to a Breeders' Cup legend in the 3,000-winner phenomenon that is Julie Krone. Jay waited his moment. 'About half an hour after Midday won,' he wrote of Henry, 'I encountered him swimming upstream, anonymous as anyone, dolphin smile. I braced him with congratulations, his smile broadened and he replied, "Took long enough, didn't it?"'

If there had not been so much before and so many highlights still to come, Midday's victory that day would be hailed as the absolute pinnacle of Henry Cecil's career. It was his first success in America and, at $1 million, was the richest race he had ever won. But giddily exciting though it may have been to those in California and to British fans watching on TV back home, it was only part of a swirling stream of success that was taking him to a public eminence not enjoyed even in the 40 per cent strike-rate days when those silky, slow-pumping Cauthen elbows ruled the roost.

Three races before Midday, Henry had run Passage Of Time's full-brother Father Time to close his career in the Breeders' Cup Marathon. That Father Time could finish no closer than sixth did not matter because he had done his bit five months earlier by becoming the first Cecil winner in seven years at Royal Ascot. The day after Midday's triumph, Tom Queally slung Twice Over off the turn to take the leaders in the Breeders' Cup Classic only to be mown down by the extraordinary Zenyatta, who had trailed the field by a street and then suddenly sprinted through and round them as if she were a sports car among trucks. That didn't matter either because a month before that Tom and Twice Over had put down their own marker in Henry's Hall of Fame.

After Twice Over had finished close up in both the Locking Stakes at Newbury and the Prince of Wales's Stakes at Royal Ascot, he had finished a disappointing seventh of ten behind the all-conquering Sea The Stars in the Eclipse at Sandown. It was his 12th race, he had not won in a year, he was a four-year-old colt. It would be easy to think we had seen the best of him. Not for Henry. Twice Over and his devoted lad John Fletcher went hacking around Newmarket on the easy list and it was two months before he saw a racecourse again. When Twice Over did it was not the Eclipse but a much easier target at Doncaster, where he won as an odds-on shot should. The ruse was repeated in similar style at Goodwood, and by the Champion Stakes

Twice Over was ready to rumble. When Henry Cecil did his victory interviews afterwards he could not keep a little smile from playing around his lips. He may not have been able to train in the physical way he used to, but he still knew what training was about.

In the New Year he was into new tricks. A blinkered chestnut colt called Tranquil Tiger had already been busier than almost any horse Henry had ever trained, running 23 times in the last three seasons. The last two of them had been on the Polytrack at Lingfield, and in March 2010 he won Warren Place another Derby – the Winter Derby at Lingfield. A week later the stable's target was bigger, bolder and a lot further away as Twice Over tilted for £3.7 million in the Dubai World Cup. As luck would have it he was drawn ten places from the rail and got trapped hopelessly wide all the way. Hopeless was what bookmakers made of Henry's filly Jacqueline Quest when she lined up for the 1,000 Guineas five weeks later. They listed her at 66-1. What followed not only showed that Henry was back as a trainer, it revealed a loser with a definite 'gift of grace'. The man who had started the last decade mired in slump and scandal was beginning the new one being hailed as little short of a saint.

Jacqueline Quest and Tom Queally did their bit. They inched out the French-trained Abdulla favourite Special Duty by a nose, but the jockey's celebrations were premature. In desperate search for more momentum he had switched his whip from right hand to left just as Ted Durcan had done with Light Shift at Epsom. But while Queally got the momentum he wanted, Jacqueline Quest lugged right, carrying Special Duty with her. In view of the narrowness of the verdict, the subsequent stewards' inquiry soon found the Cecil filly had interfered enough to cost her French rival the extra fractions for victory. In regulation terms the reversing of the first and second was the correct verdict, but for romance we were all the losers. We were denied one of the most touching stories for decades – and this time it was not about Henry Cecil.

For Jacqueline Quest's owner Noel Martin was one of the most tragic figures ever to be wheeled into any winner's circle. He had arrived in Birmingham from his native Jamaica at the age of ten, was soon fascinated from afar by the racing game, left home at 14, did odd jobs, made his money in property development and learned to ride with the impossible dream of competing in the Grand National. So far so strong, but on a visit to Germany he was rendered quadriplegic when his car hit a tree after three neo-Nazis threw a lump of concrete through his windscreen for the simple disgusting reason that they did not like the sight of a black man at the wheel.

Racehorses became Noel's escape from his horrible reality. His silks reflected the yellow, black and green colours of the Jamaican flag. His horse Baddam won two races at Royal Ascot in 2006 and now, in his 1,000 Guineas winning/losing filly, he had a living memorial to his late wife Jacqueline. Before she died they had made a joint suicide pact, but she was rushed to hospital before preparations were complete. Noel still planned to join her but he was proud of how far he had come. He related all this live on Channel 4. Then the official announcement wrecked the moment. No one watching could have failed to wipe away a tear.

Jockey and trainer caught the mood. 'It's obviously disappointing but not a tragedy,' said Tom Queally very calmly. 'There are worse things going on in the world. Of course it was a bad day and I am very sorry for the owner, but if I go around with a long face it won't achieve anything.' Henry Cecil was even more serene. He kissed Special Duty's trainer Criquette Head-Maarek and said, 'Jacqueline Quest ran really well and is improving. Maybe I will get my own back at Royal Ascot. I am pleased for Criquette and the Prince but obviously I would rather have won the race for ourselves.'

In fact Jacqueline Quest never touched glory again, ending her days refusing to race for Henry at Ascot and then doing the same

Henry Cecil with owner Noel Martin after Jacqueline Quest had passed the post first in the 1,000 Guineas in 2010.

thing when switched to Ian Williams' stable near Noel Martin's home in Birmingham.

Fate does not always pay its dues, but for Henry Cecil the dividends were now showering down. The much-fancied Oaks candidate Timepiece failed at Lingfield but the same card saw a fine Derby Trial victory for Bullet Train, a handsome son of the Prince Khalid mare Kind, a five-in-a-row winning sprinter in 2004.

Bullet Train blew out in the Derby and ended his career as a crucial trial horse at Warren Place. Meanwhile the aura around his trainer continued to gather strength. So much so that after Timepiece had pulled herself together to win at Royal Ascot, and before Twice Over's tilt at the Eclipse Stakes came over the hill, the *Racing Post* chose to launch a 'Henry Cecil Week' complete with contributions from both ordinary readers and the great and good.

Twice Over (Tom Queally) wins the Eclipse Stakes, 2010.

It even included an introductory essay from me telling the story of unpromising youth and the question 'What are we going to do with Henry?' All that was needed was for Twice Over to win the Eclipse to crown the story. With a bold strike for home from Queally, that is exactly what he did.

Long after all the back-slapping and announcements had ended, Henry and Jane stood briefly alone on the steps of the Sandown weighing room. In his strange way he looked both happy and wistful at the same time, as if conscious of his good fortune but also aware of how much water had passed beneath his bridge down the years. It had been 41 seasons since Lester Piggott knifed Wolver Hollow so enterprisingly up the inside in that first Cecil training year, 13 not always lucky ones since Kieren Fallon had met such trouble on the same route in 1997. Henry said how touched he had been by the kind things written, how happy he was to win the Eclipse again and how Twice Over 'was one of his best friends'.

What he did not dare tell was that back home there was something that would put 'Henry Cecil Week' in need of a major update. Frankel was about to hit the tracks.

13

FRANKEL

THEY ARE the racing stories that insiders most love to tell. They are the tales of being there on the morning when a great horse works for the first time and you believe you have seen a galloping version of the Holy Grail. One of them happened on the Limekilns at Newmarket during the week before the Eclipse Stakes in July 2010. It was when the Frankel legend really began.

Before that moment when the rider squeezes leg and hand to ask the horse beneath, nobody is ever sure. Sometimes it can be a major surprise, most famously one foggy morning at Chattis Hill near Stockbridge in Hampshire in the spring of 1913. The rider of a big grey two-year-old with strange white splotches all over him was told to follow a sharper bunch up the working ground but 'not to bother if he can't keep with them'. Imagine the fury of trainer Atty Persse when out of the gloom appeared the spotted colt ten lengths clear having evidently set off some way in front. Imagine the disbelief when the rider stuttered out that he had actually started at least six lengths behind. A week later Atty tried it with good visibility and could hardly believe what his eyes were telling him.

The Tetrarch, as he was called, had given a stone to a decent older handicapper and beaten it in a canter. When he first ran, in a maiden race at the Craven meeting, he was the greatest certainty in racing history. The security at Chattis Hill was so tight, and stable lads so terrified into silence, that The Tetrarch started at 5-1 against. He only ran as a two-year-old and was never beaten in seven races. They called him 'The Spotted Wonder'.

There was not much secrecy on the Limekilns in July 2010 but there was wonder just the same. Frankel was a half-brother to the Lingfield Derby trial winner Bullet Train. His dam Kind's five consecutive wins in 2004 had been for trainer Roger Charlton, but in 1993 Warren Place had themselves won three races in a row with his grand-dam Rainbow Lake, culminating in a seven-lengths rout in the Lancashire Oaks at Haydock. Everyone knew that Frankel was from one of Juddmonte's best families and most in the yard had heard that the bay colt by the 2001 Derby winner Galileo had a good stride on him but had been rather uncontrollable early on. For five furlongs Tom Queally kept the brakes on that morning. It was when he released them that the lightning struck.

'I have never seen anything like it,' says Teddy Grimthorpe. 'One moment Frankel was with them, the next he was streaking away as if the others had lead in their legs. I have to watch a lot of gallops and know how misleading it can be when you don't know all the horses, weights or instructions. But you could not mistake this. He was going so fast at the end we thought he would finish in Newmarket High Street. When we gathered afterwards, nobody said anything, and Queally was white as a sheet. What could we say?'

It was not a feeling Tom Queally would ever forget. 'It was the stride that amazed me,' he says. 'When I moved on him he did not seem to be going any quicker but he just left the others for dead. We had to be excited, but of course you can never be sure until they have passed the racecourse test.' Which, in the European Breeders' Fund Maiden Stakes over a mile at the Newmarket July course on the dark, rain-pelting evening of 13 August, is what Frankel did. The official verdict was half a length, not four lengths in a canter as The Tetrarch did in 1913, and the starting price was a well-noised 7-4 favourite, not a lock-down 5-1 against. But this was never meant to be a betting coup. It was a hoped-for starting point on a journey to much better things and, given that he'd cruised up to and passed a well-fancied colt called Nathaniel (who was to win the next year's King George VI and Queen Elizabeth Stakes at Ascot), this first soggy glimpse of Frankel was still a pretty impressive one.

Henry Cecil certainly thought so. 'We didn't know if he would go on the ground, so we are delighted with him really,' he told Racing UK at the side of the unsaddling enclosure. 'We were always going to be very easy on him and Tom hasn't really had to ask him for anything. I haven't really galloped him but he's got good engagements. Potentially he could be very nice.' It was all said in that civil but don't-declare-all-your-hand way that trainers employ as their after-race default, but there was almost a skip in Henry's raincoated step as he signed off with sing-song jauntiness, 'Thank you for talking.'

Teddy Grimthorpe had been watching in his hotel in Deauville. Beforehand he hadn't been quite so jaunty. For not only had he seen Frankel's potential for himself, he had heard of it not just from the trainer but from his stud managers and from the man who first set eyes on Frankel as a living being. Jim Power was stud groom at Banstead Manor Stud, the Abdulla breeding operation's headquarters near Newmarket. At 10pm on 11 February 2008 he had looked at the closed-circuit TV screen in his house near the foaling barn and told his wife he didn't think he would be going to bed for a while. 'I knew that Kind was near to her time,' remembers Jim, 'and I could see she was getting restless. By quarter to eleven I was all changed up and ready, and it was really a textbook foaling. I just felt inside to make sure the little nose and the two front feet were in position and then let things happen as naturally as possible. She was very straightforward. Mind you, so was her mother Rainbow Lake.'

Of such mixtures of professionalism and paternity is a stud groom's life made up. Jim had worked for Juddmonte for 20 years before finally retiring in 2010 with his finest produce heading for the stars. He was originally a would-be jockey with Brian Marshall at Lambourn in 1959, had moved on to stud work at Hever Castle in Kent, and had first come to Juddmonte's stud at Wargrave in Berkshire to break the yearlings. When that operation was transferred across the Irish Sea to Ferrans Stud in County Meath, he moved across to Banstead Manor, where he was assistant stud groom for the foaling of both Commander In Chief and Tenby in the 1990 crop. He was not easily impressed, but he was with Frankel.

The distortions of hindsight make scepticism necessary. Although I was then still wet behind the ears in racing terms, I still remember finding it fascinating but unlikely when the great Madame Couturie assured me that from the moment she foaled him she could see that her future French Derby and King George VI and Queen Elizabeth Stakes winner Right Royal was going to be a champion. Madame Couturie's Haras du Mesnil in Normandy was where the youthful Henry Cecil had spent three surprisingly badly fed months in his late teens; but in his sixties, the superfoal appeared rather closer to home. 'I am not going to claim I was saying it immediately,' says Jim Power of the future hero who clocked 123lb at the first scale, 'but he definitely had plenty about him. There are some that you do remember. Tenby was a very tenacious foal, I remember telling people about him, and we also began to think a lot of this chap – especially when he came back from Ireland.'

Frankel had to travel across the water to accompany his dam on her return visit to Galileo at Coolmore Stud in Tipperary, where she duly conceived Frankel's talented full-brother Noble Mission. With an 11-month gestation period, equine gynaecology produces a 'foaling heat' in a mare within four days of the original birth, but the Juddmonte practice is to wait until the 30-day cycle comes round. So it would have been a four-week-old and still unnamed Galileo colt who accompanied his mother in the luxury horse box off down the motorways and on to the ferry to see his father again. There is not a lot of romance in the routine but it is efficiently and sensitively done and, in crucial response to the rose tints of hindsight, the Juddmonte team have a monthly marking system for all their foals and yearlings. What was to be Frankel was already being given 8s and 7++s. Unlike the famous 9s and 10s freely allocated by the judges in *Strictly Come Dancing*, these seemingly lower marks still indicated a very high rating.

In 2008, those marks and the Galileo foal's general demeanour had a special significance, because the Juddmonte and Coolmore Stud operations had for some time been doing a 'foal share' arrangement whereby they took turns at having the pick of the crop. In the year 2000, for example, Coolmore had chosen Rainbow Lake's son of Sadler's Wells out of the Abdulla group and he had turned out to be Powerscourt, winner of the Arlington Million and the Tattersalls Gold Cup. In 2008 it was Juddmonte's turn. But there were plenty of other athletic and beautifully bred foals running around Banstead when Frankel and Kind came back to England at the end of April. Why should Frankel stand out?

'He was very inquisitive and attentive to what was going on around him whether he was in the stable or in the field,' says Jim Power. 'He was always the first one to come up to you and was the type of foal who would defy you not to take notice of him. But it became more marked after he was weaned in July. I remember him in the paddock one morning going right away from the others with this open galloping stride. You could see it then as you can see it now. The hind legs powered him forward but the front legs really reached out and pulled on the ground. It seemed to give him an extra ten or twelve inches of rotation. Yes, he certainly made an impression.'

He did on Juddmonte's Irish farms manager Rory Mahon when Frankel was shipped over to New Abbey Stud and then to Ferrans for the next stages of development and education. 'I immediately gave him a 7++,' says Rory in sober marking mood. 'He was a well-balanced colt with a very good walk and stood on good limbs, and his temperament was very good.' All this information was being fed to Philip Mitchell back at Banstead, and through him to Prince Khalid himself. The foal choice would have to be made. Kind's colt by Galileo would be the pick. Frankel would be trained in England and run in the green and pink colours, not prepared by Aidan O'Brien in Ireland in the dark blue silks of the John Magnier team.

But as summer moved into the autumn of 2009 and the Galileo colt took quickly and kindly to saddle and bridle, to trotting and circling in the covered school, and to cantering on the white-railed all-weather track, two crucial issues still needed resolving: there had to be a decision on who would train him and on what he would be called. They, as with all things Juddmonte, would be finally taken by the quiet, scrupulously polite man who likes to list himself in the owners' table as plain K. Abdulla, but with whom courtesy should never be confused with softness, nor shyness with lack of will.

One morning in Paris a year later, in the summer of 2010, he sat and talked of the racing passion first lit when friends took him to Longchamp way back in 1956. Never once did the courtesy or the self-effacing shyness slip, yet neither did the impression alter that the unique owner-breeder achievements of his international Juddmonte empire still depend on his being at the heart of it all. As he spoke, the words carefully chosen in still quite accented English, you had to think how far and yet how close he was to the thousands who also have racing as their thing. Indeed your first impression of the impassive features on the rather slight but immaculately dressed figure at the centre of the Juddmonte team might make you think he was not experiencing much buzz from it all. 'But I do enjoy it,' insisted the Prince. 'I like being in England, I like visiting my horses and going to the races. But I don't like showing myself and talking to the press. I don't think it suits me really.'

He was sitting in a silk-lined anteroom at the top of the stairs in his Paris town house on the edge of the elegant Parc Monceau, that kilometre-round showpiece immortalised by a series of Claude Monet paintings in the late 1870s. He was not half a mile from the Bois de Boulogne and ready to lunch with important visitors from his native Saudi Arabia, where his brother-in-law is King Abdullah. Yet he would be returning in time to watch a once-raced Oasis Dream colt called Uphold wing home at 100-30 in the second division of a maiden race at Nottingham. Betting shop punters who blindly back the pink and green would have been as pleased as a prince in Paris, especially those who got the early 7-1.

'It is still my only hobby,' Prince Khalid said with a degree of self-mocking sadness, 'but while I have very good people working for me I like to be involved. We have budgets on everything because you cannot say to managers that you should just go and spend, that's not good for anyone. When I first said to Lord Weinstock that I was going to have horses I did not expect to make money, and we are not really doing that, but it is all within reason. At one stage I felt the operation was getting too big. It is important for me to be able to deal with one manager.'

To that end Teddy Grimthorpe has each day to brief himself from the trainers of the 250 horses spread almost evenly between England and France, and some 40 in America, and report every evening to his patron wherever he may be in the world. By the time the manager does so, the miracle of satellites means he will be talking about a race his employer has already watched. The search is for excellence, not mere indulgence, and the key to Khalid Abdulla's interest is his fascination with how his equine families evolve. 'I have my stud book with me all the time,' he said. 'With breeding I think the dam is the key more than the stallion. With a bad dam, nothing is going to work out. We have to sell to keep the standard. With unraced mares [such as Workforce's dam Soviet Moon] it is a judgement. I cannot take any credit for Workforce [who won the Derby in 2010] but at least we did not sell the dam.'

But with Frankel, Prince Khalid cannot avoid taking credit for both the trainer and the name. For the legendary Bobby Frankel had died in America in November 2009. He had saddled the Belmont Stakes winner Empire Maker among many other fine horses for the Juddmonte flag. His flair for training and his Jewish Brooklyn humour had long made him a favourite of the Saudi Prince. As the yearling allocation arrived it was decided to let the best one honour Bobby Frankel's name. Back in 1998 Sheikh Mohammed changed the name of what he thought was his best two-year-old from Yaazer to Dubai Millennium and the big bay colt later repaid the billing with a runaway victory in the 2000 Dubai World Cup. Frankel got the right title first time.

Not many felt that the Prince had chosen the wrong trainer either, although there has to be sympathy for the uncomplaining Roger Charlton, who had trained Frankel's dam Kind to win five in a row in 2004 and who had won the Derby for Khalid Abdulla with Quest For Fame (subsequently a big US winner with Bobby Frankel) in his own first year of operations, 1990. Prince Khalid will not be drawn beyond a quiet smile and the words 'they are all good trainers but I have to choose'. However, it's hard to think that the analyst in him had not noticed Henry's fortunes were on the drift when the yearling Kind was sent to Roger Charlton rather than to Warren Place, where her own dam Rainbow Lake had won three on the bounce in 1993. Similarly, it was an unhappy coincidence that at the time of the Frankel allocation in 2009 Charlton had just endured his least successful season in 11 years with only three individual winners in the Juddmonte colours, while a resurgent Henry Cecil had 12 including Twice Over, Midday and the Royal Ascot winner Father Time.

Whatever the reasons, it was to Warren Place that Frankel headed on 14 January 2010, and his subsequent success is a huge tribute to the team Henry Cecil had recently assembled around him. For, in the wonderfully restrained wording trainers use for such things, there were times when Frankel was to prove 'not entirely straightforward'. By the time he left Ferrans the colt had been trotting and cantering up to a mile with behaviour that Rory Mahon assures us was impeccable. But he would not be the first nor the last young colt to find the wide-open spaces of Newmarket and the invitation to go slightly quicker as intoxicating as a slug of whisky in a hitherto abstemious teenager.

From being controlled, almost circumspect with the power they find in their legs and limbs, they suddenly want to rush and run a hole in the horizon. Still being new to the language of bit and bridle, they ignore all instructions from above, much to the alarm of the rider. If the central thrill of riding a thoroughbred is like having a living, thinking, jumping motorbike between your knees, this is like the motorbike with the throttle out and the brakes and steering broken. All of us ex-jocks have our horror stories. Here, with the young Frankel, was the danger of another one.

Henry and Mike Marshall went through their roster of riders and came up with Dan de Haan, the big, powerful horseman son of Ben de Haan, winner of the 1983 Grand National on Corbiere. 'I rode

Henry Cecil on the Newmarket gallops with Frankel – ridden by Dan de Haan, the first rider to experience the colt's exceptional quality.

him after a couple of weeks,' remembers Dan, 'and he was a bit keen but settled all right. Then one day in May when he had gone right across the Limekilns quite unrideable the boss asked me to ride him again. We tried him in a three-piece bridle but he was hanging out to the left and you could not steer him. I remember Mike Marshall coming to me with a long face one morning and saying, "I'm not sure he is going to make it."

'But,' Dan continues, with the relish reserved for those who have had a physical hand on equine greatness, 'we then put the cross-noseband on him and, though he was still quite keen, I thought he might come round. He's only a small horse to ride compared to big old chasers or something like Twice Over, but half his problem was that if you were sat behind something his natural stride was so much longer than theirs that you had to pull him back and as he had a temper if you took a pull he would just try and take off with you. The day I realised that he was a monster was down the Al Bahathri one morning. I had him on his own and when I found he was not actually running away I suddenly tumbled what he was. When I pulled up Mike asked me how he had gone, and I said to him, "I promise you, this is an absolute beast."'

Such tales are the hot coals around which racing people warm their hands on winter nights.

The big deal for Dan and others privy to the Galileo two-year-old was where it would run. 'I watched the first time he worked upsides on the watered gallop,' says Dan. 'Steve [Kielt] the farrier was with me, and after seeing what Frankel could do he hurried off and backed him for next year's Classics. The trouble was that, as Frankel's half-brother Bullet Train had won the Lingfield Derby Trial, Steve went and did it for the Derby itself. Looking back, Frankel was always going to be a bit too free to run in that.'

Interestingly enough, Frankel was pretty tractable in a 12-runner field first time out. And on his next appearance at Doncaster Tom Queally was able to hold him up in second place until two furlongs out, and that with only two others for cover. That day Frankel's principal rival was a Godolphin colt called Farhh, who had left his field six long lengths behind on the July course three weeks before Frankel's debut at the same track in August. But Farhh had to be withdrawn after having something akin to a nervous breakdown at the starting stalls. So while Frankel did look astonishing at Doncaster, streaking almost half a furlong clear of a filly called Rainbow Springs, it was hard to give his form a rating. It was not so difficult the next time he ran, at Ascot.

While there were still only four opponents this time, the Royal Lodge Stakes is one of the premier mile races for two-year-olds in Europe and what Frankel did to the rest of the field was nothing less than astounding. Again he was anchored off a slow pace, but if his rivals thought they might catch him out in a sprint finish, the answer came in an extraordinary move round the final turn when Queally allowed him to run and that great Frankel stride came powering home ten lengths clear of the others as if he was a greyhound who had just slipped his leash.

After this Henry was a bit more effusive than the 'potentially he could be very nice' marker first time out. 'He's a star,' he said. 'I think he is the best two-year-old I have had since Wollow. I haven't had one like this for a long time.' No one thought he was getting over-excited, and if Frankel was visually slightly less impressive in the Dewhurst at Newmarket three weeks later, he was still winning the most important two-year-old race in the British calendar by two and a quarter lengths under a hand ride and finished so strongly that Queally had trouble pulling up.

He was a star to follow, and that day the trainer was making his own celestial progress for the very next race was Twice Over's bid for a second Champion Stakes. It was to be the last time the event would be run at Newmarket before moving to the new, jazzed-up end-of-season 'Champions Day' at Ascot. A victory by 'my best friend' for Newmarket's most lauded trainer was almost too good to be true. But with Queally cutting for home down the incline from the Bushes two furlongs out that's exactly what happened and the crowd went wild with delight.

As with Twice Over's Eclipse Stakes victory, we were being presented with a perfect bookend to the Henry Cecil story. But Frankel and the man himself had quite a chapter yet to write.

When Henry Cecil is on song he tilts his head and you are not sure whether he is serious or going to make a joke about you or himself. He was on song one end-of-March day in 2011, and he was entitled to be. 'I think we could win it,' he said with that funny little smile. He was serious – and not just about Twice Over in the Dubai World Cup that Saturday. He was talking about the trainers' title. 'Why not?' he continued. 'We were close last year and had a couple of unlucky seconds. We will need a lot of luck but you have got to try, haven't you?'

At Warren Place on this Tuesday morning Henry had been up at five and on the phone to his wife Jane and his jockey Tom Queally at Meydan, Sheikh Mohammed's astonishing racecourse in Dubai, to talk through Twice Over's progress. 'He's enjoying himself and doing very well,' said the trainer, yet before you started to think he was getting mushily sentimental he dived off into elaborate detail about the problems with Twice Over's front feet and of how he had flown farrier Steve Kielt out to fit the special shoes that made such a difference.

That is the thing about Henry, he likes to wear his learning lightly. 'I don't want to be a bore,' he had said as he smoked what was clearly not his first cigarette on the patio outside the kitchen at 6.30am. It was a beautiful Newmarket morning. Clumps of daffodils splashed yellow across the garden and over in the yard Guineas and Derby favourite Frankel headed a 140-head string that was set to add to those glory years which had gathered ten trainers' titles and for which Twice Over's Champion Stakes victory the previous October had taken the Group One success total beyond the century mark. Boredom? Wonder more likely.

The first wonder, of course, was that Henry was there at all. The ink should perhaps never have run dry on how family problems, his twin brother David's cancer and then his own had reduced him and his stable to a sick shell of what it once was: remember, in 2005 just 12 winners were logged from fewer than 40 horses and most of Warren Place was either empty or rented out. 'I am still having some remedial chemotherapy,' he said briefly, 'but I am determined to stay positive. I am sure it helps your body if your mind keeps positive.' Warren Place was now again too full to have tenants and a look round that Tuesday suggested there was a lot to be positive about.

Frankel was in a barn over on the far side. 'We tried bringing him in to one of the boxes nearer the house,' said Henry, 'but he much prefers the barn. He likes to have other horses to talk to.' In a celebrated interview some years ago, Henry stated quite openly that his horses talk to him. Quite what Frankel said when his trainer pulled back the exercise sheet that morning remains between the two of them, but the shining slab of muscle across the colt's quarters was a loud enough statement of his well-being.

So too was his demeanour as he followed his half-brother Bullet Train to join the rest of the string taking their preliminary trot round the big covered ride that Noel Murless installed in the sixties for the princely sum of £10,000. Frankel is not massive but is plenty big enough and there was real power across that slightly low-set neck. Almost too much power to judge by the way he had pulled in the Dewhurst, and to control it on that Tuesday he had a cross-noseband on his muzzle and Shane Fetherstonhaugh on his back.

You will recall that Frankel was not the first Derby favourite Shane had ridden through the winter. He was the quiet figure in the saddle who had stayed calm and unflurried while Motivator did his routine whip-rounds at the bottom of the Warren Hill canter and let fly his double-barrelled bucks on the way home. Frankel was not as dance-on-the-spot volatile as Motivator, but a sudden leap as he followed Bullet Train out of the school and the arms-tugging stretch of his neck up the canter indicated some pretty high-calibre explosive at the end of the rein.

'I think it is very important to match the rider to the horse,' said Henry suddenly, all serious. 'Shane is just about the best rider we have.

He is very calm and he settles Frankel well. But the horse is growing up. They do, you know.' The words were quick and crisp but the eyes were watchful because we had driven round to Warren Hill and Henry had marched over to his normal vantage point three-quarters of the way up the Polytrack. At 68 he was still a slightly dandified figure with a dark-blue French-style cap topping a brown leather bomber jacket, yet another cigarette on the go between gloved fingers.

'Here they come,' he commented as specks began to grow in the distance. No binoculars, but no doubting the focus on what was happening in front of us. 'Frankel is going to work a mile tomorrow up the Cambridge Road Polytrack. He has done a lot of conditioning and is where I want him to be but tomorrow will be the first time we move him away from his leader. He won't work again on Saturday because I am away, but after that it will be Wednesday and Saturday up to the Greenham. He's a proper horse, but there are some other nice ones here you know.'

What followed was a recitation of horse names often unknown but always enviably related. 'That's been backed for the Derby,' Henry said casually as a handsome bay sailed easily by. 'He's called World Domination, by Empire Maker out of Reams Of Verse. That's All Time, a full-sister to Passage Of Time. That's Midsummer Sun, a half-brother to Midday by Monsun. They are all unraced, but I think they could be decent.'

It was possible to see the determination beyond the throwaway 'I don't want to be a bore' style. 'That's Panoptic, she's in the Guineas. She ran twice last year but got fizzed up both times. But she works well. She might get there but we will have to see how she gets on. I think the most important thing in training is to go with your horses, not to try to bring them with you. You have to let them want to do it.'

Warren Hill is a very public place to do your daily business and watching the horses is mixed with banter from passing owners and trainers. Former Warren Place tenant Ed Vaughan came up to say thanks for the Indian meal he and Henry's older son Noel had with Henry the night before. Michael Stoute passed complete with purple Breeders' Cup baseball cap. Not so much banter there, but then Michael had lots of business to do with his string, which had also won ten titles.

Everything about Henry that morning was a statement not just of how happy he was to be back but how keen he was to take it all the way. His life had looked as if it was dying on him, now he was almost pinching himself with the simple delight of once again playing the game. There was an ease but not an idleness about him. For he was thinking not just of that year but of the next, and for all his casualness you could sometimes almost feel the electricity crackling off him.

'Look at this,' he said back in the stable, pulling the rug off a handsome bay with a big white blaze. 'He's Frankel's full-brother. Of course we haven't done anything with him yet but he looks decent, don't you think?' There are a number of such almost rhetorical questions as he happily goes from box to box: three as yet unnamed Dansili colts belonging to Khalid Abdulla as well as one called King Of Dudes owned by Andrew Tinkler, and another called Malekov owned by the ruling family of Abu Dhabi, and a handsome Teofilo-sired son of Oaks winner Love Divine called Hologram owned by the Lordship Stud.

The world wanted Henry again, and you could understand why. Khalid Abdulla had been the most successful as well as the most loyal of all his owners, having had 389 Cecil-trained winners up to the end of the previous season. Earlier that March I had visited Prince Khalid's elegant London office overlooking Cadogan Square and asked him what made the trainer stand out. 'Henry is very special,' said Frankel's owner. 'He seems to really understand his horses and he again has a very good team working with him.'

Training a large string of racehorses can only be done if the personalities driving it truly complement one another. As the horses circled in the covered ride, Mike Marshall, Cecil's assistant of the last three years, had stood beside him as short and square-jawed as Henry was tall and languid, and there was no doubting the drive and insight he was bringing to the operation. 'Mike is down at the bottom of the canter seeing them on,' Henry later said on Warren Hill. 'He always knows what we need and won't let things slip.'

But then neither does Henry. 'Some people get the impression that Henry is floating around not paying attention,' said Shane Fetherstonhaugh once Frankel had been safely stowed away. 'But I can tell you he is deadly serious. He is in total control of what goes on and it is really interesting watching him walking around the place. He is studying his horses all the time, mornings and evenings. He somehow puts himself on the same level as them and they definitely recognise and relate to him, especially the fillies. But most of all he wants to win the big races and to win that trainers' title back. Obviously you have got to win at least a Derby or a King George but it certainly won't be for lack of trying.'

As Shane talked the mind went back to Henry walking round the yard with that strange mixture of jokey affection and firm, almost pernickety attention to detail. 'What has happened here?' he had asked sharply at one point when he spotted one tacked-up horse with its reins over its head in the box. 'Why is that light still on?' he said of a glare in the barn, before adding, 'I hate these things being slack. It's the little things that count. They all add up.'

Confronted with a lorryload of hay he pulled a handful out and sniffed and nuzzled it in such a horse-like manner that you could imagine him and Frankel chatting over dinner later that evening. 'I like to understand what is happening,' he said. 'All staff have good and bad points and if you can get the best out of each of them you will be all right. That's why I do my own list every night or early in the morning. A head lad may not change a rider because the other lad will get grumpy and give him grief. But if you keep the wrong person on a highly strung animal the horse is going to go the wrong way. If I think we need a change, I change it.'

Suddenly the authority is naked in the voice. 'If anybody strikes a horse here they don't get a warning, they are out straight away, or you get horses soured up. And you have to be careful of people who think they are jockeys and ride horses too fast to find out for themselves. I have really good head staff and have spies in the string. If I hear it is happening, I tell them that I am the man who is training the horses.'

Come 17 May it would be 42 years since the odd-tempered Celestial Cloud had become the first of all the winners to be trained by Henry Cecil, and the many who doubted the young man then and the plenty who wondered about the more battered one now should have been listening as he said, 'Last year we finished fourth in the table but we would have been closer without that Guineas disqualification and a couple of other things going wrong. This year I am a lot stronger. It is just a question of having some luck. I could actually win it again. I could. I probably won't, but I am really going to try.'

As I left Warren Place the buds and the birdsong filled the eye and ear. The air, like the stables, was full of promise. Hope is an addictive thing. The thought that Frankel might indeed prove to be a mighty new Pegasus addicted us all in the weeks that led to the showdown that would be the 2,000 Guineas up that unforgiving Rowley Mile on the last day of April. But not one of us was ready for what occurred within ten seconds of those starting gates slamming open and the 13 runners being despatched over that same straight patch of green old Charles II first galloped up three and a half centuries before.

It was the shock of it. There was Frankel, the most talked about Guineas favourite in years, the spearhead of the Henry Cecil resurgence, not just making the running at Newmarket but seemingly intent on blowing a hole in the wind. Of course we had been warned. Henry had talked about 'running his own race' and 'allowing him to use his stride'. But this was altogether different. For when the gates opened Tom Queally did not merely give Frankel his head, he positively encouraged his partner to take the race by the throat. It was the invitation Frankel had spent his young life waiting for.

It took about a furlong for the crowd to appreciate what was happening. Then an extraordinary noise went up from the grandstand as the big screen showed a close-up of that enormous stride hitting full power. It was the sound of a whole crowd gasping in astonishment. What we were seeing was not just one of those sprinters who each year try to burn off the Guineas field for a few furlongs only to fade away as the lactic bites in the final quarter. This was the 1-2 favourite out clear and awesome. By halfway he was a full 15 lengths ahead. Frankie Dettori's frantic elbows on the pursuing Casamento showed that he and the rest of the pack were already hung out to dry.

The truly iconic moment came a few seconds later when Tom Queally looked down and back between his legs. All he can have seen was an empty stretch of Suffolk turf. The first Classic had been reduced to a rout. All the hopes for the colt and all the good wishes for his trainer flooded in as Frankel swept imperiously past the winning post. It could not have happened, but it had. For months wild dreams had suggested there just might be a monster in our midst, and here was the living proof of it. Better still was the resurrection of Newmarket's favourite son. As had happened after Twice Over's Champion Stakes the crowd rushed to see the trainer make that slightly stiff 'hold back the emotion' walk to the unsaddling ring. 'Three cheers for Henry Cecil!' called out a voice. Just three hardly seemed enough.

At 7.30 the morning after, a cowboy-hatted figure of a stable lad made his slow and extremely unsteady way down Warren Hill. Up at Warren Place the trainer's face had a peaceful sobriety about it as Frankel walked the yard, the Burnett flag flying proudly above. In one weekend there had been anticipation, exhilaration and relaxation: three momentous days in Frankel's meteoric route across our horizon; just another astonishing chapter in the unique story that is Henry Cecil.

Sharing the special mixture of relief and satisfaction that pervades the morning after a major triumph is one of the sweetest pleasures that racing can give, but in, God help me, more than 40 years of such pilgrimages maybe none has matched the delight of being at Warren Place that day. It was 1 May 2011, and as the sun began to work its magic there was the feeling that this was not just what it used to be, it was what it ought be.

At Frankel's head 30-year-old Sandeep 'Sandy' Gauravaram led his horse round with the calm of a man who has already made two crucial decisions in life: the first to take his chance in Britain after an early career as champion apprentice in Hyderabad, the second to put in for the handsome Galileo yearling when he arrived in January 2010. At the trainer's side, Mike Marshall was a study of slightly hung-over concentration. And as for Henry Cecil, he wanted to look to the future rather than the past.

In the trotting ring new Derby favourite World Domination was limbering up for his date in the Dante. In the paddock Twice Over, the stable's highest-ever earner, cropped grass in anticipation of his return in the Lockinge at Newbury, and his trainer smiled at him with real affection. But even he could not avoid the Frankel images that blazed in the memory. 'It was very good, wasn't it?'

he said quickly, flicking his head in emphasis. 'Frankel has such a tremendous stride that we wanted to let him use it. And it worked, didn't it? Quite special really.' As he paced away to take another pull on the cigarette I remembered that they used to call his old Burnett grandfather 'Maxim' because of his quick-fire speech.

Mike Marshall gave a crumpled smile at the understatement. He would have been in short trousers when Bolkonski and Wollow opened Cecil's haul of 25 British Classics in 1975 and 1976, but he too knew that however impressive those victories were they had never touched the extraordinary image of Frankel in mid-flight. Even 18 hours after the event it was still almost impossible to believe that the calm, wide-faced animal walking the yard was the same massive-muscled superpower who had torn a Group One field to ribbons before halfway. But he was, and the true beauty of the morning was that they had expected it.

With one exception, no one had dared put it into words beforehand. But in several visits during the spring the impression that Frankel could be something altogether exceptional was much stronger than any sentimental wish to see Henry Cecil complete the unique journey of returning to the very top just six years after being near to Doomsday. In those build-up mornings Frankel had stalked Bullet Train like a mighty panther in the string. He came up Warren Hill with such power that you felt that if Shane so much as coughed it would be next stop Moulton. 'I think he's a very good horse,' Henry would say in the car, 'but it's a long season and a lot of things can go wrong, can't they?'

They hadn't gone wrong in his Greenham Stakes, his Guineas trial at Newbury, but some harboured reservations about how hard he pulled and how comparatively pressed he briefly was by the still underestimated Excelebration at the furlong pole. Henry had first won the Greenham with Wollow 35 years earlier. Back then victory had been instant the moment Dettori Snr released the brake. It had hardly seemed diplomatic to express such thoughts in 2011 and the more one looked at Frankel and listened to his connections, the easier it became to think we might be into something exceptional.

The clincher came on the Friday, the very eve of the 2,000 Guineas. Trainers are usually best given a wide berth on such occasions but Cecil was much more bonhomie than nail-biting banter. He came over to James Fanshawe to enquire about his injured son. He joshed John Gosden about not making the guest list for Prince William's wedding. He even asked a slightly startled Michael Stoute to share a photo 'for my book'. But then Henry and the rest of us had just watched Frankel at the breeze.

Some of us had not been paying attention. Frankel had been at the head of the string following Bullet Train for what is normally the opening canter. As he loped past us, it seemed that Shane Fetherstonhaugh's arms were less stretched than usual. Then we looked at Bullet Train. He was being ridden flat out while the Guineas favourite coasted effortlessly in the slipstream. Here was an image of raw power and easy speed only arrived at by three full centuries of sending horses up this very hill. In the car back to Warren Place, Henry was unusually animated. 'I have a plan,' he said, taking those big hands off the steering wheel. 'I don't think there is any point in worrying about the others or about the pacemaker and the draw. I want him to use his stride. If he had to, he could go all the way.'

Having been the regular work rider for both Midday and Motivator, Fetherstonhaugh is not unassociated with greatness nor quick to overpraise. But pressed on the phone a fortnight earlier he had dropped his voice to an almost awestruck whisper and said, 'You just cannot imagine the feeling of power that this horse gives. If you let him stride he doesn't seem to be going fast but then you look round and they are miles behind. I honestly think we might see something incredible at Newmarket.'

Five minutes after the call, a worried Shane rang back. 'That's not going to go in the paper before the race,' he said. It didn't. But it's in here now.

All playwrights know the problem. They write too big a scene too soon and the rest of the evening is anti-climax. That was in danger of happening with the drama that was Frankel. What could be termed the Second Act had produced the most astonishing, trail-blazing 2,000 Guineas any of us had ever seen. The satisfaction glowed at Warren Place as the family standard flew on the masthead and Henry pulled back Frankel's rugs to run his big hands lovingly over the horse's flank and quarters. The newspapers vied with one another to effect the best 'Superhorse' headline and a month later the Queen's Birthday Honours list confirmed that future winners would be trained by Sir Henry Cecil. Could there be a better closure to the story than the monarch's sword upon the shoulder?

But plenty more still needed telling, and what had been done needed to be undone. Frankel may have won the Guineas by going flat out from the beginning but his mind and body would be destroyed if that became a habit, and up at Warren Place the sense of 'we won't use those tactics again' was so palpable over the next six weeks that it almost backfired at Ascot. Everything on the gallops was planned to get Frankel to settle behind his leader again. Everything that Henry said stressed how much more controlled the plans would be for the upcoming St James's Palace Stakes at the Royal meeting. 'This time the pacemaker will lead,' he said, 'and I will follow the pacemaker. Then I can stride on once I get into the straight.' Even for someone of Henry's long experience the use of the first-person singular was understandable amid the post-Guineas euphoria, but on raceday a jockey must always be ready to react to the situation that confronts him. It all seemed a far cry from the 'you will know what to do' instructions to Steve Cauthen.

At Ascot, as so often in Flat racing, the problems at the finish of Frankel's race were actually caused within seconds of the start. At the post Queally and Frankel had only a rapidly shrinking three-quarters of a length to spare over the 20-1 Irish hope Zoffany. Out of the stalls the tilt had at first looked much more serene as Tom was able to settle Frankel easily on the rails behind the Japanese horse Grand Prix Boss with canny Richard Hughes to his outside on Dubawi Gold. However, it quickly became clear that the group he was in was taking little notice of the tempo being set by Frankel's pacemaker Rerouted, on whom Michael Hills had taken his own 'set a good gallop' instructions unnecessarily to heart and was soon way ahead of the posse.

St James's Palace Stakes at Royal Ascot, 2011: Frankel holds on to win from Zoffany.

Queally, aware that his present position could end being locked up on the rail with Richard Hughes on his outside, took the first opportunity of slipping past the Japanese challenger with the thought of then being able to coast up to and past his pacemaker. That's when the 'you don't realise how fast you are going' deceptiveness of the giant Frankel stride and the over-zealous role of the pacemaker confused the plot. For while Frankel had swept round his field and powered effortlessly all the way up the Ascot straight the previous September, that had been in a position close to a steady gallop not way off a frantic one. While it may have felt as if Frankel was swooping up and past his leader equally easily, he was actually putting in immeasurably more effort and, although a good six lengths clear at the two-furlong pole, the momentum was beginning to drain and the finishing post was suddenly stretching away. There was much relief in the cheers when he got over the line.

At the time it was all something of a public embarrassment, Henry Cecil wincing in the TV close-up and Tom Queally fudging away about 'that being the plan' and his horse having plenty left at the finish. Closer to the action, Mike Marshall shook his head as Sandy led Frankel back and remarked carefully, 'I hope we can put that behind us.' Truth be told there were some difficult days to follow, but Henry had four decades of experience and Tom put his cause right with an inspired ride on Timepiece to win the Group One Falmouth Stakes at the July meeting. She was led in by a beaming Shane Fetherstonhaugh, who had groomed her since she was two.

Best of all, Frankel was beaming. 'This is my favourite gallop,' said Henry one morning on the Limekilns as we waited alongside the Bury Road for the horses to come winging out of the rising sun. You could only get glimpses against the glare but there was that familiar set of the neck and the rapacious reach of the stride. The Hannon camp were saying bullish things about Canford Cliffs before the

Sussex Stakes showdown. But that was as it should be. Frankel had a point to prove. If he was half the horse we thought he was, he was going to prove it however and wherever Canford played his aces.

So it happened on what remains one of the most golden days of them all. Newmarket may have been the most thrilling, Ascot's Champions Day the most fulfilling, but for sweet proof that we were into dreamtime there may never be anything to match what Frankel did when those gates whacked open at Goodwood. For what was greatest about Frankel was the excitement he brought. Debate his merits if you like – and even as a miler he was still some way short of Brigadier Gerard, who won 15 races in a row and as a three-year-old took the 2,000 Guineas by three lengths, the Sussex by five, the Goodwood Mile by ten, the Queen Elizabeth II by eight, and closed the season by taking the Champion Stakes over a mile and a quarter – but no horse in all my time has ever been more consistently exciting than Frankel at his best.

There was that raw, dangerous power about him. A feeling that if he really put it together he might indeed run that famous hole in the wind. That's what he had done in the first half of the Guineas, that's what we now wanted up the straight at Goodwood. Remember, this was his biggest test to date. Canford Cliffs would arrive having won five Group Ones in a row, and last time out his finishing speed had humbled France's triple Breeders' Cup-winning mare Goldikova in the Queen Anne Stakes at Ascot. Richard Hughes had said Canford was the best horse he would ever ride. Many expected him to sit behind Frankel and slice clear before the post. Remember the doubts that lingered after Ascot? How would the horse react after what seemed such a draining experience? How would Queally take the barrage of criticism that had come from us 'riders in the stand'?

No matter that the Canford Cliffs team later found a hairline fracture that ended the colt's career, he and Hughes had still hooked on so deadly to Frankel's tail that our eyes bore into the leader to search for that rocket within. What happened next seared itself into the memory. It was the moment when we truly noticed the

Shane Fetherstonhaugh leads Timepiece into the winner's enclosure after the Falmouth Stakes at Newmarket's July Course, 2011.

enormity of the Frankel stride. It lifts and propels him forward in a wholly different rhythm to other horses. Behind him Canford Cliffs was taking almost two steps to one. Then, with Queally still coiled motionless, we saw the Hughes elbows move. We knew Frankel was going to win, but the real power was yet to come.

At the furlong pole Queally pressed his body down and asked Frankel to punch his weight. In an instant the big colt surged clear of Canford Cliffs, who reeled across the track as if a truck had hit him. I heard myself giving an enormous yell, and as Frankel stormed past Mike Marshall and I stood whooping madly by the winning line before running up and hugging Sandy and travelling head man Mike McGowan and dancing round in a silly little jig of winning happiness.

Besides Brigadier Gerard's unmatched feats, I have witnessed Sea-Bird's Derby, Nijinsky's King George, Mill Reef's Eclipse, Dancing Brave's Arc, all of Sea The Stars' 'Group One a month' progress from May to October two seasons earlier, and nothing I saw went faster

Sussex Stakes at Goodwood, 2011: Frankel powers clear of Canford Cliffs.

than little Dayjur tearing up the Knavesmire in 56.1 seconds, which is averaging 11.2s for each of the Nunthorpe's five furlongs – and from a standing start.

But none of them had quite the impact of Frankel opening his shoulders at Goodwood, and you didn't need to be a form analyst to know the merit of it. Those 300 years of selective breeding and 200 years of racing horses across these downs had not all been in vain. At its best a thoroughbred racehorse should be a thing of wonder. It should be able to do something to make you shout. The thrill about Frankel at Goodwood was that the shouting was set to go on.

As he hosed Frankel off later that afternoon, Sandeep Gauravaram was generous about the horse who had transformed his life since he left his earlier career in India. 'He's growing up all the time,' he said. 'We came down yesterday and he settled and ate all his feed with not a bother. He wants to please. He wants to get on with things. He can only get better. I am sure he will stay a mile and a quarter. To be honest I think he would have won the Derby. But for me it has just been wonderful to be part of it.'

For this writer, even if in a much lesser way, that was a feeling shared. Never more so than three weeks later when photographer Edward Whitaker and I were there before dawn. Even after a lifetime of visits this was a special one because, although Frankel was not an elephant, he was always in the room. Even as we hurried off to help Aideen Marshall feed the Fillies' Yard in the moonlit darkness of Warren Place, the biggest thought was whether all would be well when Chris Russell pulled the door in Frankel's box across the paddock.

It was. That year it always had been. Frankel's appetite was one of his key characteristics, but so too – even from those first muffled greetings under the clear harvest moon – was the whole rhythm of life that beat through the Cecil yard as it closed on the great Champions Day showdown at Ascot, which was then just four weeks

Aideen Marshall in the feed room of the fillies' yard, Warren Place.

ahead of them. There were more than 120 horses at Warren Place and more than 50 people would be present (and 16 absent) for the 'team photo' Edward had organised for later. The facts are that some team members, be they on two legs or on four, are definitely more equal than others yet everyone's effectiveness is imperilled if there is not involvement from the very bottom. And on that particular morning it had started with the cats.

Tabby and Tiny are a long way short of their colleague Felix when it comes to mice-snaffling, let alone rat-catching, but Aideen could not start the early-morning duties she shared with Chris Russell, Dee Deacon and Peter Emmerson until the moggies had been fed. Once they were pacified Aideen said, 'Today's runners first,' and we lugged the food trolley out into the moonlight. About eight boxes along she stopped and put a head collar on the rather opinionated incumbent so it would agree to walk to the manger rather than step out of the door.

This was Principal Role, a talented if slightly quirky performer who would need to win Yarmouth's big race that afternoon to maintain her exalted stabling right next to the Breeders' Cup heroine Midday and two away from the yard's other Group One filly, Timepiece.

We moved the trolley through the darkness to what looked like an aircraft hangar but turned out to be the 'Oh So Sharp Barn', named after the Cecil Triple Crown winner of 1985. 'I love feeding the fillies,' said Aideen, sensing the atmosphere of skittish feminine welcome so different from the horny snorting you get when a bunch of colts demand their breakfast.

The two runners to be fed first, the light and leggy three-year-olds Asterism and Chabada, proved to be the one pair who turned their noses up at the bowl of specially bruised oats with a handful of chaff and lovely juicy carrot which all the others so enjoy. Both fillies petulantly spurned Aideen's offering and resumed chattering to each other through the partition for all the world like two figure-conscious, overbred girls at private school. Aideen could only compare not condemn as she moved on to worthier recipients. 'She's pretty good,' she said of Midday as the £2 million winner accepted her feed with aplomb if not gratitude, 'but she likes her own space. You would not want to push her too far.'

These equine insights, including the observation 'thorough madam' about one filly whose name will be withheld, were the privileges of that early morning, as was the sight of the trainer himself wandering through the gloom at ten to five. As always he was a figure of languid, slightly rumpled chic with a mixture of quizzical interest and aloof pensiveness as he restlessly looked at lists, talked to staff, studied horses and indulged in a monologue of rhetorical musings that it seemed best not to interrupt.

'With 16 people away there's hardly any point in the photo, is there?' he said. 'We worked the horses yesterday, so they will be doing just one canter this morning. It's easy to overdo it, isn't it?'

He was 68 and had been padding round these boxes every day, summer or winter, clear or damp, healthy or sick, since taking over

Warren Place from his father-in-law in 1977. He was so evidently enlivened by the environment it was scarcely credible that we were only six years on from that 12-winner slump of the 2005 season, and that this was the first year the whole of Warren Place had been filled with Cecil horses without the need for a supportive tenant.

But there was no dwelling on the past here, only planning for the future. At York Twice Over had excelled himself by outgunning Midday in a Henry Cecil 'one-two' in the first ever Juddmonte International won by Prince Khalid, the race sponsor, and the filly Vita Nova had run a career best going a close second in the Yorkshire Oaks to the Classic winner Blue Bunting. All three horses were now pointed at Champions Day. 'The paper makes So You Think 6-4 for the new Champion Stakes,' Henry said. 'Ours [Twice Over and Midday] are third and fourth favourite. We [Frankel] are 3-1 on for the Queen Elizabeth and the other mare [Vita Nova] is third favourite for the fillies' race. It's difficult but they should run well, shouldn't they?'

Back in March there had been something slightly shocking in the way his self-deprecating modesty switched to high-vaunting ambition. He was fourth in the trainers' title chase during this team photo visit but close enough that a glory day at Ascot would wrest back the championship he had ten times made his own. As the target loomed closer he was voicing the ambition less, but the desire for it still drove him.

'He involves everyone, that's what is so special about him,' said Dee Deacon as she mixed the afternoon and evening feeds. 'This is his life and he is still so driven that it keeps him going, and all of us too.' Having been at Warren Place for 14 years and head girl for the last three, Dee has seen the good times and the bad. 'With all he was going through you couldn't imagine how he would manage, but he never missed a morning however bad he looked. Sometimes we have had to hide our feelings to keep him strong and while he watches over us we watch over him too. It's deeper than a normal work relationship. It works both ways.'

Dee was mixing what seemed to be a standard food bowl. She had stirred a handful of molasses-sweetened chaff into a plastic tub of golden Canadian corn whose husks had been slightly bruised by the crushing machine to aid digestion. There was boiled bran and electrolytes to add along with the usual vitamin, calcium and joint supplements that equine athletes take. It didn't seem any different to the rows of other bowls, until you noticed the quantity and then checked the name on the wooden tag. This was Frankel's evening feed and, surprise, surprise, he ate more than all the others.

'Yes, he just loves his food,' Dee confirmed. 'Like the other horses he will have a bowl first thing and a couple of bowls at dinner time, but for the evening feed he will take three good bowls of this Canadian corn. No other horse eats as much as that but nothing fazes him. I remember when he came back after winning the Guineas he was already hollering for his food. It's obviously part of his secret.'

Quite what makes a champion is the oldest but most renewable topic in any sport. Asking how Frankel compares with the Warren Place champions of the past is like querying senior Old Trafford hands about how Wayne Rooney rates against George Best or Bobby Charlton. Billy Aldridge was drawing down more oats from the crushing pipe in the ceiling. He teamed up with Cecil way back in the seventies and had ridden alongside all the stars. He pondered the sheer impossibility of the question and put up Oh So Sharp's achievement of winning from a mile to a mile and three-quarters before adding the intriguing personal comment 'she was bossy in her own way'. He then mentioned Kris, the master miler of 1979. 'He was a hell of a good horse,' said Billy. 'Should have won the Guineas. Joe Mercer gave him too much to do.'

But that was the past. Frankel was the present. There were lists to check, boxes to clear, horses to tack up, races to win. That was the actual point of it all.

It was half past six by the time the string began to gather at the big, circular covered ride. Cecil and Mike Marshall stood, as usual, side by side. Much would be noticed, little said. Frankel came across with exercise rider Shane deep in thought, probably as much Frankel's as his own. A filly with a hood over her ears suddenly planted her forelegs and refused to go forward. It was the volatile but very able Sun Chariot entry Chachamaidee. Martyn Peake is one of those quiet, cool riders always cherished by a stable. He leant forward and patted his filly's neck while the trainer walked over and put a big, firm hand on the bridle. Chachamaidee walked smoothly on, the knot in her mind unravelled. It was a classic Cecil mix of almost feminine sensitivity and unmistakeable masculine authority. No words had been said but the exchange had been eloquent.

It was a 40-strong first lot that Wednesday morning, and as Frankel and lead horse Bullet Train came down Warren Hill at their accepted place at the head of affairs you could see both the pleasure and the pain the superstar gave his trainer. 'I can be quite nasty you know,' Cecil said with an only half-joking laugh at the suggestion that snapper Edward Whitaker might go too close. The restless pacing to and fro, not to mention the quick drags on the cigarette, became even more of a contrast to the leisurely stalking walk that was the Frankel hallmark.

The mood lifted as we trekked across the Heath to watch the string swing up the Warren Hill Polytrack. 'He's doing very well,' Cecil said of Frankel. 'Now he's learned to settle he would get a mile and a quarter. He would get it now. Even better next year.' Frankel was only cantering behind Bullet Train but the memory went back a week to the vision of him streaking clear on his return to the grass gallop of the Limekilns.

Beside Henry, the young Italian Marco Botti shook his head as he accepted congratulations for a Group One victory in France with Excelebration, twice a vain pursuer of Frankel that season. 'That's my clever strategy,' Botti said with a laugh to Cecil's teasing, 'avoid Frankel.'

Breakfast featured plenty of teasing too, along with the quick crossword, the ever-present entry book, the large bound horse folder, and the homegrown fruit and vegetable health concoction that Jane Cecil strains each morning and whose benefits Cecil grudgingly concedes while wiping beetroot stains from his mouth. 'It must be good for me because I am still alive, or at least I think I am.' He likes to have people around him. Jane's daughter is there when in Newmarket as, every day, is her sister Sally Noseda, who in an earlier life was a skilled work rider for the Michael Stoute team. George Bell, the regular partner of Vita Nova, was at table, as was Lorna Fowler, the partner of Plato, the one and only Cecil winner at Cheltenham – albeit in a charity race. Mike Marshall came in and snatched a quick breakfast, and secretary Claire Markham picked up instructions as they fell from the trainer. The mood was friendly but there remained an element of 'man at work' and 'don't speak unless spoken to'.

Goat's milk was also on the Cecil diet and the talk suddenly turned to a filly called Juve, who had a goat as a companion way back in the seventies but contracted grass sickness so badly that the owner ruled she should be put out of her misery. 'I went round to the box,' Henry recalled in that vivid, almost childish way of his. 'She was lying down and looked dreadful, her eyes cloudy, her mouth creamy. But she looked up at me in such a way that I said, "I just can't do it now, I will wait until the afternoon." You will never believe it but when I came back she was on the mend and she went on to win five races.'

Studying the Programme Book.

It was a shaft of light from the past that held in the mind as we went out to see the two-year-olds on second lot. Among them was Noble Mission, who had to carry the somewhat unfair dual burden of being Frankel's full-brother and having the slightly dunce's-cap distinction of wearing a hood over his ears – an 'old dog learns new tricks' calming aid picked up from fellow trainer James Fanshawe. 'He's had some sore shins and a few little problems,' said Henry, 'but he is coming along and will probably run next month. He's not Frankel but he could be all right.' Many of them would not run that season as Cecil used the privilege of his experience to give them the time to develop their talent. Most will turn out no good, but one or two just might prove to be the diamonds in the dross. That's the all-absorbing dynamic of the training game.

Its darker side clouded in as we walked over the Heath to watch the canter.

First Henry sympathised with Peter Chapple-Hyam over his beaten odds-on shot the previous day at Yarmouth, only to be told that in a later race the trainer had a filly so badly struck into that she needed to be euthanised. Cecil has had his own brushes with mortality and the mournful look remained as Gay Jarvis rode up with difficult news about her much-loved husband Michael's losing battle with illness. At moments like this those two-year-olds on the gallop are just young horses cantering up a hill – but they carry dreams with them, and dreams can be a treatment too.

They promised the future, no less, but as we later gathered in the main yard for the photo we were celebrating the present and the excitements of the immediate past. There was much joshing and 'I don't want to be in the front' false modesty from the usual suspects. The sun was warm and beforehand Henry had wanted to show Edward the garden, the roses, the Tutankhamun peas, the Neolithic plant from Australia, the finest of his vegetables, and then upstairs we went in a burst of real animation to the giant wardrobe with its rows of cashmere jackets, silk shirts and Gucci shoes.

When it was all over and the car swung off the roundabout into Newmarket high street, the hands on the clock tower showed half past eleven – exactly seven hours after the headlights had stabbed through the darkness on Warren Hill. Morning had ended, but for the stable the day would stretch out until evening.

In the 3.20 race Principal Role did her bit to justify her exalted box mates Midday and Timepiece by cruising clear in Yarmouth's main event of the season. An hour later the two-year-old Feel The Difference drew clear at Beverley, and finally the Kempton floodlights looked down on those two food-faddish girls last seen spurning their breakfast. Asterism and Chabada finished first and third.

'It has been a good day,' said Mike Marshall as he celebrated with his wife and mother-in-law later that evening. It had been, but he knew – we all knew – that none of it would be enough until the Elephant had done his stuff at Ascot.

As we closed on the new Champions Day the strain was beginning to show. Not on the horse but on the trainer – and Henry Cecil would not have had it any other way. 'He's in good form,' he said as Frankel coasted up Warren Hill ten days before his final assignment in the Queen Elizabeth II Stakes on that season-climaxing afternoon. 'But this week with the sales and everybody around is completely non-stop. It's impossible really, isn't it?'

His face was showing all of its 68 years, but then it had done a lot of living, and anyway he was not the only one. A glimpse of Michael Stoute in the ever-lightening dawn was to appreciate the burden of juggling current training activity with future-prospect purchase at the yearling sales at Tattersalls each day. Even the comparatively youthful William Haggas was looking a rather drawn, sleep-deprived figure as he instructed his horses and riders at the top of the Al Bahathri. The swan system is needed: calm on the surface, paddling hard underneath. The signs that Wednesday were that Henry's legs were swirling as purposefully as ever even after an amazing 42 years on the training pond.

Of course this was a very different Cecil to the teasing, energised player who had marched across Warren Hill to watch Frankel follow Bullet Train up the Polytrack back in March. 'Tomorrow will be the first time we move him away from his leader,' Henry had said then. 'It's a long season and we have to be careful, but this horse could be exceptional, don't you think?' He had indeed been careful: Frankel had run just four races in the subsequent seven months. But if anyone had doubted the 'exceptional' tag, they didn't now.

Back then we still did not know what would happen when the bomb at the end of those stretching reins was finally detonated. The answer had been that astonishing explosion which blew the 2,000 Guineas field apart at Newmarket and which soon put ideas of the Derby out of the question. Since then tactical worries after the scrambling, muddle-paced win at Royal Ascot had been swept away by the superbly controlled front-running triumph at Goodwood. Now on this beechnut October morning there was a very real sense that the trainer believed that what he had already once, perhaps inadvertently, described as the best horse he had ever seen was in better shape than ever.

'Oh yes, he's a much better horse now,' said Henry in one of those rare moments when he produces a crushing authority out of the slightly uneven, often reticent rhythm of his conversation. 'He's relaxed, he's getting stronger, he's in really good order. Now that he is settled he can be with his leader [at Ascot it would be Bullet Train doing afternoon duty too] and then let him go two and a half furlongs from home. The main thing about Frankel is that he does quicken for a long way. From two furlongs down he will go right to the line and when he lengthens like that other horses are not going to stay with him, are they?'

The impact of these words was acknowledged with a dipped-head smile from Marco Botti, whose Excelebration had hustled up Frankel for a moment at Newbury back in April and who on form could go closest at Ascot. 'But we can talk as much as we like,' added the ever affable Teddy Grimthorpe, who of course as Khalid Abdulla's racing manager had quite a bit to be affable about. 'In the end it is the racecourse that counts and you can never be sure.' Just three days earlier Teddy had watched Workforce, Prince Khalid's Michael Stoute-trained

2010 Derby winner, finish way down among the stragglers in the Arc de Triomphe. No doubt that kept the caveats in the Grimthorpe mind, but back at Warren Place the vibrations came from a stronger drum.

Those closest to Frankel had already become too wise either to shout silly boasts to the sky or to pretend that keeping a sense of calm around what remained a highly volatile athlete did not have a sense of strain about it. 'The great thing about him is that you can't keep him away from his food,' said Sandeep Gauravaram with a smile. 'He's relaxed, and I think he's enjoying himself.'

Shane Fetherstonhaugh, whose duties as Frankel's work rider had been coupled with looking after the two star fillies Midday and Timepiece, was also very positive as what was officially the world's best racehorse stalked back into the yard. 'He seems very settled,' said Shane, 'and he's still developing. Just have a look at him.' Frankel was not the sort of placid horse you slap across the ribcage as a hearty emphasis of his well-being, but following Shane's gaze down to the slab of muscle across the loins was to see an awesome sight. For any racing fan these private moments when you feast your eyes on greatness imprint themselves indelibly on the memory. For me, having had the unbelievable luck down the years to gaze at champions as far apart as Mill Reef and Sea The Stars, that little pre-Ascot cameo was very special.

We were still two days away from Frankel's gallop on the Friday when Tom Queally would angle himself forward and Bullet Train would once again watch his brother rocket away, but the trainer was ticking over the routine like a clockmaker examining the swings of a pendulum. 'We will work on Friday,' said Henry, 'and then again on Tuesday, and then fiddle him through to have him ready for Saturday. I think that should be right, don't you?'

The pointlessness of posing the question didn't cloak the enormity of the responsibility as the countdown continued to the richest raceday Britain had ever staged, and one on which, statistically at least, Cecil could make up the £1.3 million by which he trailed Richard Hannon in the trainers' table. To do that, not only would Frankel have to do his stuff but Midday and Twice Over would have to be first and second in the Champion Stakes as well as Vita Nova collecting in the Fillies' and Mares' Stakes while Mr Hannon failed completely to trouble the scorer. Not a time, you would think, for a trainer to entertain distractions.

Welcome to Sales Week.

On the kitchen table was the catalogue, on the phone was an agent. Cecil took the phone outside and returned five minutes later with the sort of message that would numb the minds of the unfamiliar. 'I said I liked the colt,' he said to his wife Jane about one of the lots on his typewritten, note-scrawled shortlist, 'but that I would not want to give silly money for him – not more than 200,000.' Heavy questions hung in the air as he returned to the catalogue and a foaming, freshly pressed fruit cocktail with a purple beetroot base. Drop concentration now and the superstars of tomorrow will slip through your fingers. 'I have a few orders,' said Henry, almost as if it was a surprise to get any. 'Not a lot but a few, and we just have to hope for the best.'

The adjustment of focus between the immediate and the future and back again can often leave an observer stranded in space.

'How did she feel?' he asked suddenly, switching his attention to George Bell, who had been on Vita Nova. 'I liked the way she kept her head down. After that hold-up [the mare had banged a leg a week earlier] I will now work her on Saturday and again on Tuesday and that should put her right, don't you think? She is not a heavy thing, is she?'

The exchange suddenly brought us back to the images of the morning and of the athletic tinkering needed to reach raceday in optimum condition. Then the phone went again and it was sales time.

At Tattersalls sales, 2011: Henry and Jane Cecil with owner Craig Bennett.

That's if Henry could use the new mobile when he got up to Tattersalls.

The gleaming little machine was passed around the table. It was on 'lock', and after several attempts to solve that problem secretary Claire Markham tried to coax her employer through the basics of receiving messages while Jane went to the dentist and bloodstock expert Crispin de Moubray was beavering around other parts of the sales ring on their behalf. Unique among trainers, Cecil plies his trade across the Heath unencumbered by either binoculars or cellphones. It might even be part of his secret. But at that moment over breakfast it didn't hold out huge hope for good communication during the afternoon.

But first there were the two-year-olds out on second lot. In the first sortie Tom Queally had come over to ride the handsome Sir Robert Ogden-owned Thomas Chippendale, who was engaged (and would win) that week. These were less immediate prospects, although they included Frankel's hooded full-brother Noble Mission, who had now progressed enough to get a run before the season's close and so ease the burden of expectation for being so royally related. From the covered ride the string filed its way down across the hill to reach the Al Bahathri, where the trainer had taken up his usual position at the six-furlong marker. Most trainers position themselves further up to see the finish of the gallop. Looking across we could see Michael Stoute there. As so often when queried about his routine, Cecil just shrugged at the question. 'I like to see them join up,' he replied.

Five batches of twos and threes came spinning past. Each time Cecil switched from apparently languid contemplation to rapt attention. There were no notes, no tape recorders, but it was very obvious that some sort of filing process was under way before we turned and walked back, feet scrunching on fallen beechnuts.

As the horses re-gathered there was another debriefing which to the outside ear seemed little more than a version of that age-old question-and answer 'All OK?' and 'Yes, guvnor'. But back in the car with Saint-Saëns' Danse Macabre playing on Classic FM, there was a sudden shaft of training clarity.

'That third horse,' he said of one of the unraced hopefuls who had seemed to go at least as well as the others, 'I like him, but the way he sounds he just might have a problem. It could clear as he gets fitter, but we will have to be careful and might have to do something.' As so often, the statement was more a piece of mental note-taking than question, and indeed it is inside that Cecil skull that the workings of Frankel and all the others are stored. 'By now I know the ones I like,' he said of the two-year-olds, without volunteering any names.

'I don't write them down but I have them in my head. We are not usually that far out.'

The big bullets were back in their boxes, and as the trainer changed jeans and shoes and took the new mobile off for its debut run at the sales, the senior members of the Warren Place team looked ahead to Ascot with that mix of confidence and concentration which both gives them belief in their job and a determination to avoid the traps that await highly tuned athletes in any category. 'Something can happen so easily,' said Mike Marshall. 'It looks like Vita Nova is going to make it but somehow she banged herself in the box. It could have happened to anything.'

Mike was around Dubai Millennium when he was at Godolphin, and with Nashwan when he was with Dick Hern, and while he did not put Twice Over and Midday into that category, he believed both would have live chances in the next week's Champion Stakes. 'Twice Over is about confidence,' he said. 'When he didn't want to be saddled or be loaded up at Royal Ascot, I thought the signs were bad. But after his two wins at York he has got all his confidence back and he could go really well on Saturday.'

But for all his tributes to Twice Over, who at £2.4 million remains the biggest purse winner in Cecil's extraordinary training career, Marshall, like many others in the yard, could never forget his admiration for Midday. 'I just think she is better than Twice Over,' he said. 'She can be very effective when she gets that long stride going, but she has this tremendous acceleration. For all her success I don't think people realise how good she is. I think she could win on Saturday.'

It went without saying that he thought Frankel would also score, but another day with his team could only remind you just how fine a line top stables must walk as they prime their superstars for the fray. While Sea The Stars was always a model of decorum on the track, except for his hollering at the world on his arrival at the racecourse stables, no one at John Oxx's yard was ever in any doubt of the need to tread carefully around their hero with his massive 'king of the herd' personality. With Frankel the explosions were nearer the surface, and one day the previous winter one had hit Jonathan 'Stretch' Ormshaw full in the face.

'I was leading Dan de Haan out on him one icy morning,' remembers Stretch, whose nickname derives from his seemingly elasticated length, 'and he swung his head round and clocked me. Everybody said how well Dan did to sit on him but I was in hospital with five stitches and a cracked cheekbone.' Others smiled at the memory and mused on the ever-present dangers, when one kick in the stable can stymie a race if not a career. 'But Frankel has grown up a lot,' said head girl Dee Deacon with almost maternal pride. 'I think boxing over to the watered gallop has been very good for him. We take care to keep him settled and work around him and I am sure he will be even better next year.'

Ah yes, next year. Over at Tattersalls the extraordinary human comedy of the first day of the premier yearling sale was playing out, people meeting and greeting with eyes that restlessly scan for other activity. The players for the big teams huddled in little groups, deep in concentration. By the collecting ring Cecil was talking earnestly to a would-be client. A couple of hours earlier the Niarchos team had gone to £700,000 for a Galileo half-sister to Irish 1,000 Guineas winner Nightime, who would be in training at Warren Place the following season. The clock ticked on, as it always will. But if a stable is to hang on to greatness it has to do more than chime every hour. It has also to sound across the biggest stage, as Frankel had to do on Champions Day.

For those putting on the big Racing For Change promotional drive who had 'bet the farm' on rolling the great events of the autumn together for this mid-October Ascot climax, what Frankel did was little less than a gift to heaven.

Mind you, the weather smiled first. It was a gorgeous, clear, russet-leaved, song-in-the-heart afternoon at a time of year when there's a fair chance of any day having a grim, soggy, end-of-the-year feel. But fortune favoured the brave. The crowds turned out in their thousands and the horses, although not all the Cecil horses, did their stuff. Vita Nova was ninth of ten, having clearly not got over her problems. Twice Over was tenth and Midday only a closing fourth in the Champion Stakes. But the true champion of Champions Day was unquestionably Frankel himself.

He had been billed as the star attraction, and he delivered in kind.

For watchers getting used to the connections, their roles have their own delights. There's Sandy Gauravaram, quiet and immaculate at Frankel's head; travelling head man Mike McGowan, ever alert for the little detail that can lead to the big issue, his face set in concentration with the slight sadness of living for years as an Everton fan; Mike Marshall, here as a 'sweeper' for the big days; Steve 'Yarmy' Dyble, a link right back to drinking larks at Marriott Stables but now sober and ready to ensure Frankel was trouble-free at the starting stalls; and Chris Bishop, here with Bullet Train, who is making his first racecourse show since completely downing tools when last tried in his own right at Newmarket in April.

Then, of course, there is Henry. He is all in blue, as he has been for each Frankel run this season – elegant suit, dark blue shirt, white and blue spotted tie. The tension crackles in him as he paces up and down beneath the big sycamore trees in the saddling paddock, but just as evident is the easy familiarity with which he snugs Queally's saddle under his arm. He has been in this position so many times before. So many great horses, different owners to deal with, different jockeys to brief – but always the same simple

Champions' Day at Ascot, 2011: Tom Queally, Khalid Abdulla, Henry Cecil.

and yet so easily fallible routine. So much involved in just tying a saddle on.

In the paddock Queally is as white-faced as ever, but cool and calm and smiling politely as he bows to Khalid Abdulla. Cecil's face is a mask of civility, his mind elsewhere, only coming into focus when he takes his jockey away from the Prince's entourage for one final word. Then Tom is on board Frankel with Sandy and Mike McGowan as flankers to follow the familiar shape of Bullet Train's tail just as if they were filing out of the covered ride of a morning.

Not everyone took to Ascot's new £210 million grandstand when it was reopened in 2006, but as Frankel and his green and pink jockey canter past it under that glassy October sun only a curmudgeon could deny that it makes the finest of settings. Queally takes Frankel over to the far rail, the best place to handle the sudden scare or backfiring exhaust that always threatens to ignite the rocket beneath him. Down at the start he links up smoothly with Yarmy. There can be no nonsense now. But the straight mile at Ascot still takes a hundred seconds of breath and strain. The journey from the steel cage of the stalls to the soaring cheers of the grandstand may be a short one, but it is as if Frankel's very being and Henry's whole life depend upon it.

Bullet Train sets off determined to have his own seconds in the sun. Queally anchors Frankel in fourth place as the pack allows the leader to have his way. The rein-stretching, head-turned anchoring seems hardly worth the effort, except for the spectacle it provides when Tom is towed out by Frankel to head the pursuers with his stable companion as a hare all of eight lengths ahead of him. Bullet Train is quite a talented hare, though, and his six-length advantage at the three-furlong pole means there's a bit of running to do. At the two-furlong pole Frankel is almost at Bullet Train's quarters, but so too are the two main rivals, Excelebration and France's best filly Immortal Verse. What is needed now is the big punch for the finish.

And that, quite wonderfully, was what Frankel gave us.

Once again it was pointless to debate quite what this beating of lesser-rated rivals achieved in the ledgers of fame. What mattered was the manner of it. When Queally crouched low on Frankel's neck, re-threaded his reins and pumped his elbows to induce his horse to turn on the turbo, the answer was one whose lilting athleticism lifted the heart. Frankel has a natural white stocking above his near fore fetlock and when he really stretches you notice the way it peerlessly rises and reaches. The official verdict was four lengths at the line but for the record crowd it was immortality.

For the watchers the specialness of the horse could now be complemented by the uniqueness of the trainer. He went through all his usual routines – first with the horse, then the lad, then the jockey, then the owner, and then finally a quizzical turn to the besieging press before moving among them to receive the TV interview. The face was both proud and vulnerable, the manner happy yet diffident, the head dipped in acknowledgement when the traditional (now knighted) call went up 'Three cheers for Sir Henry!' There was little new to be said, but what was said was well said: 'I have been very lucky. Delighted for the Prince, for the staff, for everyone.'

Those are the days which you can shut your eyes and bring back to savour in the memory. The Ascot images were among those used for a celebratory DVD when Henry Cecil was honoured with a Cartier Award in London on the evening of the morning the Queen put the sword to his shoulder at Buckingham Palace, when it truly was 'Arise, Sir Henry'. He had not won the trainers' title but he had handled the biggest star of the season, and more than 70 two-year-olds were being sent to him for 2012. There was an air of very special satisfaction as he padded the garden at the end of one December morning in 2011 and told stories that ranged from going quail shooting in Georgia to restocking his pond after herons ate his fish. 'I am going to put a log on the fire,' he said later, 'and go to sleep and dream of Frankel winning, maybe even the King George. I think I ought to give him an entry, don't you?'

The celebratory DVD was on the screen for the Christmas party. It was at the now luxuriously appointed Bedford Lodge Hotel in the Bury Road just three doors down from Freemason Lodge. When the infant Henry was first at Newmarket this was the home of top jockey Harry Wragg; imagine even Frankie Dettori living in quite such mid-town state today. When Henry first had parties they were often in fancy dress. One year Steve Cauthen came resplendent in the white navy uniform of a lieutenant of the US fleet, and Henry was swathed in silks as some eastern potentate.

No uniforms this time, but Tom Queally bought the drinks and Henry was in his best cashmere jacket and open-necked, bright-patterned shirt alongside Jane looking devoted and lovely. Yarmy was there too, and Billy Aldridge and Joan Plant, three who linked back to the earliest days. All the team had gathered, right through to Steve Kielt the farrier and Charlie Smith the vet. Sandy Gauravaram sat smiling with his wife, sipping a glass of beer, Shane and Claire made a happy couple, and it was a night when only happiness should be spread.

The team were back where a few years earlier only their dreams could have taken them, a place to which Henry Cecil-trained horses had so often transported others before them. The memories flooded in so strong that when the trainer took the microphone after they had played the DVD you half expected him to give his own rendering of 'My Way', that greatest of all ballads of wistful, successful farewell. Instead Henry thanked everyone and told the story of how in his darkest handful-of-horses days he walked sadly away from the Al Bahathri and heard a young trainer say to his owner, 'That's Henry Cecil – should have retired years ago.'

He told them that perhaps he should have retired, but he hadn't, and he wouldn't. He said how Frankel had been a success but the other three-year-olds hadn't fired, how he had been quiet with the two-year-olds but there should be some decent ones for next season, how he was very hopeful of the bunch he was being sent for the next year. He did not strain nor have a note in hand, but no chief executive nursed through his own 'Agincourt' speech could have roused a team better. It was a long, long way from the Hopeless Henry whose childhood prize was a Muffin the Mule glove puppet.

We danced and caroused late into the night. We had been lit up by the achievements of one horse, but much more by the man who had masterminded him. There should be a word for it, I remarked. 'I have been with the man for 21 years,' said Billy Brown, Scotland still deep in his voice. 'Is this a trainer or a genius?' Billy, like the rest of us, searched for a suitable word. The best we could come up with was that we had been 'Frankelfied'.

EPILOGUE

THE 2012 season came, and with it the bitterest of ironies that while Frankel thrived, Henry didn't. After an initial scare which saw the BBC close its Grand National coverage in April with the mistaken announcement that Frankel would be retired following a training injury, the horse flourished with increasingly impressive victories at Newbury, Ascot, Goodwood and York.

Henry's health was not so good. At Newbury in May for Frankel's opening run in the Lockinge Stakes, the trainer had looked more pinched and worn than a year previously. But he still sent Frankel out to set a new benchmark against old rival Excelebration, beating that excellent colt for the fourth time, on this occasion by five lengths. Queries on Frankel's well-being had come when the colt knocked his tendon during routine work early in Grand National week. 'We hope it's just a knock' is all too often a wistful prelude for acceptance of what can be a season- or career-ending setback. Mercifully, veterinary scans and steady exercise proved the wish correct, and to watch Frankel flash past the Newbury stands with that neck set so straight and the stride so devouring was to believe that as a four-year-old he could indeed be better than ever.

For his 69-year-old trainer it was not so easy. Problems with his stomach had returned and Henry was visibly even thinner by the time he got to Royal Ascot for Frankel's tilt at the very first race of the meeting, the Queen Anne Stakes. But his team's handling of their 'superhorse' retained its masterful touch. Great horses give inspiration. This one had the seemingly impossible task of opening the finest five days' racing in the world with a headline act that would carry its song all the way to the weekend. No promoter would risk such a thing. Frankel delivered and some more. On officially good to soft going, he ran the Straight Mile in 1m 37.84 seconds, only 0.6 seconds outside the record, by far the best comparative time of the day – and he was clocked at 10.58 for the third last furlong, a faster split than any achieved by the sprinters in the King's Stand Stakes which followed. The gallant Excelebration was second again, but this time bobbing a distant eleven lengths in the champion's wake.

Frankel was already the best horse in the official world rankings, but now the respected Timeform operation opportunistically gave him a rating of 147, the highest in their history and above such giants as Sea-Bird, Brigadier Gerard and Tudor Minstrel. The Queen, fresh from the very personal triumphs of her Diamond Jubilee celebrations, had come in her carriage. We felt Frankel might still have won if he had pulled it. But most of all we felt a sense of gratitude – for being there, and for those others who had brought us a horse of such delight.

The chief of these was absent, Prince Khalid having been called back to Saudi Arabia in mourning for Crown Prince Nayef, who had died the week before. But the assorted others wore that shared possessive grin of being part-owners of such wonderment. Steve 'Yarmouth' Dyble had been down at the start to see fair play as part of Henry Cecil duties which stretched back to the 1970s and 'Yarmy's' drinking days. Mike McGowan doesn't smile a lot but there was a radiance about him as he led Frankel back for a wash-down whilst a jubilant 'Sandy' collected his own trophy. Farrier Steve Kielt didn't lose his grin even when trainer Bryan Smart spotted a missing racing plate and called out, 'That must be some horse – he's done it on three legs!' Shane Fetherstonhaugh, the solemn-faced figure who shouldered the massive responsibility of riding Frankel each morning, was on a rare outing to watch 'his' horse. Shane did not have much to be solemn about.

Neither did Tom Queally. Exactly a year earlier he had been putting a brave face on a wrecked race-plan as Frankel had pursued his over-eager pacemaker too soon and had only a shrinking three-quarters of a length left at the line. Now Tom was serenity itself as he said, 'It looks like he is getting better and I didn't think that was possible. He settled, he travelled, he got everything else off the bridle and I was still sitting there. Then away he went – it was amazing. He ticked all the boxes, he did everything right. From my point of view he's been flawless in the past but I couldn't have asked for anything more. The biggest problem I had again was pulling him up. If he gets any better I'll be pulling him up [a mile down the road] in Legoland.'

It was a time for smiles, but it has to be said that at this stage Henry's was more of strained relief than of expansive happiness. Forty-four years of handling top-class horses had made him aloof, but not immune to the pressures of housing the animal all the public want to watch. He knew that any morning, any canter, any slip on the road crossing could be Frankel's last. Remember the retirement dramas in Grand National week? Only he and his team can ever know the care that had been needed to get their champion to Royal Ascot.

Not content with getting Frankel there, and despite a continuing infection which would have kept the rest of us to our beds, Henry had also accepted something of a one-man mission to spread the word of what having such an animal represents. Interviewer after interviewer was taken into the tartan-curtained study with the model soldiers on their shelves and the moose antlers on the wall and treated to that disarming mixture of self-deprecation and candour which seemed to get more revelatory by the year. 'Frankel is always smashing his box up,' Henry told the *Guardian*'s Chris Cook: 'He breaks mangers and things like that. He's very hot-blooded. You can think it's a cold evening and you put a light under-rug on him and you find at 10 o'clock at night that he's tried to pull the rug over his head, which is dangerous. He can get tangled up and break his neck or a leg. So you have to watch him.'

In the Ascot winner's enclosure the whole circus started up again as Henry was taken from camera to camera to give his own benediction to the galloping miracle he had just set before us. Part of Henry Cecil is as patrician as the stately homes which his forbears built. But the other side is still the vulnerable, hopeless schoolboy who wants now to share the proof 'that I am not completely useless'. It was a full hour before he had finished. The rightness of his knighthood 'for services to racing' had never been better displayed.

It had been Henry's 75th Royal Ascot success since Parthenon had travelled from Marriott Stables to start the record-breaking tally way back in 1970. On the Friday of the 2012 meeting the three-year-old Thomas Chippendale outgunned Frankel's full brother Noble Mission to give the stable first and second in the King Edward VII Stakes and take the Royal Ascot total to 76. On the Saturday, Henry put family first by giving his step-daughter away at her wedding. His favourite meeting had been a triumph once again and his most favourite horse of all seemed only to be getting better.

Would that Henry had been. His stomach problems moved to his throat. He was missing from the racecourse, spent part of Newmarket's July Meeting in hospital, and was not able to make the trip to Goodwood for Frankel's almost exhibition triumph in the Sussex Stakes. Unlike 2011, when the colt was only a narrow favourite to beat the much heralded but subsequently injured Canford Cliffs, Frankel was now 20-1 on to beat just three rivals. But as exhibitions go, this was as thrilling as thoroughbreds can give and without the frisson of runaway tension that the horse had in his early days. The faithful Bullet Train kept up his gallop to the quarter-mile pole, where Queally set Frankel down to run, and for another glorious time they set the world alight.

All that was missing was the trainer, and while the stable's wider well-being was attested by Goodwood victories for Noble Mission and for the fillies Chachamaidee and Wild Coco, sightings of Henry were confined to Warren Place, Newmarket, and the treatment room. Frankel's own next mission was to be at York in the Prince Khalid-sponsored International Juddmonte Stakes. It would be his first attempt at a mile and a quarter and a last chance for him to be seen in Yorkshire. Despite gainsaying predictions, Henry announced that he 'would not miss it for the world,' and as an unprecedented number of fans flocked to the Knavesmire, he was as good as his word – although words, as the worldwide TV audience was to hear, were painfully difficult to say.

Like 'a rather frail old artist on the Riviera': Henry Cecil at York, August 2012

If ever there was final evidence of the steel beneath the Cecil charm it was on this Juddmonte day at York. He was now quite shockingly thin, but sported a beautifully cut dark-brown jacket, trademark narrow grey trousers and a striking wide-brimmed dark blue trilby of almost stetson dimensions. He looked not so much a trainer as a rather frail old artist on the Riviera. As a concession to his illness he had a steel stick with a leather handle but, being Henry, it seemed more a fashionable walking cane than an invalid aid.

He had two runners, Noble Mission and Sir Thomas Chippendale, to saddle in the Great Voltigeur Stakes. His team had three – Bullet Train, Frankel and Twice Over – in the Juddmonte. Speaking may not have been easy but he was especially animated as he joined the horses' connections in the paddock before the Voltigeur and as he waved to the crowds that cheered him as he walked across to the stands. But it was for Frankel that he and they had come, and any doubts to the horse's right to all-time greatness were sent high in the sunny skies as the colt produced a performance more mesmerisingly memorable than anything anyone had seen before.

Reputations can delude the eye, but there was never a single moment in the 2 minutes 5.69 seconds it took to run the esoterically exact distance of 1 mile 2 furlongs and 88 yards when Frankel did not impress. A stalking panther he may have looked as Tom Queally hacked him behind the others to the start, but he was a panther firmly on the leash. When the stalls slammed open he loped out at the back as Bullet Train took third place behind the trail-blazing Ballydoyle pacemakers attempting to stretch the tempo for their stablemate St Nicholas Abbey. There was pace enough, but it only seemed to suit Frankel and Queally all the more as they stalked the Breeders' Cup winning St Nicholas Abbey a good 15 lengths off the lead. York has a pitilessly long straight. The hope, such as there was one, for Frankel's rivals was that it might bottom him. One glance was all you needed as answer.

These glances are the very best of Flat racing moments. They are the instant the jockey realises that the horse beneath him is a weapon that can blow the others away. I had always thought that Lester Piggott on Nijinsky as they moved out to take the 1970 King George VI and Queen Elizabeth Stakes was the greatest of them, representing in Piggott and Vincent O'Brien the apogee of the most charismatic trainer-and-jockey partnership Flat racing has ever seen. But Frankel drawing up to St Nicholas Abbey at York now has to be the match of it.

For while St Nicholas Abbey may be better over a mile and a half, he is still a classy animal. And yet as he closed up on his field the camera moved to his right, and there was Frankel simply cruising. These closing furlongs might have been uncharted territory but Queally had no doubts what he was riding. In a hugely welcome, if forty years overdue development, the sectional times were being shown on the screen. From the three- to the two-furlong marker Frankel clocked just 11.02 seconds, his fastest fraction of the race. He was doing over 40mph and he was not stopping. There was a seven-length gap before Frankie Dettori inched Godolphin's Farhh past the battling St Nicholas Abbey. His face was wreathed in smiles. If you had to be second, this was the horse to be second to.

In so many ways this was the ultimate in racing fulfilment and for no one more than the trainer, now being helped through the crowd to greet the greatest of all the champions he had run on the Knavesmire and further afield. It was 50 years since he had fallen in love with Yorkshire whilst working with the yearlings at Burton Agnes. It was the track where he had saddled the likes of Ardross, Reference Point and Diminuendo. It was a public who appreciated him and what he had done.

As Tom Queally loosened the girths one side and Mike Mc-Gowan the surcingle on the other, a voice called for three cheers for Frankel and then three more for Henry Cecil. Twice the crowd thundered forth its acclamation, in poignant contrast to the brief whispering comments from the trainer to the Channel 4 microphone held by Derek Thompson, who had himself received chemotherapy that Monday. 'You have seen him,' croaked Henry. 'Make up your own minds. It's fantastic. Great for Yorkshire. Great for supporters of racing.'

The television close-up amidst the struggling throng was not a happy nor a flattering one. But Henry Cecil is not somebody who enjoys leaving a weak impression. Minutes later the winning connections were being brought to the victory rostrum. As the announcer called the trainer's name the stick was spurned, and when Henry stepped forward in sprightly fashion, no amount of shyness at his chemically-induced baldness could prevent the stately good manners of doffing his hat, as a gentleman should.

The cheers rang out anew but the warmth of their affection was tinged with a wincing shot of sadness at quite how sick their hero looked. To put it bluntly, he seemed like the doomed relative we all visit in the closing stages of an illness, and as the thousands left the Knavesmire there was a very real sense that this was the last we would see of Henry Cecil. Then as the weeks went by and more hospital treatment was needed and sightings even on the Newmarket gallops became fewer, most people assumed that assurances of the trainer being around for Frankel's farewell appearance at Ascot in October were mere whistles in the wind.

But the ferocious inner drive that had forced mind over matter in previous dramas would yet again win through. To have the focus to handle the last hurrah of the best horse in creation was an unbelievable incentive, and so too was the tireless and even combative support of his wife Jane, who was having to act as something of a spokesperson as well as in her ongoing roles as everything from nurse to gatekeeper.

Such pressures inevitably lead to tensions and, sadly, they in this case included a falling-out over this book.

When shown the almost completed manuscript after Royal Ascot, Jane and Henry very much took against it. They objected to my handling of some of the well-chronicled dips in the story. They felt that I had betrayed the welcome they had so openly given in 2011. There were words like 'intrusive' and 'tawdry' used to describe my approach – which was a touch ironic, as the main criticism of other readers was that the book was in danger of being too sympathetic.

However, people – especially revered public figures fighting for their lives and the crowning moments of their career – are more than entitled to their opinions. It appeared to be Henry's and Jane's understanding that the book I had spent so long in writing and to which I had put them and so many others to so much trouble in researching, was going to be little more than the 'cuttings album' format with which I had first approached them in February 2011. In fact, by April of that year it had become clear that the cuttings were far too unwieldy (and at times far too harsh) to make an attractive book, and I said they would have to trust me to tell the story as best I could.

What you have read is my affectionate, admiring but I believe necessarily realistic portrait of an extraordinary man and a quite exceptional career. In more than 40 years of journalism I have never before been accused of betraying a trust and do not intend to start now. But the book stands as a tribute to the sport as well as to the astonishing man who has been at the centre of it for so long and who in the autumn of 2012 faced what seemed the most impossible climb of all. He appeared at a public gallop for Frankel at Newmarket, but reports were of his being increasingly weak and frail. Bookies were too polite to quote odds about him making Champions' Day at Ascot in mid-October. If they had, the price would not have been a short one.

But Henry made it – and more. Incredibly, he once again took on the 'witness to the wonderhorse' role as he had done before Royal Ascot. Frankel's last bow in the Champion Stakes was attracting an unprecedented amount of attention to the racing game, and his trainer was prepared to step forward and wave the flag. It was as if the years had rolled back to some of those interviews with the young tyro three decades ago. Racing For Change, the sport's promotional arm, could hardly believe their luck as eminent scribes from the major papers took their turns to be ushered into the tartan-clad study and wonder at the courage and the charm of the embattled legend within.

Frankel himself was kept out of bounds in his box in 'The Garage', but the rest of the team were introduced to add their own testimony of the horse that had so caught the public's imagination. Steve Kielt described how he had the biggest feet; Dee Deacon told of the biggest appetite; Sandy Gauravaram of how Frankel liked his own space; and Shane Fetherstonhaugh called him 'a big alpha male, not one for petting'. Yet, of course, it was the trainer who truly fascinated and whose appearance amazed and uplifted some of Fleet Street's finest – including *The Sunday Times* star writer David Walsh:

Sixty-nine winters rest heavily on Cecil's back. His body has absorbed enough cancer drugs to stock a small hospital. But when he considers his life, it's the future he wishes to speak about.

'It was written recently in a newspaper that I will retire at the end of the season because of my health,' he says. 'It's a load of rubbish. I've had three or four sessions of chemotherapy over the last four months, one more to go, and the scans have been very good. The original cancer I had six years ago has completely gone. This was a new cancer, on my chest, and it was pressing on my vocal cord, damaging nerves and causing me to lose my voice.

'With all the chemotherapy I couldn't eat properly for a long time and lost a lot of weight. The cancer is shrinking, it's losing its strength, and the doctors are pretty confident that by the end of the year I will be 100 per cent. I look very white now and I've lost my hair, which I don't like because I am very vain. But I enjoy life and I am not ready to go anywhere.'

In the hauteur of Cecil's aristocratic manner there is also vulnerability, conveyed in eyes that often appear sad, and in much that he says. 'I appreciate the support of people,' he says. 'They have been very good to me through the years. I am surprised by it. I don't know why they are like this. Lately, when I have won a big race, they applaud me. It is almost embarrassing. I don't think I deserve that. I am glad they feel I am not a complete waste of time.

'Apart from days spent in hospital, I have never missed a day in the yard,' he says. 'Although I'd be wobbly in the morning and have used a stick a few times, I get into my car and go onto the Heath. I think you just concentrate on the good things. Without Frankel, I wouldn't have had a chance of getting to where I am now. If anybody deserves a pat on the back, it's him.'

The brave words were duly reported but most of us still had the gravest doubts about whether Henry would make Champions' Day, although Teddy Grimthorpe laughed reassuringly and said, 'You want to bet?' But fortunately the trainer's attendance was not the chief subject under the spotlight, and the run-up to the Ascot showdown gave the airwaves free rein to debate whether Frankel was the best horse anyone had ever seen.

Diverting as this was, the truth is that the case remained as unprovable as the relative footballing merits of George Best or Lionel Messi. But, as I and other hacks were able to trot out on the debates before Ascot, there was one thing we did not know. How would

Frankel handle it if he had to get down and dirty against a truly top horse in the really testing conditions which Britain's rainiest ever autumn would now guarantee? The beauty of this final Champion Stakes bow was that with the French star Cirrus Des Aigles in the field we were about to find out. Impresario Bernie Ecclestone could not have whisked up a more perfect challenger than Cirrus Des Aigles, and even the diminutive Formula One ringmaster could not lay claim to controlling the weather.

So Frankel would now for the first time both run on going officially described as 'heavy', and against an opponent already established as a fine horse on any ground and an absolute 'machine' in the very soft. How magnificent was the contrast: the four-year-old, blue-blooded Frankel on his fourteenth and last race before retiring to the £125,000-a-time coupling life of a stallion; and Cirrus Des Aigles, the six-year-old gelding from the wrong side of the tracks who took six shots to win any race and then only a minor event on the sand at Cagnes Sur Mer. But Cirrus Des Aigles' form line now showed victory in 16 of his 45 races, climaxing in a record-time victory in this very Champion Stakes in 2011 on good ground, the only three times he had been faced with heavy ground he had won by eight lengths, ten lengths, and most recently by a crushing nine lengths at Longchamp. What's more, the crafty Olivier Peslier would be in the saddle – just as he had been on the outsider Solemia in the Prix de l'Arc de Triomphe a fortnight earlier before clawing back the Japanese favourite Orfevre as the ground took its toll. For Tom Queally on Frankel, it would not be easy.

On official ratings there was just ten pounds between the two horses and if, as seemed likely, Cirrus Des Aigles was five pounds better in such conditions and Frankel were to run five pounds below his best, the maths could easily make them equal. Few, outside the opposition camp wanted such an outcome but they added to the tension as the

Ascot afternoon wound relentlessly towards its climax, and was finally almost taken to snapping point by the appearance of Henry Cecil.

He was dressed in the same style as at York, but this time with a blue coat and a brown trilby – and if it were possible, he appeared even thinner, making the figure at Royal Ascot look almost buoyant by comparison. But the commitment was absolute as he walked set-faced through the parade ring with the saddle under his arm, just as it had been since he first took a trainer's licence way back in 1969, when Nixon was President, Elvis was still singing, and Neil Armstrong would not walk on the moon until a fortnight after Henry had won the Eclipse with Wolver Hollow.

When people are concentrating that hard there is a defensive barrage that seems to insist on space around them. Even in the paddock there seemed no danger of Henry being crowded out, as in a gesture of defiance against his illness, he insisted in walking over and himself levering Tom Queally into Frankel's saddle before Sandy and Mike McGowan led the horse out through the tunnel to take a salute from the crowd massed into Ascot's multi-tiered stand.

Neil Armstrong may have taken 'one small step for man, one giant leap for mankind' all those moon years ago, but for us there was now the feeling that Frankel was on the verge of doing something nearly as historic for the racing game. All the team were gathered: Yarmy and Steve Kielt down on the track, Mike and Aideen and Shane and Claire up in the stand. Public esteem may have made Frankel 1-5 in the betting, but we all knew that in Cirrus Des Aigles he had by far his toughest opponent since Canford Cliffs in the 'Duel on The Downs' Sussex Stakes of 2011, and there were absolutely no rumours that the French horse might be harbouring a weakness such as Canford Cliffs had revealed that day.

There was this sense of finality. We knew it would be the last time and so feasted our eyes on Frankel as Tom Queally cantered him very steadily back past the stands and down towards the ten-furlong starting gate. I had thought that the sight of Mill Reef skimming across the Longchamp turf was the most perfect action I had seen on a racehorse, but the image of controlled power that emanated from Frankel that Ascot afternoon tops the lot. Yet when the gates slammed open it was not images but reality that counted, and for a few moments it looked as if Frankel was slightly out of gear. There was even a hint of reluctance as he completely missed his kick out of the stalls and needed at least three urgent shoves from Queally to ensure he locked himself into racing mode. It seemed a long while from the runaway of 18 months earlier. Could the great fires be dimming?

The fears flew around all right. Peslier had an awesome handful on Cirrus Des Aigles as he led into the straight with Nathaniel hard at it beside him and Queally with still five lengths to find on the champion. But he had seen what had happened to Christophe Soumillon when he set Orfevre down to run in the Arc and after hitting the front two furlongs out weakened to Peslier's delight in the last hundred yards. Queally and Frankel were not for weakening. The jockey was crouched but the reins were tight and the stride was sure as the horse swept past Nathaniel and arrived to take Cirrus Des Aigles at the furlong pole. In such races the absolute moment of truth is what happens when the rider asks for extra and the horse has to dig deep and make it hurt. This was Frankel's moment.

Much bilge is said about 'good horses being the same on any ground'. Brigadier Gerard was a stone worse on heavy, and only courage got him through. Frankel needed courage here, but he had the power and the class as well. There would be no ten length routing but this final, decisive but toughest victory – by one length and three quarters – was his greatest too.

As he came back the big question returned, and now the answer had to be in the affirmative. The horse we were looking at had long proved that he was as fast as any of the other legends; now he had shown that he could battle it out just as well. For me, riddled with flu, it was a strange out-of-body experience. After so many years searching for the ultimate thoroughbred, this really seemed to be the one. Memories would fade and the leaves would come off the trees. But what a wonder we had with the horse they called Frankel.

It was the result the thousands had flocked to Ascot for. They rushed to cheer around the winner's enclosure. They could touch each other just to prove that they were there, and join the mighty rejoicing that a big race could bring. They would know that Frankel was off to stud. They might giggle at the enormity of his covering fee, but when the big screen showed the trainer they realised that this was the greatest achievement of it all.

A hush fell, because the voice came only in a whisper. Just six short, rather jerky sentences which must have been difficult to deliver but which gave the occasion its benediction. 'He didn't like the ground,' Henry said of Frankel. 'He was sort of floundering on the ground. But he was very relaxed. He is the best I have ever had. The best I have seen. I would be very surprised if we ever see a better.' No more needed to be said but, even more than at York, there was a poignancy in the ever-recurring thought that we would be lucky to have any more from that quarter anyway.

Predictably Frankel and the stable swept up all the awards, and in January 2013 the World Thoroughbred Rankings gave him the official status of the highest rated horse in history, albeit by dint not of raising his own mark of 140 but demoting Dancing Brave from 141 to 138, Shergar from 140 to 136, and the dual Arc winner Alleged from 140 right down to 134. At the glittering Cartier Awards, special recognition was given to 'Team Frankel', and Dee and Mike and Sandy duly stepped on to the rostrum alongside Jane to receive the cheers. Jane was on duty again for the Sir Peter O'Sullevan Charitable Trust lunch, where Henry became the latest recipient of the great man's annual award, whose previous holders include Her Majesty The Queen. Joanna Lumley was the only royalty on show, but she raised the roof with an impassioned tribute to the winner who was not there.

In all these gatherings there was a sad assumption that the phrase 'not well enough to attend' meant that Henry's as well as Frankel's days would be over. But at the same time as Peter O'Sullevan's guests were clucking in sympathy at the Dorchester, the trainer was spotted quite twinkle-eyed at the butchers in Newmarket. At Tattersalls, the Japanese operation Ki Farm gave a December Sales top price of 985,000gns for Wild Coco and promptly showed confidence in the future by sending her back to Henry to be trained for 2013. While the trainer, radiotherapy over, recuperated in Dubai, Horses in Training 2013 showed 125 horses assigned to Warren Place, down only twenty from 2012, still more than double the total of the first Classic-winning seasons, and with 37 two-year-olds providing plenty of good reasons to get up in the morning.

In April the much-loved Craven Meeting came and with it a Henry Cecil evidently in better health than when last seen on a racecourse. Better still, good winners came too. Midday's half-sister Hot Snap won the Nell Gwyn Stakes so well that she was made favourite for the 1,000 Guineas and the four-year-old Tickled Pink started her season brilliantly by taking the Abernant Stakes from the front. The weather was windy with showers but Henry was hatless, and as the ring of press men closed in after the Nell Gwyn to ask the same 'do you think this could be another Classic winner' questions there was a huge, yearning sense of déjà vu.

Lee Mottershead was there for the *Racing Post*. He was born in 1975 between Bolkonski winning the St James's Palace Stakes at Royal Ascot and the Sussex Stakes at Goodwood. Lee's racing interest had been kindled by his factory working father idolising Henry Cecil, and he has rightly risen to high rank in his profession. 'Of course none of us had seen Henry since Champions Day,' remembers Lee. 'So it was a thrill that he was there with a new Classic contender and he seemed to be enjoying it too, that whole banter thing with him at the centre of the audience. He may have looked a sick man but he was very obviously still first and foremost a racehorse trainer.'

That weekend Henry went to Newbury for the Greenham meeting, stayed the Friday night with Henry Ponsonby, drove round Lambourn in the morning, went shopping in Hungerford and even got away with an unfortunate parking bump with his car. Frankel's brother Noble Mission once again threatened more than he delivered in the John Porter Stakes and the promising three-year-old Kyllachy Rise could not quite justify favouritism an hour later. But the horses were running well. A week later when Henry was at Sandown to watch Thomas Chippendale start his season with a splendid second to the talented Al Kazeem, we could delude ourselves that it was business as usual. Winners kept coming. Late in May Chigun won a Group race in Ireland and three days afterwards Frankel's half-sister Joyeuse won so well first time out at Lingfield that she was added to what looked the strongest Warren Place team for years at Royal Ascot.

But Sandown was the last time he would go racing. The years of mind over matter had taken their toll on what was left of his immune system and while he was still making plans and entries to the very end, on Tuesday 11 June, that end had come. Its inevitability in no way lessened its impact and the extent of the tributes was matched by the depth of them. Some of the most touching came not from the famous and those who knew him well but from many whom he had never seen or for whom he had done some instant, unasked for favour on Newmarket Heath. The man who at times had been seen even by his friends as both a fool and a genius, a saint and a scoundrel, a half-wit and a hero, had ended hailed as little short of an heroic saint.

It was the very height of the season and so Jane Cecil was granted the trainer's licence to keep the Warren Place runners on the track. At Royal Ascot the next week, the Queen stood in the paddock to lead a minute's silence on the opening day and Jane and her sister Sally saddled the favourite Tiger Cliff to run a slightly unlucky second in the Ascot Stakes. Next day Chigun was also a disappointing favourite, but on the Thursday the millions of mourners had the memory they craved. Less than an hour before the Queen had her own greatest racing moment when winning the Gold Cup with her filly Estimate, the Cecil-trained Riposte swept through to take the Ribblesdale Stakes in the Frankel colours of Prince Khalid Abdulla.

Lady Jane was not the only one wiping a tear from her eye as the unsaddling enclosure rang to a huge and sustained ovation afterwards. 'It's been a tough, tough week,' she said, 'but it's a very special day and I am sure Henry is looking down. Keeping busy is what is keeping us going. If we had nothing to do I think we would all fall to bits. Henry's been planning since last year and we are just trying to carry on what he hoped to achieve. The reception was for him – he would have loved that.'

It was all almost too much to bear but, as with so often in the Cecil story, the tale still had twists to come. On the Friday Joyeuse did the Frankel family proud by finishing third in the opening race and later in the afternoon Jane Cecil cut a sad figure as she presented the trophy for the Queen's Vase run especially in Henry's honour. That was surely drama enough but Saturday was to sign off with the ultimate example of how in racing happiness always stands above the trapdoor to disaster. Thomas Chippendale stuck his neck out in magnificent effort to win the Hardwicke Stakes only to wobble, collapse and die less than a hundred yards past the line.

Where there should have been triumph there was tragedy, what should have been an arm-waving walk back was a winching of a carcass behind a screen. It was the heaviest of reminders. Henry's own funeral was on the Monday at Newmarket and he was then taken to be buried next to his mother in the cemetery at Crathes.

Nothing goes on for ever but at the start many wondered if Henry Cecil would go anywhere at all. His has been the greatest racing story ever told because the career which he brought to a climax with Frankel has the quality that only the gods can bestow. It's called immortality.

SIR HENRY CECIL CAREER STATISTICS
1969–2013

3,432 races won worldwide

416 Pattern winners
114 Group One
110 Group Two
192 Group Three
221 Listed race wins

36 Classic wins
25 English Classic wins

Three Triple Crown winners

1985 Oh So Sharp
1,000 Guineas, Oaks, St Leger

1979 Le Moss
Stayers' Triple Crown – Gold Cup, Goodwood Cup, Doncaster Cup

1980 Le Moss
Stayers' Triple Crown – Gold Cup, Goodwood Cup, Doncaster Cup

10 Champion Trainers' Championships
1976, 1978, 1979, 1982, 1984, 1985, 1987, 1988, 1990, 1993

SIR HENRY CECIL STATISTICS YEAR BY YEAR

Statistical breakdown relates to races in Great Britain only; prize money shown is win and place, except for the years 1976, 1985, 1986 and 1987, which show win money only. Overseas winners shown are those at Group One or Grade One level.

1969

27 winners / 145 runners / Strike rate 19% / Prize money £69,950.35 / Trainer table 8th

GROUP ONES

Wolver Hollow	Eclipse Stakes *	Sandown	Mrs Hope Iselin	Lester Piggott
Approval	Observer Gold Cup (now Racing Post Trophy) *	Doncaster	Sir Humphrey de Trafford	Duncan Keith

* equivalent of Group 1; pattern not introduced until 1971

1970

35 winners / 206 runners / Strike rate 17% / Prize money £39,552.55 / Trainer table – Not in top 12

ROYAL ASCOT

Parthenon	Queen Alexandra Stakes	Sir Reginald Macdonald-Buchanan	Greville Starkey

1971

53 winners / 239 runners / Strike rate 22% / Prize money £75,780.00 / Trainer table 10th

1972

51 winners / 253 runners / Strike rate 21% / Prize money £67,962.40 / Trainer table – Not in top 12

ROYAL ASCOT

Falkland	Queen's Vase	Lord Howard de Walden	Greville Starkey

OVERSEAS

Irvine	Premio Roma	Capannelle	Charles St George	Lester Piggott

1973

39 winners / 215 runners / Strike rate 19% / Prize money £49,834.15 / Trainer table – Not in top 12

OVERSEAS

Cloonagh	Irish 1,000 Guineas	Curragh	Arthur Boyd-Rochfort	Greville Starkey

1974

50 winners / 260 runners / Strike rate 19% / Prize money £90,769.73 / Trainer table 10th

ROYAL ASCOT

Relay Race	Hardwicke Stakes	Sir Reginald Macdonald-Buchanan	Lester Piggott

1975

82 winners / 293 runners / Strike rate 28% / Prize money £241,741.92 / Trainer table 2nd

CLASSICS

Bolkonski	2,000 Guineas	Newmarket	Carlo d'Alessio	Gianfranco Dettori

GROUP ONES

Bolkonski	Sussex Stakes	Goodwood	Carlo d'Alessio	Gianfranco Dettori
Wollow	Dewhurst Stakes	Newmarket	Carlo d'Alessio	Gianfranco Dettori
Take Your Place	Observer Gold Cup (now Racing Post Trophy)	Doncaster	Carlo d'Alessio	Gianfranco Dettori

ROYAL ASCOT

Bolkonski	St James's Palace Stakes	Carlo d'Alessio	Gianfranco Dettori
Roussalka	Coronation Stakes	Nicholas Phillips	Lester Piggott
Fool's Mate	Bessborough Stakes (Handicap)	Lord Howard de Walden	Frankie Durr

1976

52 winners / 227 runners / Strike rate 23% / Prize money £261,500.64 / Trainer table 1st

CLASSICS

Wollow	2,000 Guineas	Newmarket	Carlo d'Alessio	Gianfranco Dettori

GROUP ONES

Wollow *	Eclipse Stakes	Sandown	Carlo d'Alessio	Gianfranco Dettori
Wollow	Sussex Stakes	Goodwood	Carlo d'Alessio	Gianfranco Dettori
Wollow	Benson & Hedges Gold Cup	York	Carlo d'Alessio	Gianfranco Dettori

* awarded race on the disqualification of Trepan

ROYAL ASCOT

Catalpa	Ribblesdale Stakes	Lord Howard de Walden	Alan Bond
General Ironside	Queen's Vase	Garfield Weston	Lester Piggott

1977

74 winners / 317 runners / Strike rate 20% / Prize money £245,509.37 / Trainer table 5th

ROYAL ASCOT

Lucky Wednesday	Prince of Wales's Stakes		Charles St George	Joe Mercer

1978

110 winners / 344 runners / Strike rate 32% / Prize money £555,400.28 / Trainer table 1st

GROUP ONES

Gunner B	Eclipse Stakes	Sandown	Pauline Barratt	Joe Mercer

ROYAL ASCOT

Gunner B	Prince of Wales's Stakes		Pauline Barratt	Joe Mercer
Le Moss	Queen's Vase		Carlo d'Alessio	Geoff Baxter
Main Reef	Chesham Stakes		Jim Joel	Joe Mercer

1979

128 winners / 287 runners / Strike rate 45% / Prize money £809,377.06 / Trainer table 1st

CLASSICS

One In A Million	1,000 Guineas	Newmarket	Helena Springfield Ltd	Joe Mercer

GROUP ONES

Kris	Sussex Stakes	Goodwood	Lord Howard de Walden	Joe Mercer
Connaught Bridge	Yorkshire Oaks	York	Herbert Barker	Joe Mercer
Hello Gorgeous	Futurity Stakes (now Racing Post Trophy)	Doncaster	Daniel Wildenstein	Joe Mercer

ROYAL ASCOT

Kris	St James's Palace Stakes		Lord Howard de Walden	Joe Mercer
One In A Million	Coronation Stakes		Helena Springfield Ltd	Joe Mercer
Le Moss	Gold Cup		Carlo d'Alessio	Lester Piggott
Welsh Chanter	Britannia Handicap		Jim Joel	Joe Mercer

1980

84 winners / 314 runners / Strike rate 27% / Prize money £604,147.25 / Trainer table 2nd

CLASSICS

Light Cavalry	St Leger	Doncaster	Jim Joel	Joe Mercer

ROYAL ASCOT

Pushy	Queen Mary Stakes		Lord Tavistock	Joe Mercer
Light Cavalry	King Edward VII Stakes		Jim Joel	Joe Mercer
Le Moss	Gold Cup		Carlo d'Alessio	Joe Mercer

1981

107 winners / 292 runners / Strike rate 37% / Prize money £709,254.51 / Trainer table 2nd

CLASSICS

Fairy Footsteps	1,000 Guineas	Newmarket	Jim Joel	Lester Piggott

GROUP ONES

Cajun	Middle Park Stakes	Newmarket	James Stone	Lester Piggott

ROYAL ASCOT

Belmont Bay	Queen Anne Stakes	Daniel Wildenstein	Lester Piggott
Strigida	Ribblesdale Stakes	Lord Howard de Walden	Lester Piggott
Cajun	Chesham Stakes	James Stone	Lester Piggott
Ardross	Gold Cup	Charles St George	Lester Piggott

OVERSEAS

Ardross	Prix Royal-Oak	Longchamp	Charles St George	Lester Piggott

1982

111 winners / 320 runners / Strike rate 35% / Prize money £1,022,990.17 / Trainer table 1st

GROUP ONES

Diesis	Middle Park Stakes	Newmarket	Lord Howard de Walden	Lester Piggott
Diesis	Dewhurst Stakes	Newmarket	Lord Howard de Walden	Lester Piggott
Dunbeath	Futurity Stakes (now Racing Post Trophy)	Doncaster	Michael Riordan	Lester Piggott

ROYAL ASCOT

Mr Fluorocarbon	Queen Anne Stakes	Jim McAllister	Lester Piggott
Chalon	Coronation Stakes	Michael Riordan	Lester Piggott
Ardross	Gold Cup	Charles St George	Lester Piggott
Critique	Hardwicke Stakes	Souren Vanian	Lester Piggott

1983

92 winners / 280 runners / Strike rate 33% / Prize money £634,713.65 / Trainer table 3rd

ROYAL ASCOT

Valiyar	Queen Anne Stakes	Souren Vanian	Pat Eddery
Precocious	Norfolk Stakes	Lord Tavistock	Lester Piggott
Defecting Dancer	Windsor Castle Stakes	Sheikh Mohammed	Lester Piggott

1984

108 winners / 352 runners / Strike rate 31% / Prize money £747,663.81 / Trainer table 1st

GROUP ONES

Lanfranco	Futurity Stakes (now Racing Post Trophy)	Doncaster	Charles St George	Lester Piggott

ROYAL ASCOT

Trojan Fen	Queen Anne Stakes		Stavros Niarchos	Lester Piggott

1985

132 winners / 350 runners / Strike rate 38% / Prize money £1,148,206 / Trainer table 1st

CLASSICS

Oh So Sharp	1,000 Guineas	Newmarket	Sheikh Mohammed	Steve Cauthen
Slip Anchor	Derby	Epsom	Lord Howard de Walden	Steve Cauthen
Oh So Sharp	Oaks	Epsom	Sheikh Mohammed	Steve Cauthen
Oh So Sharp	St Leger	Doncaster	Sheikh Mohammed	Steve Cauthen

ROYAL ASCOT

Gwydion	Queen Mary Stakes		Stavros Niarchos	Steve Cauthen
Lanfranco	King Edward VII Stakes		Charles St George	Steve Cauthen
Grand Pavois	King George V Handicap		Daniel Wildenstein	Steve Cauthen
Protection	Britannia Handicap		Jim Joel	Steve Cauthen

1986

116 winners / 350 runners / Strike rate 32% / Prize money £615,582 / Trainer table 3rd

GROUP ONES

Reference Point	Futurity Stakes (now Racing Post Trophy)	Doncaster	Louis Freedman	Pat Eddery

ROYAL ASCOT

Bonhomie	King Edward VII Stakes		Sheikh Mohammed	Steve Cauthen

OVERSEAS

El Cuite	Prix Royal-Oak	Longchamp	Sheikh Mohammed	Steve Cauthen
El Cuite	Gran Premio d'Italia	San Siro	Sheikh Mohammed	Steve Cauthen

1987

180 winners / 446 runners / Strike rate 40% / Prize money £1,896,689 / Trainer table 1st

CLASSICS

Reference Point	Derby	Epsom	Louis Freedman	Steve Cauthen
Reference Point	St Leger	Doncaster	Louis Freedman	Steve Cauthen

GROUP ONES

Reference Point	King George VI & Queen Elizabeth Stakes	Ascot	Louis Freedman	Steve Cauthen

ROYAL ASCOT

Primitive Rising	Bessborough Stakes (Handicap)	Stavros Niarchos	Willie Ryan
Arden	Queen's Vase	Lord Howard de Walden	Steve Cauthen
Midyan	Jersey Stakes	Prince A A Faisal	Steve Cauthen
Paean	Gold Cup	Lord Howard de Walden	Steve Cauthen
Queen Midas	Ribblesdale Stakes	Louis Freedman	Willie Ryan
Space Cruiser	Windsor Castle Stakes	Stavros Niarchos	Steve Cauthen
Orban	Hardwicke Stakes	Prince A A Faisal	Steve Cauthen

OVERSEAS

Orban	Premio Roma	Capannelle	Prince A A Faisal	Steve Cauthen
Indian Skimmer	Prix Saint-Alary	Longchamp	Sheikh Mohammed	Steve Cauthen
Indian Skimmer	Prix de Diane	Chantilly	Sheikh Mohammed	Steve Cauthen

1988

112 winners / 368 runners / Strike rate 30% / Prize money £1,588,911 / Trainer table 1st

CLASSICS

Diminuendo	Oaks	Epsom	Sheikh Mohammed	Steve Cauthen

GROUP ONES

Diminuendo	Yorkshire Oaks	York	Sheikh Mohammed	Steve Cauthen
Indian Skimmer	Champion Stakes	Newmarket	Sheikh Mohammed	Michael Roberts

ROYAL ASCOT

High Estate	Coventry Stakes	Jim Joel	Steve Cauthen
Overdrive	Queen Alexandra Stakes	Cliveden Stud	Steve Cauthen

OVERSEAS

Diminuendo *	Irish Oaks	Curragh	Sheikh Mohammed	Steve Cauthen
Indian Skimmer	Irish Champion Stakes	Pheonix Park	Sheikh Mohammed	Michael Roberts
Salse	Prix de la Foret	Longchamp	Sheikh Mohammed	Willie Carson

* dead-heat

1989

117 winners / 363 runners / Strike rate 32% / Prize money £1,671,394 / Trainer table 2nd

CLASSICS

Snow Bride *	Oaks	Epsom	Saeed Maktoum Al Maktoum	Steve Cauthen
Michelozzo	St Leger	Ayr	Charles St George	Steve Cauthen

* awarded race on disqualification of Aliysa

GROUP ONES

Be My Chief	Racing Post Trophy	Newcastle	Peter Burrell	Steve Cauthen

ROYAL ASCOT

Be My Chief	Chesham Stakes		Peter Burrell	Steve Cauthen
Alydaress	Ribblesdale Stakes		Sheikh Mohammed	Steve Cauthen
Polar Boy	Britannia Handicap		Mrs Mark Burrell	Steve Cauthen

OVERSEAS

Indian Skimmer	Prix d'Ispahan	Longchamp	Sheikh Mohammed	Steve Cauthen
Old Vic	Prix du Jockey-Club	Chantilly	Sheikh Mohammed	Steve Cauthen
Old Vic	Irish Derby	Curragh	Sheikh Mohammed	Steve Cauthen
Alydaress	Irish Oaks	Curragh	Sheikh Mohammed	Mick Kinane
Chimes Of Freedom	Moyglare Stud Stakes	Curragh	Stavros Niarchos	Steve Cauthen

1990

111 winners / 351 runners / Strike rate 32% / Prize money £1,927,881 / Trainer table 1st

GROUP ONES

Belmez	King George VI & Queen Elizabeth Stakes	Ascot	Sheikh Mohammed	Mick Kinane
Peter Davies	Racing Post Trophy	Doncaster	Charles St George	Steve Cauthen

ROYAL ASCOT

Shavian	St James's Palace Stakes		Lord Howard de Walden	Steve Cauthen
Private Tender	King Edward VII Stakes		Cliveden Stud	Steve Cauthen
River God	Queen's Vase		Sheikh Mohammed	Steve Cauthen
Chimes Of Freedom	Coronation Stakes		Stavros Niarchos	Steve Cauthen

OVERSEAS

Rafha	Prix de Diane	Chantilly	Prince A A Faisal	Willie Carson

1991

119 winners / 381 runners / Strike rate 31% / Prize money £1,223,355 / Trainer table 5th

ROYAL ASCOT

Jendali	Queen's Vase		Sheikh Mohammed	Steve Cauthen

1992

109 winners / 383 runners / strike rate 28% / Prize money £1,182,671 / Trainer table 5th

GROUP ONES

Armiger	Racing Post Trophy	Doncaster	Khalid Abdulla	Pat Eddery

ROYAL ASCOT

Perpendicular	Prince of Wales's Stakes		Lord Howard de Walden	Willie Ryan
Gondolier	Ascot Stakes (Handicap)		Lord Howard de Walden	Pat Eddery

OVERSEAS

All At Sea	Prix du Moulin	Longchamp	Khalid Abdulla	Pat Eddery
Tenby	Grand Criterium	Longchamp	Khalid Abdulla	Pat Eddery

1993

91 winners / 398 runners / Strike rate 23% / Prize money £1,859,909 / Trainer table 1st

CLASSICS

Commander In Chief	Derby	Epsom	Khalid Abdulla	Mick Kinane

GROUP ONES

King's Theatre	Racing Post Trophy	Doncaster	Michael Poland	Willie Ryan

ROYAL ASCOT

Placerville	Prince of Wales's Stakes		Khalid Abdulla	Pat Eddery
Imperial Ballet	Royal Hunt Cup (Handicap)		Robert Sangster	Pat Eddery
Ardkinglass	Jersey Stakes		Sir David Wills	Willie Ryan

OVERSEAS

Commander In Chief	Irish Derby	Curragh	Khalid Abdulla	Pat Eddery

1994

76 winners / 324 runners / Strike rate 23% / Prize money £1,646,119 / Trainer table 3rd

GROUP ONES

King's Theatre	King George VI & Queen Elizabeth Stakes	Ascot	Sheikh Mohammed	Mick Kinane
Distant View	Sussex Stakes	Goodwood	Khalid Abdulla	Pat Eddery

ROYAL ASCOT

Kissing Cousin	Coronation Stakes		Sheikh Mohammed	Mick Kinane

1995

83 winners / 334 runners / Strike rate 25% / Prize money £1,024,553 / Trainer table 8th

GROUP ONES

Bosra Sham	Fillies' Mile	Ascot	Wafic Said	Pat Eddery

ROYAL ASCOT

Stelvio	Queen's Vase		Sheikh Mohammed	Mick Kinane

1996

113 winners / 396 runners / Strike rate 29% / Prize money £1,935,217 / Trainer table 2nd

CLASSICS

Bosra Sham	1,000 Guineas	Newmarket	Wafic Said	Pat Eddery
Lady Carla	Oaks	Epsom	Wafic Said	Pat Eddery

GROUP ONES

Bosra Sham	Champion Stakes	Newmarket	Wafic Said	Pat Eddery
Reams Of Verse	Fillies' Mile	Ascot	Khalid Abdulla	Mick Kinane

1997

78 winners / 326 runners / Strike rate 24% / Prize money £1,614,357 / Trainer table 3rd

CLASSICS

Sleepytime	1,000 Guineas	Newmarket	Greenbay Stables Ltd.	Kieren Fallon
Reams Of Verse	Oaks	Epsom	Khalid Abdulla	Kieren Fallon

GROUP ONES

Ali-Royal	Sussex Stakes	Goodwood	Greenbay Stables Ltd.	Kieren Fallon

ROYAL ASCOT

Bosra Sham	Prince of Wales's Stakes		Wafic Said	Kieren Fallon
Yashmak	Ribblesdale Stakes		Khalid Abdulla	Kieren Fallon
Canon Can	Queen Alexandra Stakes		Canon Anglia (O A) Ltd	Kieren Fallon

OVERSEAS

Yashmak	Flower Bowl Invitational Handicap	Belmont Park	Khalid Abdulla	Corey Nakatani

1998

100 winners / 376 runners / Strike rate 27% / Prize money £1,726,224 / Trainer table 2nd

GROUP ONES

Catchascatchcan	Yorkshire Oaks	York	Lord Howard de Walden	Kieren Fallon

ROYAL ASCOT

Dr Fong	St James's Palace Stakes	Ascot	The Thoroughbred Corporation	Kieren Fallon
Royal Anthem	King Edward VII Stakes		The Thoroughbred Corporation	Kieren Fallon

OVERSEAS

Royal Anthem	Canadian International	Woodbine	The Thoroughbred Corporation	Gary Stevens

1999

65 winners / 276 runners / Strike rate 24% / Prize money £2,443,757 / Trainer table 2nd

CLASSICS

Wince	1,000 Guineas	Newmarket (July)	Khalid Abdulla	Kieren Fallon
Ramruma	Oaks	Epsom	Fahd Salman	Kieren Fallon
Oath	Derby	Epsom	The Thoroughbred Corporation	Kieren Fallon

GROUP ONES

Royal Anthem	Juddmonte International Stakes	York	The Thoroughbred Corporation	Gary Stevens
Ramruma	Yorkshire Oaks	York	Fahd Salman	Pat Eddery

ROYAL ASCOT

Pythios	Britannia Handicap		Mrs George Cambanis	Kieren Fallon
Endorsement	Queen's Vase		Cliveden Stud	Kieren Fallon

OVERSEAS

Shiva	Tattersalls Gold Cup	Curragh	Niarchos Family	Kieren Fallon
Ramruma	Irish Oaks	Curragh	Fahd Salman	Kieren Fallon

2000

61 winners / 257 runners / Strike rate 24% / Prize money £1,150,915 / Trainer table 9th

CLASSICS

Love Divine	Oaks	Epsom	Lordship Stud	Richard Quinn

ROYAL ASCOT

Subtle Power	King Edward VII Stakes		The Thoroughbred Corporation	Richard Quinn

OVERSEAS

Beat Hollow	Grand Prix de Paris	Longchamp	Khalid Abdulla	Richard Quinn

2001

47 winners / 256 runners / Strike rate 18% / Prize money £769,072 / Trainer table 12th

ROYAL ASCOT

| Sandmason | Hardwicke Stakes | | Plantation Stud | Willie Ryan |

2002

30 winners / 196 runners / Strike rate 15% / Prize money £367,305 / Trainer table – Not in top 12

ROYAL ASCOT

| Burning Sun | Hampton Court Stakes | | Khalid Abdulla | Richard Quinn |

2003

25 winners / 156 runners / Strike rate 16% / Prize money £353,687 / Trainer table – Not in top 12

2004

21 winners / 150 runners / Strike rate 14% / Prize money £235,969 / Trainer table – Not in top 12

2005

12 winners / 102 runners / Strike rate 12% / Prize money £144,978 / Trainer table – Not in top 12

2006

25 winners / 144 runners / Strike rate 17% / Prize money £196,340 / Trainer table – Not in top 12

OVERSEAS

| Passage Of Time | Criterium de Saint-Cloud | Saint-Cloud | Khalid Abdulla | Richard Hughes |

2007

45 winners / 215 runners / Strike rate 21% / Prize money £732,567 / Trainer table – Not in top 12

CLASSICS

| Light Shift | Oaks | Epsom | Niarchos Family | Ted Durcan |

2008

52 winners / 282 runners / Strike rate 18% / Prize money £1,179,512 / Trainer table 12th

2009

63 winners / 324 runners / Strike rate 19% / Prize money £1,411,068 / Trainer table 10th

GROUP ONES

| Midday | Nassau Stakes | Goodwood | Khalid Abdulla | Tom Queally |
| Twice Over | Champion Stakes | Newmarket | Khalid Abdulla | Tom Queally |

ROYAL ASCOT

| Father Time | King Edward VII Stakes | | Khalid Abdulla | Eddie Ahern |

OVERSEAS

| Midday | Breeders' Cup Filly & Mare Turf | Santa Anita | Khalid Abdulla | Tom Queally |

2010

62 winners / 298 runners / Strike rate 21% / Prize money £2,267,147 / Trainer table 5th

GROUP ONES

Twice Over	Eclipse Stakes	Sandown	Khalid Abdulla	Tom Queally
Midday	Nassau Stakes	Goodwood	Khalid Abdulla	Tom Queally
Midday	Yorkshire Oaks	York	Khalid Abdulla	Tom Queally
Frankel	Dewhurst Stakes	Newmarket	Khalid Abdulla	Tom Queally
Twice Over	Champion Stakes	Newmarket	Khalid Abdulla	Tom Queally

ROYAL ASCOT

| Timepiece | Sandringham Handicap | | Khalid Abdulla | Tom Queally |

OVERSEAS

| Midday | Prix Vermeille | Longchamp | Khalid Abdulla | Tom Queally |

2011

55 winners / 285 runners / Strike rate 19% / Prize money £2,750,157 / Trainer table 3rd

CLASSICS

Frankel	2,000 Guineas	Newmarket	Khalid Abdulla	Tom Queally

GROUP ONES

Timepiece	Falmouth Stakes	Newmarket	Khalid Abdulla	Tom Queally
Frankel	Sussex Stakes	Goodwood	Khalid Abdulla	Tom Queally
Midday	Nassau Stakes	Goodwood	Khalid Abdulla	Tom Queally
Twice Over	Juddmonte International Stakes	York	Khalid Abdulla	Ian Mongan
Frankel	Queen Elizabeth II Stakes	Ascot	Khalid Abdulla	Tom Queally

ROYAL ASCOT

Frankel	St James's Palace Stakes		Khalid Abdulla	Tom Queally

2012

56 winners / 289 runners / Strike rate 19% / Prize money £2,676,863 / Trainer table 4th

GROUP ONES

Frankel	Lockinge Stakes	Newbury	Khalid Abdulla	Tom Queally
Frankel	Sussex Stakes	Goodwood	Khalid Abdulla	Tom Queally
Frankel	Juddmonte International	York	Khalid Abdulla	Tom Queally
Frankel	Champion Stakes	Ascot	Khalid Abdulla	Tom Queally

ROYAL ASCOT

Frankel	Queen Anne Stakes		Khalid Abdulla	Tom Queally
Thomas Chippendale	King Edward VII Stakes		Sir Robert Ogden	Johnny Murtagh

OVERSEAS

Chachamaidee*	Matron Stakes	Leopardstown	Tony Evans	Tom Queally

* awarded race on the disqualification of Duntle

2013

17 winners / 77 runners / Strike rate 22% / Prize money £285,733

AUTHOR'S ACKNOWLEDGEMENTS

THE FIRST thanks must go to the racing game itself. Without its obsessive inspiration I would never have had the opportunities that have come my way and, more importantly, we would not have had Sir Henry Cecil.

This book, therefore, has been almost as reliant on the people who have helped me over the last 50 years as it is on those over the last two or three. I am eternally grateful for all those trainers and owners and racecourses and lads and fellow jockeys and journalists and editors and TV producers who have been my companions and workmates for more than half a century now. Many of them are no longer with us, and so I hope this volume can be a tribute to their memory as much to the extraordinary career and times of the man whose portrait it sets out to paint.

Racing is full of history, and so too is the Cecil family. To get my head round this I was hugely indebted to Henry's oldest brother Jamie Burnett of Leys and his wife Fiona, who had me to stay up at Crathes Castle and whose two books *Crannog to Castle* and *The Holly and the Horn* are a cornucopia of historical delight.

Henry's surviving brothers Bow and Arthur were illuminating about the childhood years, as were current Sunningdale headmaster Tom Dawson and Canford archivist Frank Ahern about the Cecil schooldays. Not too many of the recollections of Henry's stud and Cirencester time have made it between the covers but Alan Yuill Walker was a witness of admirable discretion.

To construct a picture of Newmarket in the 1950s and before I have been hugely helped by Tim Cox and the magnificent racing library he has created at his home near Dorking. In Newmarket itself there were unique contributions from Mark Prescott, from the indomitable Willie Snaith and, in the kindest of ways, from Julie Cecil. For, charmingly and helpfully coaxed by her son Noel, she conjured up magical images of her days as a young girl on the Heath before being vividly insightful about the challenges of setting out with Henry on the early days at Freemason Lodge and Marriott Stables before the all-conquering campaigns at Warren Place.

So helpful too was the late George Winsor, and his kindness in trawling his memory despite his illness was deeply touching. Equally encouraging was the thought and trouble put in by Paddy and Joy Rudkin as they dug back into the recollections and memorabilia of the 20 years they shared at the very heart of the Cecil training machine. They clearly laughed a lot in those years and Frank Conlon is laughing still, and I am grateful for his myriad of recollections and to his prompting of other work riders, most noticeably Frank Storey, whose memories of Reference Point remain pearls of their kind.

Steve Dyble – a.k.a. 'Yarmy' – quickly embraced the idea that this should be a story of the people and the horses as well as the man who has so intuitively trained them down the years. Thanks to Yarmy, I was able to revisit memories of Le Moss's lad Alan Welbourn and talk again to Steve Kingstree, the man who had had the mighty Ardross in his care.

Top stables attract top staff, and you could still feel the understanding when speaking with Indian Skimmer's lass Carol Litton and with Dave Goodwin, the wonderfully tough and funny man behind Derby winners Slip Anchor and Commander In Chief. Success also attracts and sustains leading owners, and I am grateful for help from many of the patrons of Warren Place – in particular to Gilly

Howard de Walden for her memories of her husband's glory years; to Philip Freedman for his lucid recollections of Reference Point and other Cliveden fliers; to Sheikh Mohammed for the continent-changing energy which he has brought to all our lives; and to Prince Khalid Abdulla for the elegant and informative hospitality he has given me in country and in town.

The jockeys too have given me plenty of insight down the years, and the very first winning one, the then 'Mr' Bill O'Gorman, could have filled a book on his own. But since his sole success for Henry Cecil I have also had much insight as well as hospitality from Joe Mercer, Lester Piggott, Steve Cauthen, Willie Ryan, Tony McGlone, John Lowe, Kieren Fallon, Richard Quinn, Richard Hughes, Ted Durcan, Tom Queally and Ian Mongan. Lester Piggott remains the most extraordinary figure in my racing life, and it was wonderful to journey back to the days when he reigned supreme. But particular thanks also to Steve Cauthen and his wife Amy who in October 2011 had me to stay on their farm in Kentucky and helped recall the magic of the golden times when Steve was the Warren Place stable jockey and the Cecil career was at its absolute zenith.

The book tries neither to hide nor accentuate what happened as Henry's first marriage unravelled during the Cauthen era. There are still strong views on the subject, but I thought it was important to meet again with Natalie Cecil, who kindly shared her memories of good days as well as bad.

Understanding the problems that have beset the horses in the story has been greatly helped by the generosity of the veterinary profession – most especially Richard Greenwood, who was assigned to Warren Place through most of the 1980s and 1990s, and his successor Charlie Smith, who led me through the problems that beset the stable at the start of this millennium. Richard kindly read and corrected relevant passages, as did my expert friend Des Leadon, as he and Professor Tom Buckley and Alan Creighton explained the Irish Equine Centre's role in clearing Warren Place of the aspergillus with which it had become infested. Not for nothing is the last-mentioned nicknamed 'Fungus Paddy'.

In more contentious areas I have been much helped by the legal wisdom and wide racing experience of Jeremy Richardson, and by the massive knowledge and recollection of Sir Peter O'Sullevan, Ian Balding and John Dunlop, each of whose thoughts and guidance have been greatly appreciated.

John's son Harry Dunlop was one of a long line of Cecil assistants which stretches back to a young and bold Luca Cumani at Marriott Stables and continued through the likes of Willie Jardine, Willie Jarvis, David Lanigan and most recently Mike Marshall, who, with his tireless wife Aideen, was such a central part of the Frankel story.

Their stories were all fascinating and there was a nostalgic thrill in going back with them down the years, especially when, as in Willie Jardine's case, the memories were backed by the record books he scrupulously kept down the years. But for written records I have also been lucky to have had the help of two tireless chroniclers in Peter Robinson and the racing historian Michael Tanner. The former's innumerable scrapbooks represent a devotion to the Cecil saga which extends to calling his house Ardross Lodge. The latter's carefully collected newspaper cuttings were much more a scholar's research than a magpie's snatchings, and they brought a necessary perspective to the tale.

Newmarket, of course, has been the central location of the story, and many people have helped the work of the last two years, not to mention the last 50. William Gittus at Jockey Club Estates and Michael Prosser at the racecourse have been as patient with my queries as they have at my presence at all sorts of inconvenient places, both morning and afternoon. The competitive streak within racehorse trainers often limits tributes to their peers, but both Michael Stoute and John Gosden were revealing and generous in their insights. So too was James Fanshawe, who as Newmarket's leading bibliophile even read long passages of the book. His public-spirited wife Jacko was especially helpful, having been both a Cecil baby-sitter and later assistant to the great Anne Scriven, the stable's devoted secretary all the way from Freemason Lodge to the glory years at Warren Place.

Writing a story that reaches back earlier than most people remember adds importance to the judgement of one's contemporaries, and in this I am grateful to the input of Julian Wilson, who for so long headed the BBC broadcast team opposite my gang on ITV and Channel 4.

Des Leadon and Tim Hailstone read all the book as it came through week by week in almost Dickensian chunks. I am grateful to them, in particular to Tim for his publishing support – just as I am to Alan Byrne and Bruce Millington at the *Racing Post* for both encouraging me forward and giving me the paper's time to tackle tasks which seemed to grow ever larger during the process.

Many other journalists and friends added to the story, especially Clare Balding, Sue Montgomery, Brian Viner, Jonathan Powell and Colin Mackenzie. The last three even read through the manuscript, as did David Walsh, to whom I am very grateful for the generous tribute on the cover of this book. Andrew Franklin, my long-standing (and long-suffering) ally and producer on ITV and Channel 4, found footage which relit the past, as did a wonderful BBC package sourced by the irreplaceable Gerry Morrison. Jilly Cooper gave terrific writer's support all the way, and it was good to link up with Nick Clarke to talk of those early trips to Dubai when Sheikh Mohammed was starting to amaze us with dreams into reality.

At the heart of all this there was always the innate vitality and the daily battle of hope against experience which remain the redeeming features of the racing game and of those who play it. To that end there was much pleasure in recalling the Bosra Sham years with Wafic Said's manager Captain Tim Bulwer-Long, and the Niarchos family's Light Shift resurgence with their Alan Cooper – never forgetting the ubiquitous Henry Ponsonby, a never-flagging enthusiast for everything at Warren Place, most especially his own syndicate horses.

The days I spent in Newmarket in the spring, summer and autumn of 2011 were amongst the most illuminating and most memorable of all my time in racing. They were made possible only by the immeasurable welcome and forbearance offered me by Henry and Jane Cecil and, notwithstanding the later differences highlighted in the epilogue, I hope they will come to view this finished book in the manner in which it was intended. To be around their operation as they took Frankel through to greatness was indeed the very best of times.

Everyone in the yard was a model of kindness to me, but especially Jane's sister Sally Noseda, still riding with rare skill; old stalwarts like Billy Aldridge, John Scott and Pete Emmerson keeping the wheels turning; Mike McGowan and Billy Brown at the races; Claire Markham and Joan Plant in the office; Jonathan 'Stretch' Ormshaw and Dan de Haan in the yard; farrier Steve Kielt at his anvil; Chris Bishop doing so much duty on Bullet Train; and then of course 'Team Frankel'.

By the end the world would rightly know them all too. Dee Deacon, who would take those massive feed bowl round before the dawn; Sandy Gauvaram, a calm but watchful presence in Frankel's box and in the big race paddock; and rider Shane Fetherstonhaugh, to whom all the publicity was even more stressful than when he took the place in Motivator's saddle in that Derby-winning year of 2005. There were many unique things about the Frankel story, and Shane was a long way from the least of them.

Prince Khalid Abdulla is almost as publicity-shy as his horse's work rider, and his team at Banstead Manor are anything but greedy headlinehoggers. But as Frankel interest grew they responded in public every bit as helpfully as they had earlier to me in private – and Frankel even had his own website. For this book Teddy Grimthorpe has been witty as well as wise, Philip Mitchell has been as unfailingly solid as he had been 18 years earlier with Tenby and Commander In Chief, and Jim Power and Rory Mahon shared glorious memories of Frankel's nursery days.

The birth and nurture of a volume like this needed a special team, too. For James de Wesselow and Julian Brown at Racing Post Books this project proved the most arduous thing that they as well as I had undertaken. We were wonderfully lucky to have Sean Magee by our side and the relentless Liz Ampairee to drive us forward, and I was blessed to have Gill Heaney to come in daily to pick up the pieces and listen to the words that had come through the mill that morning, while throughout the process the eager and inventive Sam Hanson saved me countless hours with his research and collation. When 130,000 words were finally baked and delivered, it was Daniel Balado who first took up the challenge of the editing process followed by equally important contributions from Nick Pulford and Richard Lowther. They have done their best to aid the reader, but any mistakes and infelicities must in the end be down to me.

To get the book over the line we needed a designer who was as pragmatic as he was gifted, and in John Schwartz we had such qualities in spades. He and Paulien Hosang and the rest of the team at Soapbox have delivered a look of which I am really proud. My thanks to them and everyone else may have as much exhaustion in them as exhilaration at the end of such a lengthy process, but they are heartfelt none the less.

I just hope that they will think that the result was worth it.

Brough Scott
March 2013

TEXT AND PICTURE ACKNOWLEDGEMENTS

THE FOLLOWING publications have given their kind permission to use their copyrighted material in the book.

Daily Mail / Solo Syndication Ltd: pages 205, 234, 238, 241, 242, 247
Guardian News & Media Ltd: pages 196, 331
The late John Oaksey / *The Daily Telegraph:* page 180
Paul Kelso / *The Daily Telegraph*: page 274
The Daily Telegraph: pages 196, 331
The Sunday Times / NI Syndication: pages 68, 167, 174, 221, 252
The Times / NI Syndication: page 172

Photo credits

Adam Davey: plate 17 top
Action Images/Julian Herbert: page 3
Associated Newspapers / Solo Syndication: plate 1 top
Bernard Parkin: plate 6 top, plate 8 bottom
Bill Beck/The Daily Telegraph: page 39
Chris Smith: pages 6, 267, 311, plate 4, plate 23 bottom
Cranhamphoto.com: pages 282, 304
Getty Images/Alan Crowhurst: pages 2, 274
George Selwyn: pages 136, 164, 186, 226, 231, plate 8 top
Gerry Cranham: pages 69, 86, 87, 139, plate 2 top, plate 5 top, plate 11 bottom, plate 17 bottom right

Henry Ponsonby: plate 6 bottom

Hugh Routledge: pages 280, 290, 302, 321

John Crofts: pages 51, 88, 95, 108, 116, 125, 135, 137, 159, 160, 168, 169, 182, 203, plate 2 bottom, plate 3 top and bottom, plate 5 bottom, plate 8 middle, plate 9 bottom, plate 13 top, plate 15 top and bottom

Juddmonte: plate 19 top

Laurie Morton: plate 11 top, plate 12 bottom

Mary Evans Picture Library: page 16

Mike Powell/Allsport: plate 7

Paddy Rudkin: plate 1 bottom

Press Association/Anthony Devlin: page 114, plate 22 top

Racing Post/Edward Whitaker: frontispiece, pages 251, 305, 307, 329, plate 18 top and bottom, plate 19 bottom, plate 20 top and bottom, plate 21 bottom, plate 23 top

Thoroughbred Photography Ltd: back flap, pages 161, 211, 317, plate 9 top, plate 10 bottom, plate 12 top, plate 13 bottom, plate 14, plate 16, plate 21 top, plate 22 bottom

INDEX

Page numbers in *italics* refer to illustrations. Subheadings for Henry Cecil appear in approximate chronological order; others appear alphabetically.

INDEX